Merrill Maguire Skaggs

# THE FOLK
# OF SOUTHERN
# FICTION

THE UNIVERSITY OF GEORGIA PRESS
Athens

Library of Congress Catalog Card Number: 76–190050
International Standard Book Number: 0–8203–0294–5

The University of Georgia Press, Athens 30601

Printed in the United States of America

for Calvin first
    and then
for Virginia and Edwin Barber

# Table of Contents

# *Preface*

THIS STUDY of southern American local color
fiction traces a literary tradition which heretofore has not been
recognized as a part of the southern heritage. The tradition is
important because it defines the typical southerner. Thus the
literary tradition has psychological and sociological implications,
since it affects the way in which one who views himself as a
southerner thinks of himself as an individual. To make the various aspects of this traditional definition clear, I discuss the way
in which nineteenth-century southern literature presents the economic and social status, institutions and activities, and daily
lives of a group I shall call the plain folk. Then I discuss several
literary characteristics of that fiction in which plain folk are described—the constant use of stereotypes for characters, the most
common narrative technique, the incipient experimentation with
symbolism, and the humor. Finally, I show the effects of such a
tradition in the work of three twentieth-century writers: William
Faulkner, Eudora Welty, and Flannery O'Connor. The final
chapter is not meant to be an exhaustive study of these writers,
or even to touch on all their most important concerns. Instead I
show some ways in which their work is related to, and consis-

tent with, southern writing of the previous century. In so doing, I explore a continuity in southern writing that makes the litera-ture of the region appear a coherent whole—and an entity in some ways different from other American writing.

One always looks at literature in some context. Even the critic who attempts to focus strictly on a single work looks at this work in the context of similar literary works he has read: he judges a lyric within the context of other lyrics he knows, not other novels. One also examines a large body of works in some context. One can, as Eliot explains in "Tradition and the Indi-vidual Talent," assume that any literary work belongs primarily to the realm of literature itself; and with this assumption one's context becomes all of literature and one's comments on indi-vidual works relate them to the entire western literary inheri-tance. Or, a second alternative, one can look at literary works primarily in terms of cultural context—in terms of the time and place and people that produced them. In this case one is less concerned with the way one's material is related to other litera-tures than with the way it interacts with its own culture. Using this context, one sees works being shaped by a culture and in turn shaping the culture by providing myths and metaphors and stereotypes with which the culture perceives and orders its par-ticular experience. I have chosen the latter context.

This study is therefore quite specialized. One need not ac-cede to the truth of Scott Fitzgerald's dictum—that "life is much more successfully looked at from a single window"—to believe that focusing one's attention on a limited body of material may enable one to see details that might remain invisible in the sweep of a broader panorama. And such details need not be trivial. As John Dewey remarked, "We are discovering that the locality is the only universal." Along with Dewey and the local colorists, I assume that the thorough exploration of a very spe-cial aspect of human experience can provide insight into more universal human concerns. In the case of this book I would hope that it might lead to further knowledge both of a specific ele-ment within American literature, and of the ways in which lit-erary strains are formed wherever they appear. Thus I believe that the study has relevance beyond the regional boundaries which limit the material included. When traits or attitudes of southern local color are parallel to the local color writing of other American regions, I have made appropriate comparisons; but they appear most often in footnotes. Limitations of space preclude my treating the local color impulse throughout all American writing, much less throughout world literature.

Because my study is specialized, I often discuss "firsts" only in terms of southern American writing. Many of the situations or techniques used frequently in southern literature appeared first in other literatures and in other centuries than the nineteenth. Courtroom comedy, for example, is as old as Aristophanes (or perhaps as old as Solomon). But my purpose has not been to study such universally used situations as courtroom comedy in terms of literary "types," or to determine the relationship of southern local color to universal genres, but rather to suggest some reasons why such situations and such a genre as local color writing were used repeatedly in southern American literature.

Perhaps a more troublesome issue will be my assumptions about one of the ways in which literary tradition operates. I assume that a particular complex of attitudes which is expressed in writing, and is therefore "literary," can become a part of any culture which finds it useful: so much a part that it influences writers who may not have read the original works. In fact I suspect that no "tradition" is worth detailed study which does not have this pervasive influence. Contemporary critics assume (I think quite rightly) that Freud has influenced contemporary writers, regardless of whether the writers have read any psychology, because Freudian assumptions about the centrality of sexual drive in human life, for example, or the importance of parent-child relationships have so shaped our culture's perception of itself that they underlie virtually all contemporary American literature. In the same way no contemporary critic would feel it necessary to prove that Sir Walter Scott had read Andreas Capellanus in order to make the point that the postures of courtly love are assumed by Scott's characters. Scott used such postures because the society in which he lived felt—however unreasonably—that they were what set the gentlefolk apart from the commoners.

In this book I argue that the reappearance in twentieth-century fiction of certain attitudes about the southern people and the southern region suggests a popular tradition operating among southerners. This popular tradition I trace back through nineteenth-century southern writing, particularly southern local color writing. Recent writers have reexamined these ideas and found them faulty, as Flannery O'Connor does; and recognizing their sentimentality, they have used them for ironic humor, as Eudora Welty does. But the definitions of "southern" that such writers start with—regardless of the ends to which they are finally put—remain those of popular southern culture which southerners found acceptable after they had been promulgated by southern local colorists.

Faulkner, for example, undoubtedly felt that the mountaineers of Beat Four, which he portrayed in *Intruder in the Dust*, were "true to" the hill people he had observed in Mississippi. But their exact likeness to the mountaineers depicted by southern local colorists suggests that something other than uncolored physical or social fact formed the basis of his perceptions—that he selected facts that fit his preconceptions. That undocumented influence, I believe, was the popularly accepted southern mountaineer stereotype developed in the late nineteenth century. My argument, then, is not that Faulkner went to third-rate local colorists to find out what mountaineers were like, but that the definition of southern mountaineers which the local colorists worked out became a part of Mississippi culture and in that way was absorbed by a Mississippi writer. But the fact that Mississippi writers may have received their "definitions" from popular culture rather than directly from books does not change the fact that these impressions were initially disseminated throughout that culture by fiction. It is the development of such stereotypes as the southern mountaineer, among others, that I trace in this study. And Faulkner, Eudora Welty, and Flannery O'Connor, though three of the best southern writers, provide here only examples of a continuing tradition shared by their self-consciously southern peers.

I have used terms such as *plain people, common people, yeomanry,* and *plain folk* as synonyms throughout this book. Since Frank Owsley's *Plain Folk of the Old South* furnished much of the historical background for my study, I have used Owsley's term *plain folk* most often in designating the group of people who can be described accurately neither as aristocrats nor as trash. In conversation perhaps this group would be labeled *middle class.*

Until sociologists manage to agree on a definition of the term, however, and until they develop a definition which can include a rural population, the more familiar term is useless in such a study as this.

Most of my discussion will deal with short stories because much local color took the form of sketches designed for magazine or newspaper publication. Many local color novels were also written, and novels will be included in the discussion whenever they are necessary or appropriate. But when short stories illustrate a point as well, I have preferred using the shorter form.

I should like to thank Dr. Arthur Jones, librarian of Drew University, who generously provided me with a room in which to work and with complete freedom in using the resources of the Drew University Library while I wrote the first drafts of this study. The staffs of the Duke University Library and the New York Public Library were also most helpful. Also I should like to thank my mother, Clyde Merrill Maguire, for securing useful and almost inaccessible information for me about the history of the Southern Baptists. I am particularly grateful to Professor Arlin Turner of Duke University, who directed the major part of this study as my doctoral dissertation, and whose tactful suggestions and continued support were always of enormous value. But to Louis Rubin, especially, I gratefully express my deep appreciation for his interest and help.

M.M.S.

# Introduction

BETWEEN THE LATE 1860s and the turn of the
century, a kind of literature called local color burst into print,
dominating the popular magazines and publishing lists of the
nation. Hamlin Garland, who occasionally added to the genre,
defined local color as literature with "such quality of texture and
background that it could not have been written in any other
place or by anyone else than a native."[1] Often local color *was*
written by someone other than a native,[2] but Garland's definition
is useful because it suggests that the purpose of the literature
was to exploit a particular locality by mining from it what nug-
gets of interest could be sold commercially. The local color
writer identified himself by emphasizing local peculiarities and
traditions which made the characters or physical area described
seem unique.

Many reasons have been suggested for the great popularity
of local color in the United States during this period. For one,
public education in the nineteenth century provided a steadily
increasing number of readers who were eager to be instructed
and entertained, and local color fiction was particularly satisfactory in fulfilling both desires. The stories provided not only edu-

cational information about areas remote from the reader but also entertaining accounts of romantic courtship.

American periodicals encouraged the taste for such literature. And after the Civil War, the growing number of educated readers provided subscribers for a steadily enlarging group of magazines with a national scope.[3] One of the most important of these magazines was *Scribner's Monthly*, a periodical especially receptive to local color. *Scribner's* thus helped to make local color more familiar and perhaps, therefore, more popular among readers of the period. Moreover, it was to the periodicals such as *Scribner's* that younger writers turned after the Civil War, because of the state of the book market at that time. Until the international copyright law of 1891, publishers often found it cheaper to pirate European works for publication in paperbacks than to encourage native authors who would demand royalties. The periodicals, then, left a stamp on American literature in the postwar period, because it was difficult for Americans without a reputation to get their work published in book form. This fact explains why much local color so often takes the form of short stories or travel sketches, forms suitable for magazines. Under these circumstances the taste of the average reader was doubly important. Added to the natural anxiety of any writer to find readers who would buy his work was the added pressure of the magazine editor who was interested only in the kind of fiction his readers would enjoy. This kind of fiction was furnished by the local colorists; the pallid quality of much local color is explained by the writer's need to reach a public not primarily through hardbound books, but through the popular magazines.

The Civil War itself was of enormous importance in creating the conditions under which local color flourished. The war emphasized the immensity of the nation, a fact further underscored by the completion of the transcontinental railroad in 1869. The public reacted to its new consciousness of the nation's size in several ways. First, it demanded information about the newer or more remote areas of the country, information that local color provided. Second, however, came a reaction to the problem of imaginatively grasping such immensity. Not abnormally, imaginations sometimes preferred dealing with small groups in particular localities, because of the difficulty in synthesizing the nation's diverse population into some image of a uniform "American character." Third, political and economic rivalry with the East stimulated a local pride in westerners and southerners, a pride which found expression in tales about their areas. It was the local color movement which brought both West and South into literary prominence.

The success of the so-called western school of writers—Bret Harte, Mark Twain, and Joaquin Miller—soon proved the attractiveness of stories depicting areas which had developed unique customs. Once these stories proved their public appeal, and the popularity of stories about New England village life began to be evident, it was natural enough for southerners to add their work to the growing body of regional fiction.

Still another explanation for the appeal of local color has to do with European and American economy. With the rapidly increasing industrialization of western Europe and America, and with the rapid growth of cities which encouraged a uniform pattern of life, curiosity was whetted about ways of living unlike that of the city-dwellers. Not only in this country, but also throughout Europe, writers began to treat the more provincial areas of their countries. Thus the local color movement should probably be seen in an international context.[4] By 1894 Hamlin Garland could remark, "Every great moving literature today is full of local color."[5]

Perhaps these generalizations explain as well as possible why the American local color movement occurred, and why the literature came to have the special character it did. Since it met the need of the reading public for information and entertainment, and since most of it was published in popular periodicals, it reflected the public taste of the time. As a group American local colorists preferred stories with happy or moral endings. If a character suffered misfortune at the end of the story, the misfortune was deserved: the character had brought it on himself. The local colorist either ignored such troubling subjects as neurosis, sordidness, and sexuality, viewed them from an uncompromising position of moral righteousness, or else vitiated such threats as the subjects posed by insisting on the innate goodness or harmlessness of the less-than-perfect. Consequently local color fiction is thoroughly permeated with sentimentality.

Though social criticism appears in these stories, it is usually of a general nature. Pointed social criticism is not often found in local color.[6]

But none of these generalizations completely explains the critical commonplace that the South, of all the regions in the nation, dominated American writing in the local color period. As one is often reminded, "By 1881 it was possible for an editorial comment in *Scribner's* to note that seven Southerners had been represented in a recent issue of the magazine and to declare that 'New England is no longer king. . . . The South and the West are hereafter to be reckoned upon.' "[7] By 1888 Albion Tourgée was stating that in the preceding year two-thirds of the stories and sketches in newspapers and magazines had been specifically "southern" in setting and sympathy.[8]

Certainly the Civil War had focused the nation's attention on the South: the South was largely the field of battle. And this attention was directed southward again, if that was necessary, by postwar politics, by the "bloody-shirt waving" of Republican politicians, and by the disputed election of 1876. Readers in the rest of the nation were curious to know what the South was really like, and the romantic aura quickly surrounding the vanished Old South made stories about the area appealing to readers of all sections.[9]

But there is more to the matter than northern curiosity or sentimentality. While acknowledging exceptions, we still notice that most southern local color was written by southerners who must have had other motives than to satisfy national curiosity. While much local color satisfies a taste for the pleasant, still the idyllic light in which the South is portrayed in stories of the late nineteenth century is extreme. Surely the Civil War also aroused in the losers a need to present their region in a particularly appealing manner. The southerner's fierce pride in the South, stirred by the war as well as the defeat, found its literary outlet after the reconstruction in a lament for a lost Eden. Literature was the last battleground on which the values of the Old South were tested; as critics have observed repeatedly, in literature the South won an unconditional victory.[10] For the defeated, pride in home was the last defense possible. It was a singularly effective one. As the historian Paul H. Buck puts it, "Dixie was telling in its own way the story of its life, aspirations, sentiments, tragedies, and triumphs. . . . Its aim was to convert the Northern disbeliever."[11] While he may not have been either a sympathetic or an objective observer, Albion Tourgée, the literate North Carolina carpetbagger, said of southern feeling:

> The South believed, honestly believed, in its innate superiority over all other races and peoples. It did not doubt, has never doubted, that, man for man, it was braver, stronger, better than the North. Its men were "gentlemen"—grander, nobler beings than the North ever knew. Their women were "ladies"—gentle, refined, ethereal beings, passion and devotion wrapped in forms of ethereal mould, and surrounded by an impalpable effulgence which distinguished them from all others of the sex throughout the world. Whatever was of the South was superlative. To be Southern-born was to be *prima facie* better than other men. So the self-love of every man was enlisted in this sentiment. To praise the South was to praise himself; to boast of its valor was to advertise his own intrepidity; to extol its women was to enhance the glory of his own achievements in the lists of love; to vaunt its chivalry was to avouch his own honor; to laud its greatness was to extol himself. He measured himself with his Northern compeer, and decided without hesitation in his own favor.[12]

The young southerner in the 1870s and 1880s found himself in a predicament. If not he, then his father had fought a battle for regional autonomy and lost it. His region had suffered not only the devastation of war but also the devastation—at least in southern opinion[13]—of a vindictive peace and "reconstruction." Although he probably would have had it no other way, he had no choice but to identify himself with that defeated section. His accent betrayed his region of birth, while his poverty, and probably his affections, held him there. The most obvious response to his predicament was to make the identification tolerable by making it respectable. To do that, the South had to be made respectable to other sections, for respectability is patently defined by the larger society. The nation defines the respect due a region, just as the community defines the respect due an individual. The battle for southern respectability was fought and won by southern writers.

Finally the exceptionally large number of southern women who wrote local color fiction must be taken into account. Living in a region which, even for the nineteenth century, had unusually rigid ideas about what kinds of activities were proper for ladies, the women found in writing an occupation both monetarily rewarding and socially acceptable. And if the men occasionally were extreme in their affirmation of all things southern, the women were even more so, as a glance at the work of Grace King, Ruth McEnery Stuart, Constance Cary Harrison, Virginia Frazer Boyle, or Matt Crim proves.

If one is interested in American literature in the second half of the nineteenth century, he must consider the southern local color stories which dominated the period. Furthermore these stories should prove of great interest to anyone concerned with twentieth-century American literature. Faulkner, Wolfe, Warren, Flannery O'Connor, and Eudora Welty, to name a few, do not write from a cultural and literary vacuum. In other words local color stories popularized a vision of the South which has affected most southern writers of the twentieth century. I examine some of the less frequently recognized elements in that vision and show how these elements affected specific works of three more recent writers.

C. Vann Woodward, the southern historian, may be technically inaccurate in asserting that "one of the most significant inventions of the New South was the 'Old South'—a new idea in the eighties, and a legend of incalculable potentialities."[14] Francis Pendleton Gaines dates the tradition of the Old Southern Plantation where all was grace, sweetness, culture, and light from 1832, the year John Pendleton Kennedy's *Swallow Barn* was first published.[15] The historic reasons for the birth of this myth have been traced by William Taylor, who points out that the myth first arose simultaneously with the cultural decline of the Tidewater economy. This myth provided a way both of explaining that decline (the cavalier who owned the plantation was too much a gentleman to concern himself with mundane business matters and was therefore apt to lose his money), and also of revelling nostalgically in the "Old South" of the colonial days in order to avoid the more unpleasant economic facts of the 1830s. Taylor further traces the way in which this idea of the graceful life once lived in an idyllic southern past was taken up eagerly by northerners who were looking for an antipode to the increasingly crass materialism they saw around them.[16] Both Gaines

and Taylor point out that abolitionists seized on this myth as a
means of exaggerating the horrors of a system in which an impractical or effete owner allowed his slaves to be victimized
by an insensitive, stupid, or sadistic overseer. By the time of
the Civil War the myth of the South—of a land populated by
wealthy landowners and their numerous slaves—was firmly fixed
in the more literate minds in both North and South.

Mr. Woodward is certainly correct, however, in his assumption that the Old South myth was "a legend of incalculable potentialities." He is also accurate in connecting this legend with
the local color period. Southern local colorists seized upon the
myth with enthusiasm as a way of making the scenes they portrayed more romantic or poignant, and as the means by which
they could sentimentalize their present, thereby making it more
appealing. Woodward also suggests that one appeal of this "cult
of archaism" was the opportunity it presented to ignore a revolution in southern values, brought about by the struggle to in-
dustrialize the South.[17] The fact that literature based on this
myth often found both eager public and ready publisher in the
solvent North certainly encouraged the writers working under
severe economic handicaps themselves. And the fact that many
of the stories were not only read but also written by women influenced the sentimental direction the genre took.

Although Francis Gaines has adequately summarized the
plantation legend as it first appeared and was later developed in
American literature, it is helpful to review that legend briefly by
looking at specific embodiments of it. In the years immediately
following the Civil War, the most influential writer to use a
southern setting was John Esten Cooke. The trademarks of
Cooke's fiction are an idealized view of southern life, an emphasis on romantic love displayed in scenes of rank sentimentality,
and a cast of characters who are among the landed gentry that
southerners considered aristocrats. Writers following Cooke had
only to emphasize more strongly a plantation instead of simply
a vaguely southern setting in order to idealize not only the
"southern way of life" in general, but also a particular economic
system based on the plantation unit. With this added emphasis
they were soon writing a standardized defense of the old southern plantation.

Cooke's novella *Pretty Mrs. Gaston* illustrates his approach to fiction. The primary business of the plot is to work out the courtships of three couples and to get them all married at the end. According to Cooke's novella there is no unlucky turn of fate that a happy accident cannot cure. Indeed these accidents often aid Cupid. The plot has a touch of almost everything connected with noble romances, and the work ends when it becomes clear that unremitting happiness is in store for every character. The hero is George Cleave, who breaks his engagement to Marion Ormby in the first pages because he has lost his inheritance. A touch of mystery is added when Allan Gartrell, a distant cousin who inherits the estate George had expected, appears to claim his property and gradually reveals that he is not a gentleman. In the end we learn that the real Gartrell is dead, and the false one is a slick London impersonator exposed by a Scotland Yard detective. George gets the estate after all, and the false Gartrell gets away. Gartrell's escape leaves no misfortune, even to the villain, to mar the satisfaction of the reader.

Like most sons of the plantation portrayed in later fiction, George Cleave is nothing if not noble. He thought he had inherited Cleaveland, a sizable estate, from his uncle. But the uncle had left an unwitnessed codicil to his will stating that George could not have the estate unless he married Annie Bell, his cousin. Since a slave stuck the codicil inside a book, George does not find it until after he has assumed his ownership and has become engaged to Marion Ormby. Even though the codicil is not legally valid, George turns the estate over to his cousin, Gartrell. His conversation in explaining the move to his lawyer presumably reveals how a gentleman sacrifices all for honor:

> "Not contest a paper of no earthly validity! Surrender the finest property in the county under a paper like this, not worth the ink it was written with!"
>
> Cleave shook his head.
>
> "I know you are my friend, Mr. Jobson, but your advice is bad. You acknowledge that the only flaw in this paper is the omission of a legal formality; it is plain, nevertheless, that my uncle *intended* to execute the codicil—I have nothing to do with his motives, and I will carry out his intentions." . . .
>
> Mr. Jobson groaned.
>
> "My young friend," he added with pathetic solemnity, "if busi-

ness was conducted in the way *you* conduct it the world would not
go on for a day!"[18]

The selflessly honorable, noble, and impractical young heir to a
rich estate becomes a stock character in plantation fiction.

The beautiful daughter and iron-willed father also become
regular accessories in plantation stories. In *Pretty Mrs. Gaston*
they are represented by Marion Ormby, George's first love, and
the autocratic father who breaks her engagement when George
loses his fortune. George turns to Cousin Annie for comfort
and later they become engaged, too late to save George's property. Annie has an accident while out riding, and through it
meets the young doctor who she discovers is the man she really
loves. She has loved George only as a brother, although she
planned to turn her property over to him as compensation for
the loss of Cleaveland. Through another fortunate accident, the
injured Annie is taken to the home of Jack Daintrees. Mrs.
Gaston, the pretty widow with whom Annie lives, comes to fetch
her and attracts the attention of widower Daintrees. All Cooke
must do to get the couples paired properly is to dispose of
Gartrell, return Cleaveland to its rightful owner once more, and
have George nobly break his second engagement once he realizes that Annie loves the doctor, thus making it possible for
George to return to his first fiancée. Such series of romances
become the mainstay of plantation fiction.

The life which all these noble people live in Virginia, the
state in which the most nostalgic plantation stories are set, consists of fox hunts, dances, parties, and flirtations which work
out happily. The humor of the work and the trials of the young
people are based on such accidents as repeatedly interrupted
proposals of marriage. The dialogue is stilted, for every character acts at all times in accordance with social conventions. In
the middle of his proposal, for example, the doctor states to
Annie, "I can say, and I would say it to *you* only, that I have
never forgotten the prayers I learned with my head on my
mother's knees" (p. 174). Happily each character marries one of
his own level. Marion Ormby who has been reared on a wealthy
estate, marries the wealthy George Cleave. Annie Bell, with less
property, marries the doctor, whose income is equivalent to that

of a smaller estate. Mrs. Gaston marries a widower because she is a widow. Nothing permanently mars the idyllic existence of those who live in Virginia and in the realm of "that ruler of the world—love" (p. 147).

The 1880s saw the first publication of Thomas Nelson Page's work. Although Cooke was the first important writer after the Civil War to resurrect the romantic southern legend, it was Page whose work came to seem synonymous with southern romance. To Cooke's picture of noble southern whites, Page added lovable darkies. In fact the delightfully illiterate black "uncle" became Page's trademark. Such an uncle usually commented, sooner or later, "Dem [slavery days] wuz good ole times, marster—de bes' Sam ever see! . . . Niggers didn' hed nothin' 't all to do—jes had to 'ten' to de feedin' an' cleanin' de hosses, an' doin' what de marster tell 'em to do. . . . Dyar warn' no trouble nor nothin'."[19] Page's most popular stories were anecdotes told by such a Negro, whom an unnamed white narrator meets along a road. The black describes the idyllic life he led as a slave, and his reminiscences usually include a tender romance which he witnessed unfolding between two white aristocrats. Page's most popular stories are all variations on the noble-boy-meets-beautiful-heiress theme, as told by an aging Negro.

"Marse Chan," "Unc' Edinburg's Drowndin'," "Meh Lady," and "Polly: A Christmas Variation," four of the six stories in Page's first collection, are all variations on the antebellum romance. Of the six stories in *In Ole Virginia* three are told by elderly Negro men and two more have such men as central characters. Only "No Haid Pawn" (an unusually feeble attempt at a Poe-esque horror tale) is told by a white man about a white man. "Marse Chan," "Unc' Edinburg's Drowndin'," and "Meh Lady" were probably Page's most popular stories. "Marse Chan" illustrates the Page formula and epitomizes the plantation legend as it appeared in fiction.

In "Marse Chan" a quaint old "uncle" tells of an antebellum romance between a young couple who lived on neighboring plantations and loved each other from infancy. Their engagement was broken when their fathers quarreled over politics. One father was a Whig, one a Democrat. Page makes the point that many of the southern aristocracy were against secession, since they were Whig conservatives; the war was promoted by Democrats belonging to the party of the parvenus and poor. Channing, the story's hero, is distraught when Anne, his fiancée, sends him off to war feeling unloved. When Anne hears that Channing has defended her father's name publicly, however, she reconsiders the engagement and sends him a love letter. The day after he receives the letter, he wears it over his heart and is killed leading a brave assault on the enemy. Anne dies soon after and they are buried together. The Negro raconteur concludes that there will indeed be marriage in heaven. Such a delightful couple could not justifiably be kept apart for eternity.

The components of the Page formula include a faithful slave who follows his master through thick and thin, especially through battle; the slave's master, a brave officer who fights nobly; the slave who controls his master and who is in turn controlled by his wife. The sentimentality of southern fiction is evident in the fact that any character belonging to a group which could be considered unjustly suppressed is always shown to have power of some kind: thus slaves always boss and protect their masters just as women of both races dictate to their husbands.

In presenting his Negro narrators, Page emphasizes how much the slaves of good families looked down on poorer whites. Interestingly it is always a black who labels another character "po' white trash." The contempt expressed in such a term is apparently uncharacteristic of Page's gentle southern nobility. As Page's Negroes talk to themselves, they usually mutter affectionate nothings about their masters or former masters. They are affectionate only to whites, however; they quarrel and bicker among themselves. In stories such as "Unc' Edinburg's Drowndin'" the idyllic courtship of the aristocrats is parodied by the courtship of their servants. The whites blush, dance, kiss hands, and so on; the black says of his courtship, "We all rejourned to de wash-house agin, an' got onder de big bush o' misseltow whar hangin' from de jice, an' ef you ever see scufflin' dat's de time" (p. 73). The parody furnishes the story's humor.

The major value of Negroes as narrators is that the Negro can be expected to see and tell things simply. When a Negro is talking, his creator can be excused from dealing with complexities. Negroes are supposed to be simple. When blacks place whites in oversimplified categories, therefore, the oversimplifica-

tion is consistent with the character doing the categorizing. It is
ironic, of course, that such oversimplified categories were
adopted eagerly and unquestioningly by so many whites who
read Page's stories. Page's Negroes stated that there were only
two kinds of southern whites—aristocrats and trash—and the
writers who followed Page and used the Page formula continued
to make the same statement.

By the time Ruth McEnery Stuart published "Uncle Mingo's
'Speculatioms'" a few years later, the Page formula had become
an expected part of southern stories. In Mrs. Stuart's story, also,
a garrulous old Negro talks to a cultivated white auditor, who in
turn relays the story to the reader with occasional appropriate
interjections. Humor is derived from the incongruous juxtaposi-
tion of the Negro mispronunciations and malapropisms with the
flawless English of the educated narrator, who records the comments of the Negro with presumed phonetic accuracy. Again it is
the black who voices the most emphatic convictions and prejudices which, by the time Mrs. Stuart writes, have already become central to the southern plantation myth. The Negro divides
whites into the two categories of "quality" and "trash." When
Negroes voice such convictions, the snobbery of the categories is
amusing rather than anti-democratic.

The white narrator of "Uncle Mingo's 'Speculatioms'" discovers Mingo on a New Orleans levee "jes' a-settin' out heah
teckin' a little free-nigger-fire."[20] As the story opens, Mingo explains how he gets his food: "Well, you see, boss, my markit
moves roun'! Some days hit's right heah in front o' my resi*dence*,
an' den I goes ter markit wid a drap-line an' a hook; an' some
days hit's back heah in de Jedge's giarbage bar'l, an' den I goes
wid a hook ag'in—a hook on a stick" (p. 69). The difference between the education, as well as the social and economic status,
of the white and black narrators is clear. When Mingo dies,
however, we find that another difference exists, this one a matter
of character. The white narrator says, "We pay directly or indirectly for the privilege of hearing sermons; we pay for stories of
self-sacrifice and devotion; we pay for poetry; we pay for pictures of saints. I had gotten all these [from Mingo], and what
had I given? One month's rent of an old cabin and a few crumbs
from my table" (pp. 89–90). Mingo, in contrast to the white narrator, is a living sermon, a saint, a poem. His word is certainly

to be considered reliable, his memories accurate. Mingo mainly remembers all the wonderful things his life included back before "de wah, an de breckin' up, an' all de tribulatioms we been pass froo" (p. 78).

First among his memories is the great mutual love which he as a slave shared with his owners:

> "My mammy, she nussed Miss Annie reg'lar, an' yer know she an' me is jes' a month older'n one-'n'er, an' you know how women folks is, boss, jes' changin' 'roun' an' a-nussin' one-'n'er's babies, jes' fo' fun, like. Old Miss cay'ed me roun' an' played wid me, same as you'd pet a little black kitten. . . .
>
> "Dee jes' out an' out sp'iled me. I was jes' riz up wid'em all, right in de house; an' den, all indurin' o' de war, when all we's men folks was away, I slep' at Old Miss's do', an' Calline, she slep' on a pallet in dee's room, 'twix dee's two baids.
>
> "Dat's de reason we loves one-'n'er. We's done seen good an' bad times togedder—good an' bad times—togedder." (p. 88)

Next in importance among Mingo's recollections is the merriment of slaves on the plantation. The old man describes such happiness when, his mind wandering, he imagines he is "out in de silver road wid de res', a-flyin' an' a-dancin' roun' wid all de yong boys an' gals what I knowed way back yonder" (p. 78). Certainly not least is the sense of importance which he, as a slave, derived from performing his duties: "I tell yer, boss, when I use ter git up on dat silver-mounted ca'ge, wid my stove'pipe hat on, dey warn't nobody what could o' bought me out. I wouldn't o' sol' out ter de Juke o' Englan'! I was dat puffed out wid stuck-up-ishness!" (p. 76). Indeed, these "aristocratic recollections" so charm the narrator that he cannot "treat with dishonor the spirit that soared to heights to which I had not attained" (p. 85).

First Mingo's qualifications as a judge of character are established: he is used to an aristocratic way of life and can tell the difference between good and bad, or cultured and uncultured, people. As he puts it, "Yer see, I was raised high, boss, an' I ain't nuver got over it" (p. 70). Then Mingo illustrates the basis for his social distinctions: "I don't want no better markit 'n a fus'-class giarbage bar'l an' 'scriminatiom. Ef I wants ter know who's who, jes' lemme peep in de giarbage bar'l, an' I'll tell yer ef dee's de reel ole-timers er new-sprouters er jes' out-an-out po' white trash!'' (p. 70).

An obvious objection to Mingo's system is that the garbage pail of his former owner could hardly pass muster if his assessment of her present financial condition is correct. Mingo takes care of this objection by further comment:

> "Lord, boss, does you s'pose I's a-talkin' 'bout riches? I's one o' deze befo'-d-war-yers, *an' I knows!* I tell yer, boss, hit ain't on'y de money what mecks de diff'ence, hit's de—hit's de—boss, I wisht I had de book words ter splain it de way I knows it in heah! . . . Hit's de—de diff'ence in de—in de cornsciousness. Dat's de oniest way I kin splain it. Hit seems ter me de ole-time folks had de inside cornsciousness . . . ! De outside cornsciousness, hit bristles an' swishes an' wags termenjus; but de inside cornsciousness, hit jis lay low an' keep still, an' hit's gentle in de high places, an' when de waters o' tribulatiom runs ag'in it, hit keeps a stiff upper lip an' don't meck no sign." (p. 71)

Miss Annie, the mistress who "use ter smile on ev'y nigger 'long de coas', so 'feered she mought be a-slightin' some o' she's own people, 'caze she own so many she don't know half on 'em . . ." (p. 72), is Mingo's model of one with the "inside consciousness." Miss Annie and her aging mother are now in considerably reduced circumstances, eking out a living by making pralines which Mingo's daughter Caroline peddles in the French Market. Even living in a cheaper part of the French Quarter, however, the two ladies maintain as best they can the aristocratic attitudes for which the Negroes respect them. Mingo describes their present life as one in which the two uncomplaining women live isolated from their neighbors, since the neighbors are not people of "quality." "Dat's hit—in a *soshual* way she say she fine hit's quiet, 'caze she say, she ain't made no new 'quaintances out dar. . . . An' I say ter mysef, 'New 'quaintances'—I reckin not! New 'quaintances in dat mixtry o' Gascons an' Dagos an' Lord knows what ! I reckin not. Why boss, I kin smell de gyarlic jes' a-talking' 'bout 'em! De Lord!'' (p. 73).

At this point perhaps it would not be too fanciful to speculate on the reaction of a southerner while reading this story in 1893, when it was first collected in a volume. In the prewar days which Mingo describes, many of the readers would have been only children, if they were born at all. Few would have any clear memories of the times. To the common tendency to sentimentalize or simplify childhood memories would be added the pressure of the southern society to look on antebellum days as an ideal period. Mingo's statements about the old times specifically appeal to the prejudices of the reader, and to the southern reader's desire to feel that in the Old South was found the best of all possible worlds. Mingo, who was a slave and therefore should have known what the old system was like, indicates unequivocally that he was so happy in the old regime he would not willingly have exchanged places with a servant of the "Juke o' Englan'!" Primarily he was happy because his owners were so genteel, kind, and good, and because they provided for him and gave him self-respect. Proof of Mingo's loyalty to his owners is that he is still trying to serve Miss Annie and her mother. As his final wish before dying, Mingo asks the white narrator to take his life savings to his daughter with instructions that the twenty dollars be used for burying Miss Annie's mother in style.

Mingo indicates that those whites not like his old owners are either "new-sprouters" or "poor-white trash." They differ from Miss Annie because of their characters. First they lack her uncompromising pride, which prevents social intercourse with the vulgar. Next they lack Miss Annie's dignity in the face of hardship and her reciprocated regard for former slaves. But most of all they lack her "inner consciousness." Thus defined as aristocratic by such vague requisites as pride, courage, and consciousness of former status, Miss Annie is a character with whom any literate southerner would find it difficult not to identify himself. She stands for that mystical Old South heritage which, according to Tourgée, gave to all white southerners the most valued parts of their identities.

Reinforcing Miss Annie's appeal is the description Mingo furnishes of those whites who are not "quality." They smell of garlic, their children are noisy and uncontrolled, and their garbage barrels show lack of culinary discrimination. Unless the reader is indeed a "mixtry o' Gascons an' Dagos an' Lord knows what" living in the French Quarter, and is willing to identify himself as such, it is highly unlikely that he will feel obliged to consider himself inferior to Miss Annie and the aristocracy. For the duration of the time that the story offers an escape from the present, the reader identifies himself with Miss Annie. He feels an added self-respect because of the devotion she inspires from Mingo.

This identification is further reinforced by the only other white character, the masculine white narrator. While little is told about him, one knows his heart is in the right place. For a month he cares lovingly for the dying Mingo by doing what Miss Annie would like to do but cannot. He appreciates all the virtues of both Mingo and Miss Annie, thus illustrating his own "inner consciousness." The food prepared in his kitchen (and presumably his garbage) is "quality," as Mingo declares in discussing a meal the narrator furnishes him. Furthermore, we are allowed to infer that the narrator is of good background. His property includes a cabin in good condition, appropriate for Mingo to live in. All the whites in this story, then, are aristocrats. Since Mingo points out that one can be quite poor and still be "quality," there is no barrier to any white southerner's identifying himself with aristocrats in such local color stories as this one. The alternative is to identify with the trash. "Uncle Mingo's 'Speculatioms'" suggests some of the reasons why white southerners found it flattering to accept the myth that the Old South had only two classes of whites. As long as only two classes were recognized, everyone could think of himself as "quality."

These three stories by Cooke, Page, and Mrs. Stuart illustrate the kind of fiction that southern local colorists came to be known for. Above all, the fiction created a rosy picture of life as it used to be. The admirable character of southern aristocrats was never more firmly suggested than when Negro characters referred to that numerically small group of whites called "poor-white-trash." The trash also became a well-defined part of the southern legend, and reappeared in twentieth-century works by such writers as Erskine Caldwell.

The literary uses of the poor-white have been traced by Shields McIlwaine. In describing the poor-white type, McIlwaine summarizes,

> Ignorant, dirty, lazy, badly nourished, Indian-like content—many of these slovenly outlanders, by the time parts of the South became somewhat closely settled and the planter economy established, were too much set in their lolling way to adapt themselves to any

ordered society. They did not wish to be town laborers; few cared for an overseer's job because of the overseer's embarrassing relation to the planter's hall. In 1860, a Southerner spoke what was the general planter opinion of the poor whites. "There is no longer any possible method by which they can be weaned from leading the lives of vagrom-men."[21]

The South as McIlwaine and the local colorists describe it would seem to have been a rather simple place with a simple agricultural economy, and a simple social structure—a social structure divided into the three parts of planter aristocracy, slaves, and poor whites. When a "fourth estate" is mentioned by local colorists, it is composed of the tiny number of freed Negroes who live at the mercy of the white society.

This tripartite view of the prewar southern social and economic structure has seemed so oversimplified that reputable twentieth-century southern historians have dismissed it. In view of the barrage of literary, historical, and sociological studies written in the twentieth century to disprove the myth that the Old South was full of beautiful plantations, owned by hard-drinking, hard-riding, lusty old educated gentlemen with beautiful daughters, noble sons, courageous wives, and contented slaves, it would seem to require a hardy ego indeed, or an obtuse mind, to continue placing much credence in such a belief. The concept of the poor white has gotten less attention, probably because abject poverty and degraded character are easier for the present century to accept than unqualified virtue is. Yet the stereotype of the southern poor white, as he is described in local color fiction, has also been attacked. C. Vann Woodward points out that descriptions of the group found in late nineteenth-century accounts are as vague as the areas in which the poor whites were said to live. Woodward suggests that the term *poor white* was adopted because it supplied northern intellectuals with a means "of rationalizing the poverty of an exploited region." He adds:

A Harvard professor called this "the most numerous element in the Southern population" and estimated that there were "five or six millions of Poor Whites scattered through the South." In a moment of extreme provocation, a New York editor referred to them as

"the vast majority of the Southern people." In 1879 a journalist
wrote that these degenerates had "peopled the great States of Kentucky, Tennessee, Alabama, Mississippi, Arkansas, and Missouri,
and they are now filling up Texas." They had "no progress in
them, no love for adventure, no ambition . . . and the worst of it is
that they all vote the Democratic ticket." For some reason never
fully explained the "poor whites" seem to have been more numerous in periods of economic depression than in other times![22]

Just as McIlwaine's summary of his character suggests the condescension with which anyone labelled a poor white was considered, so Woodward's statement suggests the skepticism with
which recent historians have viewed indiscriminate use of that
label.

In 1929 Ulrich B. Phillips attempted a full-scale correction of
the southern plantation legend. Having examined records of the
South painstakingly, Phillips concluded that southern tradition
greatly oversimplified the economy. He found that in 1860 the
total number of the planter class—owners of twenty or more
slaves—in fifteen slave states consisted of less than a quarter million, while three times as many families owned as few as five to
nineteen slaves. But Phillips also found that nearly six of the
eight million whites populating the South had no proprietary
touch of any kind with the four million slaves. Phillips points
out that "the non-slaveholders and the small slaveholders were
scattered everywhere . . . in widely varying proportions." He
adds that their standards of living and their mores differed from
one area to another and that in such areas as the mountains
they made up the whole population, while in rich farming lands
they lived as neighbors of planters and prosperous townsmen.
Phillips emphasizes the fact, however, that these non-slaveholders or families with only a few slaves were considered then,
as they should be in retrospect, perfectly respectable and desirable neighbors.

Joseph E. Brown, war-time governor of Georgia, emerged from a
mountain farm with a yoke of oxen as pay for schooling; John
Letcher, his contemporary as governor of Virginia, began adult
life as a carpenter; C. G. Memminger, Confederate Secretary of
the Treasury, was an orphanage boy; and Andrew Johnson a tail-
or's apprentice, illiterate until a wife took him in hand. These and

their fellow millions cannot be lumped as "poor whites" and dismissed with a phrase whether it be "ancestrally degenerate," "oppressed by the slave system," or "debilitated by the climate." Sweeping statements are likely to be as false as they are facile.[23]

Twenty years later Frank Lawrence Owsley's work effectively ended any lingering tendencies among scholars to oversimplify the economic and social structure of the antebellum South. Owsley divides slaveholders into five economic classifications ranging from "the great planters possessed of thousands of acres of land and hundreds of slaves" to "small farmers with two hundred or fewer acres and one or two slaves." He also divides non-slaveholders into five groups, only the last of which— "a 'leisure class' whose means of support does not appear on record"—would clearly fit the designation "white trash." Owsley's contention, amply supported by statistics, is that "the core of the social structure [in the Old South] was a massive body of plain folk who were neither rich nor very poor . . . [a] great mass of several millions who were not part of the plantation economy." He devotes his work to this group; and his description of them is important to this study: "These were employed in numerous occupations; but the great majority secured their food, clothing, and shelter from some rural pursuit, chiefly farming and livestock grazing. . . . The group included the small slaveholding farmers; the nonslaveholders who owned the land which they cultivated; the numerous herdsmen on the frontier, pine barrens, and mountains; and those tenant farmers whose agricultural production as recorded in the census, indicated thrift, energy, and self-respect."[24]

Thus such scholars as Phillips and Owsley have demonstrated the absurdity of assuming that whites in the Old South fell exclusively into one of two categories. As we have observed, this assumption was largely popularized by southern local colorists. Because of the second-rate literary quality of southern local color, scholars have therefore assumed that the more respected writers of the twentieth century were the first to include in their works characters who represent what Owsley called the plain folk of the South. Cleanth Brooks, for example, reads and paraphrases Owsley, and then concludes that Faulkner's unique genius is revealed by his knowledge and presentation of plain people: "Faulkner is writing fiction, not sociology or history, and he has employed all the devices for the heightening, special focus, and, in some instances, distortion that fiction demands and justifies. Still, the picture of the yeoman farmer and the poor white that emerge is perfectly consonant with the findings recorded in Owsley's study."[25] Faulkner is exceptional in that he "is also very much aware of the niceties of a social structure which distinguishes the yeoman farmer from the tenant farmer and which sees within the category of the tenant farmer a variety of types ranging from the honest and often shrewd man of poor fortune to the embittered or numbed landless peasant and on to the happy-go-lucky buffoon or the thorough-going rogue."[26]

That the massive body of southern plain folk was not discovered and acknowledged by southern writers until the twentieth century is the assumption this study disputes. The plain folk were first described approvingly and distinguished from "white trash" in southwestern humor stories written before the Civil War. In the postwar period, southern local colorists, although admittedly leaning heavily on the plantation tradition, also utilized the plain folk often enough to develop the story based on such characters into a literary tradition. By the turn of the twentieth century a comprehensive literary tradition detailing the facts about the plain man was fully developed.

The plain folk tradition was in most aspects antithetical to the plantation tradition. Both, however, exist side by side in southern local color fiction. If it is valid, and most scholars assume that it is, to view Faulkner's Compsons and Sartorises, or Warren's Beaumonts and Murdocks in the light of the plantation tradition, then it is also valid to view Faulkner's McCallums, Varners and V. K. Ratliffs, Eudora Welty's salesmen, store clerks, and hotel proprietors, and Flannery O'Connor's good country people in the light of the plain folk tradition. While a short discussion of southwestern humor will be included here, as well as representative uses to which three twentieth-century writers put this tradition, this book will concentrate on local fiction, since the local color period produced the most detailed and comprehensive portrait of plain folk.

It would be misleading to imply that the impulse to depict the plain folk necessarily sprang from the local colorist's love of

realism. It is just as logical to assume the opposite. One must
always remember that the southern local colorist was extremely
eager to present his region in the best possible light. He had
three widely recognized, accepted stereotypes to work with: the
colorful plantation owner with his variously appealing family,
the contented darky, and the contemptible poor white. One notices almost immediately, however, that Joel Chandler Harris is
virtually the only local colorist to give the poor white more than
a passing nod. While others refer often to his existence, they seldom portray him in their stories. Shields McIlwaine, having verified the fact that the poor white was an established literary type
before the Civil War, also explains his dropping out of sight
during the local color period:

> Southern writers of the Revival strove to create for the nation a
> new picture of their region, one that would be both admirable and
> lovable. A natural consequence of this was that the aristocracy, as
> the highest development of Southern culture, received the earliest
> and perhaps the major literary attention from the native authors.
> ... Thus, although the motives were different, Southern literature
> was again—as before the War—putting her best foot forward; it was
> not, of course, the bare, itchy one of the trash.[27]

In other words the local colorists were reluctant to use poor
whites as major characters because the lives of the very poor
were unpleasant and brought no honor to the area. Yet even the
most optimistic or sentimental local colorist felt the need in his
stories for characters who would serve as contrasts to aristocrats.
This need was two-fold. First, an opposite helped to define the
aristocrat and make him appear more admirable. This problem
was often solved, as Page's stories illustrate, by providing the
gentleman with a faithful Negro servant. The Negro was useful
not only in revealing the love and loyalty the leisured classes
elicited, but also in providing occasional humor for the tale. Certainly racial humor, based on condescension to an inferior, is an
omnipresent characteristic of southern local color. Second, a foil
to the aristocrat was needed to *do* something, to provide the plot.
Aristocrats could act, of course, but only nobly. Because the
aristocratic stereotype became increasingly sacrosanct, the kinds
of action the noble gentleman or lady could perform were quite

limited. If a gentleman had shortcomings, those shortcomings had to be produced by his heritage—a poor head for business, for example, or a tendency to cherish an unrequited love with such selfless consistency that physical damage or sacrifice became inevitable. If a lady had a shortcoming at all, it was the indomitable pride which proved she was a lady. From a writer's viewpoint, the trouble with unflinchingly noble characters is that their range of actions, like their range of transgressions, is narrow. Even Page eventually discovered that one can write only so many stories about fine young men who court the heiresses of neighboring plantations and either die in the war or marry. Furthermore, the faithful Negro could perform only limited kinds of action consistent with the Negro stereotype. He could act to preserve family property or health; he could even scheme to aid an aristocrat's happiness or ambitions; but he could do little more without violating the slave stereotype. He could be resourceful in defending either himself or his owners, but he could not be aggressive in initiating other kinds of action.

The obvious place for the local colorist to turn for characters capable of a greater variety of actions than the slave was to the poor white. At the opposite social and economic pole from the aristocrat, the poor white could logically serve either as admiring opposite or as foil. He was white, and therefore capable of independence, shrewdness, and originality. Furthermore, the southwest humorists had already demonstrated that a poorer white could be the subject of successful sketches. In the popular stereotype, however, the poor white was detestable; he was an improper subject for refined fiction. The rigidity of the poor white stereotype, like that of the Negro, prevented his usefulness for writers determined to populate the South with admirable people.

Facing this dilemma, the local colorist had no other choice than to portray good people of a status somewhere between aristocracy and trash. The yeomanry which appear in local color stories function in many ways as a combination of the three more widely recognized southern types. They have the respectability of the aristocrats but the more or less limited means of the poor whites; and, like the Negroes, they provide occasions for humor based on the reader's feeling of superiority. Yet being both white and self-respecting, yeoman farmers or store clerks

are capable of relatively unlimited varieties of action. The simi-
larities between southern local color and southwestern humor
suggest that what the local colorist usually did was simply to
omit the more raucous elements in frontier life and diminish
the belligerence of the frontiersman by setting him on a pro-
ductive farm, thereby making the social status of a poorer white
countryman less ambiguous. All that a slight elevation of status
required was that the relatively poor, white character be portrayed as one unquestionably worthy of respect. Thus one of
the central ironies of southern local color fiction is that the
writers' impulse to romanticize the South resulted in the development of a relatively realistic type: the plain, simple, self-
respecting, poor-but-honest farmer.

Because the plain folk were not part of the plantation myth,
they could be drawn as the writer chose to remember them.
Character, actions, and potentialities could be treated with
greater variety of approach. Since plain folk were neither wholly
worthy aristocrats nor wholly contemptible poor-white-trash,
they could have both virtues and vices—surely a requirement
for characters convincingly similar to those the reader encounters every day. The extent to which plain folk could be realis-
tically presented, and their faults acknowledged, was also affected
by another aspect of the plantation legend. Readers who had
encountered repeatedly the statement that the South had only
two classes of whites had learned even before the Civil War to
identify themselves with the aristocracy. Once this identification was a habit, no reader was particularly offended by the
revelation of foibles in a character who was not aristocratic,
who spoke in dialect. Though the southern local colorist was
always inclined to shun the shocking or distasteful, he had a
limited freedom when characterizing any figure whose English
deviated from the written standard. Thus, as we shall see, the
southern local colorists (as well as those from other regions) included in their stories characters who indulged in pettiness,
gossiping, and even occasional fornication or violence, habits
more often associated with characters created in the twentieth
century. The local colorist got away with portraying such characters by making them speak in dialect; their dialect allowed the
reader to consider himself different from the characters. Moreover the southern local colorist reassured the reader that his

violent or petty characters were really lovable, that is, really southern.

It is not so much the behavior of southern characters which changes between the local color period and the twentieth century; instead what changes are the writers' attitudes toward that behavior. The actions more recent writers have pictured as typically southern are portrayed as such by southern local colorists. The actions are, in fact, but one part of a much fuller picture of common people. Any critic struggling to define for himself the unique qualities of southern (as opposed to national) literature must go back at least as far as the local color period in his studies. By the end of the nineteenth century there was not only a plantation tradition, but also a plain folk tradition in some ways similar to that of New England or the West, from which twentieth-century southern literature grew.

# *The Beginning:*
# *Southwest Humor*

*WHILE THIS STUDY* will deal primarily with southern local color fiction, it must be clear that the roots of the plain folk tradition in southern literature are planted firmly in southwestern humor—those humorous sketches of rural southern frontier life published between 1832 and 1867 in such newspapers and magazines as William T. Porter's *Spirit of the Times,* the *New Orleans Picayune,* and the *St. Louis Reveille.* Forerunners of the tall tale—the type of story most closely associated with southwest humor—are now recognized in the work of Mason Locke Weems, James Kirke Paulding, and David Crockett. But the true southwestern humor story is usually considered to have appeared first in Augustus Baldwin Longstreet's *Georgia Scenes,* published in book form in 1835.

Two types of sketches are commonly classified together as southwestern humor. The first is the tall tale, characterized by exaggeration, imaginative invention, and zestful braggadocio. It is usually told by a "ring-tailed roarer" who considers himself "half-horse, half-alligator, with a little bit of snapping turtle thrown in." The tall tale most often describes a hunt or a fight, although it can also detail a wide variety of improbable events.

The anonymous "Where Joe Meriweather Went To," for example, describes a man who floats off through the air because his buckskin breeches with straps under his boots get wet, shrink, and pull him into the sky. More earthbound, the second kind of sketch describes the activities, customs, and manners of early southern backwoods settlers. Writers of this kind of sketch share with those of the first the common purpose of amusing the reader by recording the "natural" antics of men and women living in semi-isolation, frontiersmen who seldom come in contact with more genteel sophisticates. The second kind of story is most often told by an educated narrator; much of the humor derives from the differences between the narrator and the people he describes. Writers of this type of sketch include Longstreet, Joseph Glover Baldwin, John S. Robb, and Sol Smith. In this type of southwestern humor the backwoods activities described may seem outlandish, but the story is kept securely anchored in fact by the anxious ordering of the narrator, who not only tells but also interprets or comments on the events in the story. It is from this more realistic type of southwestern tale that the plain folk story of southern local color springs.

There is, of course, a difference between southwest humor and the humor of local color. Most obviously southwest humor is rawer, franker, more directly the result of carelessness about the significance of physical pain or psychological humiliation. Because these elements are much more pronounced in the southwest sketches than they were in later southern stories, twentieth-century scholars have found in southwestern humor the seeds of American realism or a naturalistic view of human life. To look at a recent anthology of southwestern humor like John Q. Anderson's *With the Bark On*, however, is to see that scholars experience the same selective perception of phenomena as others. That is, when interest in realism and literary naturalism was high, scholars accurately noticed the beginnings of realistic literary expression in southwestern sketches. As the subject of realistic fiction grows more familiar—or perhaps stale —other aspects of southwestern sketches grow clearer. Mr. Anderson notices the southwestern humorists "who not only did not scorn the backwoodsman but saw in him an Americanism he did not find elsewhere."[1] His anthology stresses a much more genial and approving attitude towards the country bumpkin than did earlier volumes whose compilers found Sut Lovingood or Simon Suggs more interesting creations of this early period. Anderson can therefore argue from the contents of his anthology that "the presentation of the backwoodsman is not as vicious in its class distinction as some twentieth-century critics claim. Were that not so, then it is difficult to account for [the humorists'] implicit—and sometimes stated—admiration of the plucky spirit of the man of the backwoods, especially of his skill in repartee and his refusal to be worsted by the man of the town."[2] The point is simply that as the pendulum inevitably swings from an interest in the literary expression of the painfully harsh and cruel facts of life—what Lionel Trilling calls the principle of unpleasure[3]—back toward an interest in a more comic view of the everyday, the relationship between southwestern humor and southern local color becomes easier to see.

Perhaps the most influential writer among the southwestern humorists was Augustus Baldwin Longstreet. It is an interesting coincidence that Longstreet's first sketches appeared in 1832, the same year Kennedy's *Swallow Barn* was published. Appropriately the two traditions begin in literature almost simultaneously, one describing the plantation, the other the plain folk. Longstreet's sketches form as convenient a beginning for the plain folk tradition as *Swallow Barn* did for the plantation myth; certainly the popularity of *Georgia Scenes* encouraged others to try their hands at similar sketches. A scrutiny of Longstreet helps one to understand the moods and themes of stories which later follow his in time, in subject matter, and in manner.

"Georgia Theatrics," the first story of *Georgia Scenes*, begins with a statement which can be misleading:

> If my memory fail me not, the 10th of June, 1809, found me, at about 11 o'clock in the forenoon, ascending a long and gentle slope in what was called "The Dark Corner" of Lincoln. I believe it took its name from the moral darkness which reigned over that portion of the county at the time of which I am speaking. If in this point of view it was but a shade darker than the rest of the county, it was inconceivably dark. If any man can name a trick or sin which had not been committed at the time of which I am speaking, in the very focus of all the county's illumination (Lincolnton), he must himself be the most inventive of the tricky, and the very Judas of sinners.[4]

This introduction can mislead by suggesting that the sketches of Georgia life which follow will provide a detailed account of degraded activities among Georgia backwoodsmen. Moreover, the statement implies that the narrator approaches his subject from a position of social superiority, that he considers the backwoodsmen he will describe to be "low," common (in the pejorative sense), or even trashy. The opposite proves to be the case in almost every story in the volume but "Georgia Theatrics." Longstreet consistently indicates his preference for the country farmers over the more wealthy, cultured, and sophisticated townspeople. In fact the author himself quickly corrects that first impression by insisting that "Lincoln has become a living proof 'that light shineth in darkness'" (p. 1).

"The Dance," the second story in *Georgia Scenes*, subtitled "A Personal Adventure of the Author," illustrates Longstreet's usual attitudes. This story describes an all-day frolic sponsored by a Georgia farmer whom Longstreet consistently dignifies by the title "the squire." Throughout the tale Longstreet insists almost vehemently on the superiority of the squire's family and the squire's way of life to those of any city. Since the squire is described as both prosperous and happy, it is interesting to notice that he lives in a one-room log cabin, with floors of split logs roughly smoothed by an axe, which room also provides the girls with their dance floor while their parents "camp out."

To allay any suspicions that Longstreet may be using such terms as *lady* and *gentleman* ironically, we must look at a passage in which he comments on the country custom of beginning a ball in the early morning:

> The girls, as the old gentleman informed me, had compelled the family to breakfast under the trees, for they had completely stripped the house of its furniture before the sun rose. They were already attired for the dance, in neat but plain habiliments of their own manufacture. "What!" says some weakly, sickly, delicate, useless, affected, "charming creature" of the city, "dressed for a ball at 9 in the morning!" Even so, my delectable Miss Octavia Matilda Juliana Claudia Ipecacuanha: and what have you to say against it? If people must dance is it not much more rational to employ the hour allotted to exercise in that amusement, than the hours sacred to repose and meditation? And which is entitled to the most credit; the young lady who rises with the dawn, and puts herself and

whole house in order for a ball four hours before it begins, or the
one who requires a fortnight to get herself dressed for it? (pp. 4–5)

Longstreet refers to the excellence of such country customs
throughout the story. To make his point even clearer, he ends
the sketch with an incident in which the narrator himself, when
compared to his hosts, appears vain and foolish. We learn that
the narrator once courted the squire's wife, and considered himself one of her favorites. When he plans an ostentatious display
of dancing techniques, with which he will surprise her and remind her of his identity, however, he not only makes himself
absurd but also discovers to his chagrin that the lady has no
recollection of him at all. Before this humiliating dénouement,
the narrator's thoughts and memories reveal once more the high
respect Longstreet has for such tenants of a one-room log cabin,
particularly for the squire's wife Polly:

Pleasing but melancholy reflections occupied my mind as I gazed
on her dispensing her cheerful hospitalities. . . . I compared my
after life with the cloudless days of my attachment to Polly. Then I
was light hearted, gay, contented, and happy. I aspired to nothing
but a good name, a good wife, and an easy competence. The first
and last were mine already; and Polly had given me too many little tokens of her favour to leave a doubt now that the second was
at my command. But I was foolishly told that my talents were of
too high an order to be employed in the drudgeries of a farm, and
I more foolishly believed it. I forsook the pleasures which I had
tried and proved, and went in pursuit of those imaginary joys
which seemed to encircle the seat of Fame. From that moment to
the present, my life had been little else than one unbroken scene
of disaster, disappointment, vexation, and toil. And now, when I
was too old to enjoy the pleasures which I had discarded, I found
that my aim was absolutely hopeless; and that my pursuits had
only served to unfit me for the humbler walks of life, and to ex-
clude me from the higher. (pp. 9–10)

Thus Longstreet presents an idealized picture of the joys of
country life, as it was lived not on a southern plantation but
on a small farm. The farmer appears preferable in every way
to his wealthier and more educated contemporary in the city.
The same theme in even more exaggerated form threads through

other sketches in the volume, such as "The Song," "The 'Charming Creature' as a Wife," "The Ball," and "The Shooting-Match."
Whenever, in such a sketch as "The Hunt," a cultured man of
good judgment participates in some socially fashionable activity,
he either has a wretched time or ends his attempt appearing and
feeling foolish. From the beginning of self-consciously southern
literature, then, one recognizes both the admission that many
southerners were common folk, neither planters nor white
trash, and the belief that such folk deserve admiration and respect. Longstreet's volume suggests a fact that is true of the cor-
pus of southwest humor tales: whether the backwoods inhabitants appear to be "low-life" characters or simply honest, plain
folk depends entirely on the attitudes toward them displayed by
the narrator. These attitudes vary widely enough to furnish us
a good number of stories (as Anderson's anthology demon-
strates) in which backwoodsmen are not ridiculed but extolled.

    Longstreet's volume does include several characters of whom
the author apparently disapproves, and these characters are
found among poor country people as well as among wealthy
townsfolk. The youth who is the apparent victor in "Georgia
Theatrics," who greets the narrator with "a taunting curl of the
nose" and admits that he was just imagining how he "could 'a'
fout" (p. 3), is certainly one such figure. Another is the infa-
mous Ransy Sniffle, who foments the battle in "The Fight."
Longstreet describes Ransy in detail, composing a picture which
quickly comes to represent the white-trash stereotype:

> Now there happened to reside in the county just alluded to a lit-
> tle fellow by the name of Ransy Sniffle: a sprout of Richmond,
> who, in his earlier days, had fed copiously upon red clay and
> blackberries. This diet had given to Ransy a complexion that a
> corpse would have disdained to own, and an abdominal rotundity
> that was quite unprepossessing. Long spells of the fever and ague,
> too, in Ransy's youth, had conspired with clay and blackberries to
> throw him quite out of the order of nature. His shoulders were
> fleshless and elevated; his head large and flat; his neck slim and
> translucent; and his arms, hands, fingers, and feet were lengthened
> out of all proportion to the rest of his frame. His joints were large
> and his limbs small; and as for flesh, he could not, with propriety,
> be said to have any. Those parts which nature usually supplies
> with the most of this article—the calves of the legs, for example

—presented in him the appearance of so many well-drawn blisters. His height was just five feet nothing; and his average weight in blackberry season, ninety-five. (pp. 43–44)

One important aspect of "The Fight" is that Ransy Sniffle is considered inferior to all the other townsfolk. Billy Stallings and Bob Durham, the two men whom Ransy finally manages to get into a fight, are respected citizens, both of whom have proved their mettle in many a previous battle. Moreover, while the credit for the street battle goes to Sniffle, we still notice that nobody takes exception to such fighting. All the men of the town prepare to watch the bout with an excitement approaching glee, an emotion very different from the narrator's disdain. Longstreet does not suggest that no "gentleman" would participate in a street fight. He implies that most gentlemen have the discretion to stay out of too violent a fight unless a meddlesome trouble-maker intervenes in their affairs. While the author's contemptuous impatience at the idea of violent street brawls is unmistakable, his outlook is one of moral superiority to the whole town. Even considering the fight from such a superior point of view, he still makes it clear that Stallings and Durham are in an altogether different category from Sniffle. The account of the street fight is much like contemporary accounts of duels. While he could object to either on grounds of morality or common sense, the writer was forced to concede, sadly, that "the best people" sometimes indulged in such activities.

The kind of respect for plain folk which Longstreet exhibits also appears elsewhere in southwestern humor. Even in a volume whose title would seem to indicate another attitude—such as John S. Robb's *Streaks of Squatter Life*—we are never allowed to infer that a "squatter" is automatically what southern writers would later call a "tacky." In fact throughout Robb's volume squatters are presented with sympathy as well as humor, and appear mostly as courageous frontiersmen and clever hunters. In the first section of the volume, a picaresque novella entitled "The Western Wanderings of a Typo," John, the hero, encounters a squatter's widow on the prairie south of Chicago. The woman is described as a tidy one who bustles about her log house, but whose children have faces as "yellow as saffron."[5] Although yellow faces will in later southern stories become the sign of "clay-eaters" or white trash, this particular widow is presented simply as the pitiable victim of bad luck. The cultured and charming wanderer apparently considers her his social equal, for he later invites her and her children to the wedding at which he marries a wealthy heiress. More importantly in "The Pre-emption Right" Robb describes a squatter whose two dominant characteristics—his reverence for women and his deep love for his Negro servant—are in local color stories the unfailing marks of an aristocrat. In the same volume Robb also describes a mountaineer admiringly: "Dan pulled his long knife out of his belt, and laying it before him, smoothed back his long grey hair. He was a genuine specimen of the hardy American mountaineer,—like the Indian, he dressed in deer skins and wore moccasin, while every seam in his iron countenance told of 'scapes and peril" (pp. 104–105).

This tolerant and respectful attitude towards backwoodsmen and early settlers also pervades Harden E. Taliaferro's "Ham Rachel, of Alabama," collected in a book in 1859. In this sketch squatters are described as "a poor, plain, hardy, robust, and honest people, many of them wholly uneducated. All they cared for was 'to make buckle and tongue meet' by raising stock, a few bales of cotton, and a little corn for bread."[6] One may assume that such ambitionless folk are contemptible if he wishes, but a glance at the adjectives by which squatters are described should convince the objective observer that such a conclusion would not parallel the convictions of Taliaferro.

A class structure so fluid as to allow the poor to consider themselves the equals of the rich is implied in the stories of Alexander G. McNutt, who once served as governor of Mississippi. McNutt's two hunters, Jim and Chunkey, live in backwoods huts and exist in hand-to-mouth fashion. Yet they associate freely with an unnamed governor who happily joins them on their drinking sprees and listens to their tall tales. This essentially democratic spirit running through many southwestern humor tales helps to explain a major contradiction in later local color stories. Although southern local colorists state, when the propagandistic purposes of their stories require it, that the South had only two classes of whites—planters and trash—the action of the stories themselves suggests just the opposite. Georgia writers such as Richard Malcolm Johnston, Joel Chandler Harris, and

Will Harben, in fact, speak frequently of the "democratic spirit" prevalent in their state. By remembering that one source of
southern local color fiction is southwestern humor, we can
understand why local colorists insist on an absence of class-
consciousness among white southerners almost as often as they
insist on a southern society dominated by self-consciously genteel and superior aristocrats.

One theme prevalent in southwestern humor, and later to be
taken up again by southern local colorists, is the prejudice which
plain folk entertain against a self-appointed aristocrat. Often the
humorist himself seems to share such a prejudice. In Robb's
"Hoss Allen's Apology," a folksy candidate makes a fool of
his gentlemanly opponent, to the immense delight of the voters.
In "Ham Rachel, of Alabama" country voters are told, "We are
all for Taylor; we know him; he has fought our battles; he is
one of the people; if he were to come to your cabin, he would
be at home, drink buttermilk, eat bread and butter and yam potatoes with you. As to General Cass, he's been doing nothing
all his life but scooting canoes up and down the Western waters,
and knows nothing about statesmanship."[7] Usually when an
educated character is juxtaposed to a backwoodsman in southwestern tales, the plainer man seems the better man, shrewder
and more capable of surviving. Even in the work of Joseph G.
Baldwin, whose lack of sympathy for backwoodsmen and for
frontier life often approaches contempt, we find such a passage
as the following: "But how could . . . [a wealthy Virginia Gen-
tleman] believe it? How *could* he believe that that stuttering,
grammarless Georgian, who had never heard of the resolutions
of '98, could beat him in a land trade? 'Have no money dealings
with my father,' said friendly Martha to Lord Nigel, 'for, idiot
though he seems, he will make an ass of thee.'"[8]

Some backwoodsmen are less sympathetically presented than
others, and Johnson Jones Hooper's Simon Suggs is a rascal by
any standards. Like Ransy Sniffle, however, Suggs appears the
greater villain because he contrasts so clearly with the characters
surrounding him. While the townsfolk he constantly fleeces
often seem through their gullibility or cupidity to deserve the
treatment Suggs gives them, still the humor of each sketch rests
partially on the recognition that a rascal like Suggs can outwit
his superiors. Suggs' adventures provide an interesting commen-

tary on southern social structure in the days when the South was first settled. One fact emerging from *The Adventures of Simon Suggs* is that social respectability in a southern frontier town was often based on possession of wealth. Perhaps this suggestion explains some of the contempt Longstreet displays for wealthy townsfolk, or perhaps the contempt Longstreet first expressed partially explains the existence of Hooper's observation. At any rate, when Simon Suggs begins his adventures, he goes to a lavish gambling parlor and begins to impersonate a wealthy but eccentric hog-drover: "In a few minutes, indeed, it was whispered through the company, that the red-eyed man with white hair, was the wealthy field-officer who drove swine to increase his fortune; and in consequence of this, Simon thought he discovered a very considerable improvement in the way of politeness, on the part of all present. The bare suspicion that he was rich, was sufficient to induce deference and attention."[9] The point made explicitly in southwestern humor tales, and implicitly in later local color fiction, is that a southerner's possession of wealth usually insures respect. Descent from a good old family is unnecessary. The corollary suggestion, one local colorists emphasized more explicitly, is that respectable ancestors or family are unnecessary for any man whose self-respect is based on his own merits rather than on those of his family.

Except for the relationship of southwestern humor to the humor of local color (a topic to be covered later in this study), perhaps the clearest evidence of the close relationship between southwestern humor and southern local color is the similarity of the events on which both kinds of stories are based. The following is a list, compiled by Cohen and Dillingham, of the most typical subjects in southwestern humor:

1. The hunt
2. Fights, mock fights, and animal fights
3. Courtings, weddings, and honeymoons
4. Frolics and dances
5. Games, horse races, and other contests
6. Militia drills
7. Elections and electioneering
8. The legislature and the courtroom
9. Sermons, camp meetings, and religious experiences

10. The visitor in a humble home
11. The country boy in the city
12. The riverboat
13. Adventures of the rogue
14. Pranks and tricks of the practical joker
15. Gambling
16. Trades and swindles
17. Cures, sickness and bodily discomfort, medical treatments
18. Drunks and drinking
19. Dandies, foreigners
20. Oddities and local eccentrics.[10]

The chapters which follow should make clear just how closely local colorists followed the lead of southwestern humorists, not only in the approval they expressed of the plain folk but also in the subjects or events on which they chose to base their stories. One should remember that the passive, degraded poor white, as he was stereotyped, could never have participated in most of the activities described in both southwestern humor and local color tales. He would not have had the initiative required for such group activities as militia drills, electioneering, and participating in contests and competitions. He would lack the money or goods necessary for drinking and gambling, and the strength required for fighting or frolicking. He would have been too poor to entertain anyone in his home and too depraved to participate in religious meetings. While the participants in all these activities described by southwestern humorists are often crude, rough, vulgar, and callous, they nevertheless assume their own worth, their equality with others. It is the frontiersman's self-confidence and assertiveness which allow us to identify him as the forerunner not of the white trash but of the plain folk.

# The Economic Identity

*AS I HAVE NOTED* southern local colorists, when
they consider a statement necessary, usually divide the antebellum southern social structure like Gaul into three parts: Aristocrats, Negroes, and Trash. Despite such standardized statements,
however, local colorists are capable of making much finer distinctions between types of southern whites by indicating differences of speech, education, manners, attitudes, and ways of
living. Unlike the New England communities that Harriet Beecher
Stowe presents in which a minister or minister's descendant is
granted high status regardless of his earnings,[1] the class differences in southern fiction are very closely related to differences
in income. In fact it is important to notice initially that the antebellum communities of fiction are not really different from their
postbellum avatars in this respect. Since money could as greatly
influence the status of one living in either Old or New South as
in the West or the New England local colorists portrayed, we
approach the plain folk first by determining the usual income
local colorists assign them.

As a rule, plain people neither enjoy the immense wealth

supposedly characteristic of planter aristocrats, nor suffer the abject poverty of the poor whites. The first thing one notices, in fact, is that southern local color fiction provides almost as many economic categories in which to place plain folk as later historians such as Phillips or Owsley do. In order to differentiate between wealthier plain folk and aristocrats, or between poorer plain folk and trash, one can assume that the plain folk category includes those who talk in dialect while still being described respectfully by the writers, those who have amassed wealth recently by hard work, or those an author specifically labels plain people.

Whether stories are set before or after the war, the plain folk category includes owners of relatively large plantations. One plantation with many slaves, for example, has as proprietors "plain, honest folk of the class commonly damned as "estimable' by their more pretentious neighbors. . . ." Their life involves "traditions that, so far as they went, were equal to the best— traditions of affluence as expressed in bountiful living, open doors and stables, and a retinue of lazy, happy-go-lucky servants, underworked and overfed. . . ."[2] The planter in Will N. Harben's "The Whipping of Uncle Henry" is wealthy enough to own property in several states and is enough of an aristocrat to be a loving master to his slaves. Yet his wife, instead of "pure English," speaks a somewhat ungrammatical dialect which Harben describes as "the colloquial speech of the middle class whites."[3] Ruth McEnery Stuart describes two Arkansas ladies— clearly plain folk since they smoke pipes, talk in dialect, giggle about youthful kisses, and abhor piano music—as "the sole representatives of a family that had stood with the best in the Arkansas community in which they lived. . . . Their mother and grandmother had had slaves at their call, and by frugal care had accumulated what there, in those days, was counted as wealth."[4] And in one of Richard Malcolm Johnston's stories, a Georgia planter with a hundred slaves and two thousand acres is presented in such a way that there is not the slightest need to assume he is an aristocrat: "Indeed, he had worked hard—so hard that he had never taken the time to learn any better manners than those which he had started with; and he was proud to feel that he had never needed them, and that he did not need them now."[5] The plain folk in southern local color stories, then, sometimes own prosperous plantations and are often the most respected members of a community.

These descriptions of plain but wealthy southerners suggest the importance of slaves and property, either owned or formerly owned in a particular family. In many of the stories, however, one finds farmers with much less property who are also considered prosperous by their neighbors. Indeed, it is not always easy to decide whether a character is wealthy, when one can read of a Georgian who had inherited "six Negroes and three hundred acres of well-stocked land—a fortune for those times."[6] It becomes obvious that in local color stories set before the Civil War, any slave owner, whether his slaves are one or many, has a respectable community status. We are reminded of the "portly widow Haycock" Simon Suggs encounters, "who was accounted wealthy, in consideration of the fact that she had a hundred dollars in money, and was the undisputed owner of one entire Negro. . . ."[7] Local color stories also contain characters such as the one who "lived in an unpretending one-story house, with the usual shed-rooms, and owned a reasonably good piece of land, out of which, with the help of four negroes . . . [he] got a living and something over"[8] or ones who live in a "double log-house" on a "little farm" with "two negroes"—wealth the neighbors consider "snug property."[9] Or the stories describe such folk as the Thigpens, who "had always been an industrious family. They had a good piece of ground of a couple of hundred acres. On this Allen with four negroes, a man, his wife, and their two boys, used to make good crops and was able to lay up a little every year."[10] It is important to notice that characters in local color fiction may live in cabins or log-houses, with few slaves and few acres of property, and still be considered prosperous.

But possession of slaves is not itself an unerring index of economic prosperity. Alice French describes widely respected but slaveless commoners living in antebellum Arkansas as "honest, hard-working people," one of whom "had a natural turn for business, though he could not write his name." Of this illiterate, she adds, "He prospered; he bought more land, he built a house for his mother—just the year before she died, poor soul,—and generously started his nieces and nephews in life."[11]

George Washington Cable describes the Louisiana Acadians as "simple, non-slaveholding peasants." [12] Yet Cable suggests that, as herdsmen, the Acadians also possess considerable wealth which may not be evident to one unaccustomed to their habits: "When I say . . . [an Acadian] was a man of note, I mean, for one thing, his house was painted. That he was the owner of thousands of cattle, one need not mention, for so were others who were quite inconspicuous. . . . Nor would it distinguish him from them to say he had many horses or was always well mounted. It was a land of horsemen." [13] Cable insists in *Bonaventure* that Acadians were respectable and even occasionally quite prosperous, even though they were descended from French peasantry, in contrast to the Creoles, who supposedly came from French or Spanish aristocracy. The "Cajuns" remain respectable in Acadian stories by other writers of the local color period, and therefore will be considered a part of the South's plain folk. Only in the stories of Kate Chopin, however, do Acadians ever own slaves; and even in Mrs. Chopin's work, the slaves never number more than one.

Several characters portrayed by southerners during this period not only have no slaves, but also have strong anti-slavery convictions. Harben's "A Humble Abolitionist" describes a Georgia couple who lend money to a neighboring aristocrat, hold a mortgage on his property, and get a slave in return for the investment when the planter goes bankrupt. They have never believed in slavery—hence their humorous awkwardness around the Negro. The Gills live in a three-room cabin, yet they are obviously in a better financial position than their bankrupt aristocratic neighbor. With dignity Peter Gill says of his slave, "I don't know as we-uns'll have any big hall for him to cavort about in . . . but we pay our debts an' have plenty t'eat." [14] Southern mountaineers described in the local color period not only own no slaves, but are so adamantly hostile to Negroes that many—at least in Joel Chandler Harris's stories—refuse to fight in a war which will preserve the institution of slavery.

> "Them dad-blasted Restercrats a-secedin' out'n the Nunited States."
> "They say they er airter savin' of the'r niggers. . . ."

"Well, I hain't got none, and I hain't a-wantin' none; an' it
hain't been ten minnits sense I ups an' says to Dave Hightower,
s'I, 'The Nunited States is big enough for me.'"[15]

Yet the mountaineers, though they are slaveless and poor, also
belong among the plain folk. Mary Noailles Murfree is the local
colorist most closely associated with the mountain setting because her stories were so popular, particularly her first volume,
*In the Tennessee Mountains.* Though she conveyed a rather negative mountaineer stereotype in that first volume, still she makes
the point that mountaineers are not to be confused with poor-
white-trash:

> It would have been impossible to demonstrate to them that they
> stood on a lower social plane [than educated folk from the valley].
> Their standard of morality and respectability could not be ques-
> tioned; there had never been a man or woman of the humble name
> who had given the others cause for shame; they had lived in this
> house on their own land for a hundred years; they neither stole nor
> choused; they paid as they went, and asked no favors; they took no
> alms,—nay, they gave of their little! As to the artificial distinctions
> of money and education—what do the ignorant mountaineers care
> about money and education![16]

Even an occasional tenant farmer or sharecropper is respectable enough to be classed among the plain folk of local color,
particularly if he is an Acadian. In Kate Chopin's "Loka" we
meet "a respectable family of 'Cadians"[17] who adopt an Indian
girl at the behest of the Band of United Endeavor. Though the
husband of the family "cropped in a modest way" and the
family income was modest, "the 'Cadian woman was a deserv-
ing one, with a large family of small children, who had all her
own work to do" (p. 194). The family is respectable enough for
town leaders to entrust them with the moral instruction of a
wayward Indian. The wife is impatient with slovenly Loka:
"She's vrai sauvage, that's w'at. It's got to be work out of her"
(p. 196). But the husband excuses her because, as he reminds
his wife, "We got to rememba she ent like you an' me, po'
thing; she's one Injun, her" (p. 206). The Acadian tenants in "A
Dresden Lady in Dixie" are so respectable that after it appears
the daughter of the family has stolen a Dresden figurine, she

confesses to a friend, "I tell you, Pa-Jeff, its neva been no thief
in the Bedaut family. My pa say he couldn't hole up his head if
he thinks I been a thief, me. An maman say it would make her
sick in bed, she don' know she could ever git up."[18] Though
only white trash are supposed to live in piney woods areas,
"Boulôt and Boulotte" presents "two brown-skinned, black-eyed
'Cadian roly-polies" who are both "piny-wood twins" and also
admirably industrious. The twins have apparently learned their
good habits from their family; all live in "a neat log cabin that
had a substantial mud chimney at one end" (p. 207). Thus even
the very poor, even occasionally a tenant farmer, can be considered plain folk. They are not necessarily white trash, for the
status of a character is determined by the writer's attitude
toward him, by the way in which the writer presents him. Local
colorists present many characters, both very rich and very poor,
who demand respect and who remain a part of the plain folk.

The difference which attitudes can make is illustrated in two
almost identical stories by Kate Chopin. The action, the situations described, and the plight of the characters are the same in
each. But in one the primary characters are Acadians, and are
viewed respectfully, in spite of their poverty.[19] In the other, one
character is a poor Anglo-Saxon: that makes all the difference.
In this case the national origin of characters shapes the author's
attitude and by shaping that attitude determines the class status
of the characters.

"In Sabine" is about trashy Bud Aiken, who has tricked a
pleasant and proper Acadian girl into marrying him. After the
wedding he mistreats her and she, being illiterate, cannot write
her family for help. Aiken's cabin is an index of his shiftlessness:
"The one room that constituted his home was extremely bare of
furnishings,—a cheap bed, a pine table, and a few chairs, that
was all. On a rough shelf were some paper parcels representing
the larder. The mud daubing had fallen out here and there from
between the logs of the cabin; and into the largest of these aper-
tures had been thrust pieces of ragged bagging and wisps of
cotton. A tin basin outside on the gallery offered the only bathing facilities to be seen."[20]

The Aikens possess only two spoons for silverware, and live
in a cabin exactly like that of a Negro with whom Aiken works
his crop on shares. A passing nod is paid in the story to the

good-hearted Negro, when Gregoire Santien, a Creole of good family, arrives to find the colored man chopping Aiken's wood. The Negro tells Santien, "Ef I don't chop dis heah, his wife got it to do. Dat w'y I chops 'ood, suh" (p. 79). The conclusive proof of Aiken's worthlessness is that he says in front of his wife, "That's the way with them Cajuns . . . ain't got sense enough to know a white man when they see one" (p. 83). Santien feels quite noble when he steals Aiken's one horse and takes the wife back to her family.

"A Visit to Avoyelles" also concerns a husband who "was not kind except to himself."[21] He mistreats his wife Mentine and gives her nothing but babies—and those as fast as she can have them. Yet Jules, the husband, is Acadian. Mentine had run away to marry him without his tricking her, as Bud Aiken did his wife. When one of Mentine's former suitors arrives to check on rumors about the couple, his observations are not about the shiftlessness of the husband, but rather about the sad changes in the wife. Mentine's voice has grown rough and shrill from screaming at her children. Her figure, "that had looked so trim in the wedding gown, was sadly misshapen. She was brown, with skin like parchment, and piteously thin. There were lines, some deep as if old age had cut them, about the eyes and mouth" (p. 226). At the end Doudouce leaves sadly, helpless to do more than promise Mentine's boys a mustang to ride. In contrast to "In Sabine" this story portrays a woman whose bad judgment has resulted in her becoming like her husband. When two Acadians marry, however, the marriage is sacrosanct and must be respected. Though she has made a bad bargain, Mentine sticks to it and keeps a little of her self-respect.

In the first story Gregoire Santien is well within his gentlemanly rights, is in fact performing his gentlemanly duty, in rescuing a good Acadian from her contemptible husband. In the second story, because all characters are of the same status, each respects the rights of the other. Bud Aiken, the shiftless husband, loses a wife and a horse in the first story. But the Acadian plain folk seem to enjoy a good relationship to those of higher status in both stories.

While plain folk in local color stories often live near families with great wealth, some writers depict areas in which the degree of prosperity is fairly uniform. Among Georgia settings Johnston's Dukesborough and surrounding countryside and Harris's Pinetucky District are mostly composed of people who are "sociable and comparatively comfortable."[22] Harris summarizes the economic status of these folk in a sentence: "With few exceptions, all the Pinetuckians owned land and negroes. . . ."[23] Cable presents the Acadians of the Louisiana prairies as citizens who are all more or less equally prosperous. The mountaineers in the stories of Mary Murfree, John Fox, Jr., and Joel Chandler Harris all seem poor, but they are usually untroubled by their economic level. And Charles W. Chesnutt describes Branson County, North Carolina, by saying: "Society in Branson County is almost primitive in its simplicity. Most of the white people own the farms they till, and even before the war there were no very wealthy families to force their neighbors, by comparison, into the category of poor whites."[24] A character in one of Tourgée's novels finds such a Carolinian "a thrifty farmer, with four or five hundred acres of good land, living in a log-house, with a strange mixture of plainness and plenty about him."[25] He decides that the class to which the farmer belongs is "rough and plain," but also "very good-hearted and honest" (p. 99).

Most of the passages quoted so far have suggested a rural society, and certainly the antebellum South had a predominantly agricultural economy. Here and there stories reveal an active prejudice against business and commerce, a prejudice first expressed by Longstreet and the southwest humorists. In Harris's "Aunt Fountain's Prisoner," for example, after an industrious Yankee turns the old southern plantation of his wife's family into a thriving dairy and the base of "trading and other commercial transactions in butter," the narrator states that the old people who once lived in the neighborhood "would have been horrified; and no wonder, for when they were in their prime the Tomlinson Place was the seat of all that was high, and mighty, and grand, in the social world in the neighborhood of Rockville."[26] As the mountaineer is more sympathetically portrayed in the later stories of Mary Murfree, he begins to seem superior to the valley folk who are corrupted by commerce. One says, "I ain't settin' store on the valley lands I seen whenst I went ter the wars. I kin remember yit what them streets in the valley towns smelt like. . . . Heaven's no place fur tradin', I understan', an' I *do* wonder sometimes how in the worl' them merchants an' sech

in the valley towns air goin' ter entertain tharse'fs in the happy
land o' Canaan. It's goin' ter be sorter bleak fur them, sure's ye
air born."[27]

In spite of these occasional comments, however, the plain
folk of local color stories are often engaged in occupations other
than farming. Several of the stories involve characters who are
either storeowners, as in Harben's "A Filial Impulse,"[28] or clerks
and managers, as in Kate Chopin's "Azélie."[29] A clerk is the
hero of one of Cooke's most flagrantly sentimental stories,
"Annie at the Corner."[30] Although the pretentious Bill Williams
is always a comic character in Johnston's stories, his occupation
as store clerk is respected by the country children with whom he
attended school. Just before he quits school to enter the store,
Bill is excused from a whipping because the schoolmaster, too,
respects all who work in town.[31]

Doctors and lawyers are mentioned often. Interestingly, in
fact, only medicine and law provide completely respectable pro-
fessions in southern local color literature. Prosperous merchants
rarely appear. If a man is prosperous, he is usually a farmer or
planter. Clergymen, too, appear seldom in these stories, and
when they do appear, are usually biblical fundamentalists of a
lower economic level. Perhaps here again we can trace the influence of southwestern humor. In prewar humorous sketches
the preacher is often detested by a less inhibited character such
as George Washington Harris's Sut Lovingood. Sut often makes
the circuit rider the butt of his practical jokes, just as Simon
Suggs does. When the parodies of fundamentalist sermons written by William Penn Brannan are recalled along with the adventures of Sut Lovingood and Simon Suggs, one begins to suspect
that southern local colorists, searching for pleasant characters
and uncontroversial subjects while still using the ideas developed in southwestern humor, preferred simply to avoid the
southern preacher as a type too controversial to be safe.

Even the most sentimental southern local color stories, however, occasionally admit that agricultural pursuits were not necessarily the most promising occupations. Harris and Page both
mention the possibilities of making money by working on the
railroad, though in the stories of each, a railroad worker is involved in a dangerous accident. In Page's "Run to Seed"[32] the
hard-working son of a good family realizes after the war that his

family is getting poorer and poorer, and therefore secures a job on the railroad. He sends all his money home to his mother and sister, and then dies nobly, victim of a railroad accident in which he has saved the lives of all the passengers. In Harris's "The Baby's Christmas" a young girl is forbidden to love a railroad conductor because her parents consider him below their social status. "He had been a train-hand, a brakeman, baggage-master and what not."[33] Yet in a passage in which Harris gently satirizes southern newspapers, he suggests that the conductor is considered respectable enough by the citizens of Rockville. When the couple elopes, the local newspaper runs a headline reading,

LOVE LAUGHS AT LOCKSMITHS
A LOCAL ROMANCE WITH A HAPPY ENDING

(p. 395). In both these stories, of course, the postwar setting suggests that in the better days before the Civil War, working on the railroad would not have been necessary for a respectable young man.

Other stories mention boardinghouse operators and artisans. In fact the family who disapprove so heartily of their daughter's lover (in Harris's "The Baby's Christmas") run the boarding-house where the daughter meets her conductor. Constance Fenimore Woolson's "Felipa"[34] describes a family living so far back in the Florida canebrakes that the little daughter has never seen another white woman. Yet it is with this family that three northern tourists spend a winter. The family is at least prosperous enough to be able to accommodate tourists comfortably for an extended period of time. In "Otto, the Knight," a story Alice French sets in Arkansas, the most sympathetic character is a woman who cooks meals for white workers employed in the area. The narrator describes Aunt Betsy Graham by saying, "There was not a kinder woman in Lawrence County, or, in homely fashion, a better cook."[35] The hero of the same story is a carpenter named Dake, "a young English artisan" who had come to America "to better himself" and who makes "a plain husband," but one with high "moral aspirations" (p. 16). And in Harris's "A Piece of Land"[36] the justice of the peace is a wheel-wright, while several blacksmiths appear in mountain stories.

Thus southern local color stories indicate that one did not have to be a farmer to be a respectable member of the plain folk.

Also mentioned in local color are groups of southern plain folk who live outside the towns but earn their livings from occupations other than farming. These groups represent in fiction what Frank Owsley documents as fact:

> Of course, the great error that casual travelers and later writers have made concerning the mountain and piney-wood folk of the antebellum South has been to consider them agriculturists. Had they lived upon the plains, their livestock economy would have been apparent; but because of the great forests their herds of cows and droves of hogs were seldom to be seen by anyone passing hurriedly through the country. Nor could the economic importance of their subsidiary occupation of hunting and trapping be realized except by one who tarried long and learned the ways of these taciturn folk.[37]

One later writer who "tarried long and learned the ways of these taciturn folk" instead of "passing hurriedly through the country" was George W. Cable. A careful historian, Cable toured the Acadian prairies and swamps before writing *Bonaventure*, in order to make accurate notes on the people living there. The shrewdness of his observations about this group is unique in the local color period. Cable was observant enough to notice that the Acadians should actually be divided into two groups: the prosperous herdsmen of the prairies and the poorer inhabitants of the bayous and bogs lying southward along the Louisiana coast. *Bonaventure* is divided into three long novellas, the first of which describes life on the prairie, the second life in the bayou country. Cable presents the Acadians in "Carancro," the first novella, more sympathetically than those in "Grande Pointe," the second; but in both he suggests that the Acadians should not be judged primarily as farmers. The prairie folk are herdsmen, and the bayou dwellers are hunters and trappers. One boy at Grande Pointe reads time "by hunter's signs in nature's book" (p. 91), and his father, in giving an inventory of their possessions, suggests that he lives the life of a fisherman: "Bonaventure, I don't got much. I got dat li'l' shanty on Bayou des Acadiens, and li'l' plunder inside—few kittle', and pan',—cast-net, fish-line', two, t'ree gun', and—my wife' grave" (p. 187).

At the beginning of "Grande Pointe" a Negro states that each bayou Acadian has only "a lil fahm so lil you can't plow her; got dig her up wid a spade" (p. 75). Cable suggests within the story, however, that the Negro is misrepresenting those living on Bayou des Acadiens when he suggests that a little farm is all Acadians have. They are not primarily farmers, and thus need no more than a garden plot. In "Grande Pointe" the men of the Acadian village also prepare to help out a nearby planter during the harvest season. The fact suggests one reason that Acadians in the local color stories, even when they are described as tenants, are still quite respectable: they have other means of income.

Not so observant or careful as Cable, those writing mountain stories suggest that mountaineers make what little money they have by trying to farm their rocky plots of land. This assumption leads to striking contradictions in the generalizations about mountaineers. They are presented, for example, as both lazy and proud, slow and agile, stolid and fierce, stupid and dignified. Yet the stories refer frequently to the accuracy of mountain sharpshooters and picture the hillbillies occasionally driving cattle. Perhaps in retrospect we can see that even these stories hint that mountaineers sometimes occupied themselves as hunters, herdsmen, and trappers.

Usually, however, the mountaineer's practice of illegally distilling whiskey explains his economic survival. Stills are mentioned prominently in almost every mountain story, with the exception of those in Mary Murfree's first volume. But Miss Murfree's later stories take up the subject of moonshining so repetitiously that one wonders whether it were an oversight not to make stills more central to her first tales. At any rate, from the first mountain stories to be collected in a volume after the Civil War[38] throughout the local color period, one rarely finds any story set in southern mountains which does not include a still. Especially after Harris published "Up at Teague Poteet's,"[39] southern local colorists usually took an indulgent view of mountaineer moonshining.

The plain folk of southern local color live on many and varied economic levels, and are occupied not only in farming, but also in other activities. Some are clerks in town stores, some run boarding houses or work on railroads, and some are hunters, trappers, and fishermen in the backwoods. The widest divergence of economic prosperity, however, is evident among the farmers. And it is not at all misleading to consider plain folk primarily those living in the semi-isolation of a farm. A rural atmosphere pervades even the towns described in most stories.

Throughout Johnston's stories runs a refrain about the joys of visiting Augusta:[40] "at which any man of respectable standing in Middle Georgia, during that period . . . would have been rather ashamed to acknowledge that he had never been for at least one time."[41] But Augusta is always a place one visits equipped with saucer eyes, the better to observe the marvels there for reporting back to Dukesborough. Even when Harris describes the larger towns of middle Georgia, the habits and mores of the townsfolk are essentially rural. Most of the more closely settled areas mentioned in these stories are not so much towns as villages or settlements. And the pointlessness of considering these settlements as different from the country in any important way is suggested in a gently satiric passage, typical of Joel Chandler Harris's work: "In brief, Pinetucky was satisfied with itself. It was a sparsely settled neighborhood, to be sure, but the people were sociable and comparatively comfortable. They could remain at home, so to speak, and attend the militia musters, and they were in easy reach of a church-building which was not only used by all denominations—Methodists, Baptists, and Presbyterians—as a house of worship, but was made to serve as a schoolhouse."[42]

# The Basis of Social Status

THE FACT that equally admirable plain folk are portrayed as living on widely varying economic levels suggests that in southern local color fiction social standing could be based on something other than wealth or family. Joel Chandler Harris implied as much when he called middle Georgia "the most democratic region, socially, in the world."[1] One of the most striking paradoxes of American local color, in fact, is that southern local colorists who insist in one sentence that the antebellum South was predominantly an aristocratic culture usually insist soon afterwards on its democratic fluidity; while a northerner such as Harriet Beecher Stowe, describing New England as "the vigorous germinating seed-bed for all that has since been developed of politics, laws, letters, and theology, through New England to America and through America to the world," also states that "Massachusetts was in regard to the aroma and atmosphere of her early days, an aristocratic community. The seeds of democratic social equality lay as yet ungerminated in her soil."[2]

Southern local color creates the impression that Harris could have extended his definition of democratic Georgia to the whole South, if he only excepted Virginia and Louisiana from the rule.

One "Virginian of good birth," Colonel Carter of Cartersville, still clings "away down in the bottom of his soul . . . to the belief that the poor white trash of the earth includes about everybody outside of Fairfax County."[3] But Colonel Carter has only a "fair education, and limited knowledge of the world and of men." Although he is excessively "proud of his ancestry, proud of his State, proud of himself" (p. 10), most southern local colorists concede that Virginians are different from other men. Non-Virginians in these stories more nearly fit Harris's generalization. In fact, when a story is set in Georgia, a character is portrayed as a snob only if he or his family were originally Virginians.

An explanation for so purposively democratic a milieu is suggested by one of Richard Malcolm Johnston's stories. "Careful Pleadings" implies that anti-aristocratic prejudice widespread in central Georgia would have made it unwise, even dangerous, for anyone to insist too dogmatically on his social superiority to others.[4] John Kilgore, a poor neighbor, resents the exclusiveness of a townsman, General Snow. Johnston says, "Some country people regarded . . . [the general] as a would-be aristocrat because of his solitary, luxurious living. . . . Among those who took this view, the most pronounced was John Kilgore, who often saw fit to claim that he was as good a man, every bit and grain, as old Jim Snow, whom other people might call General, but not John Kilgore, No, sir!"[5] Kilgore complains to his friends, "'It's nothin' but proud and it's nothin' but astocracy that he never goes to nobody's house, nor never invites people to his'n. If he weren't so little already, it would be a good thing to let him be took down a button hole or two lower'" (p. 238). Since the general seems fond only of a pet dog, Kilgore decides to shoot the dog. He goes to General Snow's house to swear that his sheep has been killed by the general's dog. But when he arrives, the general invites him in for a drink, and Kilgore soon withdraws his complaint. The story suggests not only that a feeling of exclusiveness was rare enough among wealthier Georgians to elicit negative comment, but also that it probably would have been senseless to flaunt such an attitude in democratic middle Georgia. In Georgia, as in most southern states, anyone who proves himself a gentleman is respected—that is, accorded enough status to meet his wealthier neighbors as an equal.

But the question of what constitutes a gentleman in local

color stories demands answering. As a rule a gentleman is anyone who conducts himself in a way of which the community
approves. Being a gentleman involves the possession not of
wealth, but of good character. And the sign of good character is
self-respect. Although narrators of southern local color stories
often seem amused when a very poor character claims to be a
gentleman, still the claim goes uncontested if the character
proves himself virtuous. This principle is amply illustrated in
Kate Chopin's "A Gentleman of Bayou Têche." In this story an
impoverished Acadian agrees to pose for a journalist who is looking for "local color." When an old Negress tells the Acadian's
daughter that the magazine caption underneath her father's
picture will read, "Dis heah is one dem low-down Cajuns o'
Beyeh Têche"[6] the daughter attempts to break her father's appointment and challenges the intentions of the amused men in
a nearby plantation where the journalist is staying. As she does
so, the Acadian appears with the wet body of the journalist's
son in his arms. The son's pirogue has upset in a bayou, and the
Acadian has saved the boy from drowning. The grateful journalist begs for a picture and assures the Acadian that he can entitle
it himself. The old man chooses as his inscription, "Dis is one
picture of Mista Evariste Anatole Bonamour, a gent'man of de
Bayou Têche" (p. 303). The narrator indicates that Bonamour
has proved his claim to the title of gentleman. In gratitude for
Bonamour's heroism, the plantation owner invites the Acadian
and his daughter to breakfast. The narrator adds, "They sat
down at the corner of the table, making no manner of objection
in their perfect simplicity" (p. 301).
    Similar poor but self-respecting men prove they are "gentle-
men" in stories set in almost every locality treated extensively
by local colorists. In one of Alice French's stories, an illiterate
Arkansan, "the best driver in 'the bottom,'" is described as a
natural gentleman: "Jeff, with his one arm and his Southern gal-
lantry, is helping the widow . . . who doesn't need helping one
whit, but accepts it as the duty of a 'man person.'"[7] This reverence for the ladies, always the highest mark of a southern
gentleman, is also inherent in a humble farmer living around
Knoxville, who proves even to the most skeptical—in Harry Stillwell Edwards' "His Defense"—that he is a gentleman. Hiram
Ard, the hero, is indicted on a charge of cursing before his

mother-in-law. The lawyer whom Ard hires is so amused at the charge that he can scarcely keep a straight face when Ard approaches him. The lawyer sees Ard as a very poor farmer of the lowest economic class who

> was tall, and in old age would be gaunt. He was also sunburned, and stooped a little as from hard labor and long walking in plowed ground or long riding behind slow mules. One need not have been a physiognomist to discover that, although yet young, the storms of life had raged about him. But ... he was neat, and ... his jeans suit was home-made, and his pathetic homespun shirt and sewed-on collar—the shirt and collar that never will sit right for any country housewife, however devoted—were ornamented with a black cravat made of a ribbon and tied like a school-girl's sash.[8]

When his trial begins, Ard's natural humility, his unwavering self-respect, his love of wife and child, and his chagrin at having spoiled a "gentleman's record" by cursing before a lady, all quickly win for him the sympathy of jury and audience. "For all the world loves a manly man, and from that moment [that Ard began to talk] their attention never wavered" (p. 8). By the end of the story Ard has so conclusively proved himself a gentleman that charges against him are dropped, the audience cheers him, and his teary-eyed lawyer returns the fee Ard had paid. The story illustrates clearly the way in which community status in local color stories is based not on money but on character.

This method of earning social status implies, of course, that anyone lacking the virtues approved by the community loses his social status, regardless of his wealth. In a body of fiction such as southern local color, in which the expected assumption is that anyone of wealth is an aristocrat, it is surprising to discover stories about villainous planters. Yet such stories were written by the same writers such as Joel Chandler Harris or Richard Malcolm Johnston who most often proclaimed the glories of the Old South. Harris's "Balaam and His Master" concerns the handsome son of Billville's leading family, who lacks self-discipline or restraint and is "sensual, cruel, impetuous, and implacable, ... the wonder of the mild-mannered people of the county, and a terror to the God-fearing."[9] The young master comes to the bad end he deserves and commits suicide in the Billville jail.

"A Piece of Land" includes as villain Bradley Gaither, a greedy planter who owns more land and slaves than the rest of Pine-tucky District put together: "He was first at church, and the last to leave; he even affected a sort of personal interest in politics; but the knack of addressing himself to the respect and esteem of his neighbors he lacked altogether. He was not parsimonious, but, as Squire Inchly expressed it, 'narrer-minded in money-matters.' He had the air of a man who is satisfied with himself rather than with the world, and the continual exhibition of this species of selfishness is apt to irritate the most simple-minded spectator."[10] In the same story old Billy Carew has also lost the respect of the community, as well as most of his property, be-cause of his habitual drunkenness.

Perhaps the best example of the way in which social status, in southern local color, is based on character rather than property is found in Johnston's "The Durance of Mr. Dickerson Prime." In this story Mr. Prime, a sycophantic farmer, makes a point of ingratiating himself with Mr. Sprowles, a wealthy planter. Yet neither man is regarded as the superior of the other because both have the same failings—they treat neither their families with respect nor their neighbors with good manners. Further-more, both are stingy. The farmer is characterized by "parsi-moniousness, and . . . a spirit notably apprehensive of harm to himself or his property."[11] Mr. Prime is determined to marry his daughter against her wishes to Sprowles's son, for he sees the match as a means of increasing his own property. Mr. Sprowles, on the other hand, is equally offensive because he does not appreciate Prime's services to his family and accepts "such service as one of the items of their dues" (p. 13). Incon-siderate of his wife, Mr. Sprowles seldom allows her the plea-sure of making the house and yard look more genteel. He so browbeats his son that the boy flees to Augusta. At the end of the story both men get their just deserts, for young Jim Sprowles returns very ill, and Mr. Prime rushes to nurse him. When the disease is diagnosed as smallpox, the community is so terrified that during the quarantine period Mr. Prime is required to stay isolated in his cottonshed. But rich Mr. Sprowles's punishment is greater, for his son is left so disfigured by smallpox that he flees westward and is never heard from again. Both men are viewed by the community (and by the narrator who speaks for the community) as equally unappealing because both lack the kind of character that merits respect.

These stories also suggest that the poor, even the trash, are judged individually, just as the wealthy are. In three Johnston stories—"A Case of Spite," "Oby Griffin," and "Mr. Eben Bull's Investments"—members of white-trash families earn community respect. The community honors the wife of Dan Hickson, a shiftless poor white in "A Case of Spite," because she "slaved herself" to provide for children her husband does not manage to support.[12] "Oby Griffin" plumbs a new depth of bathos even in the Johnston canon by describing a saintly little invalid who dies happy after his fondest wish has been granted and he has been baptized. Oby comes from a family of renters who "were . . . more rude than was common even in their class."[13] Yet when the Griffin family moved to the neighborhood, they were preceded by news of Oby's superior intellect and wisdom. "Mr. Eben Bull's Investments" describes a boy who in every way embodies the physical attributes associated with poor-white-trash:

> I noticed, moving about apparently with some anxiety, a pitiful-looking boy of about my height, but thinner. On a sort of sugar-loaf head was an irregular crop of hair of every shade of white, surmounted by a wool hat the rim of which in front for the breadth of his forehead had been torn away. His upper lip made a sort of arch over two of the biggest, longest, whitest teeth I have ever seen. His copperas-dyed, home-made clothes, short in the legs and arms, were out at the knees and elbows. His bowed legs looked like two long parentheses.[14]

Yet, in spite of bowed legs, wool hat, and badger teeth, the boy wins a foot-race, proving himself superior to the best runner Dukesborough offers. All of these stories suggest that community regard must be earned in a southern neighborhood, being neither an automatic accessory of wealth nor an attribute precluded by poverty.

Finally we receive the impression that a respect for individual human dignity, inculcated among the citizens of southern communities, makes rigid distinctions about social status unnecessary. Harris suggests that a major reason for this respect of

others is that most residents in an Old South community were
related to each other:

> Rockville ought to have been a harmonious community if there
> ever was one. The same families had been living there for genera-
> tions, and they had intermarried until everybody was everybody
> else's cousin. Those who were no kin at all called one another
> cousin . . . and so the habit grew until even the few newcomers
> who took up their abode in Rockville speedily became cousins.
> There were different degrees of prosperity in the village before
> and during the war, but everybody was comfortably well off, so
> that there was no necessity for drawing social distinctions. Those
> who were comparatively poor boasted of good blood, and they
> made as nice cousins as those who were richer.[15]

But social status is not simply based on general good character in southern local color fiction; very specific characteristics
are usually approved of. Though many virtues are occasionally
applauded, four are affirmed with great consistency—pride, courage, hard work, and common sense. Usually one of these four
suffices to make the reader respond to a character sympathetically. When a single character exhibits all four, he becomes a
paragon, as Hiram Ard is in Edwards' "His Defense."

Perhaps pride is a virtue in the local color stories because it
has been traditionally associated with aristocrats and nobility.
Virtually every aristocrat in local color stories is described as
proud. But pride is also a quality approved in common folk.
Certainly this approval is consistent with the American democratic tradition in which every man has something to be proud
of in his humanity. Of course the southerner of traditional views
would amend the statement to read "every white man," and
most southern local colorists reveal notoriously traditional southern views. Nevertheless pride in himself is almost enough, in
most southern local color stories, to compensate a character for
any other defect, particularly if his pride does not lead him to
the pitfall of snobbery. Any man who is both proud and tolerant
is a natural gentleman, regardless of his economic position.

Above all else southern characters are proud of their families. Yet this statement would seem to contradict everything
stated so far, had not Harris suggested that drawing social dis-

tinctions was unnecessary because "those who were comparatively poor boasted of good blood, and they made as nice cousins as those who were richer."[16] Tourgée, contradicting Mrs. Stowe,[17] singles out the "influence of family position" as one of the major differences between North and South: "Every family there has its clientelage, its followers, who rally to its lead as quickly, and with almost as unreasoning a faith, as the old Scottish clansmen, summoned by the burning cross."[18] The important thing about Tourgée's statement is that he describes family loyalty as an attribute of *all* southerners. Tourgée himself, perhaps because he lived among southerners for many years, fell into the habit of classifying or describing a character in terms of family background. He says of a Union sympathizer, for example, "He was of an old but not now wealthy family. His connections were good, but not high."[19]

Local color stories confirm Tourgée's statements both that all southerners possessed a family pride and that each family had its clientelage which rallied around in time of trouble. In Constance Woolson's "Up in the Blue Ridge," for example, a fundamentalist preacher who advocates total abstinence expends much effort to help the black sheep of a good family, an erring lad involved in operating a still. The preacher's philosophy is: "The Lord will forgive; it is an Eliot."[20] The minister explains that he loves the Eliot family in much the same manner that a subject is supposed to love his monarch. Because he was born upon Eliot land, he has been careful to hold the Eliot family in reverence all his life. He concludes his impassioned statement, "This son has been a sad, wild boy always—has nearly broken his father's heart. But he is an Eliot still; the little I can do for him I will do gladly until I die" (p. 321). The mountaineer feuds mentioned with increasing regularity toward the close of the local color period illustrate the same rallying of neighbors and friends to the cause of a particular family. In these stories, of course, the families are not aristocratic, though family feuds are also identified with Creole aristocrats in Cable's *The Grandissimes*.

Pride in family, then, is characteristic of southern characters, whether they are rich or poor. But when such pride is expressed by a particularly poor individual, the attitude is sometimes an occasion for humor. A woman in "a drooping gown of checked homespun . . . and a pair of coarse shoes just from the shop,"[21] announces proudly, "You've heerd me say I have good stock in me, ef I am poor. I've got own second cousins that don't know the'r own slaves when they meet 'em in the big road" (p. 21). Or a group of women whose costumes betray their poverty say with laughable smugness of a neighbor, "She is sometimes pleasant, to be sure, but if it was n't for her husband, poor man, who married her out of pity, although she was only a 'cracker' and he a man of education and standing, she would n't be noticed."[22]

Perhaps the best example of humor elicited by an expression of family pride is found in Harris's "Mingo." Mrs. Feratia Bivins, who Harris states is representative of the poor-white class, explains:

> "Goodness knows, I hain't come to that pass wher' I begrudges the vittles that folks eats, bekaze anybody betweenst this an' Clinton, Jones County, Georgy, 'll tell you the Sanderses wa'n't the set to stint the'r stomachs. I was a Sanders 'fore I married, an' when I come 'way frum pa's house hit was thes like turnin' my back on a barbecue. . . . No, sir, you won't find no begrudgers mixed up with the *Sanderses*. Hit useter be a *common* sayin' in Jones, an' cle'r 'cross into Jasper, that pa would 'a' bin a rich man an' 'a' owned *niggers* if it hadn't but 'a' bin bekase he sot his head ag'in stintin' of his stomach. That's what they useter say. . . ."[23]

Usually, however, pride in family is considered a commonplace trait of all characters in southern local color stories. Most writers, like Tourgée describing his Unionist, manage to mention of any character treated sympathetically that he comes of a good family.

Of all the special groups described in southern local color, mountaineers are particularly associated with pride. Indeed it is this quality which, in the stories written before Harris published his influential "Up at Teague Poteet's," most often saved the mountaineer from a poor-white classification. Mary Noailles Murfree speaks of a "pride, so intense that it recognizes no superior, so inordinate that one is tempted to cry out, Here are the true republicans!"[24] She states that "differences of caste are absolutely unknown to the independent mountaineers,"[25] and adds that there is among them "utter insensibility to the difference in . . . social position."[26] This last phrase explains why pride is applauded even among the poor in local color stories. A proud man confident of his own importance and worth need not be ashamed of his poverty. Pride is necessary if plain folk are to seem admirable in a land which particularly honors its wealthier ladies and gentlemen.

One of the consequences of this pride in himself or in his family is that it promotes in the proud man a sense of personal honor, an honor he will protect at all costs. We are familiar with the idea of an aristocrat who treasures his personal honor above all else, but this same sense of honor is associated in local color stories with the plain folk. Chesnutt's "The Sheriff's Children," for example, reveals the form this sense of personal honor takes in a county official. The sheriff in this story has sold his Negro mistress and his mulatto child years before. At the time of the story he is confronted by a mulatto prisoner whom the whole county suspects of having murdered a white man and who turns out to be the sheriff's own son. While the sheriff has felt no remorse about selling his son in the past, his rigid sense of honor makes him protect the young man once he is in jail. The sheriff refuses to allow a lynch mob to take the prisoner, for he believes firmly in the due process of law. Later in a scuffle, the mulatto manages to grasp the sheriff's gun and threatens to kill his father if not allowed to escape. The sheriff's sense of honor prevents his opening the cell. Chesnutt says, "It may seem strange that a man who could sell his own child into slavery should hesitate at such a moment, when his life was trembling in the balance. But the baleful influence of human slavery poisoned the very fountains of life, and created new standards of right. The sheriff was conscientious; his conscience had merely been warped by his environment."[27] The story is resolved when the sheriff's white daughter saves her father's life by shooting his mulatto son. The tale illustrates quite well the belief that a conscientious southerner would risk his life to preserve his honor, even if his actions should seem inconsistent to outsiders who do not understand southern mores.

The most dramatic examples of personal codes of honor are found in the mountain stories. In these the mountain code protects neighbors with stills from revenue officers. Not only does almost every story mention stills; but nearly every story also involves a fight between the revenuers and the hillbillies. From

the earliest local color mountaineer stories written by Sherwood
Bonner through the last feeble efforts of Mary Murfree or Matt
Crim runs an acknowledgment of the dire consequences visited
upon any mountaineer who betrayed his honor by cooperating
with federal officials and revealing the location of stills. As Matt
Crim reminds us, "According to the mountaineer's code of
honor, a man could not do a meaner, more contemptible thing
than to betray a comrade to the revenue-men."[28]

"The Case of Eliza Bleylock" and "Lame Jerry," both by
Sherwood Bonner, illustrate how strictly the fictional mountaineers demanded adherence to their "code." Eliza and Janey Bleylock, in the first story, are daughters of a man who owns a thriving still. A partner in Mr. Bleylock's enterprise is Dick Oscar, to
whom Janey is engaged. One day a peddler arrives at the Bleylock house and asks to stay a while. He tries to make love to the
girls, and succeeds in becoming engaged to Eliza, whom he often
asks for information about where her father gets his whiskey.
When Janey overhears one conversation and realizes that the
peddler is a government spy, she leads him to the still in revenge against Dick Oscar, who has retracted his promise to
marry her. Revenue agents then catch Oscar and the Bleylock
boys and take them to prison, bragging that one of Bleylock's
daughters revealed the still's location. Janey, meanwhile, has a
change of heart and walks alone all the way to the governor's
mansion to beg the release of her fiancé and family. She is such
a romantic figure that newspapers pick up the story, and because
public sympathy is aroused, the governor pardons the men. At
home again, all assume that Eliza was their Judas. Though she
could make the long journey to the governor on foot and by
herself, Janey cannot bring herself to admit that she was the one
guilty of so egregious a lapse of honor. So the men abuse Eliza:

> Afterward Eliza Bleylock seemed to wither away. She repeated her
> denial of having been a traitor, but no one ever believed her. She
> worked hard, and was used roughly. She had never been strong.
> Sometimes she stole away and nursed Janey's baby, that seemed to
> love her; but never when Dick Oscar was at home.
>     One day, sitting by the spring alone, . . . she died.
>     . . . And she was buried, with very little said about it, in the
> valley.[29]

"Lame Jerry" concerns another informer whom Janey and
Dick Oscar find beaten almost to death. They nurse him back to
health, although Dick indicates that he can never excuse a "tat-
tlin' sneak."[30] Though he recovers physically, Jerry is broken in
spirit by his beating and by a series of painful personal reversals described in the story. He ends his days totally ostracized
from human society, a kind of ghost who lacks the initiative
even to leave the mountain.

On the other hand many mountain stories, particularly those
written by Joel Chandler Harris—who always took the most
affirmative view possible—abound in the heroic feats of those
who risk their lives to warn their friends of approaching revenue
agents. Harris especially praises heroic young girls in such stories as "Up at Teague Poteet's" and "The Conscript's Christmas." Of course when the heroism of those acting upon this
code of personal honor is admired, then by extension the code
itself, even if it is an extra-legal one, is implicitly approved.

Warning men at the stills of approaching danger often takes
courage, the second major quality supplying social status in local
color stories. Courage is a quality most often associated with
men, particularly with brave soldiers. Certainly southern local
color offers a plentiful supply of brave Confederates for those
who wish to read of them. But a more interesting type is also
developed in this period—the courageous southern girl or lady.
Again we find the most dramatic examples of this type in the
mountain stories. Among tales of mountain girls who perform
remarkable feats of courage, usually walking or running many
miles—preferably through a snowy night—to save another, are
Constance Woolson's "Up in the Blue Ridge"; Sherwood Bonner's "Jack and the Mountain Pink"; Mary Murfree's "Drifting
Down Lost Creek," "The Star in the Valley," "His Day in
Court"; and Matt Crim's "S'phiry Ann" and "Silury," to name
only a few.

Courageous women are not found exclusively among the
"mountain pinks," however.[31] Another popular local color formula describes the courageous or imperious lady who singlehandedly saves her home from Yankee marauders. A good
example of such a character appears in Page's "My Cousin
Fanny," the sketch of a peppery spinster who is an accomplished
musician. When Yankees invade, a colonel promises Cousin

Fanny that he will spare her house if she will sing for him. Fanny explains how she resolved the awful dilemma in which she had to choose between performing for the enemy and protecting her property: "So I paid for my ransom, and a bitter ransom it was too, I can tell you, singing for a Yankee! But I gave him a dose of Confederate songs, I promise you. He asked me to sing the 'Star Spangled Banner'; but I told him I would not do it if he burnt the house down with me in it—although it was inspired by my cousin, Armistead."[32]

Because southern local color usually presents only the brighter side of things, those characters lacking courage are not so much contemptible as they are amusing. Johnston's Bill Williams is perhaps the most frequently used and popular coward among the fictional plain folk. When Williams is forced by his wife into a fist fight, he seems quite willing to lose until somebody assures him that his wife's former suitor will care for his family if he gets "too badly used up."[33] The most amusing incident, however, occurs when Bill is trying to decide which of two local girls to marry, and is in no hurry to make up his mind. His mind is made up for him when one of their brothers visits Bill armed with a stout hickory stick. Bill looks at the stick and confesses immediately, "It was Miss Karline I wanted all the time. . . . I always did love her the best, but which I didn't ezactly know it till jes now."[34]

Equal to pride and courage in the esteem of southern local colorists is a capacity for hard work, another source of social status for the plain folk. In spite of the antithetical plantation tradition which glorified gentlemen living a life of leisure on inherited estates, the hard-working man is the admirable man in most local color stories. Even the planters must be involved in unceasing activity of some kind if they are presented with complete sympathy. Only Harry Stillwell Edwards' Major Worthington is a planter both lazy and sympathetically presented; but the amused condescension Worthington evokes is the kind generally directed toward a character like Bill Williams. Other planters may sit on their porches drinking juleps, but first they must have earned through vigorous exercise the right to rest. In spite of the plantation tradition, southern local colorists consistently reveal a respect for the "successful" man and for the recognized avenue to success—hard work.[35]

Though in *Old Times in Middle Georgia* it is unclear whether
Johnston intended to reveal such an attitude, "Mutual School
Masters" suggests that an aristocrat is simply a man who is
"successful," that is, who is wealthy. In this anecdote two brothers serve each other as schoolmasters. Each holds the privilege of
beating the other if lessons are poorly prepared, and by this
method they learn Latin. The result of such earnestness is that
both become adults who earn a great deal of money. One brother
comments, "Many a poor boy, with scantier means, but with
superior gifts, has done far better than Dave and I. It only tends
to show what can be done by a youth of slim means and moderate understanding by searching for and making for himself opportunities instead of mouthing complaints against fortune for
not bestowing them gratuitiously" (p. 213).

This kind of statement is familiar to students of American
history. Underlying it is the assumption that any lad, by apply-
ing himself assiduously and using his brains and talents, can
achieve in the land of equal and unlimited opportunity, the
"American Dream" of wealth, power and prestige.[36] But if
the statement seems very American and very typical of the late
nineteenth century, it does not seem inherently southern, at
least if one retains a belief in a tripartite, antebellum southern
society most commonly characterized by the leisurely gentility
of hereditary aristocrats.

One may rightly object that Richard Malcolm Johnston is not
necessarily representative of southerners and that his nostalgic
recollection of his past is not necessarily accurate. Such objec-
tions seem less pertinent, however, when one glances through
the biographical sketches in *The Library of Southern Literature*, that
monument to regional chauvinism. Here, for example, Henry
Stiles Bradley, a southern University professor, extols Joel
Chandler Harris as a lad who "improved his opportunities" and
who as a newspaper apprentice "was unwilling to merely get
along": "Instead of being content to set the required ems of type
and take the balance of time for idling, he aspired to contribute
to the literary make-up of the paper. His daily question was not
'how shall I escape this disagreeable task,' but 'how shall I per-
fume this place till it shall smell of the myrrh and frankincense
of hearty service and cheerful sacrifice?' This stamped him at
once as a failure as a loafer. No man can loaf successfully with a

spirit like that."[37] Bradley finds Harris different "from the ordinary boy who does not succeed," from those who "wasted their
energies in misdirected channels . . . and are today unknown."
Harris might "have eked out a living as a lawyer or a school
teacher, but the living would have been all, if he had made that.
As it is, he has made fortune, fame, and a countless multitude of
friends."[38] Bradley thus implies quite clearly that the respected
man is the successful man, the one who directs his energies to
gaining fame, fortune, and friends. The unsuccessful man is the
one who squanders his energies in unremunerative pursuits, for
example editing Chaucer's poems, teaching school, or practicing
law. Joel Chandler Harris should be emulated because he was
successful.

Having absorbed Professor Bradley's comments, we begin to
understand why both Harris and Johnston so often portray middle Georgia as "the most democratic region, socially, in the
world."[39] Harris, bastard son of an Irish laborer, and Johnston,
son of an unpaid Baptist preacher and farmer, both experienced
that upward mobility made possible by a fluid society which
insisted on a white man's innate dignity and which revered
wealth or accomplishment more than background. In the stories
of both writers the road to wealth is traversed by means of hard
work.

The beneficent effect of hard work is preached so consistently, in fact, that anyone described as hard-working is automatically admirable. Jeff, the driver in Alice French's "The
Mortgage on Jeffy," has worked hard and prospered enough to
build his mother a house, and to start his nieces and nephews in
life. Miss French mentions that "there was money in cotton"
during the days of Jeff's prosperity.[40] But the good prices and the
prosperity are never really connected very closely. Jeff's prosperity instead is described as a product of his "natural turn for
business," especially of his willingness to work for what he desires. Though two feuding Arkansas farmers in "A Loaf of
Peace" seem very primitive in comparison to their planter neighbors, the reader understands that they are good men when their
daughters describe in great detail how industrious they are, not
only in the fields but also in the cabins, where both men help
with chores.[41] In the most sentimental stories about planters or
farmers, such as Harris's "How Whalebone Caused a Wedding,"

or Cooke's "The Wedding at Duluth," or Johnston's "The Durance of Mr. Dickerson Prime," it is the poor but hard-working suitor who always gets the girl, rather than a rich and sometimes effeminate rival.

In "Azalia," which explores the merits of a southern town, Harris even reveals his irritation at the northern assumption that southern ladies do not work. When a northern aunt and niece come to Azalia, Georgia, for reasons of health, the aunt assumes that they are entering a "wilderness," and is surprised, as soon as she arrives, to catch sight of a beautiful quilt. The niece concedes, "It is well made . . . and the colors are perfectly matched. Really, this is something to think about, for it fits none of our theories."[42] Harris identifies the source of those theories: "A course of novel-reading, seasoned with reflection, had led Miss Tewksbury to believe that Southern ladies of the first families possessed in a large degree the Oriental faculty of laziness. She had pictured them in her mind as languid creatures, with a retinue of servants to carry their smelling-salts, and to stir the tropical air with a palm-leaf fan" (p. 195). The story, of course, proves just how wrong the yankees had been in their theories about southern women: southern ladies are quite industrious.

Logically enough, any character in one of these stories who doesn't work is considered suspicious and often contemptible. As Owsley suggests, this distrust of any man who appeared to be sitting during the day instead of working probably explains why mountaineers were treated so condescendingly in the sketches of early travelers and in the first mountain stories of the local color period.[43] In her early mountain stories Mary Murfree describes the hillbillies in the most unflattering terms, concentrating on their apparent laziness. The mountaineer is "the hairy animal, whose jeans suit proclaimed him man."[44] The facial expression "very usual with these mountaineers" is one of "settled melancholy" (p. 90). Descriptive phrases such as "the languid monotony of the expression of his face" (p. 91), "the inherent inertia and conservatism of the mountaineer" (p. 174), "the vague, hazy reverie which is the habitual mental atmosphere of the quiescent mountaineer" (p. 91), or "his listless manner . . . of stolidity, not of a studied calm" (p. 90) become the rule rather than the exception in her first volume. It is not surprising to find Miss Murfree characterizing mountaineers, at one point, in terms of "their narrow prejudices, their mental poverty, their idle shiftlessness, their uncouth dress and appearance" (p. 134).

This prejudice against any who refuse to work probably explains the almost rabid anti-union sentiment in Alice French's "Otto the Knight." By the end of the story we have been led to identify labor unions with foreigners, anarchy, and violence; the good people are those who are willing to work honestly for their wages, even if working means crossing a picket line as a scab. The story relates the gradual conversion of Otto, a young boy, to more wholesome American attitudes than his uncle, a German immigrant and labor agitator, has taught him. Significantly the same story also suggests a certain prejudice against leisured aristocrats. Young Caroll, a plantation owner, "had his clothes sent him from his tailor in the North, he rode a fine horse, he polished his finger nails, he never seemed in a hurry. . . ."[45] Miss French adds, "Otto hated him." Indeed, Miss French does not seem totally out of sympathy with "Poor Otto, . . . [who] deemed it his duty to hate everybody that had very much money or very much land" (p. 23). The Caroll women reappear in *Otto the Knight*, but young Caroll is allowed to sink into effete silence. The ladies, in contrast to young Caroll, are very industrious.

In local color stories *work* usually means hard physical labor. As Johnston says in "Mr. Joseph Pate and His People," "In those days, white boys who worked at all were expected to work steadily like the negroes."[46] Will Harben, on the other hand, is more openly unsympathetic with the prejudice against those not engaged in exclusively manual labor. In "A Filial Impulse," a prospering writer returns to his home—a North Georgia cabin— to find his sick mother isolated in a hot, windowless room, and his stepfather as insulting as ever. On impulse he buys a neighboring plantation for his mother and her other children. He gains new family respect because he has enough money to make such a gesture. His stepfather replies, however, when told the visitor is a writer: "I 'lowed you mought go at some'm' o' that sort; you used to try mighty hard to write a good hand; you never would work."[47] The most effective social criticism in Harben's *Northern Georgia Sketches* appears in "Jim Trundle's Crisis," in which meddlesome neighbors decide to humiliate Jim Trundle by whipping him publicly, because they do not believe he is working properly. Their note to him states, "You are no earthly account, an no amount of talkin seems to do you any good. Yore children are in tatters an without food, an you jest wont do nothin fer them. This might hev gone on longer without our action, but last Wednesday you let yore sick wife go to the field in the hot brilin sun, and she was seed by a responsible citizen in a faintin condition, while you was on the creek banks a fishin in the shade."[48]

Jim Trundle decides that he deserves his whipping, resolves to do better, and meets the Regulators in the woods, ready to take his punishment. Harben is clearly sympathetic with Trundle, who is described as having a poet's soul. But the story illustrates the one way in which a disgraced southerner can be sure to redeem himself in the society local colorists describe: he can become respectable only by hard work. The same view is found in James Lane Allen's "King Solomon of Kentucky." A shiftless white man, formerly of a good Virginia family, is sold as an indentured servant in order that his debts can be paid. He becomes a town hero only when, during a cholera epidemic, he works digging graves until he contracts the disease and dies.[49]

Southern characters in local color stories judge almost everyone in terms of his ability to work. In sentimental eulogies of plantation life, the argument that Negroes are too lazy to care for themselves is used to defend slavery. One Page character shouts, "George Washington a slave! Madame, you misapprehend the situation. *He* is no slave. I am the slave, not only of him but of three hundred more as arrogant and exacting as the Czar, and as lazy as the devil."[50] The southern apologists also argue that the Negro's unwillingness to work hard made slavery an expensive and impractical method of cultivating land. One mistress of a large plantation "had heard some talk of the government buying the negroes from their owners and setting them free. She ardently hoped this would be done, for she was sure they could then be hired cheaper than they could be owned and provided for."[51]

Only laziness automatically makes a poor, white man into a poor white. Johnston's petty Dan Hickson, in "A Case of Spite," is trash because he won't work, just as his wife is respectable because she "slaves herself." When "good" Negroes refer condescendingly to white trash, the whites' laziness is usually mentioned. Henry, the best slave on the plantation which serves as setting for "The Whipping of Uncle Henry," objects to Cobb, the new overseer, because Cobb is too lazy to work in the fields, as we are led to infer that the absent owner does. According to Henry, "Thar ain't no pore white trash in all this valley country as low down as all . . . [Cobb's] layout."[52] Mrs. Pelham, the owner's wife, recognizes that Henry has assessed the overseer correctly. She says to herself, "Nobody kin hate a lazy, good-fer-nothin' white man like a nigger kin" (p. 49). Henry proves his superiority to Cobb by refusing to follow Cobb's orders, instead doing the work of three men in clearing a field by himself.

The fourth quality revered by the plain folk and the writers who describe them is common sense. Common sense, in local color stories, means getting maximal results with minimal labor. Perhaps this reverence for common sense can be traced back to southwestern humor tales, in which an untutored character's "horse sense" either enables him to survive in difficult circumstances or allows him to get the better of a more sophisticated companion in a trade or bargain. Regardless of the theme's source—whether in literature or contemporary society—however, approval of common sense is voiced often in local color fiction. If the plain folk approve of hard work, they still recognize that making work needlessly hard is a foolish expenditure of energy. Common sense allows them to tell the difference. In Johnston's "Weasels on a Debauch" a Georgia farmwife discovers that weasels are steadily killing her chickens. Since she cannot catch the weasels, she turns for help to Len Cane, who knows the habits of every animal indigenous to the area. He knows, for example, that after gorging themselves on chicken blood, weasels seek the nearest shelter to sleep. Simply by piling boards in the chicken yard, Cane is easily able to catch and kill the predators and save the chickens. With little effort Cane achieves an important result. But common sense can also be used to prevent tension or resolve a potentially dangerous situation. Thus Mary Murfree describes the common sense of a young boy in "A Warning." The boy's father returns from a "preaching" under the influence of the recent sermon and berates his brother-in-law for being intoxicated. When the ensuing argument is about to become violent, the small boy deftly overturns a pair of warping bars.[53] The men consider the clatter a supernatural warning and peace is restored.

Sometimes a character combines common sense with courage in a dramatic way. In Matt Crim's "Silury," for example, a young mountain girl hears that her father has been captured by revenue officers who are taking him to prison. She waits in ambush for the party, shoots her father's mule from under him, and screams at him to run. She makes such a racket that the troops assume a large party of hillbillies is shooting at them. The officers flee without bothering to recapture their prisoner.[54] It is with such simple stratagems that mountaineers usually outwit officers in these stories.

But common sense is most often employed in personal relationships, particularly to manipulate others, as two of Johnston's stories from *Old Times in Middle Georgia* illustrate. "Our Witch" describes the way in which two men manage one intractable woman. Andy Magraw is told by his homely wife that a pretty neighbor (who looks much younger than her age) is a witch. Knowing that argument is useless, Andy employs with his wife the famous "please-don't-throw-me-in-the-briar-patch" psychology. He begs her above all not to go to the head deacon of her church, the only man in the neighborhood of whom Andy suspects she is afraid. Mrs. Magraw of course goes immediately to the head deacon and is dealt with sensibly. The deacon simply tells her that her accusation is curious, since he understands that the pretty neighbor is about to reverse it. Mrs. Magraw knows that she looks somewhat witchlike, that she is unpopular with her neighbors, and that a reversed accusation might put her in some danger. Broken in spirit, she takes to her bed and dies, leaving her husband free to marry the pretty neighbor. The same psychology works in "Old Lady Lazenberry." Mrs. Lazenberry, an aging woman who finds herself a widow for the second time, knows that her chances of finding a third husband are extremely slim. In the whole neighborhood there is only one unattached man her age, and he is a confirmed bachelor. She therefore begs her gossipy daughter-in-law, above all, not to mention any burgeoning friendship between herself and the bachelor. When the daughter-in-law promptly spreads rumors about them all over the neighborhood, the surprised bachelor notices Mrs.

Lazenberry for the first time. Mrs. Lazenberry sends the poor man an apology for the rumors, denying that she has had anything to do with them, and when he calls to straighten matters out, he is promptly trapped as her third husband.

Those who call a spade a spade, rejecting inaccurate euphemisms or romantic evasions, are generally considered most sensible. Miss Jane Inchly, the spinster in Harris's "A Piece of Land," is such a stickler for fact. "Though she was neither fat nor fair, she was forty. Perhaps she was more than forty; but if she was fifty she was not ashamed of it. She had a keen eye and a sharp tongue, and used both with a freedom befitting her sex and her experience."[55] When Miss Jane's brother watches a neighbor careening drunkenly across the street, he says sympathetically, "First the limbs give way, and then the mind. It's Providence, I reckon. We're all a-gittin' old." Miss Jane replies with uncompromising orthodoxy, "Why, you talk, Ichabod, as if Providence went around with a drink of dram in one hand and a stroke of palsy in t'other one. . . . It's the old Boy that totes the dram. And don't you pester yourself on account of old Billy Carew's palsy. A man's nimble enough in the legs when he can git to the dimmy-john" (p. 243). When Squire Inchly suggests that perhaps the nagging of Carew's wife had something to do with his turning to drink, his sister replies, "A mouse'll squeal if you tromple on it." She adds that if the squealing is bothersome, then the intelligent course of action is obvious: "Don't pester the mouse" (p. 245).

Miss Jane Inchly is appealing because she voices her common-sense observations in the form of aphorisms. She is also an invaluable addition to an otherwise maudlin story. In the tale an honorable young man has been unjustly convicted of theft and has served part of his sentence in the state prison. When his good name is cleared and he returns to find his sweetheart waiting, it is Miss Jane's comment which slightly deflects the flood of bathos in which the story ends. "Go in there, Jack," she tells him. "A man oughtn't to grumble at waitin' for his dinner if he knows he'll git pie" (p. 273).

Other characters in local color possess equal amounts of Miss Jane's talent for seeing things more clearly than most, or for coining a shrewd phrase. In Page's sketch of an old maid he recalls, "She said that cleanliness was next to godliness in a

man and it was on a par with it [in a woman]";[56] or "She said
that Christ was born of a Virgin, and that every woman had this
honor to sustain" (p. 14). But common sense is not limited to
women or spinsters in these stories. When a pietistic politician
in Mary Murfree's "Electioneerin' on Big Injun Mounting"
hears of a wife-beating drunkard, he says hotly, "I can thrash
any man who beats his wife." A storekeeper quiets him by
pointing out sensibly, "That would be a mighty pore favor ter
his wife," explaining that "She hed ruther be beat" herself than
have her husband hurt or imprisoned.[57]

A character's common-sense approach to facts and events,
especially when facts are manipulated to his advantage, often
provides humor. Johnston's "Shadowy Foes" describes Penninah,
a widow for the second time, who has been subject during her
two marriages to intense fits of jealousy whenever she thought
of the hypothetical woman who would marry her husband if she
died. On two occasions when she was apparently on her death-
bed, she became so angry with the husband who would not
promise to forego another marriage that she recovered and lived
to bury both mates. Mr. Pate, one of Johnston's most successful
characters, describes the sensible way of dealing with Penninah:

> "And I have give' my advices to Harry Brister and Sammy Pounds,
> that both of them val'able young men been layin' for her ever
> sence not so very long arfter Billy Gunnell went, and was now open
> and above-board a-tryin' to over-persuade her, as both of 'em well
> might . . . I should promise P'nniny, at the very offstart, that in the
> event of her a-goin' before me I should never even think about
> takin' of another companion. And then, if the time come a'gin and
> onexpected, to leave it to the good Lord to git me out o' standin'
> up to sech a foolish promise."[58]

Another example of such humor is provided by a young mountaineer in Harry Stillwell Edwards' "An Idyl of Sinkin' Mount'in"
who has gained a local reputation as a doctor. His philosophy is
"give natur' what natur' calls fur."[59] When asked what he does
if nature calls for something which is out of season, he replies,
"Ef natur' calls fur what natur' hain't got, I argy thet hit ain't
Dr. Zeke thet's ter blame; an' I ginerally waits ontel natur' calls
fur suthin' ter hand" (p. 78).

Persons lacking common sense are also humorous. Such a character is the "born inventor" described by Edwards, who builds a cyclone escape chute for his family. It is a rough wooden shaft running from the house down a hill to an old dairy, the original entrance to which the boy plugs up. One night the inventor and his brother decide on a trial run, and grease the chute in preparation. They frighten their parents sufficiently, and soon all four have slid down into the dairy. But there they almost drown, since the dairy, stopped up, has slowly gathered a great deal of water. All four are covered with splinters and, worse still, cannot get out. One boy must crawl painfully up the chute to release them. After the mother survives the ordeal, she wrecks all her son's inventions and sends him to work in the cotton field where all good Georgia boys belong.[60]

While local colorists consider a lack of common judgment humorous, they fail to applaud common sense in special circumstances. It can never be used, for example, to deny "higher" values or to ignore good manners. In one story by Ruth McEnery Stuart a housewife is determined to sell a pair of antique candelabra, even though her husband treasures them as the dearest possessions of his dead mother. Though practical enough, Mrs. Brooks is therefore inexcusably insensitive to the feelings of her spouse when she says, "Well, the way I look at that is, if the spirits that stan' guard over things, as you say, would jest keep 'em dusted an' cobwebbed off, so's we could be sure they *was* keep-in' up with 'em, they'd be some sense in . . . [keeping family heirlooms]. Teddy took on some over sellin' the ol' things, but I tol' him he hisself was the only Brooks antic I cared to keep."[61]

A similar situation occurs in Sherwood Bonner's "On the Nine-Mile." A young girl in a precarious emotional state because she has been partially paralyzed in an accident is told by her practical but ill-mannered fiancé: "A man marries a woman ter have his meals cooked reg'lar, an' the harvestin' 'tended to, an' the lard tried out, an' the apple-butter made, an' the geese plucked, an' the house cleaned, an' the washin' done on Monday, an' the mendin' Saturday, an' the odd jobs on Sunday."[62] To Miss Bonner even the fiancé's practicality cannot excuse his insensitivity. For the most part, however, common sense, pride, courage, and a willingness to work are qualities deeply respected and amply displayed by southern plain folk described in the local color period. It is these four qualities that are considered the basis of good character. And it is good character, or lack of character, which determines social standing or respect in the communities of southern local color fiction.

Because of this emphasis on the importance of character—an emphasis suggesting a fluid social structure,[63] southern local color, when it does identify characters in terms of classes, suggests that the plain folk enjoy relaxed and easy relationships with both aristocrats[64] and poor whites.[65] Only stories set in Louisiana reveal an open antagonism between established families of the ruling class and the plain folk.

Although tension exists in fictional Louisiana between Creoles and Americans, the hostility between Creoles and Acadians is even more pronounced. Creoles assume they are descended from French or Spanish nobility in these stories, and are greatly superior, for that reason, to the Acadians of French peasant stock. Cable himself seems to have been infected to some extent with this prejudice, since he makes the noble hero of *Bonaventure* (a novel written to exploit the "color" of Acadian life) a Creole. When Bonaventure's mother offers her baby for adoption, she has the following exchange with an Acadian leader:

> "Are you an Acadian? You haven't the accent."
> "I am a Creole," she said, with a perceptible flush of resentment. So that he responded amiably:—
> "Yes, and, like all Creoles, proud of it, as you are right to be. But I am an Acadian of the Acadians, and never wished I was any thing else." (p. 3)

The difference between Creoles and Acadians is so much assumed in Kate Chopin's stories that the uninitiated sometimes have difficulty knowing which group a character belongs to. For practical purposes the reader must simply assume that the rich are Creoles; the poor, Acadians, unless they are otherwise identified. Several of these stories, however, suggest that the two groups have some relatively friendly social relationships. "Polydore," for example, portrays the struggles of the respectable (and apparently Creole) Mamzelle Adélaide with her adopted son Polydore, stupid child of "a 'Cadian hill woman" who "had begged with her dying breath" that Adélaide "watch over

the temporal and spiritual welfare of her son and above all that
he did not follow in the slothful footsteps of an over-indolent
father."[66] And in "For Marse Chouchoute" and "At the 'Cadian
Ball" young Creoles attend Acadian dances.[67] According to Mrs.
Chopin, then, the social differences between Creoles and Acadians are recognized, but not always rigidly observed.

While in most of this fiction differing classes live on mutu-
ally friendly terms, local colorists encountered several interesting
problems when portraying the relationship between plain folk
and white trash. One poor white—a rarity in southern local color
because she is both a vital and convincing character—illustrates
the trouble. The difficulty Joel Chandler Harris has in keeping
Mrs. Feratia Bivins in her social and economic place suggests
that when a poor white begins to act in a story, he begins to
seem much like any other character; that is, he no longer appears totally worthless and contemptible. Moreover, it is axio-
matic in southern local color that deliberate action—at least, hard
work—is rewarded. As Mrs. Bivins illustrates, a character who
works can be expected to prosper. And none who prospers from
his own hard work is ever convincingly labeled (as Harris allows
Mrs. Bivins to label herself) "trash." Mrs. Bivins is important
because Harris tries to make her a "representative" poor white,
because she engages in a feud based on class as well as personal
antagonisms (another rarity), and because she exemplifies the
skillful characterization of which local colorists were occasionally capable. For these reasons, "Mingo," the story in which she
appears, is worth considering in detail.

Ostensibly "Mingo" depicts the loyalty of an ex-slave who
cannot desert the granddaughter of a family he once served.
As such the story is like at least a hundred others written in this
period. It is solidly based on the tritest element of the Old South
legend—the love of slave for master. This element provides only
the frame of the story, however; the details make the story
unique. Before the tale begins, we are informed, the inconceivable has happened. Deely Wornum, whose mother was a proud
Bushrod from Virginia, ran off and married Clay Bivins, whose
mother herself characterizes the Bivins family as "pore white
trash."[68] After Deely committed the unpardonable sin of marrying beneath herself, Emily Wornum issued orders that any slave
mentioning her daughter's name would promptly be sold. Mrs.

Wornum also forbade anyone to contact the girl. Soon Clay Bivins was killed in the war, Deely died, and their little daughter was left in the care of the paternal grandmother. The story is essentially Mrs. Feratia Bivins' recollection of her confrontation with the proud Emily Wornum, formerly of Virginia. The clash of the two women is presented as a conflict of castes, in which Harris hears "the voice of Tragedy" (p. 24).

The excuse for the story is the narrator's return to the neighborhood outside Rockville in which he spent his boyhood and to the country church he formerly attended. After the morning service he eats lunch with Mingo, formerly a Wornum slave who is now working to help support Deely's child, and Mrs. Bivins. He hears the story first from the white woman and then from the Negro, who fills in details. The narrative technique is usually employed to convey a poignant reminiscence from the lips of an elderly Negro. In this story, however, we also have a white woman speaking of herself. The supposed ring of authenticity resounds through her version of the story, just as it does through Mingo's version.

According to the narrator, Mrs. Bivins is a good representative of the poor white, for her words "seemed to represent the real or fancied wrongs of a class, and to spring from the pent-up rage of a century" (p. 21). As Harris portrays her, Mrs. Bivins reveals many of the characteristics associated with poorer southerners. She is deeply antagonistic to Negroes,[69] even when she admits the superiority of Mingo and the Wornum slaves: "Niggers is niggers, but them Wornum niggers was a cut er two 'bove the common run" (p. 16). After this statement, the narrator observes, "The curious air of condescension which Mrs. Bivins assumed as she said this, the tone of apology which she employed in paying this tribute to Mingo and the Wornum negroes, formed a remarkable study. Evidently she desired me distinctly to understand that in applauding these worthy colored people she was in no wise compromising her own dignity" (p. 17). She is equally antagonistic to those whites who consider themselves her superiors. According to Mingo, "Ole Miss en ole Marster dey hed Ferginny ways, en Miss F'raishy she wouldn't 'a' stayed in a ten-acre fiel' wid um,—dat she wouldn't. Folks w'at got Ferginny ways, Miss F'raishy she call um big-bugs, en she git hostile w'en she year der name call" (p. 26). As often as the narrator comments on Mingo's inherent grace, he points to Mrs. Bivins' awkwardness. She is "tall" and "angular," "plainly, even shabbily, dressed," moving with decision, "her movements betraying a total absence of that undulatory grace characteristic of the gentler sex" (p. 10).

Most remarkable, however, is the extent to which Mrs. Bivins does *not* seem characterized by those adjectives usually applied to the poor whites: ignorant, dirty, lazy, badly nourished, content.[70] Above all Harris leaves the impression of her strength: "She had thin gray hair, a prominent nose, firm thin lips and eyes that gave a keen and sparkling individuality to sharp and homely features. She had evidently seen sorrow and defied it. There was no suggestion of compromise in manner or expression. Even her hospitality was uncompromising" (pp. 12–13).

One of the most effective devices in this story is Harris's subtle suggestion of the similarity between Mrs. Bivins and Mrs. Wornum, those women of different classes. Their pride seems to rest on the same things—their families, and the lavishness of life in their family homes. Moreover, the codes of behavior both women accept, particularly a fearless insistence on one's rights and privileges, seem essentially identical: "Em'ly Wornum, she taken on awful [about the marriage]. I never seen her a-gwine on myse'f; not that they was any hidin' out 'mongst the Bivinses er the Sanderses,—bless you, no! bekaze here's what wa'n't afeared er all the Wornums in the continental State er Georgy, not if they'd 'a' mustered out under the lead er old Nick hisse'f, which I have my doubts if he wa'n't somewheres aroun'" (pp. 15–16).

Although a fiery spirit and passionate temper usually seem to belong to the southern aristocracy in southern fiction, such is not the case in "Mingo." The unimaginable happens when Emily Wornum's pride is so broken by news of her daughter's death that she falls on her knees before Mrs. Bivins, begging to see her granddaughter. Mrs. Bivins' reaction differs from an aristocratic one only in her superior ability to use forceful language:

> "Maybe you think," said Mrs. Bivins, regarding me coldly and critically, and pressing her thin lips more firmly together, if that could be,—"maybe you think I oughter wrung my han's, an' pitied that 'oman kneelin' thar in that room whar all my trouble was born an' bred. Some folks would 'a' flopped down by 'er, an' I won't

deny but what hit come over me; but the nex' minnit hit flashed
acrost me as quick an' hot as powder how she'd 'a' bin a'houndin'
airter me an' my son, an' a-treatin' us like as we'd 'a' bin the off-
scourin's er creation, an' how she cast off her own daughter, which
Deely was as good a gal as ever draw'd the breath er life,—when all
this come over me, hit seem like to me that I couldn't keep my
paw's off'n 'er. I hope the Lord'll forgive me,—that I do,—but if hit
hadn't but 'a' bin for my raisin', I'd 'a' jumped at Emily Wornum
an' 'a' spit in 'er face an' 'a' clawed 'er eyes out'n 'er. An' yit, with
ole Nick a-tuggin' at me, I was a Christun 'nuff to thank the Lord
that they was a tender place in that pore mizerbul creetur's soul-
case.

   "When I seen her a-kneelin' thar, with 'er year-rings a-danglin'
an' 'er fine feathers a-tossin' an' a-trimblin', lettle more an' my
thoughts would 'a' sot me afire. I riz an' I stood over her, an' I says,
says I,—

   "'Emily Wornum, whar you er huntin' the dead you oughter
hunted the livin'. What's betwix' you an' your Maker *I* can't tell,'
says I, 'but if you git down on your face an' lick the dirt what
Deely Bivins walked on, still you won't be humble enough for to
go whar *she's* gone, nor good enough nuther. She died right yer
while you was a-traipsin' an' a-trollopin' roun' frum pos' to pillar
a-upholdin' your quality idees. These arms helt 'er,' says I, 'an' ef
hit hadn't but 'a' bin for *her,* Emily Wornum,' says I, 'I'd 'a' stran-
gled the life out'n you time your shadder darkened my door. An'
what's more,' says I, 'ef you 'er come to bother airter Pud, *thes make
the trial of it. Thes so much as lay the weight er your little finger on 'er,'*
says I, *'an' I'll grab you by the goozle an' t'ar your haslet out,'* says I."
(pp. 22–24)

The rage into which Mrs. Bivins works herself carries an impact which clearly contradicts the idea of a poor white as lazy,
passive, and content. And even Mrs. Bivins' poverty seems questionable by the end of the story, for Mingo says, "I tuck holt er
de little piece er groun' w'at she had, en by de he'p er de Lord
we bin gittin' on better dan lots er folks. It bin nip en tuck, but
ole tuck come out ahead, en it done got so now dat Miss F'raishy
kin put by some er de cotton money fer ter give de little gal a
chance w'en she git bigger" (p. 34). In the story the terrible Mrs.
Bivins establishes her own magnitude as a character. The narrator recognizes in the confrontation of the two women the element of tragedy. But significantly it is not the tragedy of the

devastated Emily Wornum, but of the conquering Feratia Bivins: "It was merely Mrs. Feratia Bivins who had been speaking, but the voice was the voice of Tragedy. Its eyes shone; its fangs glistened and gleamed; its hands clutched the air; its tone was husky with suppressed fury; its rage would have stormed the barriers of the grave" (p. 24).

In the anticlimactic final third of the story the soothing voice of Mingo more or less restores the narrator's sense of order. He is able to finish the encounter seeing only the "pretty picture" of faithful servant and lovely child, hand in hand, waving goodbye. The impression of what Harris has done in the first two-thirds, however, is not entirely erased. He not only has pictured the poor white conquering the aristocrat, the Snopeses overwhelming the Compsons; he also has suggested a certain primitive and poetic justice in that victory. Furthermore, he has implied that little essential difference, after all, could be discerned between the ways in which either grandmother would rear a child, for the differences in the characters of the two are negligible. The one objection to Mrs. Bivins' guardianship—that the child would develop a greater awareness of "culture" with Emily Wornum— seems met when Mingo remarks, "'T won't b'ar tellin' how smart dat chile is. She got Miss Deely peanner, en, little ez she is, she kin pick mos' all de chunes w'at 'er mammy useter pick. She sets at de peanner by de hour, en whar she larnt it I be bless ef I kin tell you . . ." (p. 34). In local color stories proof of a woman's gentility is her musical ability. While the suggestion that there is little difference in the two grandmothers seems unrealistic, yet its inclusion, as means to a happy ending, certainly strikes at the heart of the Old South myth.

Mrs. Bivins is Harris's only poor white who is memorably individualized.[71] Harris does discuss the "trash" in some detail, as few local colorists do, but the rest of his characters so labelled are more consistent with the stereotype. That means two things. First, every story in which poor-white-trash appear implies that poverty is the result of hereditary defects of character, not personality the result of poverty. Second, any such character must be viewed at some distance. The omniscient narrator must merely generalize; otherwise the trash tends to turn into a Mrs. Bivins who is entirely too strong a character to fit the stereotype easily.

In presenting poor whites Harris did three important things. First, while he used the poor-white stereotype, he sympathized with the group and did not dismiss them as pariahs. Second, he humanized the stereotype (as he did the mountaineer stereotype) so that one of its representatives transcended the type to become a memorable character. Third, in describing the strength, independence, and fierce pride of Mrs. Feratia Bivins, he perhaps inadvertently created grave doubts about the validity of the stereotype as a whole. Since it is indicated that Mrs. Bivins is no longer particularly poor at the end of the story, we infer that she is no longer particularly trashy. Perhaps Mrs. Bivins suggests as well as any other fictional personality the way in which social classes in the South tended to change shape and composition, the final status of each individual being ultimately determined by his efforts and his character.

## Chapter V

# Folk Institutions and Events

*MOST SOUTHERN* local color stories either present happy or humorous events, or conclude with a happy ending. They are usually built around occasions in which people
gather together, whether for particular holidays, novel events,
or regularly established and institutionalized activities. Perhaps
the emphasis on groups partly explains the lack of detailed characterization (in the sense of complex and/or penetrating presentation of individual personality) in the body of southern local
color fiction. For nineteenth-century southerners with a rural or
village background,[1] the most interesting thing was not individuals as such, but rather individuals as they made up groups,
and participated in community occasions. Occasions, not particular citizens, provided the "color" of the locality. Of course
we must not forget the chauvinism underlying much southern
local color fiction. On the one hand it seemed desirable to picture the South as a land where happy people lived together in
mutual accord (else that feudal aristocratic vision would deeply
offend other Americans). Thus emphasis fell on happy groups.
On the other hand superficial characterization enabled writers to
avoid suggesting that the region might produce oddities of a dis-

turbing kind. It is this absence of characters whose uniqueness is unattractive, in fact, which proves so major a difference between southern and New England local colorists. Such Yankees as Harriet Beecher Stowe, Roland Robinson, Mary E. Wilkins Freeman—or even the more genial Sarah Orne Jewett—apparently felt much freer to utilize unpleasant personalities in their fiction without feeling a concomitant disloyalty to their locales.

All these pressures undoubtedly helped minimize characterization in late nineteenth-century southern fiction. Finally what makes the world of the southern local colorist so foreign to a twentieth-century reader is its creator's basic assurance, regardless of any situation's complexities, that all things worked together for good to them that lived in the Southland—at least before the Yankee invasion. Therefore the subject matter of southern local color stories consists largely of the occasions bringing happy people together in groups. Social institutions such as the schools, churches, courts, and militia often provide these occasions, as they also do in New England or middle western fiction of the same period, and therefore are an important part of local color.

The militia is mentioned most often by Johnston and Harris. Perhaps the influence of Georgia humorists like Longstreet is suggested by this fact. Harris's Pinetucky District "was satisfied with itself. . . . [The people] could remain at home, so to speak, and attend the militia musters. . . ."[2] Harris's "Little Compton" describes the intense excitement in Hillsborough when the town militia camps in the fields, enjoying the constant attention of the women while preparing for war. Johnston, however, is the local colorist who offers the most detailed description of militia day:

> Elderly ladies were there, with joint stools at the rear of their one-horse wagons, in which were ginger-cakes, and beer made from the persimmon and the honey-locust. Elderly, or otherwise exempt gentlemen, brought in ox-carts, among other things, jugs containing what some persons then considered, as some do now, an excellent invention for the heart of man in gladsome mood or sorrowful. Other exempts had ovens for the corn pone, griddles for the hoe-cake, pots of coffee, bottles of molasses, kegs of buttermilk, and pits from which ascended and permeated hundreds of square rods of circumambient air as mouth-watering scents as ever were snuffed by the nose of man.[3]

In other words the militia is not just for the men; it is a community institution enjoyed also by the ladies. It provides a social occasion.

Probably the absence of free public education in the South before the Civil War explains the fact that Johnston is one of the few local colorists even to mention schools. A southern governor expressed the traditional southern view when he said that public schools were "a luxury . . . to be paid for like any other luxury, by the people who wish their benefits."[4] Evidence of the attitude that education was unessential is found occasionally in surprising places. For example, Constance Cary Harrison communicates in *Belhaven Tales* her deep conviction that Virginia was the birthplace of all that is best in America. Yet in "Crow's Nest" she describes the estate of a Virginia gentleman whose property is falling to ruin long before the Civil War and whose children are growing up with as little education as any backwoodsmen. Though Mrs. Harrison assures us that the family in "Crow's Nest" is aristocratic, a harassed Yankee visiting the neighborhood sees little which doesn't conform "with the shiftless style of the neighborhood."[5] Shiftless or not, the aristocratic family has little need or concern for education.

Although Cable emphasizes the many advantages of boys growing up in an Acadian household, he concludes "Carancro" by mentioning "the little schoolhouse, dirty, half-ruined, and closed—that is, wide-open and empty—it may be for lack of a teacher, or funds, or even of scholars."[6] Cable the reformer preaches of the need to bring education to the ignorant Acadians and of the advantages it will make possible for them. But the idea of public education was controversial in the South of the local color period because it bore "in many minds the stigma of a Carpetbag measure."[7] The fact that tax-supported education included tutoring Negroes, of course, did not help to popularize the concept. Southern local color reminds us, as historians do, that "the great educational awakening in the South did not come until the dawn of the twentieth century."[8]

Nevertheless, for Richard Malcolm Johnston, schools were an important part of the life he remembered living as a boy. One of Johnston's favorite subjects is the country school, and especially the kind of education offered there—memorization with the aid of a hickory stick. Several of his stories, such as

"The Goosepond School," "Mr. Bill Williams Takes the Responsibility," and "New Discipline at Rock Spring," deal with the sadistic villainies of which schoolmasters were capable, or with the extreme steps necessary if the schoolmaster kept order. Schools concluded their yearly sessions with a public examination designed to exhibit the skills pupils had learned during the year. As Johnston recalls in his *Autobiography*, "Examinations were the great days of the year. They closed with exhibitions of plays to witness which men, women, boys, girls, even children used to come as far as ten and fifteen miles. I have seen more than a thousand at one of these exhibitions on a stage under an arbor of green boughs in front of the schoolhouse."[9] Such an examination, attended by all of Dukesborough and the surrounding countryside, is an important episode in "Old Friends and New." Of course the pupils all perform admirably in the story.

But by far the most important social institutions in local color fiction are the court and the church. Again and again we are reminded that the church was the center of southern (as Mrs. Stowe says it was the center of New England),[10] society—not only of religious but also of social life. It was an institution which allowed the whole community to gather regularly and frequently. Except in stories set in Louisiana, the church is usually Evangelical Protestant. Johnston states matter-of-factly of middle Georgia, "The religious faith in the community was in general Baptist."[11] Harris is perhaps using the word *all* somewhat satirically when he says the Pinetuckians "were in easy reach of a church-building which was not only used by all denominations—Methodists, Baptists, and Presbyterians—as a house of worship, but was made to serve as a schoolhouse."[12]

Local color stories suggest that church membership, while not completely necessary, was quite desirable as a mark of social status. Discussing Andy Magraw's clever stratagem for sending his recalcitrant wife to the head deacon, the raconteur in "Our Witch" says,

> "He determ'ed in his mind that it were absolute necessity for the old man Rainey to take a hand in the business, him bein' the onl'est man in the whole neighborhood she were afeard of, because it were him that persuaded the brothern to let her in the church

when they hizzitated about her high temper and the freckwent
sloshin' of her tongue. He argied that if she didn't quite have
grace, it might come to her arfter she were took in. Of course Andy
couldn't go in, because o' his cussin' sometimes, which he never
denied."[13]

Edwards' "Sister Todhunter's Heart" and Harben's "The Heresy
of Abner Calihan" both describe procedures for turning an un-
orthodox member out of the church and suggest the enormous
loss of community prestige which this punishment involved. In
the latter story Calihan is about to be removed from the church
rolls for doubting the existence of Hell. Calihan's family wail
and sob until he relents and admits the error of his thoughts.
But the importance to the family of Calihan's good standing in
the church is indicated clearly: the father of the young man
engaged to Calihan's daughter will not allow his son to marry
into a family the head of which is not an upstanding church
member.[14]

Several stories sketch the social rivalry between the congregations of a particular neighborhood. Page's "Run to Seed" contrasts the Uptons, a family which had owned a good plantation
before the war, with the Wagoners, the overseer's family on
the Upton plantation. After the war the Wagoners grow rich and
then say publicly that the Uptons have run to seed. Mrs. Wagoner is categorized by the narrator when he mentions the
sequence of her religious affiliations: "The Billings, from which
Mrs. Wagoner came, had not been Episcopalians until Mrs.
Wagoner married."[15] In "A Humble Abolitionist" the unenthusiastic new slaveowner is told by a former friend, "Some
'lows that the havin' o' this slave is agoin' to make you stuck up,
an' that you'll move yore membership to Big Bethel meetin'-
house. . . ."[16] Both these stories suggest that social and economic
status determined the church to which the southerner belonged.
The traditional cliché has been that planters were Episcopal and
farmers were Baptist—a cliché often used by Thomas Nelson
Page. Since the wealthy or formerly wealthy families in "The
Whipping of Uncle Henry" and "The Woman's Exchange of
Simpkinsville" are apparently Baptist, and since we have the
word of Johnston that most Georgians were Baptist, some local
color implies that the cliché was inaccurate, at least when ap-

plied to states other than Virginia. It is at an all-day preaching service, attended by the whole community, that the unnamed narrator of "Mingo" meets the awful Mrs. Feratia Bivins. The church Mrs. Bivins has always attended is also the one to which the Wornums brought their slaves and their children.

Presumably one reason local colorists are sometimes vague about identifying specific denominations in their stories is that they do not wish to offend anyone. Another reason, however, is that the emotional revivalism associated then and now with Southern Baptists and Methodists is suspect enough to local colorists to be associated in their stories only with mountaineers, poor whites and Negroes. This condescension to revivals is traceable to the southwest humor stories which make of the outdoor revival a place of chicanery and practical jokes—but local colorists are reluctant to resolve the dilemma they encounter when trying to explain why only the poorest element of the community attends revivals, yet most of the community belong to evangelical Protestant congregations. One of Chesnutt's Negro characters reports, "Long 'bout de middle er de summer dey wuz a big camp-meetin' broke out on de Wilm'l'ton Road, en nigh 'bout all de po' w'ite folks en free niggers in de settlement got 'ligion. . . ."[17] Harris writes one story about an innocent mountain girl who is seduced by a gentleman from the valley while attending the annual revival camp meeting: "The old people had come to pray, but the youngsters had come to frolic, and the gayest of all was Loorany Parmalee."[18] For the most part, then, the local colorists mention constantly the importance of the church in southern communities, yet provide only the sketchiest details about the kind of theology and the type of worship services the church developed.

The view of the church's role in the community depends on the writer. Johnston and Harris present the church, as they do all other southern institutions, approvingly. Although Johnston later became a Roman Catholic and moved to Baltimore, he grew up in Georgia the son of a Baptist preacher. He portrays Georgia churches with much the same sentimentality his other boyhood memories evoke. Strict or narrow religious beliefs are mentioned only when they can provide humor. Religion remains vague in Johnston's stories, usually discussed only when a character must survive great misfortune. One such character solemnly remarks, "I shall try to trust, as I always have trusted, that the judgments of the Almighty, as the Psalmist wrote, are 'just, justified in themselves.'"[19]

Other local colorists, however, convey a less genial view of southern Protestantism. Harben's "The Heresy of Abner Calihan," for example, makes the point that the elders meeting to decide whether to run Calihan out of their church know less of brotherly love than Calihan and practice Christian doctrines less than he. The only purpose of Sherwood Bonner's "Sister Weeden's Prayer" is to expose the pettiness and hypocrisy bred by backwoods religion. Neighborhood ladies in this story are gathered to card wool, when one of them announces she has seen another backsliding. Having peeped in her neighbor's window, the informer can report that Mrs. Biscoe has been sewing on Sunday. The women are horrified:

> Sister Weeden wuz the impressivest female in the Baptist society. She wuz tall an' clean-cut, an' not a bend in her from neck to knee. What she said *wuz said*. She had high cheekbones, an' black hair coiled on top of her head.
>
> "I have listened," says she, "an' if what Sister Daggett charges shell be proved true, we must expel Dorothy Biscoe from the society an' leave her to the mercy of God."[20]

Fortunately Dorothy Biscoe was busy making clothes for a community sinner to be baptized in; thus she continues to enjoy the mercies of the Baptist ladies instead of being surrendered to the Almighty. The same petty religiosity is mentioned in Miss Bonner's "On the Nine-Mile." When the heroine Janey is partially paralyzed, her aunts tell her the accident is a judgment for her sins. Jealous of Janey's many beaux, her aunts vent their malice in gathering frequently to gossip, fight, and act in ways unpleasant to Janey and each other. After her accident the aunts are satirized in a section entitled "Janey's Comforters": "'We all deserve damnation,' says Charity, severe as a Hard-shell preacher. 'Let this turn your soul to God, an' it will prove a blessin' in disguise.'"[21]

But of all brands of southern Protestantism described by skeptical local colorists, the one presented most negatively is that practiced in the mountains. The Sut Lovingood stories of

George Washington Harris, a southwestern humorist employing an East Tennessee setting, provide a precedent for this condescending attitude; for Sut is particularly antagonistic to circuit riders and religion. In the local color period Mary Murfree's stories suggest that the religion which is a pervasive part of mountaineer life is a primitive hybrid of doctrine and superstition. In fact mountaineers described by local colorists usually seem, next to Negroes, the most superstitious people in the South.

"Over on the T'other Mounting" is based on the superstition that a nearby mountain is haunted, the devil's province, because any enterprise undertaken on that mountain fails. An old man explains, "I hev always hearn ez everything that belongs on that thar T'other Mounting air witched, an' ef ye brings away so much ez a leaf, or a stone, or a stick, ye fotches a curse with it . . . 'kase thar hev been sech a many folks killed on the T'other Mounting."[22] Finding a fish fossil in the stone of the mountain, hillbillies conclude it is the bewitched supper of a neighbor who fled justice: "'So thar's the Bible made true,' said an elderly woman. . . . 'Ax fur a fish, an' ye'll git a stone'" (p. 253). In the same story mountaineers sit placidly and watch a fire burning on T'other Mountain, convinced that they are safe because a church is built on their own mountain.

"The 'Harnt' That Walks Chilhowee" reveals the mountaineers' belief in ghosts as well as in other superstitions: that a screech owl is the sign of impending death; that seeing the shadow of a rabbit is a bad omen; that a girl can discover whether she is to marry an old or a young man by performing certain rites at a crossroads at dawn; that anyone who hears a ghost speak drops dead immediately. Such superstition usually produces various kinds of fear or prejudice. For the mountaineers Indians are particularly suspect. Of a colorful rock, we are told, "'T war painted by the Injuns,—that's what I hev always hearn tell. Them folks war mos'ly leagued with the Evil One."[23] The speaker adds that Satan allowed the Indians to stand on air in order to paint at such inaccessible heights.

Miss Murfree's later volumes reflect either the influence of the all-affirming Harris or a more genial view of mountain folk which she developed with age. In the later stories she presents this mixture of religion and superstition with more sympathy.

In "The Riddle of the Rocks," a mountaineer thinks he has found Moses' broken tablets lodged in the Tennessee mountains. He is mercilessly ridiculed by his neighbors, whose contempt robs him of a precious belief. But at the end of the story he proves more admirable than they.[24]

One reason why Miss Murfree seems less tolerant of mountaineer religion in her first volume is that it prevents the mountaineers from enjoying what few social pleasures might otherwise be available. The major theme of "The Dancin' Party at Harrison's Cove," for example, is the consciousness of all who attend that they are sinning. Mr. Harrison, in fact, has agreed to the dancing party only because it seemed the last desperate measure to find husbands for his unmarried daughters.

> Not so Mrs. Harrison; she almost expected the house to fall and crush them, as a judgment on the wickedness of a dancing party; for so heinous a sin, in the estimation of the greater part of the mountain people, had not been committed among them for many a day. Such trifles as killing a man in a quarrel, or on suspicion of stealing a horse, or a wash-tub, or anything that came handy, of course, does not count; but a dancing party! Mrs. Harrison could only hold her idle hands, and dread the heavy penalty that must surely follow so terrible a crime. (p. 227)

When a visiting Episcopal deacon appears at the party in hopes of preventing the violence likely to occur, "the pious about the walls . . . [sit] racking their slow brains to excuse their apparent conniving at sin and bargaining with Satan" (p. 237); for "even the sophistication of Cheatham's Cross-Roads had never heard of a preacher who did not object to dancing" (p. 238).

The circuit rider objects not only to dancing but also to gambling. Budd Wray, who introduces "a-playin' of Old Sledge at the settlement," is confronted by the circuit rider: "Thar is a word ez we hev laid off ter ax ye, Budd Wray, which will be axed twict,—wunst right hyar, an' wunst at the Jedgmint Day. War it ye ez interjuced this hyar coal o' fire from hell, that ye call Old Sledge, up hyar ter the Settlemint?"[25]

Indeed the subject of fundamentalist religion dominates Miss Murfree's stories. The mountain folk use their religious beliefs to explain the most ordinary facts of their lives. Mrs.

Giles of "The 'Harnt' that Walks Chilhowee" remarks at one point, "'Pears ter me ez I kin see the clouds a-circlin' round Chilhowee, an' a-rainin' on everybody's corn-field 'ceptin' ourn. . . . Some folks is the favored of the Lord, an' t'others hev ter work fur everything an' git nuthin'. Waal, waal; we-uns will see our reward in the nex' worl'. Thar's a better worl' than this, Tom" (p. 293). But this mountain religion is not the kind for which Miss Murfree seems to have much patience or respect.

Perhaps because local colorists, like southwest humorists, entertained some reservations about doctrinally narrow or rigid Protestantism, the southern church sometimes provides the setting for a humorous incident.[26] "The Self-Protection of Mr. Littleberry Roach" is Johnston's story of a prosperous bachelor who cannot decide which of two widows owning property adjoining his he should marry. When the two ladies begin to vie for influence over him, their test of power is to persuade him to supply the shingles and remaining fifty dollars necessary to complete the new church building. Mr. Roach promises both that he will subscribe the amount. He is consequently a much-honored personage at the church dedication service for the new building. In the middle of the service, however, the son of one widow crawls beneath the church and sticks a long nail through the unfinished floor and into Mr. Roach. Roach screams, disrupting the service. But the trick has turned the tide; he marries the boy's mother in order to discipline her son.[27] A similar event occurs in Ruth McEnery Stuart's "A Note of Scarlet." A cow invades a church service, eats one parishioner's best bonnet, and bellows in a deaf deacon's ear trumpet.[28]

Harry Stillwell Edwards takes special delight in presenting southern churches. The satire implicit in his stories is more genial than Sherwood Bonner's criticism. In "Sister Todhunter's Heart," for example, a naive new preacher visits Sister Todhunter and discovers that she rules her husband by means of an occasional beating. The young minister resolves to turn Mrs. Todhunter out of the church. His efforts are successful, but Sister Todhunter protests vigorously. Though the story ends when she saves the life of the preacher's baby and proves to have good in her character, still the heart of the story is the circus into which Sister Todhunter turns a church service. When she leaves the membership, she takes the reputations of most of the congregation's leaders along with her, simply by speaking some well-known truths about those sitting in judgment on her.

Edwards' "Elder Brown's Backslide" not only suggests the importance of church membership but also emphasizes the inconsistency between the narrow beliefs of Georgia churches and the practice of church leaders. Elder Brown is a respected leader in his church, honest and well-intentioned, with an industrious but shrewish wife who makes it her habit to wrest consolation from her Bible "by mere force of will."[30] The story begins with the Elder's preparing to go to Macon, get a loan, and make some purchases for his wife.

He is singing loudly as he rides along, when he is thrown because his donkey, seeing a pig in the road, stops abruptly. "Lost in a trance of divine exaltation, for he felt the effects of the invigorating motion, bent only on making the air ring with the lines which he dimly imagined were drawing upon him the eyes of the whole female congregation, he was supremely unconscious that his beast was hurrying" (p. 37). Leaving his seat, the elder lands on his beaver hat, a disaster: "The beaver was his special crown of dignity. To lose it was to be reduced to a level with the common wool-hat herd" (p. 38).

The story then proceeds along the familiar lines of the countryman-come-to-town. The elder's ignorance of the way in which the more sophisticated act is humorous, and he seems absurd to everyone he encounters in Macon. His expressions are a part of both the religious satire and the humorous effect: "Now you look here, sonny," he says to a store clerk, "I'm conducting this revival, an' I don't need no help in my line" (p. 44). But Elder Brown's special weakness for whiskey is the basis of the rambling story. After consuming two sodas, the Elder visits a tavern, where he discovers that "Whisky is higher 'n it used to be. . . . But it ain't any better than it was" (p. 49). As he is about to return home, his donkey's braying sounds as if the animal is telling everyone his master is drunk; so Brown leaves the donkey to walk home by himself. His wife predictably sends him back astride a mule to retrieve the donkey. After more drinking and two fights, the elder again climbs on the donkey and goes home, leaving the mule. By the time of his second arrival his wife is no longer angry, but laughs and puts him to bed.

The story contains many age-old jokes. The henpecked husband was an object of humor in Chaucer's day, and the innocent countryman caught in the complicated vices of a town was a familiar figure in Elizabethan drama. The would-be gentleman whose elaborate manners make him ridiculous has also been a humorous object for centuries. What makes much of the humor in this story possible, however, is not only the comic events themselves but also one's awareness throughout of the incongruity inherent in the situation: a Protestant elder thinks lovingly of the ladies and becomes intoxicated.

Since the South was overwhelmingly Protestant, traces of anti-Catholicism are evident in local color stories. The unconventional spinster in Page's "My Cousin Fanny" has religious convictions which greatly concern her family: ". . . it used to be whispered that she was in danger of becoming a Catholic. . . . I remember that she used to defend them, and say she knew a great many very devout ones."[31] The narrator recalls one evening in which Catholics came up for discussion:

> She even said that evening, under the impulse of her enthusiasm, that she did not see except that it might be abused, why the crucifix should not be retained by all Christian churches, as it enabled some persons not gifted with strong imaginations to have a more vivid realization of the crucified Savior. This, of course, was going too far, and it created considerable excitement in the family, and led to some very serious talk being given her, in which the second commandment figured largely. (p. 21)

James Lane Allen includes in *Flute and Violin* two stories which suggest that the Catholic church commits a sin against nature by requiring that monks and nuns remain apart from the world around them. In "Sister Dolorosa" a nun falls in love, though she dies chaste; and in "The White Cowl" a monk breaks his vows and marries. Allen's sympathies are clearly with the lovers. When the suitor in "Sister Dolorosa" meditates on convent life, he could be summarizing Allen's presentation of Catholicism:

> The aspect and spirit of the place: the simple graves placed side by side like those of the nameless poor or of soldiers fallen in an unfriendly land; . . . the once chirruping nests of birds here and there in the grass above the songless lips; the sad desolation of this

unfinished end—all were the last thing needed to wring the heart of
Helm with dumb pity and an ungovernable anguish of rebellion.
This, then, was to be her portion. His whole nature cried aloud
against it. His ideas of human life, civilization, his age, his country, his State, rose up in protest. (p. 217)

Cable takes an occasional swipe at Roman Catholics in such
stories as "Posson Jone'" or "Madame Délicieuse." In view of
Cable's well-publicized Presbyterian devoutness, however, he
expresses very little anti-Catholicism. Generally we can say that
the religion in southern local color stories is Protestant, that religious beliefs permeate the life described in these stories, and
that the church is perhaps the most centrally important social
institution presented.

Another institution almost as frequently mentioned is the
court, or what passes for a court. The courtroom scene, usually
comic, is employed so successfully by local colorists that it becomes one of the most popular elements of southern fiction.
Again we notice, however, that such scenes were first presented
by southwest humorists in such volumes as Baldwin's *The Flush
Times of Alabama and Mississippi,* and no doubt appeared so frequently among those early stories in part because so many of
the southwest humorists were lawyers. Probably the courtroom
humor grew out of many actual incidents in which judges tried
to bring law and order to unenthusiastic backwoodsmen.[32] In
fact a formula still used in twentieth-century fiction was developed for southern courtroom scenes. The elements of the southern courtroom formula consist of a number of country people
who gather silently to watch the proceedings; a noisy clerk who
screams for witnesses or announces cases from the courtroom
steps; a stuffy room in which an impatient judge futilely attempts to speed up proceedings; a series of witnesses who are
pleased to be the center of attention and whose garrulous testi-
mony is endlessly digressive and full of pithy folk sayings; a
jury which decides the case by determining who is the best
"pleader"; a judicial procedure, the niceties of which are either
ignored or consciously rejected. While all these elements may
not be mentioned in every local color courtroom scene, each is
mentioned frequently enough to become an expected part of the
comedy.

And comedy, or farce, the scene usually is. When Johnston's trashy Dan Hickson brings a case of spite against a respectable farmer, all of Farmer Collins' neighbors gather to watch the trial. Collins wins his case by reminding everyone of his family's honor and of his dead mother. One neighbor comments afterwards, "Had no idee Mr. Collins was sech a pleader. When he brung in his ma, I declar' I were a'most fit to cry; for I knowed her, and she were as perfec' a saint in her old age as ever trod grit in Warren County."[33] In "The Pursuit of the Martyns" a witness travels a whole day to establish the fact that the defendant in a murder trial could not possibly have been near the scene of the murder. Having come so far, the witness is unwilling to speak his piece quickly. He gives the court his whole life history in remarkable detail before he finally mentions that the defendant spent the night with him at the time the murder was committed. Afterwards the witness graciously receives the congratulations of the audience for his performance.[34] The satiric undertone of most southern courtroom scenes also distinguishes Harris's "A Piece of Land": "Squire Ichabod Inchly, the wheelwright, was prepared to hold justice-court in the open air in front of his shop when the weather was fine, and in any convenient place when the weather was foul. 'Gentlemen,' he would say, when a case came before him, 'I'd a heap ruther shoe a horse or shrink a tire; yit if you *will* have the law, I'll try and temper it wi' jestice.' This was the genuine Pinetucky spirit, and all true Pinetuckians tried to live up to it."[35]

Sometimes the courtroom jokes are bizarre, even grotesque. In Edwards' "Charley and the Possum" one Negro files suit against another for stealing his 'possum trap. Charley maintains that he did not steal the trap, but merely took a 'possum to which the trap was attached. The jury rules that Charley had a right to the 'possum; the 'possum stole the trap![36] In Page's "Pulaski's Tunament" an old Negro is almost executed for murdering his worthless son. At the last minute, however, the son turns up—not to save his father but to watch the hanging.[37] Edwards' version of the grotesque church trial in which Mrs. Todhunter is expelled from membership is simply a variation of the southern courtroom scene.

A complete example of the elaborate southern courtroom scene is found in Edwards' "His Defense." As the story begins, a respectable lawyer attempts to smother his laughter while advising Hiram Ard, who is seeking legal aid, that he would do better to plead guilty as charged and save himself the hundred-dollar lawyer's fee. Here we see the tendency prevalent in local color fiction to make trials appear anything but serious from the beginning. Although several trials described in the period are indeed life-and-death matters, the local colorist usually ignores the potential seriousness of charges in order to heighten the comic effects of the trial. Ard has been indicted on a charge of cursing his mother-in-law, a charge which makes the whole trial ludicrous from the beginning. When the day of the trial arrives, the scene is set with predictable details—the number of poorer citizens present, and the informality of the proceedings (the trial begins when the sheriff bellows from the courthouse steps the names of those involved in the case). Mrs. Gonder, Ard's mother-in-law and the state's only witness, first takes the stand. Her "narrative covered years of bitterness, disappointment, wounded vanity, and hatred, and was remarkable for its excess of feeling." [38] Although Mrs. Gonder initially makes a good impression, her excessive vituperation begins to estrange the jury. Later Ard catches and holds the audience's attention, "for all the world loves a manly man" (p. 8). This detail illustrates another important element in southern courtroom scenes. For the scene to be comic, the defendant must win his case. The local colorist guarantees this result by emphasizing the essential worth of the defendant in spite of his ludicrous predicament. The writer intensifies his desired effect by coating the heavy dialect in which witnesses speak with sentimentality. Ard begins, "So far as the cussin' is concerned, thar ain't no dispute erbout that. I done hit, an' I ought n't er done hit. No gentleman can cuss erroun' er woman, an' for the first time in my life I war n't er gentleman. I could er come here an' pleaded guilty an' quit, but that don't square er gentleman's record" (pp. 7–8).

Ard then tells his whole life story, another ingredient necessary in the courtroom scene. The life story, whether told by a witness or the defendant, must suggest a wider context in which the misdemeanor should be judged and create the impression that a higher wisdom should be applied to the case, rather than the specific law which has been violated. Ard tells that he has worked hard and prospered. Prosperity to him has meant a two-room, later a three-room, house and a sewing machine for his wife. When their first baby was due, the couple decided that Mrs. Gonder should live with them and help care for her daughter. But Mrs. Gonder was always antagonistic to Ard, considering him below her daughter's social level. When the mother-in-law's interference began to threaten the happiness of the Ards, they decided to move, leaving her the farm Ard had worked so hard to develop. In the moving, however, they left the sewing machine behind. The mother-in-law then used various stratagems to keep it for herself, even when Ard made three long journeys to retrieve it. The last trip occasioned the cursing, triggered when Mrs. Gonder told Ard once again that he couldn't take the machine with him:

> "I started ter cussin'! I cussed all the way up the walk, an' up the steps, an' inter the room, an' while I was shoulderin' that ar machine, an' while I was er-totin' hit out, an' while I was er-loadin' hit in the wagon, an' while I was er-drivin' off. An' when I thought of them seventy-odd miles, an' the three days' plantin' I'd done lost, I stopped at the rise in the road an' cussed back erg'in. I did hit, an', as I said, hit was ongentlemanly, an' I'm sorry. The only excuse I've got, gentlemen, is I did hit in self-defense, for if I had n't cussed, so help me God, I 'd er busted wide open then an' thar!" (pp. 20–21)

Perhaps there is a slight difference in this particular courtroom scene, for the dilemma Edwards creates for the jury— whether to acquit a likable "gentleman" when he admits he is guilty—is resolved when Mrs. Gonder drops her charges. Her reason for doing so, however, is consistent with other scenes. In Ard's sentimental account of his life, he has repeatedly stressed his love for his wife and son. Furthermore, he has called attention to all the generous acts he performed for his mother-in-law without her knowing of them. So Mrs. Gonder drops her charges and leaves the courtroom arm-in-arm with her son-in-law. Ard has made so stirring a defense for himself, in fact, that his lawyer returns the hundred-dollar fee with instructions that the money be used for Ard's baby.

According to southern local color stories justice is better served when law is ignored. When the law is applied strictly, the result is almost always unjust. In Harris's "A Piece of Land"

an innocent man is sent to prison, convicted when two stolen
bales of cotton are found in his barn. He has been framed, and
two implications emerge from his situation: first, good southerners never steal; and, second, justice would have been served
better had the townsfolk obeyed their intuitions about the young
man's character. Similarly, in Mary Murfree's "His Day in
Court," an old man, who after years of unsuccessful campaigns
has finally been elected justice of the peace, insults the son-in-
law who has taunted him in court. Fined for using abusive language, the old man resigns his office and returns home heart-
broken. His daughter is so horrified because her husband has
brought suit against her father in her father's own court that she
leaves her spouse. Miss Murfree manages to reconcile the couple at the end of the story, but she apparently sees nothing improper in the daughter's reactions to a legalistic interpretation of
events.[39]

In Harben's "The Convict's Return" a farmer serves part of
a sentence for horse theft. But since he impulsively "borrowed"
the horse while he was drunk and since he always planned to
return it, the state governor hears his story and pardons him.
Again the story suggests that southern courts are more just when
good men are not punished harshly for impulsive infractions of
the law.[40] And in Matt Crim's "Zeki'l" a convict who returns
from prison with "a haggard face, bleached to a dull pallor by
prison life, every feature worn into deep lines"[41] is proved to
have been unjustly convicted, in fact to have taken the blame
for horse theft in place of his brother.

A dramatic example of the assumption that justice is better
served in southern courts when laws are ignored is found in
Alice French's "Trusty, No. 49." In this story of an Arkansas
town a neighbor is being tried for shooting a man down in the
street as the result of an argument in which the defendant discovered he was being cheated at cards. When the jury retires it
is instructed by the judge to find the defendant guilty, for indeed
many witnesses have seen the murder. But as the jury discusses
the case, an educated gentleman among them reveals that he
once served a term in an Arkansas prison. He tells the jury of
the multifold horrors to which Arkansas convicts are subjected
and concludes that "in the present state of convicts in Arkansas,
if you don't find the man not guilty you had better find him

guilty enough to be hanged."[42] Since the murdered man is
identified as a former prison warden known for his sadism, the
jury returns a verdict of not guilty. One member of the jury
states afterwards, "fact er the matter is, we all got to talkin' an'
discussin' them convict-camps, an' we 'lowed 't wudn't be right
to send a neighbor to ary sich place" (p. 261). The narrator
makes this verdict seem even more just when he mentions the
pathetic face of the defendant's wife and indicates how hard she
would find life if her husband were punished. Thus in southern
local color stories there are few villains, and those who appear
to be villains usually turn out to be good men. Perhaps it is a
democratic assumption that most white men are good men,
which explains the leniency white men encounter in southern
courts of justice.

One variation of the courtroom scene involves the trial of
Negroes. This variation is not necessarily humorous. The Negro
defendant is always acquitted after an impassioned and eloquent
defense by a white gentleman. Implicit in these stories, however,
is an admission that Negroes are not usually granted equal treatment before the law, that a Negro is acquitted only when he has
a white champion. Harris's "Ananias" is the story of a mean-
looking Negro whose master has always viewed him with suspicion because of his "hang-dog look" and his "countenance
and manner [which] were . . . repulsive."[43] After the war Ananias, who has been following Sherman's army, finds that he is
not to be paid anything, and makes the tedious journey home.
On the way he meets a famous lawyer and tells the gentleman
that he left his master because he was unjustly blamed for showing the Yankees where his master's stock was hidden. Ananias
tries unsuccessfully to hold the plantation together after the
war. After the plantation is lost, he takes odd jobs to help provide his master with food. Finally he is forced to steal, but is
careful to steal only from the old plantation and from the former
overseer who foreclosed the owner's mortgage. The overseer has
sworn out a warrant for Ananias's arrest, and Flewellyn, Ananias's master, has left the Negro in jail. The famous lawyer to
whom Ananias once told his story happens to be at the trial and
"speaks the word" for him. Although the lawyer knows Ananias
has stolen, he presents a successful defense by proving that
nobody could possibly have witnessed the thefts. When the law-

yer tells Ananias's sad story, all are so moved that Ananias is
acquitted and his weeping master takes him home at last. Edwards' "De Valley and de Shadder" offers a variation on the
same theme, the Negro in this case being acquitted of murder
after his former owner tells of the slave's bravery in rescuing
his master during the Civil War.[44]

Such stories as "Ananias," "De Valley and de Shadder," and
Johnston's "Ephe" all make the point that a Negro has little hope
in a southern court unless he has a white champion. Johnston,
Harris, and Edwards all seem to suggest that when a "good"
Negro gets into trouble, there is always a paternal white man
nearby to help him. Chesnutt, a Negro local colorist, understandably takes a less optimistic view of the Negro's chances in
a southern court. In "The Sheriff's Children" a Negro suspected
of murder allows himself to bleed to death in his jail cell,
knowing that he cannot expect a fair trial in any southern neighborhood. Before the Negro dies, he says, "I have been to school,
and dreamed when I went that it would work some marvelous
change in my condition. But what did I learn? I learned to feel
that no degree of learning or wisdom will change the color of
my skin and that I shall always wear what in my own country is
a badge of degradation. When I think about it seriously I do not
care particularly for such a life."[45]

"The Web of Circumstance," the most bitter of Chesnutt's
stories, is the one with which he chose to end his satiric collection, *The Wife of His Youth.* There is little characterization in the
story, for its purpose is propagandistic: to illustrate the harsh-
ness of southern law, the inequity of treatment between whites
and Negroes in southern courts, and the helplessness of the
Negro once he falls into community disfavor. Ben Owens, a
hard-working and honest Negro blacksmith, is framed by a
jealous helper and sentenced to five years in the penitentiary for
stealing a whip worth fifteen dollars. His sentence is delivered
on the same day one white man receives one year for manslaughter and another six months for forgery. After five years
Owens returns to find his wife living with the treacherous assistant, his daughter drowned, and his son just lynched. He lies
in wait to avenge himself on Colonel Thornton, who originally
brought the suit against him. Seeing the colonel, however, he has
a change of heart. But when Owens runs to assist the colonel's

small daughter, the colonel sees a desperate-looking Negro threatening his child and shoots Owens dead. The story concludes:

> Some time, we are told, when the cycle of years has rolled around, there is to be another golden age, when all men will dwell together in love and harmony, and when peace and righteousness shall prevail for a thousand years. God speed the day, and let not the shining thread of hope become so enmeshed in the thread of circumstance that we lose sight of it; but give us here and there, and now and then, some little foretaste of this golden age, that we may the more patiently and hopefully await its coming! (p. 323)

Inherent in all the humor and sentimentality with which most southern courtroom scenes are suffused, then, is an admission that the law is treated lightly and that southern cases are decided on the basis of emotion and impulse. When a Negro is being tried, it takes a drenching of emotion to save him. Hints of unequal justice in local color stories, however, are not limited to cases involving Negroes. Mountaineers, too, seem to suffer from laws made and enforced in the valley. Usually such an admission is accompanied by some humorous comment about the ignorance of mountaineers. While Miss Murfree remarks at one point on the "prejudice of the jury"[46] which makes it difficult for a mountaineer to get a fair trial, she has one speaker describe the mountaineer's trial in the following way:

> "'Vander war powerful interrupted by thar laffin' an' the game they made o' his lawyer, an' said he didn't want no appeal. He 'lowed he had seen enough o' jestice. He 'lowed ez he'd take the seven years in the pen'tiary that the jury gin him, fur fear at the nex' trial they'd gin him twenty-seven; though the 'torney-gineral . . . 'lowed ter Pete ez 'Vander war a fool not ter move fur a new trial an' appeal, an sech. He 'lowed ez 'Vander war a derned ignorant man. An' all the folks round the court-house gin thar opinion ez 'Vander hev got less gumption 'bout'n the law o' the land than enny man they ever see, 'cept that young lawyer he had ter defend him." (p. 35)

In another of Miss Murfree's stories, the sad little man who proves to be the "harnt" that haunts Chilhowee mountain was accused years before of murder. Though it is clear that he was physically incapable of the deed, still he ran away, was hunted down by a posse, and shot. The explanation for his refusal to face trial is that "Reuben war sartain they'd hang him. He hedn't never seen no jestice from enny one man, an' he couldn't look fur it from twelve men. So he jes' sot out ter run through the woods, like a painter or a wolf."[47]

As a rule southern courtrooms are considered a proper setting for humorous events. With the exception of Chesnutt southern local colorists seem to agree that the law should take into account men's individual merits and that justice should not be meted out with the consistency of little minds. In fact, when feeling does not temper the law's application, the local colorist usually implies that a greater injustice has been committed. Admitting that emotion overrules logic in a southern court implies that the law itself is of less than paramount importance to southern jurists and judges. Also implicit in such an attitude is, of course, a condoning of any violence a community can understand the impulse to commit. And a predictable result is a great deal of violence within the community, a result to be discussed at length in the next chapter. In local color fiction courts do not exist solely to punish violent infractions of the law. Instead the courts function as social institutions primarily valuable for furnishing gathering places in which country people can be entertained.

Because of their emphasis on the occasions bringing people together, the local colorists needed more opportunities for presenting southerners in groups than social institutions alone could provide. Throughout southern local color the special, uninstitutionalized events are also important and are described as often, and with as much relish, as the social institutions.

Judging from local color fiction, the most important event of a southerner's year was Christmas. The local colorist who does not mention the Christmas holidays lovingly is rare. In fact those holidays were so important that Mary Murfree (and to some extent her imitator, John Fox, Jr.) reveals a disconcerting inclination in her later volumes to resolve every tension in her stories by referring to the blessed, peace-making influence of the heavenly season. The most extreme sentimentality encountered in southern local color typifies descriptions of Christmas festivities.

Harris suggests a reason for these recurrent outbursts of emotion: Christmas was the only national or regional holiday which every southerner recognized and participated in. Thanksgiving, for example, was in antebellum times only a New England holiday.[48] A planter in "How Whalebone Caused a Wedding" had said to his wife years before, when she was doubtful about introducing her New England holiday, 'Go ahead, honey! Cut just as big a dash as you please with your Thanksgiving. I'll enjoy it as much as you will, maybe more. . . . We'll cut a big dash and be thankful, and then when Christmas comes we'll cut a big dash and be happy."[49] Richard Malcolm Johnston describes Christmas in the typical way: "It makes an old man fond, almost to tears, sometimes, to recall the old-time Christmas-tide of the far South. Sweet in general as were the season and sun in that clime, especially were they so in the period remembered in this little story."[50] Johnston further recalls the visiting among "the half-dozen families that had most property and education in this neighborhood" and the general understanding that they would spend each day of Christmas week together. But he quickly adds, "Families in humbler conditions had their reunions also, and were as happy and felt as blessed as the rich."[51]

As these passages suggest, the keynote of Johnston's descriptions is the way in which Christmas celebrations bind the community together. The high point of the season in "The Two Woollys" is a hunt in which all the richest and poorest men of the neighborhood participate. The same note of goodwill and brotherly love sounds through Ruth McEnery Stuart's sentimental story "The Frey's Christmas Party."[52] Here the numerous children of a struggling widow plan a Christmas party for their boarding house. In spite of many mishaps, they manage to bring a ray of light into the lives of the lonely people living there. And we hear the same motif in Page's "Polly: A Christmas Recollection"[53] and "How the Captain Made Christmas."[54] Grace King, too, discusses the wholesome effects of the Christmas season, even on impoverished or immoral residents of New Orleans' French Quarter, in "The Christmas Story of a Little Church."[55]

A time of feasting and frolic, Christmas is associated in these stories with heavy drinking as well as heavy eating. The conductor in Page's "How the Captain Made Christmas" proves his inventiveness when he wires his wife to have a full punch bowl ready for the train's passengers and then dispenses good cheer from it. In Alice French's "The Plumb Idiot"[56] a postmaster's admirable character is demonstrated by his practice of suspending his assistant during the Christmas week, with full salary paid, so that the assistant can go on a spree. It is against post office rules for an employee to be intoxicated; but in return for his paid Christmas holiday the assistant stays sober for the rest of the year. In fact we are assured that Harben's farmer in "The Convict's Return"[57] is really an innocent man, because the horse he "borrowed" had been taken during the customary drunken bout at Christmas. Consistent with the local colorists' emphasis on happy people dwelling together happily is the fact that Christmas is also a much-anticipated holiday for Negroes and slaves. Ruth McEnery Stuart stresses this theme in many stories, among them "A Golden Wedding" and "Christmas Gifts,"[58] "Holly and Pizen,"[59] and "Solomon Crow's Christmas Pockets," "The Two Tims," and "Duke's Christmas."[60]

Since Christmas cannot last the whole year, local colorists also describe other events which provide diversions and a chance for southerners to congregate. More spontaneous occasions are furnished by sports and games. In stories describing planters and aristocrats, foxhunting is the most popular sport, and one in which the ladies sometimes participate. But stories of the plain folk picture humbler sports and contests involving less expensive equipment. Johnston describes foot-races in "Mr. Eben Bull's Investments,"[61] and beehunts in "The Bee-hunters."[62] With his customary thoroughness Cable furnishes a complete list of Acadian diversions:

> For 'Thanase there was, first of all, his fiddle; then *la chasse*, the chase; the *papegaie*, or as he called it, *pad-go*—the shooting match; *la galloche*, pitch-farthing; the cock-fight; the five-arpent pony-race; and too often, also, *chin-chin*, twenty-five-cent poker, and the gossip and glass of the roadside "store." But for Madame 'Thanase there was only a seat against the wall at the Saturday-night dance, and mass *à la chapelle* once in two or three weeks; these, and infant baptisms.[63]

Besides sports and games local colorists' favorite community event is a marriage. Whether the location is Dukesborough, the

Acadian prairies, or the mountains, a marriage is a celebration of great community importance and is participated in by everyone living close enough to attend. In *Bonaventure* Cable spends six pages describing in minute detail each stage of the festivities arranged to celebrate the marriage of 'Thanase and Zoséphine. Johnston waxes rhapsodic about the fun of a farmer's wedding in Georgia: "All the neighbors were invited, men, women and children; and most of them went. Pig, lamb, turkey, chicken, duck, pea-fowl, goose, partridge, pigeon, cake, syllabub."[64] After the ceremony "the fiddling and the dancing began; and then the supper. . . . The dancing went on until nearly midnight" (p. 67). Fox suggests in "A Mountain Europa"[65] that a mountain wedding is so important that even a fugitive will emerge from hiding to appear there.

All these weddings end with dancing. But dances are not reserved for weddings alone. The Acadian ball is a weekly event, to which any respectable white neighbor can come if he pays for his gumbo. Of course Page often describes balls in his idealized Old South stories. Sherwood Bonner's "The Barn Dance at the Apple Settlement" sketches mountain social customs in great detail, describing the married women, who prepare for a dance by cooking in the kitchen; the young people, who flirt and tease each other before pairing off for the dance; and the refreshments: "We tasted the Cumberland punch. It was not made on the one, two, three principle, but was even more simple. It was sugarless, lemonless, waterless. It was smoky, strong, and brought tears to the eyes. In short, it was a white whiskey mixed with white whiskey."[66]

In regard to dances held for plain folk, however, local colorists often seem bothered by the contradictions involved in presenting large numbers of dancers among communities dominated by Baptists and other evangelical Protestant groups. Of course Page's aristocrats provide no problems, since they were all supposed to be Episcopalians. In view of the fact that Baptists usually disapproved of dancing, however, we understand the predicament of writers whose stories were set in Georgia or the mountains.[67] The Baptist attitude is well summarized in the following comment:

Our honest forefathers . . . made an earnest effort to protect church members from contaminations of the world. To this end they placed some worldly amusements under the ban of stern disapprobation, and made them subjects of discipline. In making these discriminations they made, we must admit, some grave mistakes. But I think it will be found that their mistakes were in allowing some things which they ought to have forbidden, rather than in those things which they condemned. For instance, they condemned social dancing and card playing because they judged these amusements to be hurtful in spiritual growth and dangerously alluring to other and grosser vices. . . . They saw in them "a love of the world" that was intense—so intense as to crush all the elements of true piety in those who habitually indulged in them. Hence it is not strange that our fathers gave them no quarter.[68]

Richard Malcolm Johnston is particularly aware of the disapproval with which Baptists regarded dancing. When the circus comes to town in "Colonel Moses Grice,"[69] one church member seen dancing a jig in time to the music is saved from public reprimand only because other church members were equally impulsive when moved by the occasion. "The Experiment of Miss Sally Cash"[70] involves Farmer Hooks, whose somber religion makes him disapprove of a neighbor who dances. Somewhat inconsistently, then, Mary Murfree suggests that mountaineers are different from other southerners because they do not enjoy dancing and that the mountaineer's suspicion of dancing, and his lack of experience in this activity, are other indications of his social and religious backwardness. But Johnston's stories remind us that the disapproval of dancing was not limited to the mountains. Since in the Baptist view dancing inflames the passions, perhaps it is appropriate that all the respectable dances Johnston describes are held to celebrate a wedding, or to announce an engagement. Only Virginia aristocrats and Louisiana Catholics regularly indulge in dancing without qualms of conscience.

Happily for the plain folk whom local colorists portray, other amusements were not forbidden by religious dogma. Circuses and travelling shows are mentioned in Johnston's "Colonel Moses Grice,"[71] Edwards' "William Marsdal's Awakening,"[72] and Allen's "A Boy's Violin."[73] Mary Murfree suggests that some occasions, in which participation is compulsory, are turned into social events by those involved. In the mountains each able-bodied mountaineer is required by law to help care for the few roads in the area:

> The provident dispensation of the law, leaving the care of the road to the tender mercies of its able-bodied neighbors over eighteen and under forty-five years of age, was a godsend to the Settlement and to the inhabitants of the tributary region, in that even if it failed of the immediate design of securing a tolerable passway through the woods, it served the far more important purpose of drawing together the diversely scattered settlers, and affording them unwonted conversational facilities. These meetings were well attended, although their results were often sadly inadequate.[74]

The southern ability to turn any occasion into a social event explains the popularity of political rallies. Cable describes one Creole who loves political rallies because he loves southern rhetoric: "He bathed, he paddled, dove, splashed, in a surf of it."[75] Southern rhetoric is so integral a part of these writers' concept of the South that Miss French describes one character, "as distinctly a Southerner as a gentleman,"[76] as having a "voice ... as soft as silk and flexible as a whip-lash, the true Southern orator's voice ..." (p. 264). Tourgée, too, gives attention to the southern political meeting: "There were many speeches of the kind peculiar to the southern stump, full of strong, hard bite, overflowing with wit and humor, and strongly seasoned with bombast. Stories of questionable propriety were abundant, and personalities of the broadest kind were indulged in."[77] Southern political rhetoric arouses Tourgée's particular concern. Lawyer-politicians at one particular rally, he says, "told how the people, after being overwhelmed in the holiest crusade for liberty that the world had ever known, by the hosts of foreign mercenaries which the North had hurled against them, after having their fields and homes ravaged and polluted by Yankee vandals, had surrendered in good faith, and had endured all the tyranny and oppression which Yankee cunning and malice could invent, without resistance, almost without murmuring ..." (p. 241). Most of all, Tourgée reports, southern politicians and orators are upset by what they consider the enormity of any conduct which admits or reports "any thing derogatory to the honor of the South" (p. 244).

Tourgée describes political rallies in the lowlands, and Mary Murfree describes them in the mountains, where "candidates of smiling mien circulated among the saturnine, gravefaced mountaineers."[78] Also circulating, she says, "were other genial spirits, familiarly known as 'apple-jack.'" When a candidate began to speak, however, "The mountaineers hastily concentrated in a semicircle about him, listening with the close attention singularly characteristic of rural audiences" (p. 179). "Electioneerin' on Big Injun Mounting" suggests not only that mountaineers come from long distances to gather for such rallies, but also that the mountain vote is often needed to swing elections in East Tennessee. While the mountaineers' votes are often crucial, however, Miss Murfree also states that little benefit comes to mountaineers after they have helped elect a candidate. According to the story, being an unpopular candidate in the mountains is not without its perils: "Rufe Chadd hev been shot at twice in the woods sence he kem up on Big Injun Mounting. I seen him yestiddy, an' he tole me so; an' he showed me his hat whar a rifle ball hed done gone through."[79] But mountaineers, like other southerners, vote according to their emotions. Politician Rufe Chadd wins an overwhelming majority of mountain votes after he refuses to press charges against an assailant: "That sympathetic heart of the multitude, so quick to respond to a noble impulse, had caught the true interpretation of last night's scene, and today all the barriers of ignorance and misunderstanding were down" (p. 180). The reasons for the traditional popularity of southern political rallies are best summarized by Senator Herman E. Talmadge of Georgia: "'We don't campaign the way we did 30 years ago,' the Senator said. 'Political campaigns were a form of entertainment. People now have television, radio and other things to entertain them.'"[80]

In local color stories the advantages offered by each locality, when summarized, always consist of the opportunities for people to participate in groups. The "advantages" a Georgia town possesses are listed by an ironic Joel Chandler Harris as "the auction-block in front of the stuccoed court-house, . . . a quarter-track, laid out . . . [for] the pleasures of horse-racing; there were secluded pine thickets within easy reach . . . [for] the exciting pastime of cock-fighting; and various lonely and unoccupied rooms in the second story of the tavern . . . [for] dice or cards."[81]

And in James Lane Allen's remarkably sentimental story, "Two Gentlemen of Kentucky," a planter's fondest memories recall the groups and gathering places which provided some novelty in antebellum days:

> From where he sat also were seen slopes on which picnics were danced under the broad shade of maples and elms in June by those whom death and war had scattered like the transitory leaves that once had sheltered them. In this direction lay the district school-house where on Friday evenings there were wont to be speeches and debates; in that, lay the blacksmith's shop where of old he and his neighbors had met on horseback of Saturday afternoons to hear the news, get the mails, discuss elections, and pitch quoits. In the valley beyond stood the church at which all had assembled on calm Sunday mornings like the members of one united family. Along with these scenes went many a chastened reminiscence of bridal and funeral and simpler events that had made up the annals of his country life.[82]

Although southern social institutions were sometimes de-scribed unflatteringly, little social criticism of the usual type characterizes southern local color fiction. Ordinarily the under-lying purpose of social criticism is to suggest the need for change. Though local colorists admit defects in southern institu-tions—backwoods Protestant churches have a constricting influ-ence and church members become self-righteous, procedure in southern courts of law is humorously unlegal, and southern rev-erence for the law of the land is less than complete—their stories seldom include even an implicit appeal for change. When Misses Bonner and Murfree attack the ignorance and backward-ness of mountaineers, for example, they never propose that this ignorance could or should be systematically attacked through a better educational system. When southern local colorists take a critical view of some aspect of southern society or of a social institution, the criticism is unaccompanied by any suggestion that radical revision of that institution or aspect of society is necessary or even possible. As Harris says, "There was room for improvement, but no room for progress, because there was no necessity for progress. The people were contented. They were satisfied with things as they existed, though they had an honest, provincial faith in the good old times that were gone."[83]

The only social question raised by southern local colorists is the position of the Negro in southern society; and the only social institution questioned is that of slavery. But saying the question was raised is not saying it was examined critically. Southern local colorists were largely writing a defense of the South, including, of course, a defense of slavery as an institution. Tourgée, Chesnutt, and Cable are rare exceptions who suggest that the slave was anything but happy in antebellum days. Other writers concede that an occasional misfortune marred the life of the southern slave; but they never examine the institution of slavery more closely than they do any other social institution. Their assumption for the most part was that anything basically southern had to be basically good.

An exception to all rules about the tepidness of social criticism in southern local color fiction, however, is Cable's *John March, Southerner*. This novel is noteworthy for its probing examination of social hypocrisy and moral pretensions in a southern town. In order to explore the post-Civil War South from social, political, and economic angles, Cable makes his setting representative of the whole South. The town of Suez is located in "the state of Dixie, County of Clearwater, and therefore in the very heart of what was once the 'Southern Confederacy.'"[84] As the title of the novel suggests, Cable's hero, John March, is a representative southern gentleman. Thus the events which occur in March's hometown of Suez are, by implication, representative of what is happening all over the South in the postwar period; and the way in which March responds to these events represents the "typical southern" reaction. Considering the limitations of a single novel, *John March, Southerner* is remarkably comprehensive in its acute dissection of the many complex elements making up southern life. Cable differs from later southern writers in presenting Suez not only as a microcosm of the South but also as a microcosm directly affected by the outside influences of the state and the nation, the national influence taking the form of northern capital.

A major part of the social criticism in *John March, Southerner* deals with political corruption. In the reconstruction legislature Negro legislators openly take bribes and embezzle public funds, justifying themselves as the Negro leader Cornelius Leggett does: "Yass, seh, . . . the journals o' the day reputes me to have

absawb some paucity o' the school funds. Well, supposen I has;
... I antagonize you this question: did Napoleon Bonapawt
never absawb any paucity o' otheh folks' things? An' yit he was
the greates' o' the great. He's my patte'n, seh. He neveh stole jiss
to be a-stealin'! An' yit wheneveh he found it assential of his
*destiny* to steal anything, he stole it!" (p. 94). Leggett is corrupt;
but he also advocates free public schools and expansion of railroads—two schemes Cable himself seemed to favor in *Bonaventure*. Ironically Leggett even advocates a *"pyo* Legislature," a possibility in which Garnet, a white community leader, seems to
take no interest. Leggett believes that "they must be sufficiend
plenty o' chicken-pie to go round" (p. 120), because he "likes to
get [his] sheer o' whateveh's a-goin'" (p. 290). He is shrewd
enough to define the difference between a man who is willing
to have others share the chicken pie and one who wants the
whole pie for himself. In assessing the two political figures,
however, John March, the "typical southerner," is so disgusted
with the openly corrupt Leggett, and so anxious to avoid dealing
with Leggett at any cost, that he has no time to detect the im-
measurably more corrupt maneuvers of Garnet, whose reputation he defends publicly.

Cable also intermittently attacks such social institutions as
the southern churches. Full of men with good intentions and a
potential source of great influence, the churches avoid taking
action relevant to any important part of southern life, because
church leaders fear offending some member of the community.
When Negroes ask to use a white church for revival services,
Garnet strongly opposes the idea: "No sir, as sure as we try this
thing, we'll create dissension—in a church where everything now
is as sweet and peaceful as the grave" (p. 210). The unscrupulous Garnet makes gullible Parson Tombs his pawn at every
juncture in the novel. Tombs even buys shares in the land company of which Garnet becomes president and which later declares itself bankrupt. All investors but the "home folk" are
robbed of their money, and only the fortunes of the directors
mysteriously increase. Ironically, after John March is converted
at a revival to the great rejoicing of the elect, his first action in
turning over his new leaf is to become part of a company involving men so detestable that March had resolved only a short time
before to have no dealings with them. The revival is considered

"a heavenly proof of the superior vitality of Southern Christi-
anity" (p. 211). Yet Garnet, the most admired speaker in the
community's religious services, is shown time after time to be a
man whose religion consists almost entirely of outward signs
camouflaging inward corruption. Garnet is careful of the letter,
if not the spirit, of the law. Referring to a dance arranged to entertain important visitors, the author states, "Major Garnet
opposed its being *called* a ball, and it was announced as a musical reception and promenade" (p. 98).

With the exceptions of the contemptible Garnet and Garnet's
completely admirable daughter Barbara, *John March, Southerner*
contains no wholly virtuous or wholly detestable characters.
Cable's relatively complex characterizations[85] are among the
most noteworthy elements of the novel. His "good" men usually
lack both insight into the forces affecting their own lives and
awareness of what is going on around them. His other characters, while possessing some admirable qualities, usually lack
integrity. The unscrupulous characters manage to manipulate
others so shrewdly that they in effect act with the tacit approval
of their townsfolk. Thus no privately owned enterprise becomes
a "barrel" for public funds, and no unequal taxes are levied
against those who can least afford to pay them without the
knowledge and cooperation of the public. Major Garnet loses his
prestige only after he is proved to have committed a sexual
offense by seducing the wife of a friend. He has never offended
his fellow citizens by his more or less open business chicanery
in which he manipulates stocks, misuses company capital, or
accepts public funds to support his private college. In suggesting
that several varieties of corruption affect life in Suez, Cable also
implies that the whole town permits the corruption to fester.

Jeff Jack Ravenel, editor of the local paper and one of the
most interesting characters in the novel, is a man acute enough
to see through the pretenses clothed in bombastic rhetoric which
those around him encourage, although he lacks the will to do
anything about pointing out or eliminating those pretenses.
When plans are being laid to capture and punish Leggett, for
example,

> Captain Champion explained that the affair would be strictly
> select—best citizens—no liquor—no brawl—no life-taking, unless

> violent resistance compelled it; in fact, no individual act; but—
>     "Yes, I know," said Ravenel, "you mean one of those irresist-
> able eruptions of a whole people's righteous indignation, that
> sweeps before it the whining hyper-criticisms of effeminated civi-
> lizations," and the smile went round. (p. 109)

Appropriately, John March, representative of the best in
southern society, is progressively robbed of his inheritance by
his friends Garnet and Ravenel. They take advantage of his
youth, his idealism, and his trust in others, in order to capture,
piece by piece, the estate March's father left him. March's character, then, is as central to the plot of the novel as it is to the
social criticism implied. March's best qualities are also his
greatest weaknesses.

We meet March first as a barefoot boy of eight, who as yet is
totally uneducated and ignorant even of the alphabet. When he
is later exposed to formal learning at Rosemont, Garnet's college, his academic performance is completely without distinction, being neither very good nor wretchedly bad. That March
never learns to think logically becomes a fact of central importance, explaining why others find it so easy to rob him. Throughout the career sketched in the novel, in fact, he seldom thinks at
all, preferring to act on impulse, in accordance with emotion or
passion, rather than acting after he has examined issues intelli-
gently. At one point March erupts, "We men—what are we without passion—all the passions? Furnaces without fire! Ships without sails!" (p. 114).

March's emotionalism represents, by implication, a key
southern quality. The community at large never permits any
event to occur that March, too, does not advocate. March is as
overwrought as the other whites of Suez become, for example,
when he overhears Cornelius Leggett bragging, "I'd marry you
ef you wuz pyo white!—Colo' line!—I'll cross fifty colo' lines
whenev' I feels like it!" (p. 99). After Leggett's statement has
been repeated to many townsfolk Cable explains that the "affair
at the old bridge was everybody's burning secret. . . . Oddly
enough, not what anybody had done, but what Leggett had said
—in contempt of the color line—was the microscopic germ of all
the fever. From window to window, and from porch to porch,
women fed alarm with rumor and rumor with alarm, while on

every sidewalk men collaborated in the invention of plans for
defensive vengeance" (p. 108). Jeff Jack Ravenel, a cooler thinker
than most, tries without much success to argue against violence:

> ". . . if the color line hadn't been crossed already there wouldn't
> be any Leggett."
> "But he threatens to cross it from the wrong side," replied John,
> posing sturdily.
> Ravenel's smile broadened. "Most any man, Mr. March, could
> be enticed across." (pp. 108-109)

Neither logic nor common sense, however, has much effect on
southern whites in such a situation. Earlier Cable has told us,
"They did not analyze. Their motives were their feelings; their
feelings were their traditions, and their traditions were back in
the old entrenchments" (p. 54).

Because southerner March cannot think, he cannot plan for
the future. He is told, "Why, John, owning as much of God's
earth as you do, you're honor bound to plan"; he replies, "I
know it," yet goes on to reveal that he neither knows nor begins
to understand how to go about planning for his future. He is
warned several times throughout the novel that his property has
been built into the plans of others. He manages to comprehend
the information, however, only after he has lost all the land he
once owned.

March's inability to face facts is a tendency also abundantly
shared by others in Suez. When March and his father inquire
about the death of a Negro who has been shot for no good reason, they are told,

> "Why, you know, . . . how ow young men ah; always up to some
> ridiculous praank, jest in mere plaay, you know, seh. Yeste'd'y
> some of 'em taken a boyish notion to put some maasks on an' ride
> through Leggettstown in 'slo-ow p'ocession, with a sawt o' banneh
> marked, 'SEE YOU AGAIN TO-NIGHT.' They had guns—mo' f'om
> fo'ce o' habit, I reckon, than anything else—you know how ow
> young men ah, seh—one of 'em carry a gun a yeah, an' nevah so
> much as hahm a floweh, you know. Well, seh, unfawtunately, the
> niggehs had no mo' sense than to take it all in dead earnest. They
> . . . ahmed theyse'ves. . . . (pp. 68-69)

Later a Negro maid, laughingly serious, describes the southerner's ability to twist any fact to his liking: "But dass my notice 'twix Yankees an' ow folks; Dixie man say, Fine daay, seh! Yankee say, You think it a-gwine fo' to raain? Dixie man—Oh, no, seh! hit jiss cayn't rain to-day, seh! Den if it jiss po' down Yankee say, Don't dis-yeh look somepm like raain? An' Dixie man—Yass, seh, hit do; hit look like raain, but Law'! hit ain't raain. You Yankees cayn't un'stan' ow Southe'n weatheh, seh!" (pp. 136–137).

Because John March believes firmly in the chivalric code of love popular in southern fiction, he is no more able to distinguish himself in romantic affairs than he is in business. In adolescence he falls in love with Fannie Halliday, a girl who cannot listen to his protestations of affection with a straight face. Later he decides that it is theoretically possible for a man to love twice, but lacks the courage to propose to Barbara Garnet, his second love. Finally Miss Garnet herself proposes to John, being level-headed enough to break the rules of conventional romance if necessary. While Cable was forced to include a sentimental romance in his novel, the romance itself suggests the absurdity of sentimental notions about courtship and love, and becomes part of the social satire.

Finally March seems an attractive, lovable, and morally righteous man, but one totally unequipped to wage "the bloodless but aggressive and indomitable war on the men, who, he felt, had robbed, not merely him, but his mother, and the grave of his father, under the forms and cover of commerce and law; yet from whom he had not been able to take their outermost intrenchment—the slothful connivance of a community which had let itself be made a passive sharer of their spoils." (pp. 465–466). Yet in drawing John March as he did, with all his glaring weaknesses, as well as his admirable strengths of character, Cable gave the southerner a characterization of himself that is still applicable. As Louis Rubin concludes, "Before . . . [Cable] gave up trying, he wrote one book, *John March, Southerner*, in which despite its romantic trappings he was able to show his native region in the rich daylight of reality. Two generations later the same vision would provide the substance that distinguished writers would use to create a new literature, the lineaments of which Cable, before anyone else, first imperfectly sketched."[86]

## Chapter VI

# *Daily Lives*

·

SOUTHERN LOCAL COLORISTS describe the
common folk as an economic class which enjoyed friendly social
relationships with other classes and which developed particular
social institutions and enjoyed specific community events. Then
going further, they detail the usual daily lives of such commoners. Almost all local colorists mention repeatedly several characteristics which come to seem typical of the daily lives of the
southern plain men. Most plain folk lived in such isolated circumstances, for example, that any stranger was welcome both as
a news-bearer and as a routine-changing novelty. The average
southerner's eagerness for news involving people from other
areas led to his being identified as a gossip and a tale-bearer.
The favorite topic of gossip, however, was the romantic affairs
of the plain man's neighbors. But other topics were discussed
too, and one of those invariably receiving comment was any
difference which served to set one man apart from his associates.
Consistently a distinguishing characteristic of southern life is
said to be a distrust of difference—difference of opinion or action. When differences of opinion became too annoying, the
plain folk resorted to violence. Violence is accepted by local

colorists as so commonplace a characteristic of southern life, in fact, that it is often treated as a joke.

In none of these characteristics, of course, does the southern yeoman appear radically different from plain folk in other American regions. Hamlin Garland's midwestern poor, living out "the ugliness, the endless drudgery and the loneliness of the farmer's lot"[1] seem situated no worse than "the men and women who had been worsted after a long fight in that lonely [Maine] place" whom Sarah Orne Jewett depicts in *The Country of the Pointed Firs;*[2] and conversely they seem no less isolated than any southern farm folk. The resulting loneliness leads to no less eager welcome for company in Miss Jewett's New England stories such as "Aunt Cynthy Dallett" or "The Town Poor" than in any written by a southern local colorist.[3] Malicious or omnipresent gossip, far from being a southern specialty, is perhaps utilized most inventively in the New England tales of Mary E. Wilkins Freeman, whose sketches probably more frequently than any other local colorist's depict the harm a wagging tongue can inflict. Mrs. Stowe, too, recalls that any uncommon event was seized on by Massachusetts neighbors if it "gave something to talk about in a region where exciting topics were remarkably scarce."[4] While Sarah Orne Jewett and Mary E. Wilkins Freeman display infinitely more sympathy for the plight of spinsters than do most southerners, Mrs. Freeman mentions the gossip surrounding romance in "A Scent of Roses," as Miss Jewett does when a confirmed bachelor weds in *The Country of the Pointed Firs.* And New England stories state as emphatically that "everything out of the broad, common track was a horror to these men and to many of their village fellows,"[5] that is, that New Englanders felt as much hostility to small human differences, as southern tales do. Furthermore, references to the pervasive violence of the community are even more expected in the work of Twain, Harte, or Joaquin Miller than in southern mountain tales.[6] Even Miss Jewett—perhaps the most serene depicter of commonplace scenes —creates a character who reports that "one of the boys got fighting, the other side of the mountain, and come home with his nose broke and a piece o' one ear bit off,"[7] thereby using the kind of grotesque detail which one associates with early southwest humor and which southern local colorists usually found too raw to repeat. The point, then, is not that in any of these respects southern life or literature was basically different from that of other regions of America. One may conclude only that these were the elements southern writers (as those of other areas) chose to emphasize as they worked out their portrait of plain people. If such qualities came to seem "typically southern" in the twentieth century, it was probably because local colorists exerted more influence on the writers who followed them in the South than in other regions.

Southern local colorists did not approach the plain folk with the impersonal detachment of trained sociologists or professional historians. Instead they chose the method of fiction—concentrating on characters who could represent the larger group. And the quality they found most typical of a southern life was its isolation. Although usually indicated implicitly rather than explicitly, the isolation remains unmistakable. Even in F. Hopkinson Smith's remarkable panegyric portraying the Virginia gentleman as he would like to be portrayed, *Colonel Carter of Cartersville*, the colonel's sister is described as one whose manner was "a reflex of that refined and quiet life she had always led. For hers had been an isolated life, buried since her girlhood in a great house far away from the broadening influences of a city" (p. 82). The local colorists' constant emphasis on groups, on institutions, and on social life is best understood not only as a reflection of their fondest memories but also as a conscious attempt to meet the charges which for southerners would be most painfully accurate —that they lived isolated from the world and from each other.

Townsfolk as well as farmers are portrayed as living essentially isolated lives: the life of the villager seems almost as different from the urbanite's as the farmer's does. The pull Dukesborough citizens feel toward Augusta, the biggest city imaginable, is acknowledged throughout Johnston's stories. Visiting Augusta provides a momentary escape from rural isolation. Similarly, living in Dukesborough is the dream of every farm boy. Johnston's Bill Williams fulfills his life's ambition at an early age when he leaves the country to become a Dukesborough store clerk. In "Mr. Bill Williams Takes the Responsibility" we discover that children from the country suspect that residents of Dukesborough "put on airs." As Bill prepares to leave for town we see the airs being assumed.[8] There is humor in the self-satisfied rejoiner of a Dukesborough provincial who considers himself superior to farmers:

> "Eb Bull . . . you town people has a contempt of country folks like me that has to make their livin' by the sweat o' their brow; but— but"—then Mr. Huckaby shook his head, as if there were a few things in rural existence that the proudest city aristocrat could have no just occasion to despise.
>
> "M– no, Jones," answered Mr. Bull; "there you're mistaken, and it's because of our manner. M– of course we has our privileges, n– and our advantages, n– and—but yit we has our respects of some country people, n– that they has the ambition like you has, to git out, or try to git out, of their ign'ance."[9]

Indeed the provincialism of the villagers in Johnston's Dukesborough, Harris's Rockville, or Mrs. Stuart's Simpkinsville often furnishes humor in their stories. And if the townsfolk are provincial, they are so because the lives they live are isolated.

In lowland stories isolation provides quaintness and color. In mountain stories, however, isolation is specifically labelled a fault. The earlier mountain stories written by Sherwood Bonner and Mary Murfree emphasize the ignorance which results from the mountaineer's isolation. A good illustration of Miss Murfree's attitude is the way in which she describes her mountainborn politician: He "had lived seventeen years in ignorance of the alphabet; he was the first of his name who could write it. From an almost primitive state he had overtaken the civilization of Ephesus and Colbury,—no great achievement, it might seem to a sophisticated imagination; but the mountains were a hundred years behind the progress of those centres."[10] The fact that mountaineers "were silent people, and news travelled slowly in that mountain country"[11] sadly strains Miss Bonner's patience. One uncommunicative mountain daughter has eyes expressing "the melancholy of a cow's, without the ruminative expression that gives sufficient intellectuality to a cow's sad gaze. To put it tersely, they looked stupid. . . . She was not a talker."[12] There is a difference, then, between the ways in which isolation is presented in valley lands and in mountain country.

When mountaineers are portrayed with greater sympathy

after the publication of Harris's "Up at Teague Poteet's," they not only talk more and seem wiser, but also live in less isolation. One of Mary Murfree's later stories, "The Moonshiners at Hoho-hebee Falls,"[13] features a mentally quick, educated and talented youth, his new-rich uncle, and a settlement which boasts stores and post office. Except for the stills mentioned, the story could be set equally well anywhere in Georgia, the Carolinas, or Arkansas.

A change of attitude toward the isolation of his characters is also evident in Cable's *Bonaventure*. In "Carancro," the first novella of the book, Acadian life is lived on small farms, "small homestead groves that dot the plain" (p. 2), or in villages "of six or eight houses clustered about the small wooden spire and cross of the mission chapel" (p. 4). Yet Cable emphasizes the advantages such a life offers any child reared in this way: "Zoséphine Gradnego and Bonaventure Deschamps, though they went not to school, nevertheless had 'advantages.' For instance, the clean, hard-scrubbed cypress floors beneath their pattering feet; the neat round parti-colored mats at the doors that served them for towns and villages . . ." (p. 6). A special advantage is the garden of this cottage, where the children, according to Cable, learned many more lessons from the thirteen different kinds of flowers he lists growing there. When he shifts the setting of *Bonaventure* in the second novella to the bayou country south of Carancro, however, Cable also shifts his attitude toward the advantages of living in such an isolated place. The ignorance of the Acadians in Grande Pointe, which schoolmaster Bonaventure arrives to combat, Cable presents as a product of isolated living. He suggests that railroads connecting the area to the outside world are to be desired. Significantly Bonaventure's best pupil leaves Grande Pointe, in the third novella, to travel "au large" through the whole state and to cities far away from his Acadian home.

While in most local color stories isolation is so expected a part of rural and village life that writers such as Harris, Mrs. Stuart, or Edwards could laugh at the provincialisms of their good country people, they could do so because of their basic assumption that rural life was simpler, better, and purer than life in those faraway cities where temptations waited at every corner. They assume that there was a better chance of growing up unsullied in the country. In fact the rural living described in local color becomes a strong argument in behalf of the South as a lost utopia.

But George W. Cable's work presents a different point of view. Cable chose as the setting for his major work not the rural South but the city of New Orleans. In using the city as a setting Cable broke with southern precedents to introduce a new element into southern fiction. Although he criticized the culture of New Orleans, Cable still made the city seem preferable to the backwoods.

Cable's "Posson Jone'" concerns a West-Florida preacher who comes to the city and falls into the hands of wily Jules St.-Ange. The Creole sets out to fleece Jones of his money. As the prospective victim the parson is presented sympathetically in much the same way the ingenuous old darkey usually is; while sympathizing with the character, the reader is aware of his own superior sophistication. In the course of the story the parson makes of himself a laughable public spectacle. At the end Jules extracts a promise from Parson Jones that he will never again come to New Orleans; he is obviously unfit to cope with the life there. Though his morals do not fit the accepted Protestant pattern, Jules is the preferable man of the two because of his common sense, his ability to recover from misfortune almost immediately, his ready accommodation to any circumstance, his joyous outlook, and, of course, his final decision to be honest. This decision does not prevent his leaving the story singing "a merry little song to the effect that his sweetheart was a wine bottle."[14] Cable may disapprove of Creole morals when examining them in the light of his own personal morality. This disapproval, however, does not drive Cable to the conclusion that a backwoods bumpkin is superior to the cosmopolitan Creole.

But even in his favorable treatment of New Orleans, Cable charges the city with provinciality. It is not the fact that the city is different from the country which irks him, but that it is "distant from enlightened centres."[15] Cable does not wish that New Orleans were Pinetucky District but that it were Boston. Cable certainly never suggests that rural life is better than urban; for if New Orleans was distant from enlightened centers, how much more distant was the plantation! In "Belles Demoiselles Plantation" the planter Charleu's seven beautiful daughters live what

other southern writers would consider an ideal life on the ancient family estate. Yet they harass their doting father to take
them to live in "the gay city." They "vowed and vowed again
that they only laughed at their misery, and should pine to death
unless they could move to the sweet city. 'Oh! the theater! Oh!
Orleans Street! Oh! the masquerade! the Place d'Armes! the
ball!' and they would call upon Heaven with French irreverence,
and fall into each other's arms" (p. 70).

The suggestions implicit in "Belles Demoiselles Plantation"
about the appeal of life in the city as opposed to the plantation
are confirmed in Cable's *Dr. Sevier*. John and Mary Richling almost starve in a city which cannot, or will not, provide suitable
work for a gentleman. Yet the two Richlings make several
friends who generously help them. Even Narcisse, Dr. Sevier's
clerk who borrows much of their scant money supply without
returning it, refuses to drop them as friends because they are
hungry. If the poor do not find work here, Cable seems to suggest, they at least find sympathy. With the various citizens of the
crescent city, contrasts Richling's father, or his apparent father,
owner of the best plantation in Kentucky. This Kentucky gentleman has all the Creole aristocrat's vices and nothing of the
Creole's charm. When he reveals his opinion of the city, he reveals simultaneously his own autocratic tyranny: ". . . this great
fretwork of cross purposes, is a decided change from the quiet
order of our rural life! Hmm! There everything is under the administration of one undisputed will, and is executed by the unquestioning obedience of our happy and contented slave peasantry. I prefer the country" (p. 68). Richling's mother is the
subject of a later conversation: "Their mother is one of those
women who stand in terror of their husband's will. Now, if he
were to die and leave her with a will of her own she would
hardly know what to do with it—I mean with her will—or the
property either" (p. 186). Obviously, whatever the faults Cable
finds with New Orleans or with Creole society there, he finds no
better alternative in the life of the southern plantation. Both are
faulty to the extent that both are isolated.

A direct consequence of such isolation is the eagerness with
which southerners in local color stories greet every visitor. Even
the maximally affirmative Richard Malcolm Johnston suggests
in "Poor Mr. Brown" that southern hospitality is the direct result

of the isolation in which southerners live: "Most country gentlemen who dwelt near the public road were accustomed to entertain overnight belated travelers and their beasts. . . . Country
children liked such visitors, having so few opportunities to see
new faces and hear new voices."[17]

Southern local colorists tellingly emphasize the hospitality of
their characters, regardless of where a story is set. In her first
volume of stories hospitality and courtesy to strangers are the
virtues Mary Murfree never denies her mountaineers. She
speaks of the "hospitality characteristic of these mountaineers,—
a hospitality that meets a stranger on the threshold of every hut,
[and] presses upon him, ungrudgingly, its best. . . ."[18] She suggests that this hospitality is partially a result of the welcomed
novelty of any new face and partially of the self-esteem of the
mountaineer, who recognizes no superior and therefore is un-
embarrassed about offering what he has to a visitor. He assumes
everyone a friend until proved otherwise. Cable mentions the
hospitality of the Acadians, too, a hospitality characteristic not
only of the prairie herdsmen but also of the bayou fishermen
and trappers. When Bonaventure arrives at Grande Pointe, on
Bayou des Acadiens, his host tells the neighbors, *"Servez-vous!*
He'p you'se'f! Eat much you like; till you swell up!" (p. 83).

As we should expect, so appealing a quality as hospitality is
prominent in the works of southern apologists like Harris. In his
"Little Compton," for example, a hospitable friendliness to any
stranger who is not an abolitionist characterizes a whole town.
All Hillsborough makes Little Compton, a New Jersey storekeeper, feel welcome. Everyone, it appears, is more or less like
Major Jimmy Bass, who always says to the visiting Compton, regardless of the late hour of Compton's departure from Major
Jimmy's house, "Don't tear yourself away in the heat of the
day."[19] Hillsborough holds Little Compton in such esteem, in
fact, that he is brought there to convalesce (in spite of his fighting with Union troops) and is protected by force when a Confederate from Mississippi wishes to send him to Andersonville
prison.

It should also go without saying that hospitality graces the
planter life described by Virginia sentimentalists. A former slave
working in an inn after the war remembers the lavish hospitality
his master dispensed before secession and remarks, "Pears like I

ent got no self-respec', to be waitin' on po' whites, nohow; en de longes' I live, sir, I ent nebber seen money tuk befo' fur a stranger's bode en lodgin'."[20] The ticklish problem of rationalizing their need to run an inn, in the hard times after the war, is also faced far from Virginia, by the elderly Simpkins sisters of Simpkinsville, Arkansas. Only their sterling motives and exemplary business conduct excuse such an act:

> Previously it had been an unwritten law of hospitality of the town that strangers be entertained gratis. It seemed odd that its leading family—that which not only lent the dignity of its solitary gabled front to its highest eminence, but had bequeathed to Simpkinsville its name and traditions—should have been first to put a price on the bread broken with a stranger; but such is the irony of fact, for, with a sensitiveness revealed to the close observer by the slight pursing of their lips, which perhaps the wayfarer interpreted as having a mercenary meaning, these two old ladies did actually charge him twenty-five cents who consumed a hearty meal, reducing the bill with minute scrupulousness to fifteen and even to ten cents to such as failed in appetite. Further than this their most rigorous consciences did not lead them, as they agreed that it was "wuth a dime to cook things an' then not see 'em et."[21]

Hospitality, then, is almost a way of life in the South of the local colorists. Even Albion Tourgée, whose experience as a carpetbagger often led him to conclusions radically different from those which southerners generally expressed, agreed with his southern contemporaries on this one fact. He says of southern townsfolk, "There was never a kindlier, more hospitable, or more religious people. . . ."[22]

But if isolation in the South gives rise to a hospitality offered generously to strangers, it also causes less charming treatment of acquaintances. Specifically southerners in local color fiction share an insatiable love of gossip. As he endures the often dull routines of rural life, the country man breaks the monotony by seeking occasions to gather in groups. And once with his neighbors, he uses the occasion to glean news of the most insignificant or slightly varied events. If the hospitality is always mentioned by local colorists, so is the gossip.

Harris takes a genial view of rural gossip, even arguing that it serves a constructive purpose: "When occasion warranted they followed the example of larger communities and gossiped about each other; but rural gossip is oftener harmless than not; besides, it is a question whether gossip does not serve a definite moral purpose. If our actions are to be taken note of by people whose good opinion is worth striving for, the fact serves as a motive and a cue for orderly behavior."[23] Johnston's most popular and amusing characters—Mr. Pate and Bill Williams—are his gossips. Mr. Pate tells almost every Johnston story of community intrigue. Mr. Pate is fond "both of the hearing and the imparting of news, good, bad and indifferent."[24] It is therefore the tragedy of his life that he eventually grows too deaf to guess what others are saying. Then his role as community tale-bearer must be assumed by Bill Williams.

In "Investigations Concerning Mr. Jonas Lively" Bill Williams initiates investigations in the public interest. Lively is a mysterious bachelor living on the property of Bill's newly widowed cousin Melvina. "Any man that thus kept himself apart from society, and refused to allow everybody to know all about himself and his business, was, in . . . [Bill's] opinion, a suspicious character, and ought to be watched."[25] By peeping through his windows, Bill discovers that Lively smokes a pipe and wears a wig; more he cannot fathom. In carrying on his investigations Bill endures many hardships. At one point Lively purchases two vicious watchdogs which drive Bill screaming up a gatepost. But all vicissitudes are proved worthwhile when Bill is able, at the end of the story, to report his cousin Melvina's reactions to news that her boarder, Mr. Lively, has eloped with her niece: "And oh, my honest friend, ef you ever see a person rip an' rar, it war Cousin Malviny; she come nigh an' in an' about as nigh cussin' as she well could, not to say the very words."[26]

In the stories of other local colorists the right to gossip remains as central to southern life as eating or sleeping, but is not always considered so healthy an activity. John Fox, Jr., develops a character in *Hell fer Sartain* who resembles an unsympathetic version of Johnston's Mr. Pate. Abe Shivers is a trouble-making busybody whose rascality is described in five of the volume's ten stories. At the end of the first story we hear that he has been murdered and that nobody mourns him. Sherwood Bonner's stories such as "On the Nine-Mile" and "Sister Weeden's Prayer" describe strait-laced women who cloak their gossip under the guise of religion. In fact in many of these stories the Protestantism and the gossiping are inextricably related. In Edwards' "Sister Todhunter's Heart" the new minister in town "had arrived a few days before, delivered a most effective sermon, and had been called upon with the promptness common to country communities where isolation renders local curiosity unbearable after twenty-four hours."[27]

In view of the fact that most local color fiction mentions gossiping neighbors, we are slightly baffled to read occasionally in a Harris story that southerners generally mind their own business. "Where's Duncan" describes a boy travelling by wagon who gives a stranger a ride. After the two travel together several days without exchanging names, the stranger finally asks the boy about his notable lack of curiosity. The boy replies, "Well, you are a much older man than I am, and I had a notion that if you wanted me to know your name you would tell me. I had no more reason for asking it than you have for hiding it."[28] Harris also says in "Little Compton" that Hillsborough was composed of residents who usually respected each other's privacy: "The people of that town had their own notions and their own opinions. They were not unduly inquisitive, save when their inquisitiveness seemed to take a political shape. . . ."[29] But when in the same story we read that "Little Compton's disappearance was a mysterious one, and under ordinary circumstances would have created intense excitement in the community" (p. 56), we must simply conclude that Harris, in his efforts to present the South sympathetically, was sometimes self-contradictory. For the most part southern local colorists agree on the existence of extensive gossiping, just as they agree on the existence of bounteous hospitality.

Predictably the primary subject of community gossip is romance—or the romantic involvements of neighbors. In their interest in other people's romantic affairs southern plain folk perhaps differ little from any other class or group in history. But it would be difficult to discuss southern local color without mentioning the importance of romance and marriage in this fiction. In the first place the nineteenth-century public was fond of romances. More important, romance and marriage were useful thematic devices symbolizing the union of North and South. "Azalia" and "Aunt Fountain's Prisoner,"[30] "The Comedy of

War" and "An Ambuscade,"[31] and "The Old Bascom Place"[32] are all stories by Joel Chandler Harris which end with a south-erner marrying a Yankee. Constance Fenimore Woolson, too, uses the romance between a proud southern woman and a northern soldier to suggest the attitudes of both sections toward each other. "Rodman the Keeper," however, ends with Rod-man's recognition that the war has left too much hatred to make a marriage possible, whereas "Old Gardiston" has the more con-ventional happy ending.[33]

While romance and marriage are perhaps the most popular subjects for fiction throughout the local color period, we quickly discover in southern stories an unresolved conflict between two ways of approaching or viewing romance. Particularly for those local colorists who specialized in plain folk characters—and almost every southern local colorist drew such characters at one time or another—the conflicting views of love presented a prob-lem. On the one hand there was the idealistic or chivalric view.[34] The South, nourished by the romantic novels of Scott and others,[35] was perhaps the last area of the world to accept seri-ously those attitudes toward love developed in the courtly love tradition. Central to that tradition is a certain masochism, in which joy stems not from the fulfilment but from the pursuit of love, a pursuit preferably prolonged and painful. Once found, the love can never be duplicated. Once lost, the lover suffers until death. Such a system is impractical for the same reasons that unrestrained masochism, being self-destructive, is impracti-cal. And anything extremely impractical is difficult to advocate successfully in rapidly changing or frontier communities. Para-doxically, however, much of the South was composed of rapidly changing communities, while the type of novel most popular there suggests that the chivalric tradition exerted a strong appeal. One explanation for the apparent contradiction is that chivalric ideals were associated with the upper classes; and through most of her history the South was struggling to maintain and dissemi-nate the conviction that she was populated by aristocrats. Those deciding that they were "ladies" or "gentlemen" deliberately assumed the attitudes they felt would be consistent with the title. Miss Clisby, an elderly Johnston character, summarizes these popular chivalric attitudes by assuming that love's pleasure lies in its struggles. When told by a young visitor, just engaged,

"Oh, Cousin Margaret, I've got something so interesting to tell you, and it's about love!" Miss Clisby replies, "Interesting subject, my dear; but I supposed you had gotten over the most exciting stage."[36]

To judge by the stories of Thomas Nelson Page, chivalric idealism about love gained even more appeal after the Civil War. At this time impracticality was no longer a deterrent. Among other things the courtly love tradition furnished a sympathetic explanation for the large number of spinsters the war left husbandless, by suggesting that a lady would never marry once her first love was dead. But whether discussing spinster or blushing belle, the true gentleman in southern fiction is always identified by his reverence for the ladies. *Colonel Carter of Cartersville* ends with the toast, "Fill yo' glasses, gentlemen, and drink to the health of that greatest of all blessings—a true Southern lady!" (p. 208).[37]

On the other hand, the plain folk of these stories generally take a much more sensible view of love than such sentimental reverence for the opposite sex allowed. A common-sense approach to romance was undoubtedly more typical of the plain folk the local colorists were supposedly describing accurately. Marriages were important to the community for chiefly practical reasons. First, as the stories suggest, marriage was an acceptable method of acquiring property, and property was the major tangible value in an agricultural community. Second, common sense indicated to a hard-working farmer the advantages of a wife who would provide company and do housework; and even greater were the obvious advantages of a husband who could work the land left to a widow. Third, a rationalization for all the hard work involved in acquiring property was provided by the presence of legitimate heirs who could inherit the property. But the importance of marriage, for whatever reasons, is evident in the fact, previously discussed, that a wedding is an event for widespread community celebration in every southern locality from the mountains to the Acadian prairies.

The tension between the idealistic and practical views of love and marriage was increased in local color stories by two factors. First, southerners bred on the chivalric tradition generally associated the practical view with "low" characters. But second, most local colorists were busily engaged in idealizing all southerners.

In elevating the group southwestern humorists sometimes presented as low, rowdy, or vulgar to the status of plain folk, local colorists found it necessary on occasion to credit them with the same idealism formerly associated with aristocrats. Yet hardworking farmers could not always be convincing characters if they consistently cherished such idealism. In local color stories, then, first one view of love and then the other is held by plain folk, and the tension is never resolved, just as it was probably unresolved in southern society. In Constance Woolson's "Bro.,"[38] Johnston's "Mr. Cummin's Relinquishment,"[39] and Mary Murfree's "Drifting Down Lost Creek," "The Star in the Valley," and "The Romance of Sunrise Rock"[40]—to name only a few examples—we find plain folk lovers who sacrifice themselves to benefit their beloveds, or who remain faithful to their sweethearts until death.

Most plain folk, however, keep an eye for the main chance and are more or less content to love the one who is near. This fact is nowhere more apparent than in the stories of Richard Malcolm Johnston. Of all subjects marriage seems dearest to Johnston's heart. Several of his stories such as "Mr. Joseph Pate and His People" or "The Experiment of Miss Sally Cash" end with an orgy of marrying, with three or four couples united simultaneously. Johnston's work occasionally leaves the impression that Georgians spent most of their waking hours marrying and giving in marriage. His stories also suggest the distinctive way in which plain-folk romance is usually presented: the courtship of a commoner is funny. By making yeoman romances comic, the writer can ignore the conflict between chivalric and practical attitudes toward love.

In Johnston's "Mr. Gibble Colt's Ducks," for example, Mr. Colt arrives at the house of two old maids and announces that he wants a little duck of his own. The oldest says she does not raise them, and Colt replies that he meant the younger sister. They are married and the three live happily together for twenty years. Then the wife dies and Mr. Colt decides to take the sixty-year-old spinster for his second little duck. She acquiesces.[41] In another story, Woolly of "The Two Woollys," who is almost a midget, decides one day to marry: "And so without neglecting his little farm, and his two negroes . . . he went about at odd times, trying first one girl, then another, until one day he was surprised in a very agreeable way."[42] The tall woman who accepts Woolly decides he is "almost handy enough to be carried about in a tall woman's pocket" and announces, "Woolly, I've about made up my mind to have you" (p. 146).

The difference between practical and idealistic views of love is nowhere more clearly indicated, nor the comic possibilities of plain-folk romances more thoroughly exploited, than in Johnston's "Old Friends and New." At every stage of the story Bill Williams acts in a radically different way from George Overton, who woos and weds lovely Lucy Parkinson. Each set of characters encounters the other only rarely, but with each switch from one to the other Johnston contrasts the frivolity of the plain folk to the high seriousness of the aristocrats. Whatever he implies about the two groups, however, Johnston makes Bill Williams' wedding much more appealing than Lucy Parkinson's. While the Parkinsons have a small, quiet, "holy" ceremony, Bill Williams has a rollicking dance which ends as a joke: Williams challenges a former sweetheart to a dancing contest; she dances him down until, by the time the guests leave, the bridegroom is so exhausted that he can scarcely breathe.

It takes Lucy Parkinson and George Overton over a year to fall in love. Their friendship is cemented when Overton gives the young belle lessons in Latin, an activity providing them with something to discuss. Lucy occasionally voices her disapproval of such characters as Dido, who not only falls in love twice, but also enjoys a second passion without benefit of matrimony. Lucy and George take long, well-chaperoned walks together and further develop that teacher-pupil relationship which Johnston states is the ideal one for members of opposite sexes. Sorrow mars their romance when Lucy's brother Jack contracts a fever and dies. But Jack does not pass away until he has begged the two of them, with his last breath, to marry. They pledge their troth kneeling by his bedside as he expires. Their courtship is slow, staid, proper, and chivalric. George finally overcomes the last objection to their marriage by discovering that his dead father left him more money than at first he had thought.

In contrast, Williams' halting progress toward the altar consumes a year for a different reason—he cannot make up his mind between Betsy Ann Acry and Caroline Thigpen. The indecision is not unpleasant to him, however; he brags that he is "flurritin'

... with the female mind."[43] All the neighbors take an active interest in Bill's affairs, and most advocate his choosing Caroline because he so desperately needs a wife with more sense than he has. One neighbor observes, "he would do a cash business to get her. Bill is getting to be a very little account there in Dukesborough" (p.54).

Johnston says of Lucy and Overton, "It was pleasing to see the gradual approximation of these two natures towards each other. It was inexpressibly sweet to feel it. Not that they understood it fully, or could foresee what it was to become" (p. 54). He leaves no doubt, however, that Bill Williams both understands and enjoys his own folly. In contrast to Bill's trifling, Overton "had resolved, even if he should ever come to suspect that his passion was reciprocated, to abstain from all mention of it while he should remain in the family, and, indeed, to abstain from proposing marriage until he should become established in his profession . . ." (p. 61). Bill, on the other hand, ends by proposing to both girls and being rejected by both. He is in danger of remaining a bachelor, until his mother intervenes and secures a wife for him.

Thus Johnston presents in "Old Friends and New" a "noble" courtship in contrast to a "common" one. For every sublime thought and exalted sensation of Overton's, he provides a parody in Bill Williams' speeches. In spite of his intentions, however, Johnston finds it difficult to keep Lucy's gradual discovery of a suitable husband on a totally ideal plane. During a public examination at the end of the school year, a neighbor's whisper injects common sense into Lucy's romance: "honey, you listen to me. Don't you let that chance slip. . . . Him and you was *made* for one another" (p. 61). Even in this flattering portrait of aristocratic life and values, therefore, Johnston sometimes intimates that a similar pattern of life and thought existed in both southern aristocrat and poorer neighbor.

The ideals of chivalric love are not always presented with unquestioning approval in southern local color. Constance Woolson, at least, seems occasionally skeptical about the value of southern romanticism. When an engagement is announced in "Bro.," a fond mother's tears of joy seem absurd, especially because "to her, as to most Southern women, the world is very well lost for the sake of love."[44] Miss Woolson adds in "Up in the Blue Ridge," "The old-time South preserved the romance of conjugal love even to silver hairs; there may have been no more real love than at the North, but there was more of the manner of it" (p. 307).

Even in her exasperation, however, Miss Woolson confirms the enormous importance which the southern community attributed to love and marriage. One result of this attitude is a great condescension to unmarried women, a condescension several local colorists reveal. The admirable Mrs. Hickson "slaves herself" in Johnston's "A Case of Spite," "as if she felt bound to be everlastingly thankful for her escape from old-maidhood and the Scroggins name.[45] In Mrs. Stuart's "A Note of Scarlet" a middle-aged maiden wins the community's respect instead of pity only after she secures a deaf deacon as a prospective husband.[46] Miss Woolson's sentimental mother in "Bro." weeps for joy that her daughter has found a worthy love. But Miss Woolson tells us that the mother is also profoundly relieved that her daughter has found love at all: she had worried endlessly that her daughter would never marry. Page's sketch "My Cousin Fanny" nicely summarizes the attitude. Everyone comments that Cousin Fanny would be remarkably nice, intelligent, and talented—if she were not an old maid. The narrator adds,

> She knew a great deal. In fact, I recall now that she seemed to know more than any woman I have ever been thrown with, and if she had not been an old maid, I am bound to admit that her conversation would have been the most entertaining I ever knew. She lived in a sort of atmosphere of romance and literature; the old writers and their characters were as real to her as we were, and she used to talk about them to us whenever we would let her. Of course, when it came from an old maid, it made a difference.[47]

Probably this emphasis on marriage explains as well as anything James Lane Allen's anti-Catholicism. Although Allen seems to be able to overlook much done in the name of religion, he cannot forgive the requirement of clerical celibacy which he sees as unnatural, and even un-American. Quaint marriage customs, such as the early marriages of mountain or Acadian girls, are sometimes viewed critically by various writers.

But early marriages never receive criticism so intense as that Allen directs at Catholics for refusing to allow the clergy to marry at all.

Allen's anti-Catholicism exemplifies another quality of a plain person's life which local colorists often illustrate—an intolerance of differing opinions, beliefs, and attitudes. The southerner's sense of outrage when criticized or contradicted was more recently the subject of James Silver's *Mississippi: The Closed Society*. It is interesting to note that Mr. Silver's criticisms, like other more contemporary views of southern society, were voiced by southerners before the twentieth century, and even figure in southern local color—that body of literature not usually associated with criticism of any kind. Harris excuses the intolerance, as he excuses all southern traits. But he still portrays Hillsborough as a town with "but one idea, and that was that slavery must be defended at all hazards, and against all enemies. That was the temper of the time."[48] Cable's Joseph Frowenfeld preaches in *The Grandissimes*, "One great general subject of thought now is human rights,—universal human rights. . . . Human rights is, of all subjects, the one upon which this community is most violently determined to hear no discussion. It has pronounced that slavery and caste are right, and sealed up the whole subject" (p. 143). Frowenfeld adds later, "Here is a structure of society defective, dangerous, erected on views of human relations which the world is abandoning as false; yet the immigrant's welcome is modified with the warning not to touch these false foundations with one of his fingers!" (p. 152).

Tourgée particularly concentrates on the southerner's intolerance of differences. He describes the predicament of Servosse, his Yankee hero, who settles in Carolina after the war:

> He was to all that portion of the South which arrogates to itself the term Southern, not only an enemy, but the representative in miniature of all their enemies. And this he was of course, and by consequence of his Northern nativity. It is true, he might in part relieve himself from this imputation; but it rested upon him to do so. The presumption was against him; and, in order to rebut it, he must take the gaelic oath to "love whom thou lovest, hate whom thou hatest, bless whom thou blessest, and curse whom thou dost anathematize."[49]

As Tourgée points out, the southern intolerance of difference stretches beyond the subject of slavery. Not only critical carpet-baggers like Tourgée, but also proud and self-conscious southerners such as Harris make the same point—although Harris's tone is admittedly rather different from Tourgée's:

> The history of Pinetucky District in Putnam County is preserved in tradition only, but its records are not less savory on that account. The settlement has dispersed and disappeared, and the site of it is owned and occupied by a busy little man, who wears eyeglasses and a bob-tailed coat, and who is breeding Jersey cattle and experimenting with ensilage. It is well for this little man's peace of mind that the dispersion was an accomplished fact before he made his appearance. The Jersey cattle would have been winked at, and the silo regarded as an object of curiosity; but the eyeglasses and the bob-tailed coat would not have been tolerated.[50]

Chesnutt seems to sum up the matter by stating, "Nowhere more than in a Southern town is public opinion a force which cannot be lightly contravened."[51]

When public opinion is contravened, the result—even in southern local color stories—is violence. Those accustomed to thinking that southern violence was first acknowledged by more realistic writers of the twentieth century need to take southern local color into account. Even in this most saccharine period southern writers described violence as characteristic of every section, every state, and every class. As a characteristic present in southern life generally, violence is also part of the fabric of the plain folk's daily lives. If the reader begins with stories set in the mountains, however, he might conclude that violence was limited to the southern Appalachians; for this suggestion is conveyed by local colorists using the mountain setting. Seven of eight stories in *In the Tennessee Mountains* contain either committed or narrowly averted acts of violence. In Constance Woolson's "Up in the Blue Ridge," the first mountain story to be collected in a volume in the local color period, violence is presented as a major characteristic of mountain towns. The heroine sees a man shot down in the street outside her window:

> "But what does it all mean?" asked Adelaide.
> "Moonlight whisky, of course. The detective has been hunting

for the stills, and these outlaws will kill the man as they have killed half a dozen before him."

"What an outrage! Are there no laws?"

"Dead letters."

"Or officers to execute them?"

"Dead men."[52]

While Harris changed the local colorists' attitude toward mountaineers by presenting Teague Poteet sympathetically, he still portrayed Teague as a man who had gained community esteem primarily through violence: "By knocking the sheriff of the county over the head with a chair, and putting a bullet through a saloon-keeper who bullied everybody, Poteet won the reputation of being a man of marked shrewdness and common-sense, and Gullettsville was proud of him, in a measure."[53] By the end of the local color period, when the hillbilly had become an admirable character, the mountaineers of John Fox, Jr., often use violent means to accomplish worthy ends. For example, the hillbilly narrator in "The Message in the Sand" explains that he and his son do not allow anyone to malign a poor orphan who was once seduced by her employer. Though their motives are charitable, their methods of enforcing Christian charity are violent. The narrator says modestly of himself and his son, "One of 'em is the shootines' man on this crick, I reckon, 'cept one; an', stranger, that's t'other."[54]

A casual glance through local color fiction will prove that violence is not limited to mountaineers. In presenting violence as a dominant factor in southern life, local colorists simply include in their fiction an observation later substantiated by such southern historians as C. Vann Woodward. The statistics Woodward computed bear repeating:

No paradox of the New South was more conspicuous than the contrast between the earnestly professed code of shopkeeper decorum and sobriety and the continued adherence to a tradition of violence. For violence was, if anything, more characteristic of the new society than of the old. In the place of the code duello, the traditional expression of violence in the Old South, gunplay, knifing, manslaughter, and murder were the bloody accompaniments of the march of Progress. The old state of South Carolina, with less than a quarter of the six New England states' population, reported nearly three times their number of homicides in 1890. For all its cities and slums and unassimilated immigrants, Massachusetts had only 16 homicides as compared with 65 in Virginia, 69 in North Carolina, 88 in Kentucky, 92 in Georgia, and 115 in Tennessee. Yet none of the Southern states mentioned came within a quarter of a million of the population of Massachusetts, and all were among those having the highest percentage of native, rural population. In the western tiers of states, Michigan had 31 homicides and Alabama 108, Wisconsin 20 and Mississippi 106, Minnesota 21 and Louisiana 98. Kansas and Nebraska were no further removed from frontier conditions than was Texas, but the Northern states reported respectively 34 and 23 homicides and Texas 184. Yet the census figures were admittedly unreliable, since they fell far short of the actual number of homicides, especially those of the rural, sparsely settled areas. A Kentucky editor published figures in 1885 demonstrating that there had been an average of 223 murders a year for the past six years in Kentucky, though the census returned only 50 for 1880; and a Mississippi paper declared in 1879 that there was an average of a murder a day in that state, while the census of the following year reported only 57. It is not improbable that the amount of homicide was two or three times that reported. Italy, with what appeared to be the highest homicide rate in Europe, did not have in her prisons in 1890 as many convicts charged with murder as did the South Central states, which had less than a third of Italy's population. The South seems to have been one of the most violent communities of comparable size in all Christendom.[55]

Woodward goes on to warn against attributing the record of violence exclusively to the Negro; he finds that racial violence was only a part of the general milieu of southern violence. In South Carolina, Kentucky, and Texas, for example, white men killed proportionately more often by far than did Negroes. Woodward also cautions against placing the blame on lower-class whites and reminds us that "the newspapers of the day were crowded with homicidal frays between lawyers, planters, railroad presidents, doctors, even preachers, and particularly editors." The violence in which the middle or upper classes participated did not take the form of the relatively civilized duel, but more often of "shooting on sight." Woodward ends his account: "According to the Southern editors dedicated to reform, the practice of toting a pistol was 'almost universal in some parts.' The state auditor of Alabama in 1881 reported the valuation of tools and farming implements in his state to be $305,613; that of guns, pistols and dirks, $354,247. Turning the chronicles of Southern communities . . . one is reminded forcefully at times of Marlowe's London, or the Highlands of the wild Scots."[56]

A representative story illustrating the way in which violence is treated in local color is Joel Chandler Harris's "Little Compton." As in many of Harris's later stories the propagandistic purpose of "Little Compton" is clear. In trying to promote the reconciliation of North and South, Harris centers his story on a friendship between Little Compton, a Jersey storekeeper settled in Hillsborough, and Jack Walthall, the wealthiest and most outstanding young man of the town. Compton arouses Walthall's admiration because he is a peacemaker. And Compton is eagerly welcomed and made to feel "at home" in the Georgia community. Not all strangers, however, elicit the same regard. We are told, "There came a stranger to the town, whose queer acts excited the suspicions of a naturally suspicious community."[57]

Fortunately the suspicions of Harris's Georgians are almost always well-founded; this particular stranger turns out to be an abolitionist whom Little Compton must later rescue from a tarring and feathering. Through Compton's efforts the man's fate is ameliorated so that he is simply given a coat of lampblack on face and hands, decorated by a sign reading "ABOLITIONIST! PASS HIM ON, BOYS" (p. 44), and put on the stage to Rockville, "where, presumably, the 'boys' placed him on the train and 'passed him on' to the 'boys' in other towns" (p. 45). All is done in a spirit of good clean fun. But there may be a moment of fleeting apprehension in the reader who recalls that Hillsborough men first felt the abolitionist should be hanged. Furthermore, at the beginning of the story Harris reveals that lynching was not an uncommon fate for abolitionists, even in Hillsborough: "The young men, in their free-and-easy way, told him the story of a wayfarer who once came through that region preaching abolitionism to the negroes. The negroes themselves betrayed him, and he was promptly taken in charge. His body was found afterwards hanging in the woods, and he was buried at the expense of the county. Even his name had been forgotten, and his grave was all but obliterated" (p. 31).

Harris intimates that an abolitionist in Hillsborough gets only what he deserves. Yet Harris's acknowledgment of this colorful

characteristic—the swift and permanent settlement of any difference with outsiders—seems a crack in the idyllic southern image.
And this crack, partially smoothed over by Harris, is not one
about which he seems happy. But at least he does not ascribe
all violence to a negligible number of poor whites. The best
young men of Hillsborough are behind every activity. One of
these young men, incidentally, is named Rowan Wornum,
whose proud Virginia family conflicts with Mrs. Bivins in
"Mingo." The leader of the Hillsborough men is Compton's
aristocratic friend Jack Walthall.

Walthall leads the townsmen not only when they deal with
the abolitionist, but also when, as the war becomes inevitable,
they send Compton an anonymous warning. Of course, it is only
Compton's "simple nature" which prevents his recognizing "the
humor of the young men" in the note which begins "The time
has arrived when every man should show his colors," and is
signed "NEMESIS" (p. 51). This southern penchant for violent
settlements becomes a dominant theme in twentieth-century
fiction. Such stories as "Little Compton," however, illustrate the
fact that violence was acknowledged in self-consciously southern
fiction from the beginning. Certainly no picture of the daily lives
of plain folk would be complete if violence were omitted.

In many local color tales, violence is treated humorously, as
it was in stories of southwest humorists. Sometimes, in fact, the
influence of southwestern humor is both direct and obvious.
Sherwood Bonner's "The Gentlemen of Sarsar" could be considered a transitional story. Its humor, like that in many southwest
stories, is based on physical pain, while the story is "framed" by
a romance described in the most extravagant and chivalric language. A young lover, Ned Mereweather, is promised that he
can keep a thousand-dollar payment due his father if he can collect it from Andy Rucker of Sarsar. Sarsar is described as "nothing more than a backwoods settlement in the hill country." It is
a "pretty rough place" in which "there are a lot of rough fellows
. . . calling themselves 'the Gentlemen of Sarsar' who regulate
things after their own fashion."[58] When Ned arrives in Sarsar he
seems to need regulating, and that task is performed under the
direction of Andy Rucker. Rucker explains that Sarsar's favorite
sport is a "nigger-hunt" in which twenty hounds are used to
catch any Negro who escapes from jail. Since one has just es-

caped, most of the townsmen, with Ned a reluctant addition to the party, arrange a hunt for the next morning.

Before dawn all the men gather at the tavern and get Ned as drunk as possible on harsh whiskey. He has to drink and hunt in order to be sociable; otherwise he has no hope of getting his money. When the hunt begins, with whooping townsmen chasing a naked Negro through the woods, Ned, in spite of himself, begins to enjoy it. Their prey cornered, Mereweather shoots at the fugitive in the excitement, and then is told by a disapproving Andy Rucker that he has killed, when he was supposed only to help capture, their prey. He realizes with horror that he has murdered a man and is to be jailed. Making matters harder, Rucker forces him to accompany the group as they take the news to the convict's mother. Stricken by grief, she reveals that the hunt was initially arranged by Rucker as a joke at Ned's expense; then turning truculent, she demands money to cover the funeral "an' odder matters" (p. 27).

Soon Bud Kane's fiancée, preacher, doctor, and mistress all solicit payment for their services to the deceased. Later after Rucker has thoughtfully posted his bond and Ned is hastily riding out of town, another woman stops him and introduces herself as the mother of Bud Kane's children. She has not married him "because he didn't belong to the church!" (p. 33). Weeks later Ned is still licking his wounds at home; he has lost all the money he had to begin with, and has failed to collect the debt besides. Then a well-dressed messenger appears who turns out to be Bud Kane, the man Ned supposedly killed in the hunt. Kane explains:

> "Mars' Andy tole you I wus dead; but dat was jest a joke o' his. Somebody axed him what made him act so hateful to you, an' he said onct dar was two men standin' on de Court-house steps, an' one of 'em ups and knocks de odder off de steps; an' dey had him up fur 'salt an' battery. An' de judge says, 'What made you knock dat man offen de steps? He was a stranger ter you, an' not a-doin' no harm.' An' de man says, 'I knows it, judge; I don't have nothin' agin de fellow; but de truth is, *he stood so fair I couldn't help it.*'"
> (p. 35)

Rather than limiting violence to the lower or poor-white classes, southern local colorists continually associate a hot and

violent temper with aristocrats. Perhaps this fact partially explains their attributing the characteristic also to plain folk: a
propensity for violent actions, like the ability to experience chivalric love, becomes proof that a plain man can also be a "gentleman." The most melodramatic example is found in Sherwood
Bonner's "Marse Colton's Lesson," a story frightening in its context because it is part of a collection designed primarily for children. It does have a happy moral ending—the young boy of the
story learns that violence solves nothing and resolves never
again to commit an act of aggression. Before learning this lesson,
however, Colton has argued with his personal slave and has almost killed the Negro in a fit of anger: "Colton was mad to the
verge of insanity. He gave one spring. He had snatched his keen-
bladed penknife from his pocket, and seizing Little Jason by the
throat, he plunged it twice into the boy's bare bosom, from
which the ragged shirt had fallen away. Then he flung him aside
like a weed."[59] Of course Colton repents his impetuosity. Nevertheless he is seen as the true son of his ancestors, each of
whose proud blood forbade him to do anything but "die with
his boots on" (p. 207). Because he is an aristocrat, Colton seems
not injudicious but heroic instead.

In "Up at Teague Poteet's" it is the young man of education
and good manners who appears more prone to violence than the
mountaineers. Woodward is both the romantic lover of the story
and also a revenue officer. He respects mountaineers, but realizes
that after his occupation has been revealed he can no longer
expect them to trust him in return:

> He would have preferred violence of some sort. He could meet rage
> with rage, and give blow for blow; but how was he to deal with the
> reserve by which he was surrounded? He was not physically help-
> less, by any means; but the fact that he had no remedy against the
> attitude of the men of Hog Mountain chafed him almost beyond
> endurance. He was emphatically a man of action,—full of the enter-
> prises usually set in motion by a bright mind, a quick temper, and
> ready courage; but, measured by the impassiveness which these
> men had apparently borrowed from the vast, aggressive silences
> that give strength and grandeur to their mountains, how trivial,
> how contemptible, all his activities seemed to be![60]

This penchant for resolving the slightest difference violently is meant to be an endearing quality of Smith's Colonel Carter. With pride Colonel Carter tells of a friend who shot down a postmaster for refusing the loan of a three-cent stamp: "Well, suh, what was there left for a high-toned Southern gentleman to do? Colonel Talcott drew his revolver and shot that Yankee scoundrel through the heart, and killed him on the spot."[61] The narrator of Colonel Carter is so highly entertained by this anecdote that he "lay back in his chair and roared." The colonel is presented as one obsessed with protecting his honor. He feels quite cheated if he is denied the privilege of dueling: "I of co'se am not familiar with the code as practiced Nawth—perhaps these delays are permis'ble but in my county a challenge is a ball, and a man is killed or wounded ez soon ez the ink is dry on the papah. The time he has to live is only a mattah of muddy roads or convenience of seconds. Is there no way in which this can be fixed? I doan't like to return home without an effo't bein' made" (p. 133). The southern gentleman's love of duels and violent settlements is satirized in Twain's *Pudd'nhead Wilson* as it is in Cable's work. For the most part, however, violence is not only a characteristic but also a privilege of any southerner whose name, as Colonel Carter says, "is known all over the county as a man whose honor is dearer to him than his life, and whose word is as good as his bond" (p. 21).

Perhaps the most publicized result of southern violence in the postwar South was the emergence of the Ku Klux Klan. Tourgée emphatically makes the point that the Klan was composed, not of poor whites, but of common folk and respectable community leaders. In *Bricks Without Straw* a Negro who chances to see the Klan gathering says, "Dey wuz all good men. I seed de hosses, when dey mounted ter go 'way. I tell ye dey wuz good 'uns! No pore-white trash dar; no lame hosses ner blind mules ner wukked down crap-critters. Jes sleek gentlemen's hosses, all on 'em" (p. 263). Tourgée goes on to explain why the Klan came into existence, and also to suggest that its victims were not only Negroes, but also any white man who aroused the antagonism of his neighbors:

> It was not the individual negro, scalawag, or carpet-bagger, against whom the blow was directed, but the power—the Government—the idea which they represented. Not infrequently, the individual vic-

tim was one toward whom the individual members of the Klan who executed its decree upon him had no little of kindly feeling and respect, but whose influence, energy, boldness, or official position, was such as to demand that he should be "visited." In most of its assaults, the Klan was not instigated by cruelty, nor a desire for revenge; but these were simply the most direct, perhaps the only means to secure the end it had in view. The brain, the wealth, the chivalric spirit of the South, was restive under what it deemed degradation and oppression. This association offered a ready and effective method of overturning the hated organization, and throwing off the rule which had been imposed upon them. From the first, therefore, it spread like wildfire.[62]

By juxtaposing Tourgée's comments to those of southerners like Harris, Will Harben, and Sherwood Bonner—all of whom mention organizations of "Regulators" in their stories—we begin to understand that such an organization as the Klan was a natural outgrowth of the southern milieu and that loyal southerners as well as critical carpetbaggers suggested as much in the fiction of the local color period.

Other southerners also admit along with Tourgée that the most respected members of a community participate in less organized lynchings and mob violence. In Alice French's "The First Mayor" Mayor Atherton is almost lynched by his town when unwise speculations cause his bank, and most town businesses, to fail. The mayor escapes lynching only by dying of a heart attack. In Miss French's "The Plumb Idiot" an unpopular southern politician is spared a lynching only because abuse would force his soft-hearted opponent to the politician's side. A white man occasionally proves his worth in such stories as Johnston's "Ephe," when he protests the lynching of a helpless Negro. But when one surveys local color fiction as a whole, he must conclude, as Tourgée does, that in spite of his many virtues, the average southerner has a strong capacity for unthinking violence which can trigger bloodshed almost instantly. The following incident occurs in Bricks Without Straw when Negroes decide to march to town, in orderly fashion, to vote:

Within the town there was great excitement. A young man who had passed . . . [the plantation owned by Negroes] while the men were assembling had spurred into Melton and reported with great excitement that the "niggers" were collecting at the church and Nimbus was giving out arms and ammunition: that they were boasting of what they would do if any of their votes were refused; that they had all their plans laid to meet negroes from other localities at Melton, get up a row, kill all the white men, burn the town, and then ravish the white women. This formula of horrors is one so familiar to the Southern tongue that it runs off quite unconsciously whenever there is any excitement in the air about the "sassy niggers." . . . Its effect upon the Southern white man is magical. . . . It takes away all sense and leaves only an abiding desire to kill. (pp. 152–153)

From their reminiscences and formal analyses of the lives lived by plain folk of the South, local colorists constructed a picture of daily life in the region which included more than social institutions or community events. According to their picture the defining characteristics of lives lived by plain folk in the South are isolation, a generous hospitality offered strangers, an indulgence in gossip, a consuming interest in romance, an intolerance of differing opinions, and a propensity for violence.

# *Stereotyped Characters*

PERHAPS the most common characteristic of
southern local color fiction is its use of stereotyped characters.
With the exceptions of two novels—*John March, Southerner* and
*The Awakening*—it is virtually impossible to find a piece of southern local color fiction not peopled by stereotypes. While a great
deal of attention has been given to three southern stereotypes—
the planter, the Negro, and the poor white—few critics have
commented on the great variety of stereotypes employed by
southern local colorists—or the extent to which stereotypes were
used. One reason local color fiction is important in southern literary history is that it added several new stereotypes to southern
literature, or at least filled out the stereotypes sketched by prewar writers. As has been suggested earlier, well-developed characterization—individualized portrayals of specific characters who
are not representative of any class, group, or idea—is rare in
local color fiction.[1] The individual character generally represents
a larger group. In fact the plain man as depicted in southern
local color is himself a stereotype, embodying the more lovable
and virtuous elements in a mythical southern personality. The
plain folk come into literary prominence in the local color peri-

od to illustrate the good qualities southerners in general possess.

The main elements in the Negro stereotype are generally familiar to the American public. The Negro is pictured as simple, childlike, lazy, dependent, often clever but never ambitious, content with his life and with the innocent or amoral merrymaking in which he indulges. He is loyal to his white friends and reciprocates their affection. He is often comic because he is often a buffoon. His common sense makes him wary of too much education or sophistication, but he has the wisdom of simple creatures, which he is always willing to impart to a sympathetic, condescending, or bemused white listener. He may even seem to the white a kind of saint, because of his capacity for self-sacrifice when the good of a white lady or gentleman is at stake. He has a weakness for alcohol and for the opposite sex, although he never allows his desires to stray (at least in southern local color fiction as opposed to southern political rhetoric) to white ladies. Above all, the good Negro (and there are few of any other kind in local color fiction) never under any circumstances wishes to challenge, upset, or change any aspect of the southern social, political, and economic structure.

The stereotyped planter lives a gentlemanly life of leisure and sips his julep every afternoon on his front porch. He is testy, opinionated, firm in his willingness to fight or die for his ideas whenever they are challenged. He is sustained by an indestructible pride in his honor and his good name. He loves God, his family, and his country—or at least his county. He is quaint, courtly, and hospitable. He loves the pleasures of the hunt and the table, and has a gentleman's weakness for drinking and gambling. His son is less colorful but more idealistic. His daughter is beautiful and womanly, always trembling in innocent wonder on the brink of romance. His wife is busy and satisfied, and is seldom mentioned more than is absolutely necessary.

The poor white is a sluggard and a clay-eater. He lives in an isolated and filthy cabin, and is seldom seen or noticed by respectable southerners. He is characterized by his laziness, his lack of domestic pride and ambition. His identifying marks are his sallow complexion, his ragged clothes, and his wool hat. Unlike the planter he hates Negroes and is in turn held by Negroes to be beneath contempt. He too is content.

I have traced the various elements of a fourth stereotype

which became increasingly useful to southern writers during
the local color period—the plain man. This stereotype was admirable, as were all southern stereotypes with the exception of
the poor white. The plain man is neither rich nor poor, but
hard-working, independent, self-respecting, cooperative, and
generally law-abiding. He is ruled more by heart than mind,
but so is the planter. His foibles are the predictable and not too
pernicious shortcomings of those in a rural society. His virtues
are southern, and his heart is usually of gold. He encounters few
obstacles in his upward rise which cannot be overcome by hard
work and common sense. Since he accepts the aristocrat's values
and applauds them, he is a true gentleman.

All these stereotypes are based either on economic class or
on caste distinctions. Within the limits imposed by these broader
stereotypes, several more limited stereotypes—particularly of
plain-folk characters—were developed in the local color period
and were based on geographical divisions. Mountaineers of the
southern Appalachians, for example, are a distinctive type. Although sharing in fiction the same general social status as Georgia crackers, Carolina tarheels, or Arkansans (such terms as
cracker, tarheel, and hillbilly have largely lost their more pejorative
connotations, at least in the minds of those to whom the terms
are applied), they remain distinctly different from the lowland
farmers. The Georgia farmers have more variety than the mountain folk. While the farmers are sometimes garrulous, the mountaineers talk little. While the farmers are usually eager to be
merry, the mountaineers are solemn even in social gatherings.
While the farmers are industrious, the mountaineers are lazy.
The farmers are often mentally quick, but the mountaineers are
usually slow-witted. Although both groups are provincial, the
mountaineers are the more ignorant of the two. Both groups are
fiercely democratic and proud, but the farmer strives for social
advancement while the mountaineer refuses to recognize any
social distinctions. The farmer's wife can be shrewd and sharp-
tongued; the mountain woman is usually submissive and
obedient.

As noted earlier, local colorists' attitudes toward the mountaineer change during the local color period. Probably this
change was possible because the mountaineer was not a clearly
defined stereotype until after the Civil War, and therefore was

not so sacrosanct a figure as the planter or the Negro. The southerner did not necessarily think of the mountaineer when he
mentioned the South. Most southern writers seem aware of the
fact that residents in mountainous areas were often Unionist in
sympathies during the war, and this fact in itself made them
appear different from other southerners. As I have indicated
previously, however, the change in the local colorist's presentation of mountaineers was not a change in stereotype but instead
a change of attitude toward the stereotype. Constance Woolson's
"Up in the Blue Ridge" (collected in 1880) suggested that mountaineers made most of their money running stills, that they did
not hesitate to kill anyone meddling with such operations, and
that they protected each other from outsiders. The mountaineer is still doing exactly the same things in the same way at the
end of the local color period. In the interim, however, Harris's
"Up at Teague Poteet's" made it fashionable for writers to overlook the less happy aspects of mountaineer violence while applauding mountaineer courage, pride, and independence. By
the end of the local color period it was possible for John Fox,
Jr., to state that the mountaineer is probably the purest White,
Anglo-Saxon, Protestant type left in America:

> Gradually it had dawned upon him that this last, silent figure,
> traced through Virginia, was closely linked by blood and speech
> with the common people of England, and, molded perhaps by the
> influences of feudalism, was still strikingly unchanged; that now it
> was the most distinctively national remnant on American soil, and
> symbolized the development of the continent, and that with it must
> go the last suggestions of the pioneers, with their hardy physiques,
> their speech, their manners and customs, their simple architecture
> and simple mode of life.[2]

The extent to which those living in a mountain setting came
to be acceptable, as southerners and to southerners, is indicated
by another of Fox's stories. "A Purple Rhododendron" is a romantic tragedy in the southern chivalric manner. Yet this tale,
though based on the attitude toward women typifying the
most florid Old South stories, occurs in the mountains. Grayson,
the hero, is widely-travelled, well-educated, and noble; he is also
a part of the mountain society. He conforms to the most ex-

treme, chivalric ideals of southern manhood, and thus exemplifies the gentility usually associated with Virginia cavaliers. Grayson is jilted by a Kentucky belle with a long history of broken hearts behind her. The narrator clearly thinks Grayson is well rid of her, but for Grayson the broken engagement is an irremediable tragedy. "He believed that he owed it to the woman he should marry never to have loved another. He had loved but one woman, he said, and he should love but one."[3] As a true courtly lover Grayson begins his search for death as soon as he is rebuffed. He remembers that he has promised his former lady a purple rhododendron, a blossom growing only in two inaccessible places in the vicinity. All winter Grayson watches for the first sign of spring and the first rhododendron bloom. Finally one appears in a high crevice which can be reached only by a snake-infested trail. Grayson persuades the narrator to accompany him part of the way, and the frightened narrator, lying precariously on a ridge, watches Grayson climbing higher and higher. When Grayson's hand finally clutches the bloom, the narrator hears the warning hiss of a rattlesnake. He watches in horror as Grayson tries to avoid the snake, loses his footing, and falls smiling to his death, still clutching the flower. By the end of the local color period it was possible to set this kind of romantic melodrama in the mountains without the plot's seeming totally incongruous to the setting.

One of the several ways in which the South has been historically different from other areas of the country has been its lack of sizable groups who were not of Anglo-Saxon or Scotch-Irish extraction. Thus, while the South has certainly endured a great share of racial problems, it has confronted relatively little social conflict between those of the same race but different national origins. The South has included few "foreign" elements even in the twentieth century. As C. Vann Woodward explains,

> Considering the amount of effort put into the immigration movements [at the end of the nineteenth century], the results were insignificant. While the greater part of the railroad campaign was in the West, where some success was attained, much of the propaganda attempted to divert southward part of the great tide of European immigration. The flood tide of European immigration, in 1899–1910, swept past the South leaving it almost untouched and further

isolating it in its peculiarities from the rest of the country. New Hampshire received more European immigrants in that decade than the total received by North Carolina, South Carolina, Tennessee, Mississippi, Georgia, and Kentucky; Connecticut got many more than the whole South combined and New Jersey twice as many. In the interchange of native population by internal migration, moreover, all the Southern states, save Oklahoma, Florida, and Virginia, lost more than they gained. The railroads were a path of emigration as well as immigration.[4]

To one southern state, however, these statements were not applicable. Louisiana was settled by French-speaking people, and still, in particular areas, retains vestigial signs of a French culture. A mutated French patois is still spoken in the more isolated areas of the Louisiana bayous and coastal islands. Moreover, New Orleans, still one of the nation's important ports, received a steady influx of non-English immigrants through several periods of her history. The chronicler of the city, George Washington Cable, mentions these immigrants often. Cable gives most of his attention, however, to the two distinct groups among Louisianans of French extraction—the Creoles and the Acadians. The Creoles trace their origins to France's upper classes; the Acadians are descendants of French peasants. When we turn to Louisiana we see stereotypes based not only on class and geographical setting but also on national origin.

George W. Cable was an innovator, and one of his most important innovations was his introduction into southern literature of two stereotypes. Cable's Creole stereotype will be discussed at length in the next chapter. Though less important, his Acadian stereotype is also interesting for several reasons. First, whereas every other stereotype discussed so far seems to have had literary ancestors somewhere, the Athena-like Acadian springs to life full-grown from the head of Cable. The Acadian is the only type developed entirely within the local color period. Second, while a rather complex series of motives controlled the shape other southern types took, the Acadian seems to have been created simply to fulfill the national demand for local color, for information about quaint or exotically different types. Other southern types were useful in conveying certain facts and attitudes toward the South which southern local colorists were trying to instill in the nation. The Acadian serves no such purpose; he is simply colorful. Third, while the presentation of most stereotypes in southern literature is affected by the preconceptions or prejudices of the writers, Cable seems to have approached the Acadians with few deeply-felt attitudes toward them. Thus, as stereotypes go, the Acadian stereotype seems more reasonable and realistic than others. Fourth, since other local colorists who wrote of Acadians, such as Grace King and Kate Chopin, took most of their cues from Cable, we have in the Acadian the one stereotype of a very poor class of people who were never presented negatively.

To gather material for *Bonaventure*, Cable traveled through Acadian country on several occasions, taking notes and asking questions. He had an anthropologist's eye for detail, a sociologist's love of statistics, and a historian's interest in generalizations. It was these details and generalizations which admirers of local color required and which went into Cable's book. Thus, while *Bonaventure* is poor literature it is excellent local color. More importantly its details appear to be more accurate than is usual in local color fiction.

As a literary effort *Bonaventure* is unsuccessful. It consists of three novellas, published first as magazine stories, which share the same characters but have unrelated plots. In form the book is neither fish nor fowl, neither novel nor collection of separate pieces. It is further marred by its apparent purpose of describing a unique group of people, for Cable's lengthy descriptions and digressions are draped over the plots like Spanish moss on an oak. Like moss they sap the vigor of the plots and often seem near killing them altogether. But a moss-decked oak is often more interesting than a sturdy birch. If Cable's descriptions sometimes seem to have a parasitical effect on the stories, they have an interest of their own. The book is sometimes inconsistent and often sentimental, but seldom dull.

Other flaws are equally visible in *Bonaventure*. Cable's conception of Bonaventure, the major character, changes between the first tale, "Carancro," and the second, "Grande Pointe." In "Carancro" Bonaventure is "the slender, the intense, the reticent" (p. 17). "He had no playmates—no comrades—no amusements" (p. 34). He speaks only when he can argue and develops a talent for casuistry: "He would debate the right and wrong of any thing, every thing, and the rights and wrongs of men in every relation of life" (p. 35). He broods silently through several years of his childhood sweetheart's marriage and widow-hood before he finally is able to break away from home and from her. In "Grande Pointe," however, Bonaventure is remark-ably similar to Raoul Innerarity in *The Grandissimes*. He is en-amored of long words which he often uses incorrectly. He never stops talking. He is volatile, gregarious, impulsive, occupied with winning friends and influencing people. He never argues but teaches, never questions but preaches. In the interim between the two stories he has found the truth and thereafter sticks to it. In the first story he is aloof, secretive, tortured, and full of po-tential. In the second he is happy, selfless, energetic, and some-what absurd.

The same shifting of tone and emphasis between "Carancro" and "Grande Pointe" is evident in Cable's presentation of the Acadians. This shift can partially be explained by the fact that Cable describes Acadians living on the "short-turfed prairies of Western Louisiana" (p. 1) in the first tale, while the setting of the second is the swampy land to the south, lying along the coast. We should remember that Cable actually presents two different types of Acadians.

A careful historian, Cable furnished in *Bonaventure* the major facts about Acadian history: ". . . in France their race had been peasants; in Acadia, forsaken colonists; in Massachusetts, Penn-sylvania, Maryland, Virginia, exiles alien to the land, the lan-guage, and the times; in St. Domingo, penniless, sick, unwel-come refugees; and for just one century in Louisiana the jest of the proud Creole, held down by the triple fetter of illiteracy, poverty, and the competition of unpaid, half-clad, swarming slaves" (p. 101). The peasant heritage of the Acadian is never completely forgotten. Cable refers to them as "simple, non-slaveholding peasants" (p. 9), and describes one character as "a man who on the other side of the Atlantic you would have known for a peasant of Normandy" (pp. 86–87). Yet Cable makes it clear that the Cajun's background is honorable and should not be held against him: "My friend, what was it, the first American industry? Was it not the Newfoundland fisheries? Who inaugu'ate them, if not the fishermen of Normandy and Bretagne? And since how long? Nearly fo' hundred years!"

(p. 76). Cable is often able to turn these historical facts into local color: "for these descendants of a maritime race call their homestead groves islands" (p. 10).

Cable stresses both the Acadian's present respectability and his potential usefulness to the state. He mentions that Louisiana has had three Acadian governors by the Reconstruction period (p. 114), and begins *Bonaventure* by introducing an Acadian who has served the state as "Senator, Governor, President of Convention, what you will" (p. 3). Yet the peasant origins of the Acadian which encourages in the Creole a sense of superiority, constituted a difference in their respective classes which is also mentioned more than once.

Cable's attitude toward this subject of class is not entirely clear. The fact that Bonaventure is Creole suggests that Cable himself believed in Creole superiority. Though Bonaventure is reared in an Acadian household, he is always introduced as the "little Creole." The Acadian exgovernor finds Bonaventure unique enough to insist, "He ought to go to school" (p. 8); but the great man makes no similar suggestion about any Acadian child. When schooling is finally arranged, Bonaventure, whether because of his inherited acumen or his acquired need for self-punishment, certainly learns faster than his Acadian sweetheart: "Zoséphine had hardly yet learned to read without stammering, when Bonaventure was already devouring the few French works of the curé's small bookshelf" (p. 34). When Bonaventure loses his sweetheart to a rival, the curé admits to being glad. In comparing the two men the curé suggests that Acadian Athanase is good, but Creole Bonaventure is better: "I never wanted you to get her, my dear boy; she is not your kind at all. . . . Do you imagine she could ever understand an unselfish life, or even one that tried to be unselfish? She makes an excellent Madame 'Thanase. 'Thanase is a good, vigorous, faithful, gentle animal, that knows how to graze and lie in the shade and get up and graze again. But you—it is not in you to know how poor a Madame Bonaventure she would have been" (p. 65). The difference between the two rivals is the difference between horsemanship and scholarship. Though Zoséphine admires the former, Cable reveals his preference for the latter: "Zoséphine found her eyes, so to speak, lifting, lifting, more and more as from time to time she looked upon the inoffensive Bonaventure. But so her satisfaction in her own husband was all the more emphatic. If she had ever caught a real impulse toward any thing that even Carancro would have called culture, she had cast it aside now" (p. 68).

Cable fills in his portrait of Acadians with great care, describing their sources of income, their daily routines, their amusements, even the varieties of their food and of the plants in their gardens. Generally the Acadian life on the prairies seems a particularly good one. Of course Cable glamorizes it in phrases such as "a turfy, cattle-haunted lane between rose-hedges" (p. 58), in exuberant descriptions of a young girl's beauty (p. 11), and in presenting characters who, with the exception of Bonaventure, are always happy. Though life is not quite so rosy at Grande Pointe, Cable describes the variety of good things which come even there as the seasons roll by (pp. 103–104). The difference in Cable's attitude toward the two places seems the result primarily of the difference in Bonaventure's role in each. At Grande Pointe Bonaventure must struggle to convince a suspicious settlement of the benefits of education; at Carancro he is respected and honored.

When describing the Acadian, Cable refers to his "gentle, brown-eyed, wild-animal gaze" (p. 6), and speaks often of his ignorance. Yet the virtues Cable assigns him are far more numerous than his faults. The men are characterized by bravery and valor (p. 16, p. 33), the women by thrift and, occasionally, taste (p. 6). The girls mature young—"at fifteen girls get married!" (p. 93)—but never outgrow the urge to be hospitable to strangers, an impulse they share with their husbands. A Negro encountered by Bonaventure delivers a summary of the Acadian character with which Cable appears to agree:

> "Oh, dey good sawt o' peop', yes. Dey deals fair an' dey deals square. Dey keeps de peace. Dass 'caze dey mos'ly don't let whisky git on deir blin' side, you know. Dey *does* love to dance, and dey marries mawnstus young; but dey not like some niggehs: dey stays married. An' modess? Dey dess so modess dey shy! Yes, seh, dey de shyes', easy-goin'es', modesses', most p'esumin' peop' in de whole worl'! I don't see fo' why folks talk 'gin dem Cajun'; on'y dey a lil bit slow." (p. 76)

The Acadian is also the subject of one story by Grace King,

and of many stories by Kate Chopin, who is probably as important a force as Cable in securing the Acadian a place in southern literature. But the Acadians of both these women are not significantly different from those of Cable. In fact, in "The Story of a Day,"[5] several of Miss King's phrases and comments appear to have been lifted almost verbatim from *Bonaventure*. The Acadian again reappeared in southern literature as recently as 1958, in Shirley Ann Grau's *The Hard Blue Sky*, an excellent example of more contemporary local color.

Occasionally we find traces in nineteenth-century local color fiction of a popular stereotype which was troubling both to writer and to readers, and which hovers ghost-like around the stories without being fully embodied in a character. An example is the sexually promiscuous mountain girl. One of the first signs of this stereotype appears in Sherwood Bonner's "Jack and the Mountain Pink," the purpose of which is to explode an apparent myth about mountain girls—that they make good mistresses. Jack Seldon, residing in a Nashville hotel when the story opens, decides that he is bored and should seek diversion in the mountains: "'I envy you,' said a decrepit old gentleman, with whom he was shaking hands in goodbye. 'I was brought up in the mountain country fifty years ago. Gay young buck I was! Go in, my boy, and make love to a mountain pink! Ah, those jolly, barefooted, melting girls! No corsets, no back hair, no bangs, by Heaven!'"[6] Although Jack meets a mountain girl, he concludes wearily, "A mountain pink! . . . Oh no, a bean-stalk—a Cumberland bean-stalk" (p. 187). As far as Jack is concerned, she is "stolid as a wooden Indian" (p. 186). Since the only mountain folk for whom Mary Murfree has much sympathy in her first volume are the mountain girls, they emerge, predictably, with unblemished reputations. They often fall in love with visiting hunters, but the hunters never press their advantage; so the girls all end by languishing away for love.

Vestiges of the myths about promiscuous mountain girls reappear, however, in Joel Chandler Harris's mountain stories. In "The Cause of the Difficulty"[7] a mountain girl is seduced and abandoned by a dandy from the valley. In "Trouble on Lost Mountain"[8] a burgeoning flirtation between mountain girl and valley visitor ends tragically because of the suspicions of the girl's mountain lover. And even in the extremely sympathetic

"Up at Teague Poteet's"[9] Teague automatically assumes that his daughter has been seduced when she grows melancholy after a young revenuer leaves the mountain.

Apparently this idea of the mountain girl which local colorists never deal with very explicitly had rather widespread currency. We find an interesting defense of her morals in two stories by John Fox, Jr. "The Message in the Sand" concerns the happy fate of an unwed mother who is forgiven her indiscretions because "Rosie hadn't no daddy an' no mammy; an' she was jes a-workin' at Dave's fer her victuals an' clo'es. 'Pears like the pore gal was jes tricked into evil. Looked like she was sorter 'witched—an' anyways, stranger, she was a-fightin' Satan in *herself*, as well as in Dave. Hit was two agin one, I tell ye, an' hit wasn't fa'r."[10] "A Mountain Europa"[11] describes a rather masculine mountain lass named Easter who attracts the attention of a cultured young man sent to the mountains as a mining supervisor. Their romance proceeds in genteel fashion until Easter learns that Clayton is about to leave the mountain. Desperately she follows him home one night and throws herself in his arms. They consummate their love, watched by Easter's mountain suitor. But Clayton, a man of honor, promises to marry Easter when he returns from a visit home. Neither of the couple is presented as either immoral or foolish, and neither is scarred by the experience. Easter's actions are the product of her innocence, her child-like lack of inhibitions, and her generous spirit which refuses to dole out love in small doses once she has acknowledged the emotion. She is the kind of mountain pink Sherwood Bonner's old man remembered nostalgically. She trusts Clayton completely and never doubts that he will marry her.

Clayton, too, is presented sympathetically. When he returns to New York, he recognizes the social gulf separating his family from Easter's. He also realizes that practicing restraint during nights on the mountain has advantages, but he returns to Easter anyway. He is repelled by Easter's uncouth father and appalled by the crude wedding ceremony the father arranges. But he submits to the humiliation because he is confident that he can make Easter into a socially acceptable wife. Fox resolves the social dilemma by having Easter's father fly into a drunken rage after the wedding, try to shoot Clayton, and kill Easter instead. At the end of the story the honor of both Easter and Clayton has been saved by the marriage, yet Clayton is conveniently rid of his wife. Fox's interest in the sexual practices of mountaineers is also apparent in "Courtin' on Cutshin," a sketch which details the amusing courtship customs among hillbillies. Several of Fox's stories, in fact, involve the titillating inconveniences involved when mountain families and their visitors must all sleep in the same room, a possibility first exploited by the southwest humorists.

The stereotype of the promiscuous mountain girl flits alluringly in and out of southern local color fiction; but the local colorists never quite summon the courage to grasp, to pursue, or even to admit the existence of her. The liveliness of this unacknowledged specter is revealed in a more recent story by Eudora Welty. In "A Piece of News"[12] a Mississippi farmer's wife, accustomed to sleeping with traveling salesmen whenever depressed, is subtly associated with Tennessee and, by extension, with the mountains.

But one of the most interesting, unusual, and influential of all the stereotypes developed by local colorists is that of the Creole. Like the Acadian, the Creole owes his creation and his characterization primarily to Cable. We explore this stereotype in detail, for in creating the Creole stereotype Cable approached the South's plain folk from a new, and radically different, direction.

## Chapter VIII

# *The Creole*

GEORGE W. CABLE WAS probably the most important southern writer working in the last third of the nineteenth century. His talent makes him outstanding in the local color period as an American as well as a southerner. Moreover, his work stands up fairly well when read today. But Cable would be important historically even if he had been less gifted, for he introduced several noteworthy innovations into southern fiction. Two of these innovations we shall discuss in this chapter, noting also the effects they had on writers who followed Cable.

Often highly praised when first published, Cable's work has attracted critical attention again in the last decade. His social criticism, particularly of southern treatment of Negroes, seems a major factor in this revival of interest. Historically, however, this criticism was the element of Cable's work least influential on southern local colorists. The contribution most easily traced in the work of other writers was Cable's addition of the Creole stereotype to American fiction.

It is important to keep in mind that Cable's Creoles are definitely stereotyped. In one's anxiety to praise any southerner courageous enough to plead for the Negro during the nineteenth

century, one must not make the mistake of assuming that southerner absolutely fair or objective, or necessarily trustworthy on
all aspects of southern society. As Arlin Turner points out,
Cable's "fiction was inspired by a sympathy for the dispossessed
around him. . . ."[1] This sympathy for the victims of injustice
formed a large part of Cable's temperament, leading him to
advocate reform not only of southern attitudes toward race but
also of the antiquated prison system and similar social ills. In
other words Cable was temperamentally inclined to play the
reformer.

But a part of the reformer's temperament is surely the inclination to see himself as different from those living happily in
the society which needs reform. Over the years, with reactions
varying from exasperation to violent hostility, southerners have
noticed that reformers sometimes oversimplify the problems
they wish to correct. These tendencies to oversimplify and to see
oneself as different from those responsible for the iniquity at-
tracting attention are part of the George W. Cable we glimpse
through his presentation of Louisiana society. Especially in his
development of the Creole stereotype Cable writes as an outsider, one who differs from and who (it follows almost necessarily) considers himself superior to the Creole.

Any stereotype is an oversimplification. Portraying any character as one automatically possessing certain qualities because of
his racial or cultural inheritance is insulting, whether the character is a happy, childlike Negro or a proud, aristocratic Creole. The insult increases in proportion to the amount of condescension involved in such characterization. George Washington Cable soon became more outcast than outsider to Creole
society, for his condescension is unmistakable. Indeed the noted
Creole historian Charles Gayarré wrote in a lengthy attack on
Cable, "When the 'Grandissimes' appeared, we were requested
by the editor of THE TIMES-DEMOCRAT to review the work. We
refused from motives of delicacy. Mr. Cable having heard of it
and having requested us to change our decision, we replied that
we would, if he could name two Creole families with whom he
was intimately acquainted. He could not."[2] To understand
Cable's oversimplified presentation of the Creole, one must first
examine the outlines of the stereotype he created and popularized.

In his study of Creole history Cable defines a Creole as "any native, of French or Spanish descent by either parent, whose non-alliance with the slave race entitled him to social rank."[3] He adds that the term implied "a certain excellence of origin" which made convenient extending it to the Spanish, as well as to the French who originally claimed it exclusively. In spite of a period of Spanish rule the Creole retained his original language and became "the French-speaking native portion of the [Louisiana] ruling class."[4]

In the opening paragraphs of *The Creoles of Louisiana* Cable describes Louisiana society as "a Latin civilization, sinewy, valiant, cultured, rich, and proud. . . ."[5] All these adjectives appear affirmative, yet each trait they suggest is qualified in his fiction to the extent that its applicability to the Creoles seems questionable; even if Cable admits each trait's existence, he questions its virtue. Indeed, when Cable's fiction is considered as a whole, the Creole's apparent virtues seem to have been transformed into vices. Cable concentrates on pride, for example, as the Creole's dominant attribute. Dr. Keene of *The Grandissimes* says, "Show me any Creole, or any number of Creoles, in any sort of contest, and right down at the foundation of it all, I will find you this same preposterous, apathetic, fantastic, suicidal pride. It is as lethargic and ferocious as an alligator. That is why the Creole almost always is . . . on the defensive" (p. 32).

Dr. Keene's statement illustrates Cable's technique for developing his Creole stereotype. If a Creole character has a particular trait which Cable chooses to emphasize, he traces the characteristic to the Creole's ancestry. Moreover, if one Creole has a certain trait, then Cable suggests that all other Creoles can be identified through their possession of the same trait. Pride is a quality which appeals to an American public sharing, to varying degrees, the assumptions that all men are born equal and that all have something to be proud of in their human dignity. Local colorists consider pride an especially appealing characteristic of southern plain folk. When characters apparently speaking for Cable describe Creole pride, however, it is called "preposterous" and "suicidal." It is not the pride of an eagle but of an alligator.

The cause of the Creole's pride, according to Cable's fiction, is his unlimited vanity about his family. Again family loyalty is a trait usually admired both in English and southern fiction. Yet

Cable makes the possession of this trait a weakness in the Creoles, because they carry it to excess. For Cable their loyalty is excessive because it accepts without question any indiscretion or sin which has been part of an ancestor's past. In "Belles Demoiselles Plantation" the omniscient narrator states, "One thing I never knew a Creole to do. He will not utterly go back on the ties of blood, no matter what sort of knots those ties may be. For one reason, he is never ashamed of his or his father's sins; and for another—he will tell you—he is 'all heart'" (pp. 64–65). *The Grandissimes* is largely based on this fanatical family loyalty and the iniquities such loyalty leaves uncorrected. One reveller states at the masked ball with which the novel opens, "Blood is a great thing here, in certain odd ways. . . . Very curious sometimes" (p. 15).

In *The Grandissimes* Honoré Grandissime, manager of his family's fortune, jeopardizes it in order to restore to a pretty and destitute widow the money his uncle once won gambling with her husband. Since the gambling was unaccompanied by any dishonesty ("withal the Creoles are such gamblers, they never cheat; they play absolutely fair" [p. 31]), Honoré's romantic gesture seems to suit Cable's morality more than it suits the facts of the case: Cable disapproved of gambling. In this and other situations Honoré is presented sympathetically only when he acts, as he often does, in ways which are contrary to family custom. Some of Cable's work does not present this Creole loyalty to relatives negatively—"Jean-ah Poquelin" is the story of a Creole who sacrifices his life to nurse a leprous brother. As a rule, however, Cable disapproves of the lengths to which a Creole goes to protect members of his blood, primarily because he disapproves of the values upheld by Creole society, and therefore of the actions he feels the loyal Creole is probably protecting.

According to the evidence offered by his fiction Cable was particularly annoyed by the Creole's assumption that his blood was somehow purer than that of others and was unpolluted by admixture with that of society's lower orders. When characterizing Agricola Fusilier, symbolic in *The Grandissimes* of the most arrogant Creole traditions, Cable dwells on the fact that one of Agricola's ancestors was an Indian princess: "And now, since this was Agricola's most boasted ancestor—since it appears the darkness of her cheek had no effect to make him less white, or qualify his right to smite the fairest and most distant descendant of an African on the face, and since this proud station and right could not have sprung from the squalid surroundings of her birth, let us for a moment contemplate these crude materials" (p. 18). Cable goes on to contemplate the crude materials at some length, clearly implying that the Indian princess is no better, and comes from no more advanced culture, than an African princess. Thus Agricola's vanity is, at the least, illogical.

The story of Bras-Coupé, an African prince who is treated unjustly by Agricola and others, further emphasizes the absurdity of making rigid distinctions between Indian and African ancestry. This story was written independently and inserted in *The Grandissimes* after no editor would publish it. Yet Bras-Coupé's history—and his proud and violent reactions when thwarted—parallel the history and actions of Agricola's Indian ancestors. Cable further ridicules Creole pretensions to gentility by emphasizing the fact that most Creoles are descended from the *filles à la cassette*, "maidens from the hearthstones of France,"[6] who were sent in boatloads to Louisiana in the early days of the colony to provide wives for the Frenchmen already there. While these girls were undoubtedly honorable, their marriages were obviously based more on expediency than romance. The *filles* could hardly be considered aristocratic ladies, courted and wed in an aristocratic way.

One of the greatest evils resulting from this pretension to gentility, according to Cable, is the Creole's contempt for honest labor. Joseph Frowenfeld, the self-righteous immigrant so sympathetically presented in *The Grandissimes*, delivers several sermons on this subject. For example: "Nothing on earth can take the place of hard and patient labor. But that, in this community, is not esteemed; most sorts of it are contemned; the humbler sorts are despised, and the higher are regarded with mingled patronage and commiseration. . . . Industry is not only despised, but has been degraded and disgraced, handed over into the hands of African savages" (pp. 141–142). In *Dr. Sevier* the Creole accountant Narcisse asks rhetorically, "You thing I'm goin' to kill myseff workin'?" To which question "Nobody said yes, and by and by he found himself alive . . ." (p. 47). When a poor friend points out to Narcisse that there are always two sides to a question, his reaction is, "Yes, . . . and what you muz look out faw, 'tis to git on the soff side" (p. 163). The same point is made in "Posson Jone'." This story presents Jules St.-Ange, an "elegant little heathen," who had learned as a schoolboy only that the "round world is a cheese to be eaten through, and Jules had nibbled quite into his cheese-world already at twenty-two."

> The trouble was he had been wasteful and honest. He discussed the matter with that faithful friend and confidant, Baptiste, his yellow body-servant. They concluded that, papa's patience and *tante's* pin-money having been gnawed away quite to the rind, there were left open only these few easily enumerated resorts: to go to work—they shuddered; to join Major Innerarity's filibustering expedition; or else—why not?—to try some games of confidence. At twenty-two one must begin something. (p. 171)

With his pride in his family and his contempt for labor the Creole of Cable's fiction places a disproportionate emphasis on appearance, especially on keeping up appearances of prosperity, even when he is in dire financial straits. When Honoré saves the Grandissime fortune by the unprecedented act of making his wealthy quadroon half-brother an acknowledged business partner, many relatives remove their capital from the family corporation. Cable says of these, "You may see their grandchildren, to-day, anywhere within the angle of the old rues Esplanade and Rampart, holding up their heads in unspeakable poverty, their nobility kept green by unflinching self-respect, and their poetic and pathetic pride revelling in ancestral, perennial rebellion against common sense" (p. 282). This novel makes it clear, however, that this emphasis on appearance is not limited to the Grandissime family, which is only an example of all Creole families: "Frowenfeld's window was fast growing to be a place of art exposition. A pair of statuettes, a golden tobacco-box, a costly jewel-casket, or a pair of richly gemmed horse-pistols— the property of some ancient gentleman or dame of emaciated fortune, and which must be sold to keep up the bravery of good clothes and pomade that hid slow starvation . . ." (p. 113). This point is made in the action as well as in the narration of *The Grandissimes.* We follow the fortunes of the last two Nacanous, mother and daughter, who in most of the novel are in danger of eviction and without adequate food. They may go hungry, but they still live as ladies, continuing the hopeless struggle for proper appearance until they are rescued by Honoré's unexpected largesse. Dr. Mossy of "Madame Délicieuse" is unlike other Creoles and therefore a misfit in Creole society. His eccentricity consists of an inability to *show himself* to his social profit" among a people "spending most of their esteem upon animal heroisms and exterior display" (p. 125). A third quality of Cable's Creole, then, is his insistence on a proper appearance.

Because the Creole has a hearty contempt for labor, his energies are consumed in the pursuit of pleasure. Cable especially identifies this pursuit with the Creole gentleman. A genteel example is Jean Albert Henri Joseph De Carleu-Marot, the planter in "Belles Demoiselles Plantation": "He had had his vices—all his life; but had borne them, as his race do, with a serenity of conscience and a cleanness of mouth that left no outward blemish on the surface of the gentleman. He had gambled in Royal Street, drunk hard in Orleans Street, run his adversary through in the duelling-ground at Slaughter-house Point, and danced and quarrelled at the St. Philippe Street Theater quadroon balls" (p. 64). And in "Madame Délicieuse" the heroine summarizes the reasons why Dr. Mossy has gone unappreciated: "Here in Royal Street, in New Orleans, where we people know nothing and care nothing but for meat, drink, and pleasure, he was only Dr. Mossy, who gave pills" (p. 143).

Since the Creole's chief end in life is the pursuit of pleasure, he loves not only meat and drink, but also that kind of license to which Cable constantly alludes with the euphemistic phrase "the quadroon balls." Cable bases two of his stories—"'Tite Poulette" and "Madame Delphine"—on the existence of this institutionalized sexual license and on the moral problems which the existence of quadroons creates. Though not a central concern in novels such as *The Grandissimes* and *Dr. Sevier*, the Creole's sexual promiscuity is often mentioned, particularly in the former novel. When the ancient De Grapion family in *The Grandissimes* objects to a plan for marrying Palmyre, a slave, to the magnificent Bras-Coupé, because she *shared the blood of the De Grapions*" (p. 176; Cable's italics), Cable seems horrified not only that Creoles indulge in miscegenation ("I know there is a natural, and I think proper, horror of mixed blood" writes Kristian

Koppig in "'Tite Poulette" [p. 87]) but also that they openly acknowledge the illegitimate offspring.

When depicting such offspring, however, Cable idealizes the beautiful quadroon woman. Like Madame John of "'Tite Poulette" or the heroine of "Madame Delphine," she is always true to her one white love. Thus the quadroon is capable of greater virtue and fidelity than the Creole man. Cable quickly skims over the fact suggested obliquely in "'Tite Poulette" that when her means of support was withdrawn because of the death or indifference of her white lover, the quadroon was expected to return to the balls and find a new mainstay. When Madame John put on widow's weeds, "her glittering eyes never again looked through her pink and white mask, and she was glad of it; for never, never in her life had they so looked for anybody but her dear Monsieur John" (pp. 83–84).

Cable treats the quadroon male differently. Quadroon Honoré Grandissime is an effete, somewhat silly figure who dies of unrequited love. Kookoo, "an ancient Creole of doubtful purity of blood" in "'Sieur George," is cowardly and inquisitive. The narrator describes him as "a sort of periodically animate mummy" (p. 48). On the other hand Poulette and Olive, the daughters of Cable's faithful quadroon women, are too virtuous to do less than marry respectably. To marry respectably is to marry a white man, as both do. In his romantic presentation of the helpless quadroon ladies, if not of the men, Cable does leave himself open to the charge that he "proclaimed his preference for colored people over white and assumed the inevitable superiority—according to his theories—of the quadroons over the Creoles."[7]

Cable's Creoles refuse not only to abide by the sexual mores of a Protestant America but also to observe any rules whatever that are not part of family custom. Captain Lemaitre of "Madame Delphine" is told from infancy, "Remember, my boy, . . . that none of your family line ever kept the laws of any government or creed" (p. 195). This young man's grandfather "had cultivated him up to that pitch where he scorned to practice any vice, or any virtue, that did not include the principle of self-assertion" (p. 195). Cable's point, stated repeatedly throughout the story, is that such an upbringing is accepted by all Creoles and that "this whole community ought to be recognized as part-

ners in [Lemaitre's] moral errors" (p. 199). A priest summarizes
Lemaitre's training: he "was carefully taught, from infancy to
manhood, this single only principle of life: defiance. Not justice,
nor righteousness, not even gain; but defiance: defiance to God,
defiance to man, defiance to nature, defiance to reason; defiance
and defiance and defiance" (p. 204). In "Café des Exilés" a group
of Spanish Creoles plan a smuggling expedition which is foiled
when one of the group betrays them to the police. But the police themselves, as a part of Creole society, share the Creole
attitude toward the law. A police chief tells the group's leader
years later, "Major, there was only one thing that kept your
expedition from succeeding—you were too sly about it. Had you
come out flat and said what you were doing, we'd never a-said
a word to you. But that little fellow gave us the wink, and then
we had to stop you." Creole justice is meted out to the little fellow, however, for he "was drawn out of Carondelet Canal—cold,
dead!" (p. 170).

Such emphasis on self-assertion, defiance, and the protection
of one's honor against real or imagined insult results both in the
swift revenge which befalls the traitor in "Café des Exilés" and
in a more formal *code duello* of which Cable strenuously disapproved. The haste to duel characterizes his most pompous Creoles—General Villivicencio of "Madame Délicieuse" and Agricola Fusilier of *The Grandissimes*. In fact only the right-minded
harangue of Joseph Frowenfeld prevents Agricola from killing
one of his kinsmen. For taking trouble to prevent the duel Joseph is rewarded by having his shop wrecked by a Creole mob.
The sad fortunes of the De Grapion family in the same novel,
who cannot keep a son alive to middle age, are explained by the
fact that "they were such inveterate duelists, such brave Indian-
fighters, such adventurous swamp-rangers, and such lively free-
livers" that the legitimate line faces extinction as the novel opens
(p. 23).

This reluctance to obey any law except one's own at one
point in New Orleans history made respectable such illicit enterprises as smuggling. It is historical fact, which Cable dwells on
in *The Creoles of Louisiana*, that the famous privateers, the Lafitte
brothers, were at various times respected members of New Orleans society. John, the younger, "was cool and intrepid and had
only the courts to evade, and his unlawful adventures did not

lift his name from the published lists of managers of society balls or break his acquaintance with prominent legislators."[8] The Lafittes were finally declared outlaws. But when John refused to betray the Creoles to the English in 1814, he became a Creole hero, renowned for his patriotism. The respectability of smuggling in the early nineteenth century is a subject Cable returns to almost as often as to the quadroon balls. Smuggling is a major element in "Madame Delphine," "Café des Exilés," and "Jean-ah Poquelin." The last story takes place "in the first decade of the present century, when the newly established American Government was the most hateful thing in Louisiana—when the Creoles were still kicking at such vile innovations as the trial by jury, American dances, anti-smuggling laws, and the printing of the Governor's proclamation in English" (p. 102). Poquelin is a man who was faced in his earlier days with the fact that growing indigo on his plantation was no longer profitable. Searching for some new enterprise, he "saw larger, and, at that time, equally respectable profits, first in smuggling, and later in the African slave trade. What harm could he see in it? The whole people said it was vitally necessary, and to minister to a vital public necessity—good enough, certainly, and so he laid up many a doubloon, that made him none the worse in the public regard" (p. 104). The Grandissime family also has its smuggler whom Cable describes with heavy irony: "Capitain Jean-Baptiste Grandissime was a man of few words, no sentiments, short methods; materialistic, we might say; quietly ferocious; indifferent as to means, positive as to ends, quick of perception, sure in matters of saltpetre, a stranger at the custom-house, and altogether—*take him right*—very much of a gentleman" (p. 311). Perhaps Cable's early employment in the New Orleans customs house explains why smuggling and piracy often seem to him symbols of the disgraceful lengths to which a Creole's refusal to work, or to observe society's laws, may take him.

Cable suggests that a certain brutalizing of the sensibilities resulted from the Creole's code of values. "The whole Creole treatment of race troubles," for example, begins and ends with the injunction "Shoot the black devils without mercy!"[9] The traitor Mazaro's fate in "Café des Exilés" is certainly not a merciful one. The man barely saved from a lynch mob in *Dr. Sevier* almost loses his life only because he mistakenly exhibits for sale, before the election of 1860, a Lincoln badge. Again Cable seems to indicate that unthinking lawlessness is a central fact of life in New Orleans, and that it leads to a disregard of human life. One of the most dramatic episodes illustrating this disregard occurs in *The Grandissimes.* Clemence, a peddler of cakes and a beloved familiar of the Grandissime family, is caught in a bear-trap while conveying voudou effigies to frighten Agricola. Several men of the family prepare to hang her, despite her frantic reminders that such a procedure is against the law. At the last a Grandissime rescuer arrives and cuts her down, still alive. She struggles away, laughter following her limping footsteps. As she stumbles along, someone shoots her in the back. Nothing is ever said or done about the murder.

Whether the Creole is brutalized or only slightly tainted by his inattention to the rules preserving order, he is clearly characterized by a willingness to adjust facts to his liking. Actually he has no regard for objective fact at all. One Creole calls looking at both sides of a question "a miserable practice."[10] Agricola Fusilier habitually boasts, "I have these facts . . . by family tradition; but you know, sir, h-tradition is much more authentic than history!"[11] The Creoles are tellers of tales in both praiseworthy and pejorative senses. Of one raconteur in "Café des Exilés" the narrator says, "What tales that would have been tear-compelling, nay, heart-rending, had they not been palpable inventions, the pretty, womanish Mazaro from time to time poured forth" (p. 154). Cable adds, "but I should fail to show a family feature of the Café des Exilés did I omit to say that these make-believe adventures were heard with every mark of respect and credence" (p. 154). Most of the humor in *Dr. Sevier* is generated by the slippery accommodations—sometimes made in the middle of a speech—which Narcisse makes to suit his audience. This tendency to adjust the truth, to tell—as Tennessee Williams' Blanche DuBois does—not what is true but what ought to be true, is characteristic also of the Creole ladies. In the case of Madame Délicieuse this little vagary is a part of her charm; for if "she could at times do what the infantile Washington said he could not, why, no doubt she and her friends generally looked upon it as a mere question of enterprise" (p. 126). Again we notice the difference in Cable's presentation of men and women;

he smiles genially over the stratagems of the ladies, but refuses to excuse the equivocations of the men.

The male Creole's refusal to face or acknowledge openly unpleasant facts, to be objective, self-critical, or honest about himself is a heinous fault leading to the inevitable destruction of his society. Cable's insistence on this outcome is substantiated by history; the tight-knit Creole society was eventually absorbed into the American, just as the slave-owning southern Confederates in other states were. Of course Cable was writing after the Civil War, with the benefit of hindsight. Nevertheless Joseph Frowenfeld preaches these sentiments in *The Grandissimes,* which is set before the sectional conflict occurred. Frowenfeld's speeches also suggest that the Creole's (and the southerner's) self-indulgent refusal to examine "true fact" leads to abysmal ignorance. Even one of the Grandissime family, which sends its favored sons to France for the best of educations, is illiterate—a fact causing much joking at family gatherings (p. 165). According to Frowenfeld, the unquestioned perpetuation of regional customs has produced "a bondage . . . which compels a community, in order to preserve its established tyrannies, to walk behind the rest of the intelligent world! . . . When a man's social or civil standing is not dependent on his knowing how to read, he is not likely to become a scholar" (p. 143). According to Cable's fiction, the Creole is ignorant, and his ignorance results directly from his outlook, his values, and his traditions. When Cable states that the Creole is cultured, he seems to mean that the Creole is indoctrinated into the values of a culture which encourages men to stay ignorant.

A direct consequence of his ignorance is the Creole's superstition, a quality ascribed in other southern stories only to Negroes and illiterate mountaineers. Yet the charming heroine of *The Grandissimes,* Aurora Nacanou, is a good example of a superstitious Creole aristocrat. When she buys thyme from Frowenfeld, Honoré Grandissime explains, "You know what some very excellent people do with this? They rub it on the sill of the door to make the money come into the house." He adds, "Many of our best people consult the voudou horses" (p. 55). Aurora even goes to a voudou friend for a love charm, which, as a matter of fact, appears to have worked by the end of the novel. That vainest of men, Agricola Fusilier, is afraid of Palmyre, the voudou, and is almost frightened to death before his relatives discover how Palmyre is conveying her voudou charms to Agricola's quarters. Frowenfeld himself is horrified to learn that both Negroes and Creoles consider him a voudou because he is an apothecary. In "Jean-ah Poquelin," Poquelin's isolation makes him suffer because of his neighbor's superstition: "To the Creoles—to the incoming lower class of superstitious Germans, Irish, Sicilians, and others—he became an omen and embodiment of public and private ill fortune. Upon him all the vagaries of their superstitions gathered and grew. If a house caught fire, it was imputed to his machinations. Did a woman go off in a fit, he had bewitched her" (p. 111). As this passage makes clear, Cable equates the superstition of the Creoles with that of the most ignorant element among European immigrants. Cable suggests in *The Grandissimes* that the Creoles learn their attitudes from the blacks with whom they play as children, just as Aurora Nacanou played with Palmyre. Thus the Creole's ignorant superstition is a direct result of the corrupting influence of slavery.

In many more remarks Cable tabulates other weaknesses of the Creoles. Usually he makes such remarks parenthetically, and they consist of only a sentence or two. But in almost every reference to a character as *a* Creole, Cable inserts a generalization about *the* Creole. His generalizations most often concern qualities of little merit. For example, a San Domingan often tells of the massacre of his entire family "with that strange, infantile insensibility to the solemnity of his bereavement so peculiar to Latin people."[12] Aurora Nacanou utters "a genuine laugh, under that condition of mind which Latins usually substitute for fortitude."[13] Narcisse proves a brave nurse in a yellow fever epidemic, though he happily extracts ten dollars a night from his patients; but "Dr. Sevier, it is true, could not get rid of the conviction for years afterward that one victim would have lived had not Narcisse talked him to death."[14] Indeed "no power or circumstance has ever been found that will keep a Creole from talking."[15] Other characters are described in a similar vein: "The stranger was a gesticulating, stagy fellow, . . . an incessant talker in Creole-French, always excited on small matters and unable to appreciate a great one."[16] In another story we read, "The Spanish Creoles were . . . both cold and hot, but never warm."[17] Perhaps the most biting comment of all Cable includes in "'Sieur George." When the major character simply appears in military uniform, "the Creole neighbors rush bareheaded into the middle of the street, as though there were an earthquake or a chimney on fire. What to do or say or think, they do not know; they are at their wits' ends, therefore well-nigh happy" (p. 50).

When remembering that Cable wrote for an American audience, in fact, we begin to realize just how much he has loaded the dice against his Creole characters. Hardly a story passes without a comment on the Creole's contempt for Americans. Cable makes abundantly clear the absurdity of such prejudice. When Creoles seem particularly un-American, the fact adds to their discredit; for example, "One American trait which the Creole is never entirely ready to encounter is this gratuitous Yankee way of going straight to the root of things."[18] Frowenfeld points out critically that New Orleans is "distant from enlightened centres" and "has a language and religion different from that of the great people of which it is now called to be a part."[19] Although Cable concedes that most Creoles are bilingual, the blunders they make speaking English are a major source of Cable's literary humor. Readers are allowed to feel superior to any character whose speech is not represented as standard.

This matter of New Orleans speech Cable treats in *Dr. Sevier*. Mary and John Richling bitterly observe that Narcisse laughs at them, and that "had they been talking French, Narcisse would have bitten his tongue off before any of his laughter should have been at their expense" (p. 163). Yet the Richlings' awareness of the unjust social distinctions which allow Narcisse to laugh at them does not prevent their laughing at Narcisse's English, or their amusing themselves by imitating the accents of Sicilians, Irish, and Italians encountered in the course of the day. Cable seems to feel that although it is unjust for Creoles to laugh at Americans, it is acceptable for Americans to snigger about Creoles. More than once the Richlings make Narcisse the butt of their private jokes, while they are in his presence. This ability to be subtle, to insult Narcisse without his being aware of the fact, supposedly indicates their youthful charm and high spirits in the face of hardship.

In one sense Cable gives the Creoles their due, for he speaks often of their charm; for example, "The Creole, true to his blood, was able at any time to make himself as young as need be, and possessed the rare magic of drawing one's confidence without seeming to do more than merely pay attention."[20] But Creole charm is the charm of the erratic, the volatile, the quaint or exotic. Cable often mentions Creole beauty, but usually implies a loveliness more of the body than of the spirit. Narcisse, of *Dr. Sevier*, embodies all these qualities:

> Mary labored honestly and arduously to dislike him—to hold a repellent attitude toward him. But he was too much for her. It was easy enough when he was absent; but one look at his handsome face, so rife with animal innocence, and despite herself she was ready to reward his displays of sentiment and erudition with laughter that, mean what it might, always pleased and flattered him. (pp. 169–170)

> The young Latin's sweet, abysmal ignorance, his infantile amiability, his artless ambition, and heathenish innocence started the natural gladness of Richling's blood to effervescing anew every time they met, and, through the sheer impossibility of confiding any of his troubles to the Creole, made him think them smaller and lighter than they had just before appeared. The very light of Narcisse's countenance and beauty of his form—his smooth, low forehead, his thick, abundant locks, his faintly up-tipped nose and expanded nostrils, his sweet, weak mouth with its impending smile, his beautiful chin and bird's throat, his almond eyes, his full, round arm, and strong thigh—had their emphatic value. (pp. 178–179)

Narcisse may be incapable either of working hard or of repaying debts, but he is good for one thing. In a "typically Creole" manner he makes a brave soldier and dies a valiant death—a death both dramatic and heroic, we infer, and, as Cable tells us, one he would have chosen for himself.

We have seen, then, how Cable attributes to the Creoles many traits usually admired. But in his examination of these traits each turns into a fault. Pride becomes blind adherence to outmoded customs; bravery becomes foolhardy propensity for violence; family loyalty becomes pompous pretension to gentility; independence becomes defiance of order. The Creoles form a "Latin civilization," and Latins, by Cable's definition, are incapable of moderation. They must be hot or cold, never warm. Finally those charming differences which make the anti-American Creoles so unlike Americans also make them absurd. For example, when elegant General Villivicencio, a respected leader of Creole society, decides in "Madame Délicieuse" to run for public office:

> No explanation was considered necessary. All had been done in strict accordance with time-honored customs, and if any one did not know it it was his own fault. No eulogium was to follow, no editorial endorsement. The two announcements were destined to stand next morning, one on the English side and one on the French, in severe simplicity, to be greeted with profound gratification by a few old gentlemen in blue cottonade, and by roars of laughter from a rampant majority. (p. 129)

It is Cable's reduction to absurdity of the "best in Creole society" that must have been, from the Creole point of view, the most intolerable affront of all.

With the exception of "Belles Demoiselles Plantation," which takes place both in New Orleans and on an estate across the river, the setting of every piece of Cable's fiction mentioned in this chapter is in the city. This use of a southern city as his setting is another major innovation Cable introduces into southern fiction. In a sense the city of New Orleans occupies the real center of Cable's Creole stories. Not only the Creoles, but also Cable's quadroons, his immigrants, and to a lesser extent even his Americans, remain stereotypes representing the many different kinds of people who contribute to New Orleans' rich diversity.

Since Cable's urban setting is unique in southern local color, it is interesting to notice his view of the city. A sense of liveliness dominates its atmosphere, a sense of many enterprises carried on by bustling men. In a story set about 1810 we read— conscious of the irony intended—of "the good old times of duels, and bagatelle clubs, and theater balls, and Cayetano's circus."[21] Certainly it is the liveliness of the city which attracts the belles demoiselles. Parson Jones is given a grand tour of the city's attractions available to the pleasure-seeking crowd from early

Sunday morning throughout the day, though the parson ends his travels in the calaboose. Cable's stories refer continually to the city's various attractions—the serenades in "'Sieur George," the coffee houses in "Madame Délicieuse," the restaurants and cafés such as the Café des Exilés, even the less harmless customs such as the charivari in "Jean-ah Poquelin." There is always movement in Cable's city, whether toward amusement or business opportunity: "The main road to wealth in New Orleans has long been Carondelet street. There you see the most alert faces. . . . It is there that the stock and bond brokers hurry to and fro and run together promiscuously—the cunning and the simple, the headlong and the wary—at the four clanging strokes of the Stock Exchange gong."[22]

In Cable's stories the city is not only lively but also a thing alive, constantly growing, constantly enclosing and gulping up the surrounding countryside. The city changes "like a growing boy" or spreads "like a ringworm" or overruns the country "like coco grass."[23] The major cause of this expansion is the constant infusion of immigrants, "that army of gentlemen who, after the purchase of Louisiana, swarmed from all parts of the commercial world, over the mountains of Franco-Spanish exclusiveness, like the Goths over the Pyrenees, and settled down in New Orleans to pick up their fortunes, with the diligence of hungry pigeons."[24]

> The alien races pouring into old New Orleans began to find the few streets named for the Bourbon princes too strait for them. The wheel of fortune, beginning to whirl, threw them off beyond the ancient corporation lines, and sowed civilization and even trade upon the lands of the Graviers and Girods. Fields became roads, roads streets. Everywhere the leveler was peering through his glass, rodsmen were whacking their way through willow brakes and rose hedges, and the sweating Irishmen tossed the blue clay up with their long-handled shovels.[25]

These immigrants, as well as the Creoles, give the city its color:

> In the high upper seats of the rude amphitheater sat the gaily decked wives and daughters of the Gascons, from the *métairies* along the Ridge, and the chattering Spanish women of the Mar-

ket, their shining hair unbonneted to the sun. Next below were
their husbands and lovers in Sunday blouses, milkmen, butchers,
bakers, black-bearded fishermen, Sicilian fruiterers, swarthy Portu-
guese sailors in little woollen caps, and strangers of the graver sort;
mariners of England, Germany, and Holland. The lowest seats were
full of trappers, smugglers, Canadian *voyageurs*, drinking and singing; *Américains*, too—more's the shame—from the upper rivers—
who will not keep their seats, who ply the bottle, and who will
get home by and by and tell how wicked Sodom is; broad-
brimmed, silver-braided Mexicans, also, with their copper cheeks
and bat's eyes, and their tinkling spurred heels. Yonder in that
quieter section, are the quadroon women in their black lace
shawls. . . .[26]

Cable's New Orleans, then, is a city of many faces. It is often
the scene of great wickedness; Cable speaks of the "loose New
Orleans morals of over fifty years ago"[27] and of Poulette's living
"a lonely, innocent life in the midst of corruption" (p. 87). But
wicked or not, and including the scenes of Creole decay as it
does, Cable's city exerts a unique fascination.

One must now ask how the Creole stereotype and the city
setting are related to the common folk of southern literature.
The answer is implied by the phrase Cable uses to define *Creole*—"the French-speaking, native portion of the ruling class."[28]
While identifying a Creole as one of the ruling class and developing an essentially aristocratic stereotype for him, Cable proceeds simultaneously to portray in his fiction a number of Creoles as clerks, shopworkers, and petty officials: "for your
second-rate Creole is a great seeker for little offices."[29]

Cable's procedure is exactly opposite the one typical in
nineteenth-century southern fiction. By holding that the South
had only two classes of whites and that the "trash" were a numerically tiny class, southern writers managed the wholesale
elevation of the commoners to the aristocracy. As we have seen,
anyone who was financially solvent and acceptable to his neighborhood could claim to be a gentleman. And if his money were
gone, genteel manners alone would suffice to keep his status
intact. Cable does the reverse. He starts with a group whose
claim to gentility could often be traced back through several
generations, who were possessed—according to Cable—of all

the imperious pride, dignity, and valor one is accustomed to associate with fictional nobles, and then he shows how "plain" and "common" they often were.

The few New Orleans businesses Cable describes are staffed by Creole workers. Most of these workers hold unimportant positions; they are both Creole and salaried employees. Dr. Sevier's clerk Narcisse and Joseph Frowenfeld's assistant Raoul are excellent examples of the Creole worker. We are told in *The Grandissimes* that Honoré's offices are filled with petty clerks who are his own kinsmen. When Honoré breaks precedent to ride with the American governor in public, he does so to secure in the new administration the unimportant political sinecures held by his relatives. In all these instances, Cable suggests the existence of a sizable number of Creoles who are quite commonplace, doing commonplace jobs in a commonplace way. After establishing the aristocratic Creole stereotype, then, Cable reduces the average Creole to the ranks of the plain folk.

This demotion is actually demanded by Cable's urban setting. It was possible for southern local colorists to oversimplify the class structure of the antebellum past, since that society no longer existed to furnish unwanted contradictory facts. But to suggest that a flourishing commercial city had only two classes of whites would have been patently absurd. If Cable was to describe New Orleans as a Creole-dominated city shaped by Creole traditions, then he had to supply it with Creole workers. If New Orleans was the thriving commercial seaport Cable described, then Creoles had to be a part of that commerce.

Strains of the traditional southern gentleman's prejudice against commerce do appear in Cable's work, though Honoré Grandissime is an exceptional Creole *because,* among other reasons, he is unapologetic about being a merchant. But without exception Cable's most aristocratic Creoles either own or have had in their background a family plantation. Richling protests to Dr. Sevier, "You've never tried . . . [working in an office job]. You've never encountered the mild contempt that people in ease pay to those who pursue the 'industries.' . . . You don't know the smart of being only an arithmetical quantity in a world of achievement and possessions" (p. 315). In furnishing *Dr. Sevier* with minor characters of ease and rank who live in New Orleans without being involved in industry there, Cable is hard-pressed to explain the basis of their incomes. He mentions the occupations only of a bank president and of the doctor himself. For the most part those of ease and rank exist only in hazy contrast to the impoverished Richlings. By admitting this regional prejudice against commerce, however, Cable heightens the irony that many Creoles are commercially employed.

Just as Cable questions the assumption that the Creoles were descended from uniformly noble ancestors, so he questions the assumption that the Creoles of the nineteenth century were living an especially aristocratic life. Philip Butcher reminds us: "Only superficially is he writing about olden times. . . . He chose to depict Creoles like those he might have seen in the neighborhood [of the French Quarter] in his own time, not like those who resided there in its days of elegant respectability."[30] In his thorough discussion of "'Sieur George'" Mr. Butcher reminds us that Cable creates in his first-published story "the aura of a bygone day hanging over the scene" and portrays "a class of persons who, even in the past, looked to a remote time as the source of their respectability and whose decline is symbolized by the physical decay of their surroundings. . . ."[31] Butcher goes on to point out that in "'Sieur George'" "the Creoles are represented as proprietors of fifth-rate shops in streets overrun by innumerable children. The wives are 'passably good-looking women' in cotton gowns; the husbands are 'keepers of wine-warehouses, rent-collectors for the agents of old Frenchmen who have been laid up to dry in Paris, customhouse supernumeraries and court clerks' deputies."[32] This atmosphere of decay pervades not only "'Sieur George'" but also most of the Creole stories which followed it. Cable connects the atmosphere specifically with the Creoles living in New Orleans. His association of Creoles with decayed neighborhoods becomes one of the most important aspects of his presentation of Creole society. After Cable wrote, the slightly tawdry surroundings were always an element in any story featuring a Creole character.

Although Cable makes it clear in his definition that the word *Creole* could be applied to descendants of either the French or the Spanish, he appears to distinguish between the two groups in his stories. Just as the contrast between the Creole and the cracker in "Posson Jone'" clearly favors the Creole, so the occasional contrast between the French and Spanish Creole favors the Frenchman. The "gesticulating, stagy fellow" of "'Sieur George," who is "an incessant talker in Creole-French, always excited on small matters and unable to appreciate a great one" (p. 53), is apparently—in spite of his French—of Spanish extraction. He is mistaken for a Mexican or a Cuban, and must be identified as "a genuine Louisianan" who is no more fit to marry the lady of the story "than rags are fit for a queen" (p. 55). But the story in which Cable gives most attention to the Spanish Creoles is "Café des Exilés." D'Hemecourt, the proprietor of the café, is half Castilian Spanish and half Martinique French. Though all but one of the regular habitués of the café are Spanish refugees, D'Hemecourt prefers this one—an Irishman—to the others. "The Spanish Creoles were, as the old man termed it, both cold and hot, but never warm. Major Shaughnessy was warm" (p. 150). Cable seems to agree with D'Hemecourt's view of the Spaniards. He describes them toward the end of the story as that "double row of languid, effeminate faces" in comparison to which "one would have been taxed to find a more harmless-looking company" (p. 166). It is hardly an accident that Cable makes Shaughnessy the leader and director of the smuggling project. Thus, although his spokesman Joseph Frowenfeld inveighs against the Creole concept of class and caste in *The Grandissimes*, Cable himself seems to make certain class distinctions in his stories. One class for which he has little respect is composed of the Spanish Creoles.

In depicting the South, Cable, an innovator in southern literature, established patterns soon to be followed by others. Besides writing one novel of extensive social criticism and introducing the Louisiana Acadian to southern fiction, he developed a detailed Creole stereotype, wrote as southerner (occasionally using such phrases as "we of the South") while utilizing a city setting, and went a step further by suggesting that living in the city was preferable to living on the plantation. Then, having done all that, he indicated that his region's ruling class was sending many of its sons to fill the ranks of the plain folk. Lastly he implied, especially in "Café des Exilés," that the Spanish Creoles as a group were not members of a middle class, but lower than that in the varied strata of New Orleans society. Keeping these innovations in mind, we must examine their effects on the

writers who dealt with New Orleans' Creoles after Cable passed
on to other subjects.

Lafcadio Hearn came to New Orleans in 1877, after Cable
had already begun publishing his stories. He must have met
Cable fairly soon after his arrival. "Their relations are not easy
to trace, but it is clear that they were closely associated through
several years, respected each other, planned literary collabora-
tion, and helped each other whenever possible."[33] In his biography of Cable, Arlin Turner states that "Hearn often wrote
in the newspapers of Cable favorably. Some of the views he
printed are so close to Cable's as to leave little doubt that . . .
they exchanged literary opinions and found much to agree
on."[34] How much they agreed on, particularly about the Creole,
is evident in Hearn's "Creole Papers," especially in the sketch
entitled "Quaint New Orleans and Its Inhabitants."[35] A few of
Hearn's comments will illustrate the similarity of their views:

> Formerly the Louisiana Creoles excelled in exercises demanding
> grace and quickness of eye; they were fine dancers and famous
> swordsmen. . . . (p. 50)

> The beauty of the women is peculiar; they possess a *sveltesse*—a
> slender elegance that is very fascinating. . . . (p. 50)

> Creole temperament is one of great nervous sensibility; phlegmatic
> characters are anomalies; a disposition to violent extremes of anger
> or affection is often masked by an exterior appearance of listless
> indifference. (pp. 50–51)

> There are few educated Creoles who cannot speak two or three
> languages well. . . . Love of the mother-country is not dead among
> the Creoles, and their attachment to ancient French customs has
> but little abated. (p. 51)

The alarming thing about a stereotype is that once created, it
is virtually impossible to lay to rest. Not only is it echoed in the
thoughts and words of the sympathetic, the creator's friends.
Phoenix-like, the stereotype rises from the fires of attack as
strong as ever, to take another, but familiar, form. This fact is
evident in contemporary literature. James Baldwin, for example,
whose militant attacks on American stereotypes of the Negro

have won him both praise and notoriety, includes in his strident protest play, *Blues for Mr. Charlie,* a Negro protagonist who exhibits his "natural rhythm" dancing to juke-box music and who explicitly describes his sexual superiority over a plain folk character whose wife he insults. In attacking one aspect of the Negro stereotype—that he is happy and content—Baldwin reintroduces other aspects—his innate sense of music and rhythm and his amoral lack of inhibitions. Similarly in Philip Roth's "Goodbye, Columbus" the Jewish protagonist discovers various facts about himself by coming into contact with a family who epitomize the rich, ostentatious, aggressive Jewish stereotype of English and American tradition. The awesomeness of a stereotype, then, lies in its power to remain alive, shaping the self-image of those identifying themselves with the typed group as well as the image of that group held by outsiders. This fact can also be demonstrated by exploring the work of writers who portrayed Creoles after George W. Cable had defined the Creole type.[36]

In the local color period two women in particular[37]—Grace King and Kate Chopin—tried to correct what they considered Cable's negative and unfair presentation of the Creole. Certainly Miss King leaves no doubt that correction was the primary goal of her fiction. She tells in her autobiography of a walk she once took with the *Century's* editor, Richard Watson Gilder, then a visitor to New Orleans. Suddenly Gilder asked her why Creoles hated Cable:

> I hastened to enlighten him to the effect that Cable proclaimed his preference for colored people over white and assumed the inevitable superiority—according to his theories—of the quadroons over the Creoles. He was a native of New Orleans and had been well treated by its people, and yet he stabbed the city in the back, as we felt, in a dastardly way to please the Northern press. . . . He listened to me with icy indifference and the rest of our walk was accomplished in silence, except for one remark. "Why," he said, "if Cable is so false to you, why do not some of you write better?"[38]

Miss King continues by telling of the restless night she spent after her walk:

> "Why, why, do we not write our side?" I asked myself furiously at home before going to bed. "Are we to submit to Cable's libels in

resignation?" I could not sleep that night for thinking of Gilder's rankling taunt.

The next morning I was resolved to do at least my share in our defense, a mighty small share I felt it to be, possibly a hopeless effort. Brave with the courage of desperation, I got paper and pencil, and on the writing-table in my bedroom wrote my first story with not an idea in my brain except that I must write it or forfeit all my allegiance to self-respect.[39]

Miss King summarizes the emotions she felt after finishing that first story: "I will show Mr. Gilder that we in New Orleans can at least make an effort to show what we are; we are not entirely dependent upon Mr. George Cable's pen!"[40] Though Kate Chopin never made such a statement as Miss King's, her son wrote in a letter dated August 18, 1931, "She read Cable with interest and regretted that his artistic ability was superior to his sense of justice. My mother did not believe he was true to the Creole life he wrote about."[41]

In view of their antagonism it is ironic to notice how "dependent upon Mr. George Cable's pen" these women apparently were. Upon examing their work carefully, we see that the only matter which really bothered them was Cable's sympathetic treatment of quadroons. Neither actually develops in her stories any aspect of Creole life which contradicts Cable's generalizations. If differences exist between him and them, the differences lie in the fact that the Creoles the women portray are often more extreme than Cable's were. But the direction the extreme takes was mapped in Cable's stories. That is, the women assume, in line with southern stories popular at the time, that the reader will view sympathetically anyone of aristocratic background or family. Once they established that Creoles belonged to an aristocracy, the women apparently felt free to criticize their Creole characters as Cable had done before them. Instead of attacking Cable's presentation of Creoles, therefore, the pro-Creole women reinforce, by restating, Cable's generalizations.

In several ways the Cable story sniping most pointedly at Creoles is "'Sieur George." Grace King's "In the French Quarter, 1870" seems designed in part to answer "'Sieur George." Yet the neighborhood is still characterized by an atmosphere of decay. Miss King describes the boardinghouse which serves as a

setting: "How bravely and pathetically the building rose in the
moonlight, with its rooms full of tired, sleeping, homeless
lodgers! Itself an aristocractic outcast, exiled in poverty, trading
its shabby beauties, its comforts, the shelter of its roof, for a
mere pittance. The skeletons of former romances, the ghosts of
former sentiment, seemed yet to flit across the galleries, look
from the windows, and lurk in the dark corners."[42] Like Cable's
Kookoo, Miss King's landlord Grouille is stingy and unwilling to
make needed repairs. The neighborhood is appropriately described in Cable's words, as one "given up to fifth-rate shops"[43]
which are run by Creoles. One shop in Miss King's story belongs to the Carlin family, all of whom rush out into the street
when they hear that Prussia has invaded France. When Miss
King says, "It was like the Carlins to rush out thus heedlessly
from their work at the first cry of news" (p. 259), her sentence
reminds us of one of Cable's: "The Creole neighbors rush bareheaded into the middle of the street, as though there were an
earthquake or a chimney on fire" ("'Sieur George," p. 50). In
Cable's story a German blacksmith finds out for his neighbors
why Monsieur George is wearing a military uniform. Miss
King's story also includes a German boarder, present when the
news arrives. But he is ostracized by his neighbors because he
represents the aggressor against France. This "plodding young
professor of Latin and Greek" (who reminds us of Kristian Koppig, the "simple, slow-thinking young Dutchman" of "'Tite
Poulette" [p. 85]) is restored to neighborhood favor only when
he makes up false news reports about French victories to read to
a blind, dying Creole gentleman.

Monsieur Villeminot, the gentleman Wilhelm Müller protects from the truth, differs in no way from one of Cable's Creoles, except that his fortune is even more depleted and his
circumstances more pathetic. He is "a decrepit octogenarian,
prostrate upon the cushions of an easy chair, quartered in a
wretched, isolated closet on a servant's gallery" (p. 257). He is
apparently suffering the results of a riotous past (in contrast to
such characters of Cable's as Colonel De Charleu of "Belles Demoiselles Plantation" who never reveals outward signs of past
indiscretions). Despite his present circumstances Villeminot is a
proud gentleman who has married the common little Margot
because she nursed him through a long and serious illness.

Margot says proudly, "I marry him, madame? I! I have that pre-
sumption? No, thank God! He married me. Oh, no, madame,
you do not know him. My 'patron' is a gentleman, an aristocrat,
a man of letters!" (p. 281). The date affixed to the title emphasizes the time difference between Miss King's story and Cable's.
Yet the two stories leave essentially the same impression.

"A Drama of Three" in Miss King's second volume portrays
an old Creole general and his wife, who could not be more
consistent with Cable's stereotype. The general is impatient and
given to vituperative attacks upon his servant. Life in Paris is to
him an ideal existence; he cites incidents which once happened
to him there as irrefutable evidence allowing him to win every
argument. He berates the American government for all its imagined evils. He is particularly vain about his family, referring to
the landlord as "a fellow of means, but no extraction."[44] Central to the story is the mysterious fact that the old couple's sole
means of support is an anonymous check which arrives every
month. The general's income is exhausted, "for in truth he had
been irresistible to excess" (p. 20). As soon as his check arrives,
the general, with infinite condescension, turns over the rent to
his landlord, a man whose grandfather was an overseer on the
general's family plantation. We learn at the end of the story that
the landlord always goes away convulsed with laughter at the
general's absurd pretensions; for the landlord is the anonymous
friend who sends the monthly check.

One of Cable's more offensive charges against Creoles was
their ignorance. Yet Miss King also mentions Creole ignorance
and lack of common sense. The Creoles of "In the French Quarter, 1870" ignorantly reject poor, good-hearted Wilhelm Müller,
and the old couple in "A Drama of Three" are "not original
in . . . thoughts" (p. 19). Cable seemed annoyed by the Creole's
lack of respect for the fine arts. Yet in her preface to *Balcony
Stories* Miss King describes the weather of New Orleans as a
"languor-breeding climate" which reduces women to sitting on
balconies and telling each other stories to save themselves "the
ennui of reading and writing books" (p. 3). In Miss King's "A
Delicate Affair," one character has been talented, like Cable's
Dr. Mossy of "Madame Délicieuse," at more than military
games: "It had been said of him in his youth that he wrote
poetry—and it was said against him."[45]

Although he criticizes Creoles, Cable treats individual Creole ladies with sentimental sympathy. Because Miss King makes no such illogical distinctions between the sexes, her version of the Creole stereotype is even harsher than Cable's. Cable's Madame Délicieuse, for example, is delightful, even "if she could at times do what the infantile Washington said he could not" (p. 126). In another context Cable states, "the Creoles never cheat."[46] In contrast the major character in Miss King's "A Delicate Affair," unlike Madame Délicieuse, is a shrewish dowager of eighty years whose major talent consists of insulting others. She also has other failings: "She played her game of solitaire rapidly, impatiently, and always won; for she never hesitated to cheat to get out of a tight place, or into a favorable one, cheating with the quickness of a flash, and forgetting it the moment afterward."[47] We learn that such cheating has typified the Creole lady since her youth; she cheated her best friend by marrying the friend's lover. Cable's Creole ladies, however impoverished, are like the Nacanous in *The Grandissimes*—always pretty and charming. In "La Grande Demoiselle" Miss King draws an incredibly exaggerated picture of waste on a wealthy plantation before the war. Then she takes a woman's revenge on the daughter of the plantation who was once the toast of New Orleans. The once-grande demoiselle is reduced after the Civil War to teaching a Negro school and to living in humiliating poverty. As Tourgée states elsewhere, "So far as the 'ladies' of . . . [a southern town] were concerned, the 'nigger teachers' . . . stood on the plane of the courtesan—they were *seen* but not *known*."[48] In a sense Miss King's demoiselle is rescued when a misogynist condescends to marry her; but the story ends with repeated comments about how grotesquely ugly the former beauty has become.[49]

Sooner or later Miss King repeats most of Cable's negative observations about Creoles. The debutante's family in "La Grande Demoiselle," for example, is much like the ill-fated De Grapions in *The Grandissimes.* The hot-headed son of the family goes to war and is the first killed. We are told that this early dying is something of a family habit, "so much so that it began to be considered assassination to fight a duel with any of them" (p. 29). And in "Bonne Maman" Miss King describes, in more melodramatic detail than Cable ever dared, the abject poverty in which a proud Creole lady lives with her granddaughter while trying vainly to cling to the old way of life. The young granddaughter of Miss King's story is so desperate that she sews for a Negress and even sells her customer an ancient lace collar which the family has preserved. Perhaps the difference between the writers is that Cable believed starving Creoles ought to change their manner of living, whereas Miss King apparently found their hunger ennobling.

We notice in Miss King's recollected statement to Gilder, however, that she was mainly offended by Cable's sympathetic presentation of quadroons. Only in her depiction of mulattoes or Negroes is Miss King significantly at odds with Cable. In "'Tite Poulette" Cable puts the blame for the hard fortunes of Madame John and Poulette on three causes. First is their lack of education: "as Madame John had been brought up tenderly, and had done what she could to rear her daughter in the same mistaken way, with, of course, no more education than the ladies in society got, they knew nothing beyond a little music and embroidery" (p. 84). Second is their lack of practicality, "that priceless worldly grace known among the flippant as 'money sense'" (p. 84). Third and most important is their inability to use such skills as dressing hair or teaching dancing, because they are "ever beat back by the steady detestation of their imperious patronesses" (p. 84). At least Miss King confirms the existence of "the steady detestation" righteous white women felt towards the quadroons. When the heroine of "The Little Convent Girl," reared strictly by nuns, finds that her mother is a quadroon, she drowns herself at the first opportunity.[50] The rest of Miss King's quadroons and mulattoes are prostitutes.

It is amusing that in her efforts to make clear the differences between virtuous white and amoral quadroon women, Miss King is the only local colorist to refer in some detail to brothels. John Fox, Jr., describes in "Through the Gap" a woman "hideously rouged and with scarlet ribbons," and Joel Chandler Harris admits the existence of "snake nation," a part of Atlanta serving to corrupt young men. A champion of white purity, Grace King describes large, opulent brothels in New Orleans rather alluringly. The young granddaughter in "Bonne Maman" thinks the music emanating from a nearby house of ill repute very gay and appealing. After Cable, Miss King also portrays a quadroon who appears to be white, in "Madrilène; or, the Festival of the

Dead." This beauty desires to be virtuous and wishes she were dead. She almost gets the latter wish when she is attacked by a mulatto prostitute whose son she struck in public. A white rescuer arrives in time to hear the harlot confess that Madrilène is actually white. But to perform the rescue, Madrilène's admirer must follow her to the "boardinghouse-brothel" where she lives. Madrilène's unaccountable retention of virtue in this environment is accredited to her white blood; Miss King leaves little doubt that, had Madrilène inherited any characteristics of the Negro race, she too would have been a prostitute.

"Bayou L'Ombre" suggests the same view of Negro morality. It describes a practical joke played at the expense of black women. The Negroes are promised white husbands if they will leave their black mates. None hesitates to do so. "Bonne Maman," "Madrilène," and "Bayou L'Ombre" are three of the five stories in Miss King's first collection. By putting these stories together, one realizes that Miss King's efforts to correct Cable's work were efforts to correct his presentation, not of the Creole, but of the mulatto. The fifth story, "In the French Quarter, 1870," does not correct but instead rewrites Cable: it is completely consistent with his presentation of Creole society.

Though Kate Chopin apparently felt less strongly than Miss King the impulse to correct Cable, her work also gives ample evidence of the debt she owes to Cable for first defining the Creole. Mrs. Chopin differs from both Cable and Miss King, however, in frequently setting her stories in the up-river plantation or farm country. The first three stories in her first volume[51] deal with the three sons of the old Creole Santien family, and clearly illustrate the fact that she never really challenges the Creole stereotype. "A No-Account Creole" concerns the middle brother, Placide. The setting is the ruined Santien plantation, a plot of ground loved only by Euphrasie, the caretaker's daughter. Euphrasie in turn is loved by Placide, who is now a common laborer. Placide has all the now "traditional" Creole irresponsibility and ineptness at business. Born to luxury, he finds that "it was a deliverance to all when . . . creditors relieved them of the place with the responsibility and indebtedness which its ownership entailed" (p. 5). As we have now come to expect, Placide is also completely incapable of sustained hard work: "Maybe it was because of his talent, and his indifference in turning it to good, that he was often called 'a no-account Creole' by thriftier souls than himself. But no-account creole or not, painter, carpenter, blacksmith, and whatever else he might be at times, he was a Santien always, with the best blood in the country running in his veins" (p. 10).

Because his inheritance has been exhausted, Placide gives little outward evidence of noble ancestry. In occupation, he is obviously a member of the common folk when the story opens. "... He did not seem to mind in the least that young men who had grown up with him were lawyers now, and planters, and members of Shakespeare clubs in town. No one ever expected anything quite so humdrum as that of the Santien boys" (p. 11).

The story describes a conventional love triangle. Wallace Offdean, a young businessman, comes to inspect the Santien estate after the mortgage is foreclosed. Aristocratic Placide has an "instinctive sense of the courtesy due a stranger" (p. 17), but dislikes Offdean and assumes the man is a "d____ Yankee" (p. 19). When Euphrasie falls in love with the new arrival, Placide, in hot-blooded fashion, prepares to kill his rival. But Offdean, thinking fast, tells Placide he doesn't know how to love a woman if he doesn't think of her happiness first. Placide is so deeply offended that anyone would try to tell a Creole how to love that he lets Offdean escape and gives Euphrasie her freedom.

Decaying Santien morals, as well as finances, figure in "In and Out of Old Natchitoches." This haphazardly constructed story ends anticlimactically when we find that Hector, the oldest Santien brother, lives under the assumed name of Deroustan and is the most notorious gambler in town. Another character in the story who exemplifies the Creole stereotype is Laballière, a romantically tempestuous figure struggling to establish a sugar and rice plantation, who starts gossip and offends his neighborhood by fraternizing with his mulatto workers. Furious at the gossip, Laballière forces a Negro boy to accompany him to a neighborhood school, where he asks that the youth be enrolled. The schoolmarm, a recently impoverished aristocrat, is so offended that she disbands the school and flees to New Orleans. A hot-headed Creole to the end, Laballière follows her. He gets the girl back by threatening to shoot Hector Santien if Santien ever again walks on the streets with her. Remembering his evil

reputation as a professional gambler, Santien recognizes that
Laballière's position is just.

Grégoire Santien, the third son of the family, is the hero of
"In Sabine." His humble social rank is suggested by the fact that
he stays overnight at the home of Bud Aiken, a poor white, who
pronounces the name *Sanchun*. When Grégoire discovers that
Aiken mistreats his wife, he gets Aiken drunk, plays cards
with him through much of the night, and then uses Aiken's one
horse to carry the wife back to her parents. This kind of revenge, we are told, is considerably more subtle than that which
Grégoire's first impulse suggested: "he was wondering if it
would really be a criminal act to go then and there and shoot the
top of Bud Aiken's head off. He himself would hardly have considered it a crime, but he was not sure of how others might regard the act" (p. 88).

Kate Chopin shows the same drifting of Creoles into the
ranks of the poor, the plain, the common as Cable did. Her
Creoles remain aristocratic to the extent that they remain improvident, proud, and violent. They remain charming by retaining the social forms and graces learned in childhood. But the
fact that none of the Santien brothers marries suggests an awareness that the Santiens retain their claims to gentility only by
remaining bachelors. To create and provide for a family would
doom each irrevocably to life in the lower strata of society. Perhaps both Miss King and Mrs. Chopin are fairer to Creoles than
Cable was, in that they do not use one Creole to generalize
about all Creoles. But their Creole characters still share the characteristics which Cable first elaborated.

For the most part, then, Mrs. Chopin's Creole stories follow
the same subjects and themes Cable first employed and Grace
King imitated. Cable's pietistic observations about wicked New
Orleans and Creole immorality are confirmed not only by Miss
King's red-light districts but also by Mrs. Chopin's stories. These
Creoles are all alike, as are any people or characters viewed
through the distorting lens of a stereotype. Occasionally Mrs.
Chopin does include wealthy and stable Creole families in her
stories, but only when the story deals primarily with people of a
lower status, such as the Acadians. Only when the Creole is an
incidental character is he both rich and morally respectable as in
"A Very Fine Fiddle,"[52] "A Rude Awakening,"[53] and "A Dres-

den Lady in Dixie."[54] The best example of a respectable Creole taking the role of minor character, however, is the heroine's husband in Mrs. Chopin's novel *The Awakening.*

From the perspective of another century Mrs. Chopin's stories seem both dated and contrived. But she will continue to be of literary importance because of her novel. *The Awakening* is the best novel to be published by a self-consciously southern writer before the twentieth century. It stands up particularly well for the contemporary reader because it meets many currently familiar criteria for good fiction: careful development of symbols, careful and sensitive characterization, carefully selective use of detail, and careful exploration of several themes which have often been examined in twentieth-century fiction and drama. However, the novel is not in any real sense "local color." Though the setting is New Orleans and its nearby resorts, and though the initially languid summer scenes help explain the heroine's undefined dissatisfactions, the "color" of the setting is minimized in the novel as a whole and descriptive details are used only when they explain some pertinent fact about a character. Instead the novel emphasizes that aspect of fiction which local colorists, almost by definition, ignored—the psychological development of a limited number of personalities.

In hackneyed terms the story depicts a "new woman." Like Ibsen's Nora in *A Doll's House* the heroine, Edna Pontellier, discovers that her marriage is preventing her emotional development and keeping her as ignorant, or innocent, as a child. With unexpected subtlety, however, Mrs. Chopin makes it clear that the fault lies not with Edna's husband, a man Edna respects but cannot love. Instead it lies with the institutional nature of the family and with the mores of society. This society demands of a wife and mother that she live only vicariously, effacing her own individuality while serving her husband and children. Edna discovers at the beginning of the novel that she could die for her children, but that she cannot live selflessly for and through them. In the course of the novel she makes a series of painful and complex discoveries about herself and the society she lives in, and awakens to her own potential for passionate desire, which her husband cannot satisfy. At the end she chooses to die, rather than bring on her children the scandal of her now inevitable future conduct. She swims nude out to sea until she

drowns. This ending is saved from melodrama by the characterization of Edna, steadily elaborated throughout the novel,
which makes her decision to commit suicide seem both ines-
capable and appropriate to her circumstances. Furthermore, the
effect of the ending is ambivalent, instead of being either sad or
tragic; for in making her final gesture Edna at last finds the freedom and release from restrictions for which she has been
searching.

Mrs. Chopin characterizes Edna partially by emphasizing her
difference from her Creole husband and friends. In the process,
of course, both Edna and the Creoles are defined. One of the
most useful means of characterization is the recurrent contrast
drawn between Edna and her Creole friend Madame Ratignolle. Edna is from a Kentucky Presbyterian family. Apparently
her Presbyterian upbringing has made her take herself and her
life too seriously for her to immerse herself fully in the casual,
or frivolous, Creole culture, a culture held together mostly by
social forms and customs. For instance, Edna cannot indulge in
harmless flirtations and emerge unscathed, as Madame Ratignolle does. Robert Lebrun, who initiates with Edna the casual
flirtation it is his custom to develop in the summer, finds that
she is falling deeply in love with him. "She reminded him of
some beautiful, sleek animal waking up in the sun."[55] Certainly
a major part of Edna's awakening stems from her growing
awareness of the physical drives she possesses. Another of her
differences is that Edna finds no particular happiness in her
children. Her attitude toward them varies in the novel from mild
dislike to mild enjoyment. Madame Ratignolle, on the other
hand, seems to exist in order to produce offspring. Yet Edna sees
in the maternal role only "an appalling and hopeless ennui"
(p. 145).

Like Edna's Creole husband, Madame Ratignolle is sympathetically drawn. Yet Edna cannot imitate her: "She was moved
by a kind of commiseration for Madame Ratignolle,—a pity for
that colorless existence which never uplifted its possessor beyond the region of blind contentment, in which no moment of
anguish ever visited her soul, in which she would never have
the taste of life's delirium" (p. 145). Unlike Madame Ratignolle,
Edna especially objects to a Creole society which allows every
male an absolute freedom to come and go as he pleases, while

it decrees that a woman is, in effect, the "possession" of her husband. Although Edna's husband is as thoughtful and considerate as it is possible to be, granted his conditioning, and further is a shrewd businessman, an ample provider, and a solicitous companion, she finds that he is not enough to capture her imagination.

A minor but interesting character in the novel is Mademoiselle Reisz, a truculent spinster who is disliked by all but Edna. Mademoiselle Reisz comes to love Edna deeply and seems also in other ways somewhat lesbian. She plays the role of unacknowledged go-between for Edna and Lebrun. She urges Edna to visit her in order to read the letters she gets from Lebrun, then plays passionately erotic music while Edna devours the messages. After Edna decides to become an artist, even if only an artist at living fully, Mademoiselle Reisz tells her, "To be an artist includes much; one must possess many gifts—absolute gifts—which have not been acquired by one's own effort. And moreover, to succeed, the artist must possess the courageous soul, . . . the brave soul. The soul that dares and defies" (p. 165). Edna remembers these words just before she dies and thinks, "How Mademoiselle Reisz would have laughed, perhaps sneered, if she knew!" (p. 302). For Edna has not possessed that soul which dares and defies, and therefore she ends crippled, like a bird men wound because it flies too low.

Despite her suicide Edna is no moralistically-drawn example of what happens to women whose affections stray from their husbands. She is as appealing as any other complex heroine of the nineteenth century. When she awakens to the value illusion has in making livable the lives of most people, Edna tells Robert, "It was you who awoke me last summer out of a lifelong, stupid dream" (p. 283). She concludes before she dies, "perhaps it is better to wake up after all, even to suffer, rather than to remain a dupe to illusions all one's life" (p. 292). Thus the novel becomes a studied indictment of any society which decrees that one of Edna's independent mind and spirit must conform to rigid social rules. Edna is an intense individualist who finds herself nearly suffocated by the role she is expected to play—the correct hostess, the loving wife and mother. The price of her declaration of independence is, of course, her death. And the deceptively casual Creole life she must live is to a large extent what requires her to make an irrevocable break with convention. But the novel is an exposé neither of the "new woman" nor of the Creoles, but rather of any society in which the rights of one individual are automatically less than those of another. Thus the novel has a timelessness and a universality of implication which continue to make it, years later, a significant work of art.

## Chapter IX

# *Stylistic Techniques*

*NO READER* interested primarily in exploring the varied possibilities of fictional style and technique would normally choose southern local color as his field of study. While acknowledging the quality of such novels as *The Awakening* or *John March, Southerner,* we can safely judge most southern local color fiction as esthetically unsatisfactory. The typical prose is verbose, undisciplined, marred by hasty construction and careless revision, sometimes turgid, and often highly exclamatory. Some aspects of the typical style of southern local colorists are pertinent to the present study, however; for certain techniques and devices, used by more than one writer, directly shaped the way in which plain folk were presented. In this chapter I consider the typical method of narration, the occasional use of symbolism, and the common types of humor found in southern local color fiction.

The prose in which narrators of southern local color fiction speak is arch and artificial. Partially the impression of artificiality results from the length of the sentences. Certainly the impression increases with the gratuitous use of "literary" quotations and references. Generally the quantity of such references is in inverse proportion to the talent of the writer: Sherwood Bonner inserts more literary allusions than any other local colorist. But the archness and extreme artificiality of the story's narrator result primarily from the narrative technique most commonly used.

One typical kind of southern local color short story is told by a double narrator. An unnamed but educated white narrator encounters a "colorful" personality and records that character's story exactly as the person tells it. In this technique we see the most direct influence of the southwest humorists. Kenneth Lynn has written an excellent account of this narrative technique. Although Lynn insists much too rigidly on his thesis that southwest humor is disguised political propaganda, his discussion of the narrative technique southwest humorists developed is accurate and useful. Of primary importance in southwest stories is the "frame," the device by which an educated narrator recalls a story once told by another.

> For Longstreet and his successors found that the frame was a convenient way of keeping their first-person narrators outside and above the comic action, thereby drawing a *cordon sanitaire*, so to speak, between the morally irreproachable Gentleman and the tainted life he described. Thus the fact that the Gentleman found recollections of violence and cruelty both interesting and amusing did not imply anything ambiguous about his own life and character. However hot-tempered the author might be in private life, the literary mask of the Southwestern humorists was that of a cool and collected personality whose emotions were thoroughly in hand.
>
> By containing their stories within a frame, the humorists also assured their conservative readers of something they had to believe in before they could find such humor amusing, namely, that the Gentleman was completely in control of the situation he described as he was of himself.[1]

The moral contrast between the Gentleman and the youthful Clown is brought out in several ways. First of all, by the *cordon sanitaire* of the frame; secondly, by the superior point of view from which the story is told, a device which coerces the reader into laughing at—rather than sympathizing with—the boy; and finally—and most importantly—by the language. The language of the narrator is as urbane as Addison's; the cool elegance of the diction, the meas-

ured rhythms, the familiar yet reserved tone, are the credentials of
an impeccably civilized man.[2]

Mr. Lynn's analysis is helpful to those interested in the techniques of southern—or even western—local colorists, as well as
southwestern humorists. He rightly emphasizes the fact that the
highly "literary" style of the first narrator (who introduces and
"frames" the story, and whom we shall call hereafter the *recorder)*
is exaggerated to make the personal, social, and economic differences between the two narrators more obvious. Such exaggeration makes it possible to view the second narrator in a comic
light. The artificial prose of local color stories in which a recorder introduces the anecdote of another is in large part a product of this exaggerated difference between the two narrators.

While the frame device characterizes Thomas Nelson Page's
most popular stories, it was used most effectively by Joel Chandler Harris, not only in his Uncle Remus stories, but also in such
tales as "Mingo." The recorder of "Mingo" returns to his boyhood church, observing as the story opens, "I was amazed at the
changes which a few brief years had wrought. The ancient oaks
ranged roundabout remained the same, but upon everything else
time had laid its hand right heavily."[3] His vaguely archaic diction and syntax immediately establish his dignity, his education,
and his conservative trustworthiness. He continues to reminisce,
at one point suggesting his own good breeding when he recognizes in Mingo, formerly a respected slave, "that familiar and
confident air of meritorious humility and unpretentious dignity
which is associated with . . . gentility the world over" (pp. 8–9).
After a section of restrained generalizations on the sad anxieties
so evident in Rockville faces, the narrator introduces Mrs. Bivins
—not by descriptions (which come later) but by a sample of her
conversation: "Mingo 'lowed he'd ast you up . . . an' I says,
says I, 'Don't you be a-pesterin' the gentulmun, when you
know thar's plenty er the new-issue quality ready an' a-waitin'
to pull an' haul at 'im,' says I" (p. 11). The contrast between the
two manners of speaking, the recorder's and Mrs. Bivins',
could not be more dramatic. Mrs. Bivins instantly appears
coarse, salty, and truculent—an excellent vehicle for humorous
twists of phrase, and an object initially evoking a smile.

Often when the form of the local color story most closely resembles southwestern humor, the major (or second) narrator is an elderly Negro man. At the end of Harris's "Mingo," in fact, this standard form is employed and Mingo himself finishes up the story. It would be laboring the obvious to discuss the reasons southern writers might wish to make the differences between white and black narrators as dramatically clear as possible. But in part, at least, the motive was different from those Mr. Lynn imputes to southwestern humorists. Lynn suggests that the southwestern humorist relied on the contrast between the two narrators to discredit the type of person the second, major narrator represented. In local color this major narrator is usually presented with the greatest sentimental affection. His statements, however, reinforce the implicit worth of the recorder, and of the recorder's background and values, just as a Negro's references to the "good ole times" make the romanticized version of those times seem more believable.

Telling a story in the first person usually creates an air of authenticity. At no time was this aura more needed or more desirable than when the story affirmed the institution of slavery. The effort in local color fiction is to make the Negro's recollections as natural and unstrained as possible. Thus the Negro talks quietly and nostalgically, with many rambling digressions. But the white narrator's presence not only serves subtly to remind the reader of the vast differences between the races; it also explains how the story was recorded. Creating a Negro literate enough to write his own story would have offended southerners, implicitly challenged the darkey stereotype, and strained credulity even in the North.

The technique of using a double narrator, however, was much too valuable to be limited exclusively to stories of aging "uncles." Indeed, the almost infinite artistic possibilities in this kind of narrative technique have been amply demonstrated in such works as Conrad's *Heart of Darkness*. Since the technique had been fully developed by southwestern humorists writing stories in which both narrators were white, it was natural enough for local colorists also to use the technique in sketches about the plain folk. Richard Malcolm Johnston, for example, uses the technique to great advantage in stories told by colorful Mr. Pate. Because Mr. Pate believes that fiction is "a kind of a

book that the half of 'em is lies, and, what's more, the fellow
that writ it knowed it,"[4] he is as much in need of an amanuensis
as any of Page's Negroes. Still there are some rather interesting
differences between stories told by a double narrator in which
the major raconteur is Negro and those in which he is white.
These differences are significant in shaping our attitudes toward
the major white narrators. The differences often suggest some
reasons for considering such characters as Mr. Pate plain folk
instead of white trash.

The relationship between two white men—one who speaks
and one who records—differs widely from that between a white
recorder and a Negro narrator. Always, when the story involves
two whites, their relationship is the easy one between social
equals. In contrast the Negro raconteur is always humble, ami-
able, eager to please his audience and willing to approve their
values. A major narrator who is white expresses his opinions
much more positively, often growing testy or irate. The white
major narrator is always opinionated, though he is quite willing
to instruct the less experienced but more educated person he
addresses. (Page's Negroes talk to adults; Mr. Pate talks to the
young boy, Philemon Perch.) The forcefulness and originality of
his observations are what make him interesting and what elicit
our sympathy. On the other hand the refined and inhibited recorder seems dull. In local color stories involving two white narrators, moreover, the recorder takes a more prominent part in
the story. In contrast to stories in which the major narrator is a
Negro, tales involving two whites most often suggest that the
refined recorder is anxious to please his instructor, the major
narrator. Mr. Pate tells his stories to Philemon Perch only because Perch cultivates his friendship so carefully. No doubt
exists that both consider Mr. Pate to be Philemon Perch's equal,
if not his superior. At times Johnston also uses double narrators
when both speakers are educated and refined. Lacking the interest provided by Mr. Pate's language, however, these stories
usually read more like moralistic tracts.[5]

Southern local colorists worked the double narrator device so
hard that it began to affect the way in which any kind of narrator related a tale. The recorder of a southern local color story
tells only what he once saw or heard; he mentions neither what
he himself once did, nor even what he felt about another's ac-

tions or comments. The kind of story in which double narrators seem appropriate—that is, stories of action or of a series of events—become standard in southern local color. The narrator's reaction to an event is never mentioned. The reader is never informed of subtle emotions aroused by an action. Sometimes, in fact, when two narrators are used, even the major narrator tells the recorder someone else's story. Thus Mr. Pate usually discusses with Philemon Perch the intrigues in which others in the neighborhood are involved. But even when a single narrator tells an anecdote, he is never its major actor. The story always centers about another. Because of the extremely reticent and self-effacing personalities of their narrators, therefore, southern local color stories emphasize external action rather than internal thought or feeling. Thus the narrative technique begins to influence the choice of subject matter, just as subject matter influences the choice of narrative technique.

Even when a story contains only one narrator speaking in the first person, that narrator generally resembles in type the recorder of another's story. Though one notes possible exceptions to the rule, the local colorist's apparent fear of being personally confused with the narrator prohibited his allowing his first (or only) narrator to present events significantly affecting the narrator's own life or way of thinking. Under any circumstances we see events from such a distance that we are left only with the hazy impressions of a dimly remembered pleasure. Such a technique is obviously useful in stories written specifically to recreate the lost southern Eden. But the technique also proved its utility in plain folk stories. The common subjects of gossip remain a pleasant part of a pleasant social order, the perfection of which is unmarred by dangerous, perhaps psychologically disruptive, motives or impulses in the people described.

It has been suggested that a primary difference between southern and national American literature is the "oral tradition" evident in southern stories. While it may be true that more stories are told for group entertainment in rural than in urban areas, the possibility still does not explain why such a tradition marks southern literature more than it does midwestern or rural New England literature. Mrs. Stowe states in *Sam Lawson's Oldtown Fireside Stories,* for example, that "chimney-corner storytelling became an art and an accomplishment" in early New England (p. 2). From such a statement one might assume that an "oral tradition" would be even more influential on New Englanders than other writers, since it would have had longer to develop there. But in fact local color fiction suggests that instead of reflecting aspects of popular culture, this semblance of oral storytelling was a carefully cultivated (and artificially contrived) literary technique. One of the several reasons for its usefulness was its hospitality to the pithy folk-saying of such a character as Mr. Pate. While it would not do to have a refined gentleman talking as Mr. Pate did, still Mr. Pate's talk was obviously the most interesting and entertaining kind of conversation. Indeed it seems a pity that Mrs. Stowe did not cultivate the technique more consciously and consistently, since Sam Lawson, easily a New England counterpart of Mr. Pate, is one of her most interesting characters, though he never reaches Mr. Pate's comic level. But however that might be, southern writers developed this narrative technique, using double narrators and the "frame" device, which *seems* simply the record of a conversation. The conversational tone, the oral tradition apparently behind the story, is the development of a literary tradition. And a major component of that tradition is the fiercely independent plain man whose opinionated outlook is unaltered by sophistication.

The first-person narrative technique is so ingrained a part of southern local color that an omniscient narrator usually behaves as if he had identified himself to us. He stops the story's action to chat and comment, in the manner of Thackeray, and never hesitates to insert an opinion if so inclined. Although this kind of narration may offend the craftsman who likes unflawed consistency in fiction, it nevertheless had two advantages for the local colorist. First, it allowed him to soften the action, or even by sleight-of-hand, to expurgate the rougher parts of the action, whenever a detailed account might upset the tenderhearted. Second, this underhanded censoring also functions in transforming the plain character into a potential gentleman; at least we are allowed to forget or ignore his rougher edges.

As an apt illustration of this narrative tendency in local color, the contrast between the Johnston and Longstreet versions of a Georgia fist fight springs readily to mind. In "The Fight" Longstreet's account of a match between two Georgia townsmen is so detailed, specific, and vivid that it is almost overwhelming. At

the height of Longstreet's battle, previously developed blow by
blow,

> I looked, and saw that Bob had entirely lost his left ear, and a large
> piece from his left cheek. His right eye was a little discoloured, and
> the blood flowed profusely from his wounds.
>     Bill presented a hideous spectacle. About a third of his nose,
> at the lower extremity, was bit off, and his face so swelled and
> bruised that it was difficult to discover in it anything of the human
> visage, much more the fine features which he carried into the ring.[6]

Bill nearly wins, having bitten off Bob's finger; but Bob ultimately triumphs and is "in the act of grinding . . . [dirt and sand]
in his adversary's eyes" when Bill cries "ENOUGH!" (p. 51).

Johnston, obviously modelling the wrestling match in "King
William and His Armies" on Longstreet's version, gets his opponents into the dirt and then modestly averts his eyes. He tells us
many things that the onlookers say and do, and remarks in-
formatively, "Whoever has not seen a combat between two
powerful, irate men, with no weapons other than those supplied
by nature, has missed the sight, though he may not regret it, of
a thrilling scene. The blows, the grapplings, the struggles of
every kind are as if each combatant had staked every dear thing
upon the result, and set in to save it or die."[7] By the time the
narrator has finished generalizing, the fight is over and the fighters are shaking hands.

Both Longstreet and Johnston also describe schoolroom battles between master and student. But once again, Johnston's narrator allows us to know what is going on without providing any
really explicit information. The narrator interrupts the fight to
exclaim histrionically, "Oh, Mr. Meadows, Mr. Meadows! you
don't know the boy that grapples with you. You have never
known anything at all about him. . . . You blow, Mr. Meadows!"[8]
Apparently Johnston felt such exclamations would arouse the
necessary excitement in the reader, while sparing him the gore.
In both of Johnston's stories the narrator is more or less omniscient. But unlike the Almighty he speaks often and at length.

The second advantage of using a narrator who is both dis-
cursive and omniscient is that he makes satire and irony much
easier to handle. Take, for example, Grace King's discussion

in "Bayou L'Ombre" of the emotions of young southern girls
living at the beginning of the Civil War:

> The great advantage was having God on their side, as the children
> of Israel had; the next best thing was having the finest country, the
> most noble men, and the bravest soldiers. The only fear was that
> the enemy would be beaten too easily, and the war cease too soon
> to be glorious; for, characteristic of their sex, they demanded noth-
> ing less than that their war should be the longest, bloodiest, and
> most glorious of all wars ever heard of, in comparison with which
> even "le grand Napoleon" and his Capitaine Picquet would be
> effaced from memory.[9]

The women writers apparently preferred this kind of omniscient point of view more than the men. The most noteworthy
of the southern local colorists using the omniscient point of view
almost exclusively were Kate Chopin and Mary Noailles Murfree. Miss Murfree often inserts editorial opinions about mountaineers and mountains, and her observations are often heavily
ironic. Perhaps Kate Chopin was most consistent, or at least
more than usually subtle, in her handling of narrative point of
view. In her work we are told something of what goes on in the
minds of the characters, but the narrator, at least in comparison
to the narrators of other writers, seldom intrudes into the story.

Along with Harry Stillwell Edwards the two southern local
colorists of greatest talent—Joel Chandler Harris and George
Washington Cable—often use a narrator neither quite omniscient
nor quite the finite observer, yet distinctly different from Johnston's amalgam. They develop instead an omniscient narrator
with a distinct personality, a persona. The dominant qualities of
the persona are humor, aloofness, amiability, and either a simu-
lated or a genuine tolerance for the foibles of the characters described, particularly when those characters are plain folk. Thus,
while we can identify the narrative techniques typifying southern local color, those techniques obviously vary from writer to
writer and from story to story; the general impression remains
one of a story told orally, rather than of a written tale. Our interest is quickened not only by the events but also by the personality of the teller as his personality is revealed in his choice
of words and phrases. When the narrator is one of the plain

people, his language and unique way of expressing himself help establish his admirable qualities.

As I have observed earlier, southern local color stories are not notable for subtle characterization. To a large extent the narrative technique used makes subtle characterization impossible. Kate Chopin's novel is the only work to which this statement does not apply. *The Awakening* stands in sharp contrast not only generally to the work of the period but specifically to Mrs. Chopin's own short stories. While her stories are singular (for they often contain the suggestion of psychological conflict), they are also incomplete. Finally, either Mrs. Chopin's own limitations or the demands of the local color genre, as the nineteenth century understood those demands, prevented her from pursuing the psychological complications in any but a fragmentary way.

Two stories involving the kinds of plain people Mrs. Chopin often deals with will illustrate the point. "Athénaise"[10] is a forerunner of *The Awakening*. The Acadian heroine Athénaise is an independent young girl who decides soon after her wedding that marriage is constricting because it allows her no privacy. She runs away from her husband twice, and finally is helped by her brother to flee to New Orleans. There an affair almost develops between Athénaise and a journalist.[11] But when, in the nick of time, she discovers she is pregnant, the discovery resolves all her doubts about marriage. She returns to her husband sublimely happy. Using a fetus as *deus ex machina* is surely no more satisfactory a solution to the problem implied than any other which does not grow out of the psychological make-up of the characters. "Cavanelle"[12] is another such incomplete story, sketching a shopkeeper whose life is completely centered in his sister. He is convinced that his sister is almost ready to become an opera singer and talks only of her future career. After hearing of this talented woman for months, the narrator (the only one of Mrs. Chopin's narrators to tell the story in the first person) goes to Cavanelle's little house to meet his sister. There the narrator discovers that the sister is frail, with a figure unsuited to opera, and that she cannot sing. The narrator goes away disgusted with Cavanelle for his inability to face the obvious. Abruptly the story ends happily. The sister dies, making it unnecessary for Cavanelle to face unpleasant facts about her; and Cavanelle is enabled to turn his attention to an aging aunt, who needs caring for but who has no talent that can be exaggerated. The story illustrates the kind of happy ending Mrs. Chopin often devises, as well as the way in which she hints at complicated psychological relationships and then fails to explore them.

Occasionally an undeveloped character or situation suggests interesting possibilities which other writers have explored more thoroughly. Alice French's "The First Mayor"[13] tentatively outlines the kind of figure—a symbol of absolute power who is both benevolent and ruthless and by whose iron grip the smallest activity of a town is controlled—later filled in so brilliantly by Robert Penn Warren in *All the King's Men* or so hilariously by Larry L. King in *The One-Eyed Man*. The ambivalent master-servant relationship Johnston happily left unexamined in "Travis and Major Jonathan Wilby"[14] reminds us both of Melville's "Benito Cereno" and of Robert Lowell's dramatization of that story. But for the most part we spin such associations and uncover such possibilities for ourselves. The local colorist, following Hawthorne's advice instead of his literary practice, never meddles with the human heart, mind, or spirit. Even when we are occasionally jolted by the appearance of such a character as Harris's Mrs. Bivins—a figure who is revealed, if not in depth, at least in breadth—we still notice at what a distance we are kept from her. Not only are her words siphoned through the intelligence of a recorder, but everything we know of Mrs. Bivins she tells us herself while she is defensively explaining her actions to an incredulous auditor. When Mingo, an eyewitness who might have furnished objective analysis of Mrs. Bivins, takes up the story, he simply fills in events. Since Mingo is the only individual who has lived close enough to Mrs. Bivins to understand her thoroughly, we are left to guess the less obvious components of her personality.

The southern local colorists were not experimenters. As a group they are not remarkable for originality either of theme or technique. When original talents such as Harris or Cable, or even Page, appeared, others followed their formulas almost slavishly. The plots of local color fiction were vitiated by a heavy coating of sentimentality, and the subject matter was shaped to suit the requirements of the public. Trying new subjects was often disastrous. When in 1880 Sherwood Bonner published "A

Volcanic Interlude," this Gothic tale of a promiscuous Mississippi planter supposedly lost *Lippincott's Magazine* half its subscribers. Occasionally, however, some bolder spirit experi-
mented slightly with techniques which other writers such as Poe
had found very useful, particularly with modes of narration and
with symbolism.

Toward the end of the local color period John Fox, Jr., in *Hell*
*fer Sartain*, tried dispensing with that recorder whose function
was to relate someone else's anecdote. When a story of his is
set outside the settlement and on the mountain, the story is told
as a monologue in mountain dialect. Five mountaineer monologues alternate with five stories told by an educated narrator.
But when the monologue is addressed to a stranger who never
appears at all, the result is an immediate lessening of the distance between reader and speaker. The dialect is no longer especially funny, and the speaker sounds much more intelligent.
The wry humor is generally directed at another whose antics the
speaker describes. Since there is no other narrator whose comments must be taken into account, all the mountaineer's generalizations which are not heavily ironic go unchallenged and
pass for wisdom. To make this monologue convincing Fox must
omit all those "colorful" details which would seem commonplace to a mountaineer. The few details about local customs
mentioned at all must be included in the briefest, most pointed
manner. Since Fox's emphasis falls on plot rather than character, the stories are short and swift. They are about the length of
the average anecdote—quickly sketched and quickly over. The
spareness of these monologues makes them stand in interesting
contrast to other stories of the period.

About a decade before Fox published *Hell fer Sartain*, Sherwood Bonner was experimenting with a similar, but more difficult, form of narration in her two best stories—"The Gentlemen
of Sarsar" and "On the Nine-Mile." "On the Nine-Mile" is
told directly to the reader by a southwestern farm woman. It
differs from Fox's monologues in that Miss Bonner attempts
to reveal the personality of the speaker in the way the speaker
phrases her observations. The technique is tricky because the
speaker is not always supposed to be conscious of what she is
revealing. Her unsympathetic account of life in a farm com-

munity obviously suggests her own attitudes and prejudices. She certainly tells us as much about herself as she does about others: "'Why, uncle, didn't you have a thrashin'-machine?' cries Elick, stickin' his knife between his teeth, an' proddin' a piece o' pork with his fork, simultaneous with stretchin' out his other hand for a biscuit."[15] Since this statement implies that Elick has three hands, it reveals not only Elick's vulgarity and the narrator's exasperation with his manners, but also her tendency to ignore finer details in the interest of her major point. Generally the narrator comes off rather well in this story: she seems mostly an ordinary, talkative, amusing, and kind old lady, given to quoting maudlin poetry in moments of stress.

Miss Bonner tries less successfully a more daring experiment in "The Gentlemen of Sarsar." The narrator and protagonist of this story is Ned Mereweather, an inexperienced but complete gentleman. The story consists of a detailed account of the way in which Ned is made to look foolish by the townsmen of Sarsar. The joke on Ned would be neither convincing nor funny, however, unless the reader also considered him a fool. Otherwise Ned would seem the pathetic victim of a practical joke. In order to gain the reader's sympathy for Ned, which is presumably necessary to sustain our interest in a lengthy account of a fool's undoing, Miss Bonner is hard put to explain his foolishness without concurrently arousing contempt. Her solution is to make Ned foolish because he is a young man and a lover, and then trust that young love will be interesting enough to keep the reader's attention until the prank gets underway. There is little doubt that love has affected Ned's judgment. Unfortunately his speeches are excessive, even for a fool:

> As befitted my slim purse, I was madly, unutterably in love—
> in love with Angie Bell, the prettiest girl, I would swear, among a
> million picked beauties. With the thousand dollars fairly mine, I
> should be able to offer those delicate attentions man delights to
> lavish on the woman he adores—buggy drives and bonbons, new
> music, books and bouquets. Thus I should weave myself, as it
> were, into her life, keep her little heart in a perpetual simmer of
> kindly feeling, and dispose her to look tenderly on my encroach-
> ing passion, nor resist when its tide should sweep her from her
> moorings into my arms. Unless—reflected I—it might be better

to trust to winning her solely on my merits, and, the betrothal an
accomplished fact, spend all the sum in the purchase of a troth gift
in some degree worthy of her inspiring beauty.[16]

The story is interesting not only because of Miss Bonner's
experimentation in narrative technique, but also because of a
subsidiary theme: Ned is foolish *because* he is a real gentleman
who loves in the gentlemanly manner and trusts others to treat
him as honorably as he treats them. Therefore gentlemen—at
least gentlemen in love—can be very foolish. Miss Bonner seems
aware of the excesses in Ned's rhapsodies, using them as a
direct means of characterizing him. Certainly Ned seems inferior
to the plain men who play the joke on him. One interesting
effect of the technique is that the narrator himself, as well as
the people he discusses, can be the object of satire. The technique Miss Bonner struggles with here, Eudora Welty later
handles deftly in *The Ponder Heart* and "Why I Live at the
P. O."[17]

Again we turn to John Fox, Jr., to find a third type of experiment with narrative technique. The five stories in *Hell fer
Sartain* which are not mountaineer monologues are told by an
educated narrator who speaks straightforwardly and seriously.
Yet this narrator has an ambivalent role in the volume, for he
seems neither particularly wise nor well-informed. Rather than
acting as our instructor or guide, he often appears as fallible as
the reader. In one story, for example, he reveals a callous ignorance of human nature. If nothing else, Fox's depiction of this
narrator reveals his more sophisticated attitude toward the
limitations of the educated gentleman.

Fox achieves an interesting result by alternating mountaineer
monologues with stories told by his more cultured narrator. The
cultured man considers mountaineers much like white trash,
whereas the mountaineer monologues go further than any other
local color stories in establishing the mountaineer's dignity.
Switching from one type of story to the other begins in itself to
create some doubts about the judgment of the educated man.
Such doubts are confirmed in "Grayson's Baby." Since the story
is set in a Cumberland settlement, it is told by the gentleman.

"Grayson's Baby" describes a mountain family which
creeps to the edge of a settlement without anyone's knowing

of them, and almost starves to death there. The narrator says, "They were hill people, who sicken, suffer, and sometimes die, like animals, and make no noise" (p. 29). The father has died and the mother and children are almost dead before anyone discovers them. Then the children are parceled out among the neighbors. The small baby is adopted by a mysterious bachelor named Grayson, who nurses it back to health. After the adoption a subtle change in the presentation of the mountaineers begins. Once the family members are seen as individuals, not as an unfamiliar group representing an even more unfamiliar way of life, they no longer appear animal-like. Each member comes to represent something admirable. The difference, it is clear, is not in the mountaineer but in the reactions of the onlooker. Although the baby is as yet too young and too sick to have a very distinct character, the narrator begins to project a great many of his own values onto him: "Never for one instant did its look change—the quiet, unyielding endurance that no faith and no philosophy could ever bring to him. It was ideal courage, that look, to accept the inevitable but to fight it in just that way" (p. 32).

The mother also becomes more interesting. The townsfolk feel that she is not properly appreciative of their charity because they do not understand her granite-like pride. When they suggest that she go to the poorhouse, she replies that "she'd go out on her crutches fust, and that the people who talked 'bout sendin' her to the po'-house had better save their breath to make prayers with" (p. 35). She makes an impossible servant because "She wasn't goin' to work a lick while . . . [her employer] was a layin' in bed . . . [or] while that woman was a-struttin' the streets" (p. 36).

After the baby begins to improve in health, Grayson returns it to its mother. When he is out of town on business, he always leaves the narrator in charge. Once when Grayson has been gone a particularly long time, the baby almost dies again and is saved by the quick action of the narrator. When Grayson returns, he goes straight to see his small ward. But the baby holds out his arms not to Grayson but to the narrator. Thereafter Grayson continues to provide money for mother and child, but he refuses to see the baby again. After Grayson's visits have stopped and the mother and child disappear back into the mountains, the narrator dismisses them with the condescending phrase, "They don't grieve long, . . . these people" (p. 39). When Grayson is killed, however, the woman reappears, having walked for two days to find whether reports of his death were true. The narrator meets her in the road, confirms the news, and leaves her standing there motionless. It is not necessary for him to point out how wrong his assessment of her has been, for the picture of the silently grieving woman speaks for itself.

By creating a somewhat obtuse narrator for his settlement stories, Fox is able in "Through the Gap" to use anticlimax for a cleverly wrought effect. While anticlimactic endings are quite familiar to the reader of southern local color fiction, the anticlimax in this story seems both controlled and deliberate. In "Through the Gap" a mountain couple appear one day and ask for a preacher but never visit one. Although they live to-gether, townsfolk soon observe the man with "another woman, hideously rouged and with scarlet ribbons fluttering from her bonnet" (p. 13). A half-breed reports this fact to the mountain girl, who after ascertaining its truth, runs off with her informant. The mountaineer sullenly waits for her return. When his former mistress comes back, everyone (including the narrator) assumes the mountaineer will kill her. As a group of women, joined by the narrator, wait outside the cabin expectantly, one states, "He hain't seed her yit. . . . He's goin' to kill her shore. I tol' her he would. She said she reckoned he would, but she didn't keer" (pp. 15–16). When the cabin door closes behind the couple, all listen for a scream and a shot. But suddenly the cou-ple reemerge and head for the preacher. In this story as in others, we notice how much more effectively the uncolored sentences Fox sometimes employs communicate facts about mountaineers. In this case we are reminded of the autocratic position of the mountain man—and of his woman's passive ac-ceptance of his rule.

Occasionally, then, we encounter in local color stories an experimental approach to narrative technique. Fox's five moun-taineer monologues in *Hell fer Sartain* are not "framed" by an educated narrator. When such a cultured narrator disappears, the image of the mountaineer changes. His sensible grasp of the facts of his life appears to increase. Sherwood Bonner occasion-ally attempts a more complex narrative technique in which the narrator, as well as the people and event he describes, are the targets of satire. And Fox, in a few of his stories, goes one step further, presenting a respectable and educated narrator whose judgment is so humanly fallible that he proves an untrustworthy authority on the people and events he sketches. Though Miss Bonner's narrators are amusing, we trust their accounts. Such is not the case in Fox's settlement stories.

Sometimes we also find in local color fiction experiments with symbolism. Local colorists especially emphasize the details of their stories' setting. Occasionally the setting not only serves the usual purposes of making action and character more definite, concrete, and seemingly realistic, but also operates to suggest symbolically the themes of the story, the primary facts about the characters, or the influences shaping their lives.

Cable often uses the decaying New Orleans neighborhoods in which Creoles live to suggest his views of Creole culture and personality. Thus the way in which he describes the Creole neighborhood parallels the way in which he reduces Creoles to plain folk status.

> [In "'Sieur George"] Cable strikes the notes that resound in his later writing, so much of it about New Orleans, the aura of a bygone day hanging over the scene and diffusing the sharpness of the images. Here is the rented room, the habitation of so many of his characters. Here, too, is a class of persons who, even in the past, looked to a remote time as the source of their respectability and whose decline is symbolized by the physical decay of their surroundings as well as hinted at by the author's suggestive "solemn look of gentility in rags" and "faded fop who pretends to be looking for employment." The impact of . . . [the first paragraph] is rather a different thing than the specific statement; its effectiveness lies in what is suggested rather than in what is denoted.[18]

In "'Sieur George" as well as in other stories we find a rather obvious kind of incipient symbolism, composed of Cable's description of setting. *Dr. Sevier* opens by describing the bustling business men on Carondelet Street, the commercial center of New Orleans in which John Richling, who is incapable of bustling, must try to make his way in the business world. *The Grandissimes* includes a picture of the "funereal swamps" around New Orleans, swamps out of which come periodic yellow fever

epidemics which sweep the city and carry away Joseph Frowenfeld's family at the beginning of the novel. Both the swamps and
the fever suggest the unhealthier aspects of life in southern
Louisiana, a life explored rather critically in the rest of the novel.
In all of Cable's better novels and stories this suggestive use of
setting symbolizes events to come and themes to be explored.

Such obviously symbolic settings are exceptional in southern
local color. Minimizing characterization as they did, southern
local colorists seldom made any direct connection between setting and personality. In *Rodman the Keeper*, however, Constance
Fenimore Woolson underlines the symbolic aspects of setting
even more strongly than Cable. She links the natural setting with
specific commoners rather than merely connecting the setting
with the society the characters represent, as Cable does. Her
"Felipa" is set in "a wild place . . . yet not new or crude—the
coast of Florida, that old-new land . . ." (p. 198). Felipa, the central character in the sketch, is described in the opening paragraphs as both a product and an embodiment of the environment: "She was a small, dark-skinned, yellow-eyed child, the
offspring of the ocean and the heats, tawny, lithe and wild, shy
yet fearless—not unlike one of the little brown deer that bounded
through the open reaches of the pine-barren behind the house"
(p. 197).

Miss Woolson connects the personality of a man with that of
a place even more directly in "The South Devil." In this
story a consumptive musician is brought to a wild section of
Florida by his step-brother, who is trying to create a prosperous
farm in the deserted Florida canebrakes. The musician soon declares himself haunted by a particularly dangerous swamp. Unable to see the snakes, alligators, and spiders in the swamp, he
notes only its beautiful tropical flowers and plants. For Carl the
swamp is like "a beautiful woman, falsely called a devil by
cowards, dark, languorous, mystical, sleeping among the vines
. . . with the great red blossoms dropping around her" (p. 154).
The languid, lazy Carl falls in love with the swamp, and he
wishes more than anything to capture the music of the place.
His brother must rescue him twice from the certain death he
invites in the bogs; for "death lives there"—in the air, the water,
the treacherous ground. But Carl is also more than a little in love
with death, especially the exotic kind of death the swamp sug-

gests. Before he finally dies, he requests that he be paddled
through the marshes to his burial place: "I particularly want to
be carried through the swamp. Take me through in the canoe, as
I went the last time. . . . I want to go. And do not cover my face,
either; I want to see" (p. 173). Carl's intense, irrational love of
South Devil Swamp symbolizes effectively both the morbid and
the esthetic sides of his character. As Carl's dead body is carried through the South Devil, "The air was absolutely still; no
breeze reached these blossoming aisles; each leaf hung motionless. The atmosphere was hot, and heavy with perfumes. It was
the heart of the swamp, a riot of intoxicating, steaming, swarming, fragrant, beautiful life, without man to make or mar it"
(p. 174).

Perhaps the most interesting use of setting to provide symbolic echoes of a plain person's character distinguishes Mary
Murfree's "Drifting Down Lost Creek." In most stories set in
mountains, the setting is merely a convenient device to explain
what special stereotype the story will treat. Miss Murfree
uses setting differently, however, to gain several fresh and seemingly "modern" effects in "Drifting Down Lost Creek." The
mountains in this story are picturesque in their grandeur, but
like Miss Woolson's South Devil Swamp they also have a distinctive personality. They are a "somber, changeless mystery"
(p. 1), becoming such an intense presence in this and other
stories in *In the Tennessee Mountains* that they are virtually per-
sonified. The character of the mountains determines the lives
of the mountaineers. In "Drifting Down Lost Creek" the setting
also symbolizes the individual facts about the life of one girl—
Cynthia Ware.

Two components of the natural setting which become symbolic—Pine Mountain and Lost Creek—are described in the
opening sentences. Initially the description is useful in establishing the melancholy mood of the story:

High above Lost Creek Valley towers a wilderness of pine. So
dense is this growth that it masks the mountain whence it springs.
Even when the Cumberland spurs, to the east, are gaunt and bare
in the wintry wind, their deciduous forests denuded, . . . Pine
Mountain remains a sombre, changeless mystery; its clifty heights
are hidden. . . . Whether the skies are blue, or gray, the dark,

austere line of its summit limits the horizon. It stands against the
west like a barrier. It seemed to Cynthia Ware that nothing which
went beyond this barrier ever came back again. . . . She beheld love
go hence, and many a hope. (pp. 1–2)

Pine Mountain is a natural barrier symbolizing the barriers
of her mountain life which prohibit Cynthia's finding fulfill-
ment. The mountain stands to the west, a fact Miss Murfree
plays on as she suggests the traditional association of West and
death. Cynthia finds an even more pertinent symbol in the west-
running brook, which vanishes after furnishing a place in which
the most prosaic tasks, such as washing clothes, are performed:
"Even Lost Creek itself, meandering for miles between the
ranges, suddenly sinks into the earth . . . and is never seen again.
She often watched the floating leaves, . . . the broken wing of a
moth, and wondered whither these trifles were borne, on the
elegiac current. She came to fancy that her life was like them,
worthless in itself and without a mission; drifting down Lost
Creek, to vanish vaguely in the mountains" (p. 2).

The seasons also symbolize Cynthia's life. The story opens in
the spring, as the youthful Cynthia helps her mother wash
clothes and meets her suitor by the creek. In the following
months he is taken to prison, unjustly convicted of receiving
stolen goods and assault with intent to kill. As Cynthia, despair-
ing, watches winter approach, the season reflects the girl's mood:
"[The mountains] were laden with snow before she heard aught
of him. Beneath them, instead of the ducky vistas the summer
had explored, were long reaches of ghastly white undulations.
. . . When the wind rose, Pine Mountain mourned with a mighty
voice. Cynthia had known that voice since her birth. But what
new meaning in its threnody!" (p. 31). With the approach of
spring, hope returns once more. Cynthia visits the neighbor
whom her sweetheart Evander supposedly attacked, and hears
him admit that Evander's idiot brother was his assailant. She
troubles his conscience until he makes a sworn declaration to
the local justice, absolving Evander of any guilt. But time drags
on and Cynthia can get nobody to take action on the case. In
late summer she herself undertakes the arduous trip necessary
to place a petition for clemency in the hands of the governor.
Then as autumn approaches, Cynthia returns to the mountains

to wait. Her hopes die in the season of dying; Evander never returns.

Finally a mountaineer who has encountered Evander in prison casually reports that 'Vander had not minded the penitentiary in the least. As a blacksmith he had learned there many new ways of working with iron. In fact, says the neighbor, "he 'lowed ter me ez one year in the forge at the Pen war wuth a hundred years in the mountains ter him" (p. 67). While imprisoned, 'Vander was hired out as convict labor and managed to invent a gadget which would make him some money. When he heard of the governor's pardon he assumed his family had secured it, and set up a shop in the valley. He married an educated wife and gave no further thought to Cynthia. Not even 'Vander's money does anyone good; when he sends money to his father, the old man buries it "fur fear he'd be pulled out'n his bed fur it, some dark night, by lawless ones" (p. 70). Poor Evander ends his days tied to a nagging wife who is ashamed of his origins. The irony, of course, underscores the implications of Miss Murfree's natural symbols.

Such heavy symbolic emphasis on setting becomes a distinguishing characteristic of southern fiction in the twentieth century. To consider hastily a single writer as an example, Robert Penn Warren begins his novels with a formula which gradually becomes predictable. In the first paragraphs or pages he presents the major themes and symbols to be developed throughout each work. Most often, the symbols are elements of the setting. *All the King's Men* opens, for example, with Governor Willie Stark and his cohorts being driven down a road Willie has been responsible for building. The heat is intense, and intensely southern, and the car passes scene after scene suggesting the impoverished life led by the nearby farmers and field workers who provide the votes keeping Willie in power. These squalid scenes contrast with the new highway, Willie's sleek limousine, and the frivolity of the men inside it. The farms suggest Willie's humble origins and the immense distance he has traveled, with the same breakneck speed at which his chauffeur is driving the car, to arrive as an almost apotheosized, though now corrupt, governor. The opening pages of *The Cave* describe a pastoral glade, equipped with archetypal Freudian symbols of cave and giant beech, to which two lovers come to find a privacy disturbed only by the buzzing of locusts. Later they notice an inconsequential pair of boots and a guitar by the mouth of the cave, recognition of which shatters permanently their idyllic trysting place and their simple lives. The cave, the beech, the boots, the guitar, and the locusts all take on increasingly complex symbolic overtones almost immediately, and dominate the novel thereafter.

Though there is no reason to assume that southern writers of the twentieth century learned such techniques exclusively from local colorists, still the use to which talented moderns put setting, particularly settings which can be employed on symbolic as well as realistic levels, is foreshadowed by the work of Cable, Constance Woolson, and Mary Murfree. Of the three, the one seeming most contemporary in her use of setting is Miss Murfree, in such stories as "Drifting Down Lost Creek." Miss Murfree starts with a familiar scene from which symbolic overtones develop naturally, then draws specific parallels between Pine Mountain, Lost Creek, and the life of Cynthia Ware. Because the way in which Miss Murfree uses symbols in characterizing a plain person has become associated with twentieth-century southern fiction, her experiment is historically important. The symbols give added significance to the life of an ordinary mountain girl.

But perhaps the most interesting of all the stylistic components of southern local color is its humor. Only the stories of Cable and Harris include anything approaching wit—or verbal humor consisting primarily of intellectually interesting turns of phrase. Philosophers and psychologists have already explored many kinds of humor, and they may define many more. But the humor of southern local color rests almost exclusively on a heightened sense of incongruity. The humor is directly related to plain folk, because its most obvious source is dialect, not only of the Negroes but also of the plain folk. And dialect can be funny because of its incongruity with standard speech.

Dialect is conveyed by phonetic spellings, and its artful use often separates the more talented writer from the mere propagandists. Phonetic spelling is, however, a two-edged weapon. When its use becomes an end in itself, it is often offensive; more than one writer mars his story by such carelessness. To spell *wait* "wate," or *wrong* "'rong," or *action* "akshun" is simply a

lapse of good taste because it implies an ignorance while revealing only standard pronunciation. It is also artistically dishonest,
suggesting differences where no differences exist. While this
kind of dishonesty often marks southwestern humor, however,
such excesses are not common in local color. At least in writing
dialogue, local colorists usually attempt to be accurate, though
the temptation to indulge in wildly irregular phonetic spellings
often seems irresistible when written messages are recorded.
More often, misleading phonetic spellings seem the result of
the particular writer's careless listening habits. When Mary
Murfree entitles a story "Up on the T'other Mounting," she is
probably making two mistakes. To give her due credit, however,
she makes them consistently. The backwoods speaker pronounc-
ing *other* "t'other" would never use an article before the word;
the article is replaced by the *t'*. Second, the pronunciation implied by *mounting* is much less likely than *mount'in* or *moun'n*,
spellings preferred by Harris, Edwards, and Fox. Writing accurate dialect becomes an art in itself in this period, and of the
authors considered in this study the unquestioned master was
Joel Chandler Harris. Harris is still worth reading for his dialect
alone: his ear for speech is remarkable. Besides Mark Twain he
was the only southern writer of his time who could make subtle
social distinctions between two characters by using two different
dialects. The speech of Mrs. Bivins, the poor-white, is as distinct
from that of Squire Inchly, the wheelwright, as it is from that of
Teague Poteet, the mountaineer. Harris even devises a convincing Irish brogue for a Yankee soldier who appears in several of
his later stories.

In most local color tales humor results only when a character speaking in dialect appears. One reason the plain folk of
these stories are appealing is that they provide such humor. The
fact suggests, however, that one cause of the humor in local
color is the human tendency toward condescension. The incongruity between the recorder-narrator and the plain man serving
as major narrator automatically allows the reader, by identifying
with the recorder, to condescend to the plain man. The careful
control of such condescension in most of these stories reveals
that local colorists have their cake and eat it, too. Although the
plain folk are presented as culturally inferior to the recorders,
the stories display the many virtues of such commoners. There-

fore the reader can feel doubly smug: he can condescend to the plain folk speaking in dialect while he still respects them, thus avoiding the moral pitfall of snobbery.

While dialect is both incongruous and funny in itself, it is generally heightened by other kinds of incongruity such as the difference between what the folksy speaker is expressing and the words he chooses to do so. Teague Poteet means that a low-lander is courageous when he says, "Look in his eye, an' you wouldn't see no muddy water; an' he had grit."[19] Praising a former neighbor, a Georgia woman says, "I knowed her, and she were as perfec' a saint in her old age as ever trod grit in Warren County."[20] Or a farm woman, admitting that she finds it difficult to be silent when a discussion is underway, says, "I, likin' always to hear my bob in conversation. . . ."[21] Perhaps the best example is a romantic conversation between a mountain couple in Edwards' "An Idyl of 'Sinkin' Mount'in'":

> "I declar' ter goodness, D'rindy" he said, seeking for some way to express his gratitude, "yuh han' 's es sof' es er moss-patch an' yuh es putty es th' sunset on th' mount'in."
> "Shet yer jaw, Zeke; yer pokin' fun at me!"[22]

Three other varieties of incongruity used by southern local colorists for humorous effect should be mentioned. The first—an incongruity between an action described and the language used to convey or acknowledge the action—we generally find most broadly underlined in stories written by the Georgians. Harris's "The Cause of the Difficulty" provides a good example of this source of humor. The story is also remarkable for other reasons, since it indicates particularly well Harris's adeptness at shaping unpromising materials to fit his own purposes. As a southern local colorist Harris was committed to the happy ending. This story, however, includes a seduction, a bastard, and two murders. How Harris manages to make the story funny provides a lesson in itself. Partly he does so by mentioning all the unpleasant facts and the sadder consequences in the opening paragraphs of the story. Then he is free to fill in details at leisure, without making us anticipate a pleasant resolution to the conflicts. To a lesser degree he refuses to take a serious view of such subjects as illegitimacy and murder. By treating them flip-

pantly, he softens the more upsetting facts with humor. At the
end of the story the seducer—a slick young cad from the valley
—reappears at the mountain scene of his villainy leading a
band of conscript officers. In most of Harris's stories even Confederate conscript officers are considered treacherous cowards
afraid to stay in the front line of battle. By leading the con-
scriptors, Hildreth obviously proves he deserves anything that
happens to him. When Hildreth arrives on the mountain, intent
on betraying the mountaineers to the officers, he is awaited by
two local residents—Loorany Parmalee, the girl he seduced,
and her mountain sweetheart, John Wesley Millirons. When
Hildreth is shot, the following colloquy takes place over his dead
body:

> "Was you gwine to kill him?" Loorany asked.
> "Well, sorter that away, I reckin."
> "Did you have the notion that I'd marry you atterwards?"
> "I wa'n't a-gwine to ax you," said John Wesley.
> "Will you take me now, jest as I am?"
> "Why, I reckon," he replied in a matter-of-fact tone.
> So they went home and left other people to look after Hildreth
> of Hall.[23]

The same incongruity between action and language heightens
the humor in Johnston's "Old Friends and New." Bill Williams,
hastily edging away from an armed and angry brother come to
avenge his family for Bill's flirting, suddenly bursts out, "I always did love her the best, but which I didn't ezactly know it
till jes now."[24]

This kind of incongruity between act and language is not always unconscious on the part of the speaker. In Harris's "Trouble on Lost Mountain," when a mountaineer catches sight of a
well-dressed stranger riding his way he soliloquizes:

> "He's a mightly early bird . . . less'n he's a-headin' fer the furder
> side. Maybe he's a revenue man . . . They say they're a-gwine to
> heat the hills mighty hot from this on.
>     . . . I hain't kindled no fires yit, but you better b'lieve I'm a-
> gwine to keep my beer from sp'ilin'. The way I do my countin',
> one tub of beer is natchally wuth two revenue chaps. . . .
>     "That hoss steps right along, an' the chap a-straddle of him

is got on store-clo'es. Fetch me my rifle, Babe. I'll meet that feller half-way an' make some inquirements about his famerly, an' maybe I'll fetch a squir'l back."[25]

Sometimes the incongruity exists between the language of the narrator and the actions he describes. This deliberate heightening of incongruity for comic effect is well illustrated by Edwards' "Elder Brown's Backslide." The elder's feet are dragging the ground on either side of his donkey when the narrator says he "bestrode his fiery steed." The satiric intent of this narrative tone, however, was not entirely congenial to southern local colorists. We find less blatant forms of it in both Cable's and Harris's work, but for the most part it is not especially typical of southern local color. When southern local color narrators make ironic comments, they are more often in dead earnest.

A second kind of humorous incongruity sometimes exists between action and setting. The church-house humor we noticed earlier could be classified in this category, as could most of the courtroom humor. Any disorder in a setting supposedly characterized by heightened formality is always a potential source of humor. The usual effect of this form of humor is to make all the actors comic. Plain folk seldom participate in tragedy because they are not noble enough. Since local colorists generally shied away from situations in which plain men and women might appear pathetic victims of overwhelming forces, mishaps occurring to the plain folk were generally considered funny. Such comic scenes are often based on actions incongruous with their settings.

A special variation is the violent action occurring in a tranquil natural setting. Harry Stillwell Edwards uses this kind of humor to advantage in his Major Worthington stories. In these stories Edwards, as John Pendleton Kennedy had done in *Swallow Barn*, makes his squire comic enough to appear less than the solemn, dignified aristocrat. Edwards indicated that his most popular story was "Two Runaways." In this tale a Georgia plantation owner forces his personal slave to run away with him for two weeks every year. The incongruity of two thoroughly lazy men trying to live like fugitives in a placid Georgia countryside provides the basic humor of the story. The same kind of humor exists in "The Woodhaven Goat."[26] After establishing the soporific atmosphere of Major Worthington's front yard, Edwards has a frightened goat upset a beehive. The major is clever enough to lie still, but Isam, his servant, tries to run from the bees and finally must jump into a well to escape them, while the major lies near apoplexy with laughter.

This humorous incongruity between action and setting can be turned into sentimentality, however, as easily as other techniques of local color. Ruth McEnery Stuart often uses a form of sentimentalized incongruity in her stories. In "Blink," for example, a Negro maid smuggles a chicken into her handbag when she accompanies her mistress and family to their new home in New Orleans. The chirping which enlivens their train ride apparently amuses Mrs. Stuart, for she includes the story in two different volumes.[27] The real point, as becomes clear, is that the old Negress is so concerned for the welfare of her white family that she seeks to provide for them in the only way she knows. In another of Mrs. Stuart's stories, "The Frey's Christmas Party,"[28] a good-hearted family of children plan to entertain all the boarders in their rooming house at a Yuletide party. Humor is derived from the incongruity between the formal preparations for the party and the minor mishaps which later accompany it: those invited are unaccustomed to entertainment, and the younger children make embarrassingly candid observations in front of the guests. The story becomes especially sentimental when a prostitute who was invited leaves the party as soon as she sees the true innocence of the children.

A third and closely related type of humor is generated by the simultaneous occurrence of two incongruous events. "Dr. Jex's Predicament,"[29] by Sherwood Bonner, describes Uncle Brimmer, an old Negro who follows his young mistress to Kentucky just after her honeymoon. Since Mabel, the young matron, has not been expecting him, Uncle Brimmer must sleep in the loft over the outhouse kitchen. When Uncle Brimmer falls ill, Mabel summons a doctor before she remembers that the doctor will have to climb a ladder to get into the loft. As the doctor ascends, Uncle Brimmer considerately sticks his head out the window to save the portly physician the trouble of climbing into his quarters. But while the doctor is checking Brimmer's tongue and pulse, a runaway bull enters the yard and knocks over the ladder. Suddenly the doctor is left dangling and kicking, holding on to Brimmer's neck. The crafty Brimmer begins to bargain with the doctor for rewards, while the doctor begs for mercy. Before any servant will go for help, Mabel herself must promise to give away many prize possessions. One is left with a vision of the doctor's dangerous position directly above the head of an angry bull, while intense bargaining begins everywhere around the house.

A similar predicament occurs in "Two Runaways." When Edwards' two fugitives are returning from a forage on a nearby corn and melon patch, they are suddenly confronted by a stag loping toward them. Isam manages to skip aside, but fat Major Worthington gets entangled with the deer, cannot escape, and is in danger of being killed. He screams to Isam for help; but Isam prefers to remain an onlooker. While the major struggles, Isam loudly commends his soul to Heaven, piously enumerating all the major's peccadilloes in great detail, but requesting mercy for such an undeserving sinner. The incident remains funny because the major manages to escape. In these stories the characters who provide humor—such as Uncle Brimmer's doctor or Major Worthington—by serving as the object of satiric laughter, quite clearly function as plain folk. A similar situation develops when Bill Williams is bragging about the great virtues and intelligence of his mare, and of his mare's colts, in "The Stress of Tobe";[30] suddenly the newest foal wanders away from his mother and mistakes an old stallion for his dam. He takes refuge under Tobe, an action which understandably distresses the stallion. The ensuing hullabaloo increases as Bill conscientiously tries to retrieve the colt, Tobe frantically tries to escape the colt, and the colt sticks closer to Tobe than ever.

A refinement of this kind of incongruity consists of the disparity between the expected and the actual outcome of a situation. Edwards' "An Idyl of Sinkin' Mount'in"[31] again provides an example, in which a mountaineer protagonist is tricked by his own vanity. He accepts a ride across the mountain with a travelling salesman when he goes to court a sweetheart recently widowed. For the duration of the ride he brags to the "furriner" about his expected conquest. As they approach the widow's cabin, however, the salesman remarks that he has just married her himself. Zeke prepares to beat up the lowlander, for it is common knowledge that any mountaineer can lick any valley man. Instead Zeke is beaten. Later he has become engaged to another when he hears that the "city feller" had only been teasing and that the widow is still unwed. Again Zeke encounters the traveller, prepares to punish him for his low trick, and again is soundly beaten. Throughout the story the unexpected reversals provide an interesting variation in the use of incongruity for the sake of humor.

As many of these examples suggest, traces of southwestern humor—a humor often based on physical discomfort or pain—persist in southern local color, perhaps because plain folk are the objects of humor in both types of stories. The more sadistic elements of southwestern humor are vitiated, but the sadism still runs through southern local color. It is simply kept well hidden. Nobody is ever seriously hurt: at worst a character is only mussed up a bit. Nothing is allowed to happen which will seriously disturb more delicate readers. In spite of this layer of gentility, however, the humor still remains rooted in action, in event, in occurrence; it remains rooted in the physical rather than the intellectual. And when physical action is the primary source of humor, then physical pain—if it is not too intense or too debilitating—is always a little funny too. Consequently the humor in local color fiction often seems either boisterous or grotesque.

To understand the plain folk tradition which developed in southern literature, one must consider the stylistic techniques by which the tradition was conveyed, as well as the dominant ideas it disseminated. One cannot separate form and content in southern local color any more easily than in other literatures. Those aspects of style most closely related to the promulgation of the plain folk tradition are the form of narration used, the kind of symbolism introduced, and the type of humor incorporated. One of the most useful devices in plain folk stories is the double narrative perspective, one narrator telling the story and one recording and relaying it to the reader. This narrative form suggests an oral tradition behind the story, and it is especially useful in keeping the reader at a maximum distance from the characters, thus keeping the characters ordinary, without disturbing thoughts or mannerisms. A stereotyped conception of character can be conveyed more easily if no individualizing traits are associated with the typed character and if he is introduced in terms of actions rather than thoughts or feelings. This effect of a story told orally became so integral a part of local color fiction that it was cultivated even when a single narrator told the story directly to the reader.

Incipient symbolism and humorous incongruity are also basic ingredients of southern local color fiction. In the late nineteenth century such writers as Cable, Constance Woolson, and Mary Murfree learned to suggest connections between setting and individual commoners, thereby making the situations of the characters more vivid and meaningful. But the stylistic element with which the plain folk tradition is perhaps most closely connected is humor, since humor is most often furnished by plain folk characters. Virtually all the humor in this fiction can be explained by some kind of incongruity. Particularly evident is incongruity between dialect and standard speech, between meaning and vocabulary, between action and setting, and between disparate actions occurring simultaneously. Since local color was popular because it entertained, since it entertained because it was usually funny, and since it was most often funny when plain folk were involved, we see once again how central the plain folk are to southern local color fiction.

## Chapter X

# The Tradition
# in the Twentieth Century

*A LITERARY TRADITION* worth tracing should
be relevant to the work of authors of genuine literary merit. And
without doubt, the twentieth-century South has produced many
of these—writers whose work must be judged excellent according to the most stringent standards, from a national as well as a
regional perspective. Ellen Glasgow, William Faulkner, Robert
Penn Warren, Thomas Wolfe, Katherine Anne Porter, Eudora
Welty, Carson McCullers, Truman Capote, Flannery O'Connor,
William Styron, Peter Taylor, Walker Percy—these have been
among the most important American writers of fiction in this
century. For if southerners once dominated late-nineteenth-
century periodicals, they have been equally prominent on twentieth-century publishers' lists. Most of these artists, of course,
do not limit themselves to a regional perspective. Thus isolating
the influences on them which are exclusively southern, from
others American or European, begins to seem at best artificial.
Yet all grew up in the South, and all show signs at some point
of having been affected by (even if they chose later to reject) the
southern milieu. That milieu reflects in its popularly accepted
attitudes and values the flattering definition of "the southern

way of life" earlier local color promulgated. Furthermore, local color dictated what one looking for "The South" would see. Thus whether directly—from being read—or indirectly—from being absorbed into popular culture—southern local color fiction has influenced twentieth-century southern writers.

It should go without saying that the visions of human life, as well as of the life of their region, which twentieth-century writers express are often radically different from those of the preceding century. Under no circumstances could one expect otherwise. Among reflective people the prevalent view of man himself differs from the one commonly held one-hundred years ago. And just as obviously, as the South's defensive armor grew unnecessarily cumbersome, her writers were able to shed it for less restricted intellectual movement, an accompaniment of which was the ability to admit southern faults.

Because more recent southern writers have seemed to contemporary readers so much more open about southern imperfections, even harshly critical of the milieu and its values, readers have sometimes assumed that the twentieth-century "Southern Renascence" blossomed miraculously rootless in the stoniest ground. Yet that assumption is as absurd as the refusal would be to recognize changes within the fiction of two different centuries. While this chapter assumes that radical change has indeed occurred between the southern literature of the last century and the present one, it also assumes that the present is an outgrowth of the past—that continuity can also be traced here. Assuming, then, that the changes are obvious enough—that they often include a view of man struggling hopelessly or helplessly against a hostile natural environment, a repressive culture, and crippling personal circumstances—then my task in the present chapter must be to pursue the continuities.

As we have already suggested, southern fiction of the present century presents such an abundance of riches that discussing any aspect of it in the scope of a single chapter becomes difficult. Since the purpose here is only to suggest (not treat comprehensively, for that would require another volume) some of the evidence for assuming that there is a significant relationship between nineteenth-century local color and twentieth-century southern fiction, the discussion is limited to three writers who appear most unquestionably to merit attention.

Their literary status aside, William Faulkner, Eudora Welty, and Flannery O'Connor are useful for this study because they remain so closely tied to the South as a geographic region. While all ventured away for some periods of time, all continued living in the South while producing their major works, and all continued through such periods to identify themselves as southerners. All can be considered more exclusively southern than more "cosmopolitan" writers such as Truman Capote or Katherine Anne Porter, or even than those such as Warren, Wolfe, and Mrs. McCullers—whose later residences outside the South naturally affected their views and interests. While the three to be discussed should in no sense be considered narrow or parochial, still they are as nearly "pure southern" as the century offers. What is true of their debt to traditional southern literature is true in varying degrees of the other southerners; but it is perhaps easiest to see in those who, for the most part, stayed home.

William Faulkner, the giant dominating twentieth-century southern fiction, is especially pertinent to this study because his novels and stories contain traces of every part of that older literary tradition describing the plain folk of the South. Often the details, characters, even the plots of his works are formed in the molds first cast by local colorists and their predecessors. In works not set in Yoknapatawpha County such as *Pylon* or *Mosquitoes*, for example, details about the French Quarter of New Orleans appear authentic because they are what one expects to read of the French Quarter, one's perspective, like Faulkner's, having been affected by George Washington Cable's work. The neighborhood is still decaying, still exotic, still foreign. Charles Bon's quadroon mistress and son are described in *Absalom, Absalom!* with the Mississippi farmboy's titillated sense of forbidden sensuality that Cable could certainly have recognized; and the details of that opulent arrangement are probably about as realistic as Cable's were.

The mountaineer stereotype is crucial to *Intruder in the Dust*, the plot of which largely depends on the reader's understanding what it means for the Gowries and their relatives to be hill people, conforming in every respect to the standardized mountaineer first portrayed in local color fiction. Foremost in importance is the assumption in the novel that any hill man will immediately avenge the death of a member of his family or clan. One's awareness that such a clan as the Gowries can be expected to lynch anyone who has killed one of their group, especially to lynch a Negro (for mountaineers, we remember from Joel Chandler Harris's work, were always suspicious of Negroes), gives the novel its tension and sense of urgency. If Lucas Beauchamp, a Negro, appears to have shot a Gowrie in the back on Saturday afternoon, then the county can assume he will be lynched on Monday night. (Saturday night would be unsatisfactory because of the rush necessary to complete the business before violating the Sabbath. According to Mary Murfree mountaineers always respect the conventions of the church.) The narrator therefore states that the spot in which the murder occurred "was the last place even in Yoknapatawpha County a nigger with any judgment—or any other stranger of any color—would have chosen to shoot anybody least of all one named Gowrie."[1]

Other expected details reminiscent of mountaineer stories of the previous century thread throughout the novel. Characters frequently reveal the mountaineer's traditional antipathy toward the federal government, for example, or toward any form of conscription. The mountaineer's propensity for running a still is also referred to often. The Gowries, in fact, make up "a family of six brothers one of whom had already served a year in federal penitentiary for armed resistance as an army deserter and another term at the state penal farm for making whiskey" (p. 35). They are

> a species which before now had made their hill stronghold good against the county and the federal government too, which . . . had translated and transmogrified that whole region of lonely pine hills dotted meagerly with small tilted farms and peripatetic sawmills and contraband whiskey-kettles where peace officers from town didn't even go unless they were sent for and strange white men didn't wander far from the highway after dark and no Negro at any time—where as a local wit said once the only stranger ever to enter with impunity was God and He only by daylight and on Sunday—into a synonym for independence and violence. (pp. 35–36)

Here, then, is virtually every element of the mountaineer stereotype—the independent spirit and the violence being keys to the clan who make their own rules as well as their own whiskey, and allow no stranger, no government, to say them nay. As do Joel Chandler Harris, Mary Murfree, and John Fox, Jr., Faulkner actually presents the hillbilly sympathetically, in spite of his obvious laziness and lawlessness. Faulkner elicits our sympathetic responses to the Gowries in *Intruder in the Dust* when Charles Mallison observes in astonishment the genuine grief which Old Gowrie, the "violent foulmouthed godless old man" (p. 161), feels for his dead son Vinson.

Throughout *Intruder in the Dust* and the entire Yoknapatawpha saga runs the assumption that all readers will recognize the democratic spirit—a spirit acknowledging the plain man's worth—on which Yoknapatawpha society rests. In *Sartoris*, for example, Banker Sartoris's best friends are Old Man Will Falls and Loosh Peabody, a broken-down and aging doctor. Although the Sartoris family considers itself better than anyone else, the banker stays on convivial terms only with these two friends. Falls walks into town from his old folks' home regularly to chat with Bayard, and Loosh Peabody comes to dinner on holidays. Young Bayard is welcomed warmly into the MacCallum family, though the MacCallums are hunters who live in a small cabin with dogs underfoot. Yet they feel no sense of unworthiness when offering Bayard their hospitality or the privilege of sharing a shuck mattress with one of the sons. If the Sartorises consider themselves superior to others, they also refuse to make invidious social distinctions among those ranking below them. Young Bayard drinks with V. K. Suratt, son of a tenant farmer and forerunner of V. K. Ratliff, and Suratt pronounces him "all right." As in former stories about Georgia aristocrats each Sartoris must earn community respect separately. Young Bayard is liked by the townsmen because he embodies their standards or fulfills their fantasies about reckless living. And Aunt Jenny Dupre commands the women's respect by sheer strength of will.

Insisting on one's superiority too openly can be stupid or even dangerous in Yoknapatawpha, as it was in the Georgia of the local colorists. Thus we learn that the old Colonel Sartoris, in contrast to present Sartorises who get along well with their neighbors, was voted out of his command because "he wouldn't be Tom, Dick and Harry with ever' skulkin' camp-robber that come along with a salvaged muskit and claimed to be a sojer."[2] Colonel Sartoris, as is commonly known, was based to some extent on Faulkner's greatgrandfather, Colonel William C. Faulkner. But as Elizabeth M. Kerr concludes, "In comparison with either facts or legend, Colonel Sartoris is a diminished version of Colonel Faulkner as a military leader and railroad builder, a man of violence who met a violent end."[3] Such a fact is worth mentioning only because it reminds us that Faulkner the writer used exclusively the historical details which suited his purpose. In this case the most useful details were the ones conforming with the plain folk tradition, the ones which made his story and his character the more "southern." At any rate, in Faulkner's first novel to introduce Jefferson, the society has definite upper and lower classes; but it also boasts an easy and democratic relationship between them. From the beginning of Faulkner's work the plain folk tradition emphasizing democratic standards is as relevant as the plantation legend. Both traditions must be kept in mind if one is to understand thoroughly the social attitudes underlying Faulkner's fiction.

While *Sartoris* presents an aristocratic family, *As I Lay Dying* portrays the other extreme—the family of an impoverished dirt farmer. To classify the whole Bundren family as poor whites, however, would be to ignore their individual differences; for *As I Lay Dying* also suggests that every individual deserves to be judged on his own merits. Certainly Addie, the schoolteacher mother who speaks in grammatical sentences, cannot be classed as "trash." Nor can her three oldest sons, each of whom has too much self-respect to be dismissed in such a manner. Cash, for example, is a painstaking craftsman, shaping wood as if he were blowing glass, never complaining, and taking immense pride in the workmanship which goes into Addie's coffin. His craft and his patience merit and receive the community's high regard. Darl arouses the reader's sympathy most thoroughly in early sections of the book because Faulkner allows him to speak somewhat "poetically." In spite of the fact that people consider him odd, he appears generous and sensitive, the latter characteristic perhaps explaining his schizophrenic breakdown at the end of the work. Even Jewel, though he is vicious, manifests the tenacity and pride approved in southern fiction. Furthermore, by his willingness to work exhaustingly for months in order to buy himself a horse, he gains what he desires in the most sacrosanct manner defined by southern fiction—hard work.

If there is "trash" in the Bundren family, it is Anse, the

father, who prides himself on his lucklessness and constantly takes advantage of others' generosity. Yet even Anse can proudly say, "I always have fed me and mine and kept a roof above us."[4] The two youngest children, Dewey Dell and Vardaman, fit the poor-white stereotype best because they are least likable. As we have noticed earlier, the classification of a southern character usually depends on how sympathetically he is portrayed. But the important thing to notice is that the family is not presented as a unit—with uniform characteristics and therefore with uniform status. Their neighbors consider them individually, and the reader must follow suit.

As he is in *As I Lay Dying,* the cracker—the plain folk character already defined in nineteenth-century southern literature—is important in most of Faulkner's best work. He is crucial, moreover, in the Snopes trilogy. *The Hamlet,* the first of the three novels, best displays the literary uses to which the plain folk tradition can be put. Though the characters in *The Hamlet* range from Will Varner, who is quite wealthy, to the destitute tenant farmer Henry Armstid, all must be classed as plain folk. In fact, as much as any other twentieth-century southern work, *The Hamlet* is the outgrowth of a point of view which has itself been shaped by that plain folk tradition of southern local color.

Will Varner, for example, though he is the richest man in Frenchman's Bend (rich enough we later learn to control a third of Colonel Sartoris's bank in Jefferson), could never be considered aristocratic. He is "shrewd, profane and lazy"; Judge Benbow says of him that "a milder-mannered man never bled a mule or stuffed a ballot box."[5] Varner is simply the wealthiest among his peers—not superior to them in the graces, manners, or habits of mind associated with the aristocrat. His wife, the best homemaker in the area, is nearly illiterate and sees no need for educating women at all. Although Varner controls all the elections and most of the commerce in Frenchman's Bend, therefore virtually owning the farmers thereabout, he is careful to deal with them respectfully. He is "the fountainhead if not of law at least of advice and suggestion to a countryside which would have repudiated the term constituency if they had ever heard it, which came to him, not in the attitude of *What must I do* but *What do you think you would like for me to do if you was able to make me do it*" (p. 5).

At the other economic extreme Mink Snopes and Henry

Armstid are luckless tenant farmers whose futures, like their pasts, are marked for the grinding labor required to produce their almost worthless crops. They are interesting in the degree to which they do *not* conform to the white-trash stereotype. Both are ferociously proud. Snopes kills a more prosperous farmer for apparently taking unfair advantage of him by demanding a pound fee on Snopes's stray cow. Armstid, hopeful of finding gold on the worthless property he is tricked into buying, finally goes mad as he frantically searches for buried treasure. But both ask no quarter, asserting themselves as they are compelled to do, asking no man's help or advice. Armstid loses his farm as a result of his unfortunate partnership with Bookwright and Ratliff, both of whom are obviously solvent and able to recover from their financial mistake. But what is interesting is not so much that Armstid could be cheated but that he would be taken into an equal partnership with his financial superiors, a partnership in which none is subservient to the others.

Throughout the Snopes trilogy the social structure of Frenchman's Bend seems transposed from the Georgia of Joel Chandler Harris or Richard Malcolm Johnston. Faulkner's village exists to serve "that nethermost stratum of unfutured, barely solvent one-bale tenant farmers which pervaded, covered thinly the whole county on which in fact the entire cotton economy of the county was founded and supported."[6] The community is dominated by "incorrigible nonconformists"—the Baptists and Methodists who "hadn't quitted home and security for a wilderness in which to find freedom of thought" or "to escape from tyranny as they claimed and believed, but to establish one."[7] The churches, however, are not more successful in Faulkner's Mississippi than elsewhere in elevating human character. Mrs. Varner runs her church "with the cold high-handedness of a ward-boss."[8] When a Snopes preacher seduces a fourteen-year-old girl, the predictable violence erupts, and as Harris would also have predicted, the preacher is tarred and feathered: "There had been talk of castration also though some timid conservative dissuaded them into holding that as a promise against his return."[9] There is in Frenchman's Bend the same mistrust of education that Johnston's Mr. Pate once voiced, and the same reverence for the land, too, even though that land is continually presented as the means of slow death to those who try to farm it. As Faulkner patterns the folk of Frenchman's Bend, they appear cut from the cloth woven by southern local colorists:

> The people . . . came from the north-east, through the Tennessee mountains. . . . They took up land and built one- and two-room cabins and never painted them, and married one another and produced children and added other rooms one by one to the original cabins and did not paint them either, but that was all. Their descendants still planted cotton in the bottom land and corn along the edge of the hills and in the secret coves in the hills made whiskey of the corn and sold what they did not drink. . . . County officers did not bother them at all save in the heel of election years. They supported their own churches and schools, they married and committed infrequent adulteries and more frequent homicides among themselves and were their own courts, judges and executioners. They were Protestants and Democrats and prolific: There was not one Negro landowner in the entire section.[10]

The real subject of *The Hamlet*, as the title suggests, is the village itself and the life which exists there. In the finest sense *The Hamlet* exemplifies local color: the vividness of the novel results from the concrete details of life observed in an isolated spot. The details Faulkner singles out are those the local colorists first described. Central to the action of the novel and to the lives of its characters is Varner's crossroads store. Here the people of the community buy their wares, share their gossip, and observe each other. And Varner's store porch is filled with those same circumspect squatting men who congregate in Mary Murfree's or Will Harben's tales. From the porch they watch the young Eula Varner go by, watch Flem Snopes bring his spotted horses to town, watch young Snopes announce his cousin Ike's sodomy. They watch Ratliff arrange his trades with Flem Snopes, watch the sheriff inquire about Jack Houston. On the porch the men hear Ratliff tell the tall tale of the trade between Pat Stamper and Ab Snopes. The store porch becomes an excellent vantage point from which to see the life of the town; and the narrator of the novel, who often seems simply a spokesman for the town, relates the story as if he too were perched in some inconspicuous part of Varner's store porch.

*The Hamlet* also includes descriptions of other rural institutions and events first elaborated in the fiction of the preceding century. County fairs and church services provide the young people with places in which to gather and court. An auction, memorialized in "Spotted Horses," also brings together virtually all the men in the district. The country school, which nobody takes seriously, operates for the children "only when there was no work for them to do at home" (p. 102). It boasts at one point, however, an impoverished schoolmaster whose belief in education, whose ambition, and whose willingness to work superhuman hours are so great that he commutes by horseback each week to the university some fifty miles away.

The Hamlet is not a novel constructed around the introduction, development, and resolution of a single action. Instead, as the first part of a trilogy tracing the rise of Flem Snopes, its function is to present the small-scale community which is the first stop in Flem's journey. The whole community—its events and its characters, its routine and its rhythm—makes up the subject of the novel. But within the spectrum of life portrayed there, one character seems especially important—V. K. Ratliff. Ratliff is an amalgam of all the best qualities of the "typical southerner." Retaining his important position throughout the trilogy, he is a kind of ideal—the plain man as hero.

Faulkner's description of Ratliff is a summary of plain folk virtues. Ratliff is "pleasant, affable, courteous, anecdotal and impenetrable. He sold perhaps three machines a year, the rest of the time trading in land and livestock . . . or anything else which the owner did not want badly enough, retailing from house to house the news of his four counties with the ubiquity of a newspaper."[11] The adjective Faulkner seems to apply most often to Ratliff throughout the trilogy is shrewd. He is the man who would never be caught on the street without the answer to anything that was none of his business. He is sublimely inquisitive and supremely wise in his insights into the characters of others. He is always right in his assessment of personalities. Above all, Ratliff's character exudes common sense, that most characteristic of yeoman virtues. Thus, by the end of The Mansion, Faulkner's idealistic aristocrat Gavin Stevens finds it virtually impossible to act decisively in an emergency without first consulting Ratliff. In fact Ratliff is one of the few Faulkner creations presented with complete approval. He is unable to out-trade Flem Snopes, of course, and ends their bargaining by conceding defeat. But he possesses the ability to recognize his own foolishness and admit his own greed. As one of the Olympiads on Varner's porch remarks, "Anybody might have fooled Henry Armstid. But couldn't nobody but Flem Snopes have fooled Ratliff."[12]

It is important to note, then, that Ratliff is the son of a tenant farmer. The sympathy with which Faulkner portrays him underscores the fact that one should never automatically characterize a tenant and his family as "poor-white-trash." Ratliff obviously rises to a high economic level by the end of the trilogy: at one point in *The Town* he is able to save Wallstreet Snopes's business by loaning him money, and in *The Mansion* is able to buy two seventy-five-dollar ties when he goes, on impulse, to New York. Making even more emphatically the point that the individual shapes his own status, Faulkner described Ratliff as the "spiritual son" of Will Varner, Varner, of course, representing the highest level of Frenchman's Bend.

Ratliff epitomizes the plain folk hero developed in nineteenth-century southern local color stories; but he has also been adjusted to the requirements of the twentieth century. Like Bill Williams, Ratliff is garrulous, inquisitive, gossipy, fascinated with the details of neighborhood life, especially with the romantic attachments of others. Like Mr. Pate or Teague Poteet, he speaks in a regional dialect of sorts (rendered by Faulkner mostly by mildly aberrant grammar), his colorful language characterized by humorous exaggeration and amusing idioms and analogies. In the later two novels he has his educated straight-man in Gavin Stevens, who listens to and appreciates his conversation. The humor of the works, as one would expect, stems mainly from Ratliff's anecdotes and observations. He is as shrewd a dealer, as hard a worker, as virtuous a member of the community, and as confident of his own worth, as any of the other plain folk of Harry Stillwell Edwards or Mary Noailles Murfree or Ruth McEnery Stuart. The twentieth-century addition consists of Ratliff's unusually intense interest in motivations, as well as actions. But we are kept as far away from those Ratliff inspects as we were from the subjects of local color stories, since they are seen through Ratliff's eyes and characterized through his conversation.

In contrast to Ratliff, for whom "the pleasure of the shrewd dealing . . . far transcended mere gross profit,"[13] Flem Snopes trades with a ruthlessness which makes possible his meteoric economic rise. Though both their fathers at one time rented farms from the same man and though they come from similar backgrounds, Flem Snopes and Ratliff appear opposite in every way. Most obviously Ratliff is garrulous and Flem Snopes silent. We learn in a later novel that Ratliff believes "Snopeses had to be watched constantly like an invasion of snakes or wildcats,"[14] that in fact Snopeses can be defined as "a family, a clan, a race, maybe even a species, of pure sons of bitches."[15] What Ratliff hates in the Snopeses is their "long tradition of slow and invincible rapacity."[16] Snopeses will do virtually anything for money, and Ratliff hates them for their soulless greed. In fact the parable in which Flem, while bargaining with the devil, reduces Satan to hysterics because of his inability to produce Flem's hypothetical soul for tormenting, is one of *The Hamlet's* most masterful comic tall tales.

One must note in passing, however, that Flem Snopes can no more be considered "white trash," at least according to the nineteenth century's version of the stereotype, than Ratliff can. The trash, according to the stereotype, were to be detested and dismissed because of their weak-willed contentment with their particularly shiftless mode of living. Though Ratliff certainly detests Flem, he does so partially because he cannot dismiss Flem. Ratliff hates Snopes because he fears him. He fears him because "you can't beat him."[17] If Flem is "trash" at all, then, he is so by a very significant alteration of the tradition. The assessment of his "trashiness" becomes entirely a judgment of his morals, his character, his soul. That he is socially mobile is what makes him a menace. And in admitting the existence of the menace, Faulkner affirms even more dramatically the South's essentially democratic economic and social structure.

Significantly, although Faulkner labels *The Mansion* "a novel of the Snopes family," we hardly glimpse Flem within the novel except as a specter haunting the ruminations of Ratliff and Gavin Stevens. The reason Faulkner must keep us at a distance from Flem—must, for the sake of consistency, portray him only through the opinions of Ratliff— has become clear at the end of *The Town.* Here Flem comes near metamorphosing into an admirable character of the self-made-man variety. He suddenly appears sympathetic in his determination to make a life for himself in

spite of his handicaps. Of Flem's business methods, for example,
we are told:

> It was simply to save his money—that money he had worked so
> hard to accumulate, too hard to accumulate, sacrificed all his life to
> gather together from whatever day it had been on whatever worn-
> out tenant farm his father had moved from, onto that other worn-
> out one of Will Varner's . . . —from that very first day when he
> realized that he himself had nothing and would never have more
> than nothing unless he wrested it himself from his environment
> and time, and that the only weapon he would ever have to do it
> with would be just money. (p. 263)

By the end of *The Town* Flem's character appears to be composed
of

> Humility, and maybe a little even of regret—what little time there
> was to regret in—but without despair, who had nothing save the
> will and the need and the ruthlessness and the industry and what
> talent he had been born with, to serve them; who never in his life
> had been given anything by any man yet and expected no more as
> long as life should last; who had no evidence yet that he could cope
> with and fend off that enemy which the word Education repre-
> sented to him, yet had neither qualm nor doubt that he was going
> to try. (p. 264)

In presenting Flem as humble but fearless, a man who works
with the only weapon he can possibly use, Faulkner comes near
making him admirable. The other characters' hatred of the
Snopeses throughout the trilogy is generated by Faulkner's presenting them as symbols of a menace within the county. But a
menace, by definition, exerts a certain power. By virtue of their
power to threaten seriously the things Ratliff and Stevens value,
the Snopeses rise above the trash category, at least as the nineteenth century defined it. And unless one recognizes this fact,
he cannot explain Flem's power to advance, nor Stevens' later
love for Linda, who at least believes herself a Snopes.

Perhaps the most interesting of all Faulkner's characters of
the plain folk type is Thomas Sutpen of *Absalom, Absalom!* Sutpen is the self-made man who prevails through his own hard
work and indomitable will. He is interesting as a kind of in-

verted apotheosis—even a parody—of the plain folk hero, a man
with all the virtues of the type, whose very obsession with his
virtuous goals turns him into a monster. He achieves his goal of
building himself a fortune not once but twice, and loses his
status twice, before he tirelessly begins a third time to rebuild
his estate and is murdered. Indeed one can perhaps better understand the metamorphosis of the plain folk hero into a human
monster by comparing Sutpen to a prototype outside the southern local color tradition, such a moral monster as Conrad's
Kurtz. Even the narrative structure of *Absalom, Absalom!* is reminiscent of *Heart of Darkness.*[18] Both works consist of long stretches
of monologue interrupted by short conversations: Quentin and
Shreve talk far into the night in their Harvard dormitory, just as
Marlow talks on board his sloop. But the most important similarity between the two novels is the way in which Sutpen resembles Kurtz. Both are men of exceptional powers who go deep
into the heart of a wilderness to carve personal empires: both
participate in "unspeakable rites" with the blacks who surround them, and both end totally corrupted, losing their souls as
they conquer their dark kingdoms. Both are inhumanly gifted
and demonic personalities who seem gods to those living around
them. Quentin constantly uses demon and god imagery, in fact,
to describe Thomas Sutpen.

Such superhuman qualities might seem thoroughly incon-
gruent with the plain man stereotype; but Sutpen is also cut to
the plain folk pattern. He is born an ignorant and uneducated
mountaineer, whose family returns to Virginia's east coast after
the mother's death. To the eastern shore he brings his sense of
equality with all men, "his sober watchful mountain reserve"
and "a good deal of latent insubordination."[19] Then, rebuffed
by the Negro butler at a plantation mansion when he is about
thirteen years old, Sutpen becomes obsessed with the dream of
having a house as grand as the one in which the butler served.
Part of his vision, of course, involves an impeccably respectable
wife and a son who can propagate his name. In pursuit of this
dream, having almost grasped it once and then failed, he comes
to Yoknapatawpha County. Through his trading abilities (abilities one assumes in the shrewd yokel, after the southwestern
humor period), he acquires "that hundred miles of land which
he took from a tribe of ignorant Indians, nobody knows how . . ."

(p. 16). Then, having managed to erect a house through inhumanly intense work with a handful of Negro savages, he begins to seek a wife.

The democratic spirit controlling antebellum Mississippi is clear throughout the book—if only by virtue of Sutpen's ability to achieve what he does. When he searches for the impeccably correct family to marry into, he finds it in the household of a smalltown Methodist merchant whose moral character is unquestionable. The best family for Sutpen's purpose is the most respectable one, and respectability is determined by the character, not the wealth, of Coldfield, his future father-in-law. Moreover, once again, Sutpen's shrewdness at bargaining is evident. His practicality gains him "at the lowest possible price the sole woman available to wive him" (p. 166). Sutpen manages all this even though, as Quentin repeats, "He wasn't a gentleman. He wasn't even a gentleman" (p. 15).

Another sign of the democratic life local color has conditioned one to expect is the fact that Sutpen makes a habit of drinking with Wash Jones, a stereotyped figure whom Shreve identifies as "white trash" (p. 181). The discussion of the plantation amusements Sutpen enjoys—primarily fighting savagely with his Negroes (p. 29)—makes it unclear whether such episodes are abhorrent primarily because of their violence and animality or because of the implicit equality between two opponents in such a fight. At any rate the crudeness of Sutpen's life in his first years on his land never affects his relationship to the men of the county. Later, after marrying, he is accepted by polite society—by the women—because "he obviously had too much money now to be rejected or even seriously annoyed anymore" (p. 72).

Against a background furnished him partly by Mississippi history, partly by popular culture, and partly by literary tradition, Faulkner moves his creation of Thomas Sutpen—mountaineer, madman, devil. Sutpen represents the exaggeration of all the typical southern virtues, turned vicious by being pursued monomaniacally. He represents the plain folk tradition carried to its extreme, and he is frightening, as extremes generally are. He is also a creation of the first magnitude in the nightmarish vividness with which Faulkner brings him to life.

While his view of his characters and the society which nourishes them is often clearly ironic, Faulkner still follows the lead of southern local colorists in portraying the "typical southerner" and the southern mountaineer. He also repeats the local colorists' observations about New Orleans, the ingredients of southern rural life, and the interests of those who live it. But a writer whose literary debts to the nineteenth century are perhaps even more evident and more obviously related to her success as an artist is Eudora Welty.

The remarkable range of tone, style, and technique in Eudora Welty's fiction parallels the inventive ways in which she uses literary traditions, especially those of southern local color. Almost every stereotype or convention developed in nineteenth-century southern fiction reappears in her work, though each usually transcends the purposes for which it was originally used. Since Miss Welty takes her craft quite seriously, she does not hesitate to fold into it any ingredient at hand which might add flavor to the final product.

No one could overlook the elements of southwestern humor in *The Robber Bridegroom*: Mike Fink and the Harp brothers are as easy to trace back to their sources as is the joyous spirit of exaggeration and magic permeating the novella. Similarly, once the parallels are pointed out, nobody should overlook the elements of southern local color, and the stereotypes of the plain folk tradition, which are found in Miss Welty's other work. These traditional subjects and attitudes emerge in her first published story, "Death of a Traveling Salesman."[20]

Whether the events of this story actually occur or take place only within the mind of Bowman, the central character, the narrator still describes Sonny, the young husband of the couple Bowman encounters, as a "typical" southern mountaineer. As in Faulkner's fiction the hill country of Mississippi is the setting substituted for the more rugged Tennessee mountains; but except for the difference in the terrain, the characters live the same life described in earlier local color fiction.

Sonny's poverty is his first identifying characteristic. Bowman is shocked to find him wearing an old Confederate coat. Almost immediately, however, Sonny reveals a second characteristic appropriate to his prototype—his self-sufficiency: he is able to retrieve Bowman's car singlehandedly from the ravine into which it has rolled and to get his own fire from a neighboring home, scornfully spurning Bowman's matches. Sonny's taciturnity equals his self-sufficiency. He also possesses the fierce pride one expects of a hill character; he rejects Bowman's money, offered for Sonny's rescue of the car. Miss Welty's story even includes that detail without which no portrait of a mountain man could be complete: Sonny has his own still, and proudly offers Bowman a drink of his own whiskey.

Sonny's wife also conforms to the mountain-woman stereotype. She has aged so quickly that Bowman, who prides himself upon guessing women's ages accurately, mistakes her for a woman in her fifties, instead of Sonny's young wife. So silent as to appear feeble-minded at first, she shyly acknowledges Bowman's right to address her only by lowering her eyes. Her own intense pride in her husband's abilities parallels her pride in the humble food and facilities they can offer a stranger. The couple seem to feel their life a good one. In fact it is Bowman's recognition of a fruitful marriage existing in a satisfying home that so tortures him it sends him running out into the night and to his death.

Another story in which traditional details provide a rather standardized background for psychological events is "No Place for You, My Love." Set in the Acadian country south of New Orleans, the story contains proportionately more descriptive detail than almost any other of Miss Welty's works. Miss Welty concentrates on the heat, the insects, the poverty, the darker skin of the people, the sight of naked children and of laughing boys with bright shirts. Appropriately, as the story unfolds, the little village at the end of the road is preparing for a shrimp dance—that much-loved form of entertainment described first by Cable and Kate Chopin. And the owner of the place in which the couple in the story eat is cooking gumbo for the night's refreshments. On its walls are articles from newspapers: "One of the clippings was an account of a shooting right here. I guess they're proud of it," states the visitor.[21]

The story suggests the use to which the best of twentieth-century writers put the accoutrements of nineteenth-century local color: the details furnish economically a background convincing one that the action explored is probable. As Eudora Welty herself has stated, using specific details to make a place seem lifelike is "the readiest and gentlest and most honest and

natural way" in which a writer can make "the world of appearance . . . *seem* actuality."[22] Protesting that such observations do
not make Eudora Welty a local colorist is unnecessary. She is a
writer who cleverly and justifiably takes what local color offers
her and bends it to her own ends.

One of the most important of the stereotypes developed in
southern local color, of course, was that of the aristocrat. Miss
Welty reveals her knowledge of such local color by working the
stereotype into several stories; her characters represent several
sub-categories the nineteenth-century stories made familiar.
"Asphodel" features the iron-willed matriarch and dowager who
freely orders affairs in the little southern town she dominates by
her superior wealth and prestige, as Harris's Emily Wornum
once did.[23] "The Burning" depicts two old-maids-at-the-mercy-
of-Yankee-invaders, women in the situation Page described in
"My Cousin Fanny," or Constance Woolson portrayed in "Old
Gardiston." One sister is a soft and fragile belle, the other an
equally familiar older-sister-with-acid-tongue. Again, however,
Miss Welty adjusts the stereotype to her own needs by reversing
the expected outcome: the two women do not repel the marauders and preserve their home, but rather are raped and driven
from the house, which burns to the ground, consuming the body
of a Negro child apparently born to one of the aristocratic family. At the end of the story the two sisters hang themselves,
though the elder goes to her death as imperiously high-handed
with her servant as ever.[24] "Old Mr. Marblehall" and "Clytie"
also deal with the remaining members of once-proud southern
families, the decaying aristocratic family in both stories portrayed with touches of the Gothicism associated with southern
literature since Poe.[25]

Poor whites dominate "The Whistle" and "A Piece of News."[26]
The former story captures the isolation of an aging couple who
make a meager living growing tomatoes, who make ill-fated attempts to achieve comfort, and who find themselves at the end
in an even worse plight, facing a drearier future. As local color
stories have already amply demonstrated, however, no poor
white should be called "trash" until the narrator presents him in
that light. The old couple in "The Whistle" are pathetic, but
too sympathetically presented to be dismissed as trash. "A Piece
of News" features a younger couple, though this story also dra-

matizes the tedium of life on an impoverished farm. Rather than presenting such monotony as "The Whistle" pictures it—the bone-tired couple continuing to work through the night—"A Piece of News" describes a wife so bored with her uneventful life that she grows excited while reading of a young woman with her own name, who has been shot in the leg by her husband somewhere in Tennessee. Even the wife's occasional promiscuity fails to suffuse her days with satisfying variety. At the end every vestige of drama, including the storm outside, passes into the humdrum "like a wagon crossing a bridge" (p. 31).

In addition to such broad categories as aristocrats and poor whites, Miss Welty's stories abound in plain folk types. "Ladies in Spring," for example, presents a female rain-maker who successfully ends a drought and who appears the self-possessed and independent old maid at home in local color stories. The rain-maker's activities, in fact, provide the most interesting experiences encountered by a young boy who is *not* initiated into compromising facts of adult sexuality simply because he fails to perceive the probable reason his father goes fishing when the river is dry. The details of the setting are all rendered with the precision of good local color, just as the comic character of Miss Hattie, the rainmaker, is an example of the best in such stories. But here the resemblance to local color is deliberate and thematically important: the perceptions of the young boy remain consistent with those of sentimental local color tales because he fails to comprehend anything but the external appearance of life around him. Thus he, as well as many a reader, fails to understand what impulses actually underlie the story, fails to realize that his presence has foiled a liaison his father had arranged. He sees only the town of Royals "spread out from Baptist church to schoolhouse";[27] he perceives only that "The brightest thing in Royals—rain was the loudest on all the tin roofs—was the empty school bus drawn up under the shed of the filling station. The movie house, high up on its posts, was magnesia-bottle blue. Three red hens waited on the porch" (p. 93).

"Kin" is another work especially interesting in its deliberate references to local color. In this tale Miss Welty contrasts the more recent present of the story with the comfortable, yeoman-populated, family-oriented South of the local color past, a South with an aura of peace and happiness, of lavish family dinners on

Sundays. To develop her contrast, the author often employs
not only the details but also the style of nineteenth-century
southern local color. The story begins by emphasizing the name
of the old family farmhouse—a name also associated with a
once-well-known story by Joel Chandler Harris. The name is
repeated to reveal the fact that one member of the family—the
Yankee cousin Dicey—at first thought *Mingo* a word for a thing,
rather than a place. Throughout the story Dicey discovers repeatedly that she has forgotten most of the beautiful or gentle
aspects of life at Mingo (and, by extension, of traditional southern life). She remembers only the grotesque—that Sister Anne,
her remote kinswoman, once fell in a well during a wedding.
While visiting the old place, Dicey sees and recalls objects
which suggest the former happy life at Mingo; but evidence that
such a life can never be experienced again—especially by those
under the influence of Yankee habits—is offered when Dicey
herself destroys the last healthy relative living at Mingo by an
unparalleled act of rudeness. The act is doubly ironic since
Dicey, as a southern child, was known for her "sweet manners"
toward her elders.[28]

Through specific details Miss Welty reminds the reader of
the period in which southern local color was popular. The
townsfolk live, for example, "as if they had never heard of anywhere else, even Jackson—in houses built . . . in the local version
of the 1880's" (p. 114). At first it appears as if such a life has
escaped the changes that time brings elsewhere, for Miss Welty
emphasizes time's standing still. Sister Anne has written on an
"old-fashioned correspondence card" a request for an old-
fashioned family visit. In her bed Aunt Ethel looks to Dicey "as
if . . . she were riding in some old-fashioned carriage or litter"
(p. 113). As Alfred Appel notes, a series of images and incidents
seems to suggest that the past is just as vividly alive at Mingo as
the present—not only in Uncle Felix's confusion of Dicey with
Daisy, apparently a former love with whom he imagines he is
arranging a tryst, but also in the corner clock which Dicey notices is wrong, or the banjo she sees "hung like a stopped clock"
(p. 134), or a Civil War musket which stands "like a forgotten
broom in the corner."[29] This sense of the past perpetuated into
the present is heightened by the narrator, for Dicey is the kind
of belle one expects in a Sherwood Bonner story: "But I had

only arrived the day before yesterday; and we had of course had
so much to catch up with, besides, necessarily, parties" (p. 112).
The story opens like a scene out of Thomas Nelson Page or
James Lane Allen, with the ladies of the house all "reclining"
after dinner. The narrator Dicey exhibits the same artless com-
petitiveness over beaux, and prejudice against old maids, which
such young ladies displayed in nineteenth-century stories: "Kate
and I were double first cousins, I was the younger, and neither
married yet, but *I* was not going to be an old maid! I was already engaged up North; though I had not yet come to setting a
date for my wedding. Kate, though, as far as I could tell, didn't
have anybody" (p. 113).

Yet from the beginning of the story, equally prominent details emphasize the fact that times *have* changed, that the girls
have grown up, that the former "generation knew more how to
visit" (p. 116). Uncle Felix, after all, has grown so old he is
nearly dead, Aunt Ethel is slowly dying, and even the good
country people gathered at Mingo at the end of the story look
like "passengers on a ship already embarked to sea. . . . Their
faces were like dark boxes of secrets and desires . . . but locked
safely, like old-fashioned caskets for the safe conduct of jewels
on a voyage" (p. 154).

Dicey finally destroys the illusion that the past can remain
unchanged in the present when she fails to observe the rules of
the past. She maliciously attacks Sister Anne, whom the reader
sees as a pathetically lonely old woman vainly trying to provide
herself with some reason for living—even if she must nurse an
endless series of dying relations and must cheerfully do the
chores others refuse. Thus Dicey proves positively that the grace
of the old manner is dead. Having delivered their blows and fled
Mingo, the two cousins Kate and Dicey laugh at the incident
until they can hardly stand. Then Dicey says she noticed the
sweet evening air "I took so for granted once, and when had I
left for ever, I wondered at that moment, the old soft airs of
Mingo as I knew them . . ." (p. 150). Shortly thereafter she says,
"I seemed to reel from a world too fragrant, just as I suspected
Aunt Ethel had reeled from one too loud" (p. 152). It is indeed
the too-fragrant world of the past which Dicey has effectively
obliterated. Reminded of the gracious aunt who used to present
a bouquet of flowers to those leaving Mingo, Dicey murmurs

with tears of laughter running down her cheeks, "I don't remember her" (p. 154). Then the two girls perform the act sever-
ing themselves from the old forms and manners when together they label Sister Anne *common*, and move off thoughtlessly
toward their present concerns, Dicey thinking of her Yankee
sweetheart. Thus Miss Welty seems to suggest that if the old
way of southern life described in long-forgotten local color was
far too sweet to seem real or vital, it still required a grace lacking in today's silliest young ladies who once might have been
portrayed as participating in it.

Apparently a result of the same literary interests which produced "Kin," *Delta Wedding* differs from local color written fifty
years earlier primarily through Miss Welty's concession that life
on a delta plantation, while sweet, is not idyllic. The happy tone
of the novel and the genial tolerance for the foibles of the attractive family portrayed therein, however, allow us validly to
associate the work with more saccharine stories and novels of
southern life preceding it. The small details which are the es-
sence of local color especially mark the first fifty pages. And
while it is difficult to see a purpose beyond the depiction of
local color in *Delta Wedding*, the novel records beautifully a colorful existence which cannot last intact forever. Although the
life Miss Welty portrays undeniably has its share of troubles
and crises, it appears full and rich, primarily because the family
members adhere to one another through mutual love.

The Fairchilds of *Delta Wedding* are remarkable because of
their indestructability. They absorb any newcomer or outsider
without changing their family's essential character. One event
illustrating this trait occasions the novel: Dabney, a Fairchild
daughter, marries her father's overseer Troy Flavin, a hill man
ranking below her socially and economically. But Troy's character is sound, if unromantic, and the Fairchilds finally accept him
for what he is: "He is from the mountains—very slow. . . . He is
not a born gambler of any description."[30] One antagonistic
neighbor considers the Fairchilds "a spoiled, stuck-up family
that thinks nobody else is really in the world!" She adds, "But
they are! You're just one plantation. With a little crazy girl in the
family . . . You're not even rich! You're just medium. Only four
gates to get there, and your house needs a coat of paint!"
(p. 163). As a "medium-rich" and joyously self-confident family,

however, the Fairchilds dominate life in the area and manage, somehow, occasionally to experience happiness themselves. While the novel suggests the local color tradition of the South, it also reveals the alterations a sensitive writer must make when working within that tradition, while still finding valid the tradition's assumption that a certain sweetness characterized life on a plantation.

*The Golden Apples,* on the other hand, uses traditions in a different way. It does present the "typical southerners" of a small town mostly as local color fiction first defined them—still making the most of any excuse to gather, turning even a funeral into a festive occasion, gossiping endlessly about one another, endlessly interested in romance and family connections, and the small events of one another's lives. The town includes such standard characters as a nosy old maid who dispenses unsolicited marital advice in public, and such standard vices as the provincial cruelty which turns the townsfolk against a harmless lady because she is of German origin, belongs to a strange church, never allows herself to be called by her first name, and never marries. Also nostalgically recalled are small-town festivities such as public concert, a recital, a political meeting, or an averted disaster when a camper almost drowns. For these details of background, this presentation of small-town southern life, Miss Welty learned from and relied on the literary tradition of the nineteenth century.

The local colorists' insistence on a fluid social structure within southern society is particularly evident in *The Golden Apples.* Morgana's democratic spirit shines through Mrs. Kate Rainey's prattling as narrator of the first story, "Shower of Gold," and in Miss Kate's funeral in the last story, "The Wanderers." In the first Miss Kate discusses the MacLains, one of the area's oldest families, with the familiarity and condescension of one who is sure of her equal status. Although Miss Kate made money peddling produce and butter around town or beside the road, her funeral in the last story still brings together the whole white population of the town as well as visitors from a distance. The mayor attends, for he is a MacLain twin who once lived across the road. Although the town has clear social ranks, equally clear movement between those ranks is commonplace. Miss Kate is dressed for burying by Snowdie MacLain, "now as at all times a

gentle lady."[31] Miss Lizzie Stark seems the arbiter of propriety
among the women of Morgana; and Miss Lizzie acknowledges
when Kate Rainey dies, "I hope I know what any old woman
owes another old woman. It doesn't matter if it's too late"
(p. 204). Thereupon Mrs. Stark takes over funeral preparations
by sending her maid over to work, complete with instructions
which include ignoring Virgie Rainey, Miss Kate's daughter.

Virgie Rainey represents the best of Morgana—by extension,
the best of the small-town South. Virgie's fate in the volume exemplifies the best to be expected in the town. In "June Recital"
we learn that as a wild and appealing girl Virgie Rainey seemed
to all to have promise, to be gifted, to be destined to accomplish
great things somewhere beyond Morgana's bounds. At the end
of the volume, in "The Wanderers," we see forty-year-old Virgie
still homebound. When her mother's funeral breaks her last
tangible tie to Morgana, leaving her free to wander at last, Virgie
gives away all her possessions but travels no farther than Mac-
Lain, a town seven miles away, where she sits reminiscing in the
rain.

*The Golden Apples,* probably Miss Welty's best work, far sur-
passes the level of most local color. It is a poignant book, suggesting the endless frustration as well as the endless promise of
living within the microcosm of Morgana. A fulfilled dream and a
fruitful life—the golden apples of the title which all live their
lives longing to pluck—are denied as firmly to the homebound
of Morgana as they are to Yeats's Wandering Aengus. While
acknowledging the underlying sadness of *The Golden Apples,*
however, one should not overlook its flashes of the satiric humor
that is Miss Welty's hallmark. Above all else her humor capi-
talizes on provincial grotesquerie: a child at a funeral makes herself a dangling earring by forcing a live lizard to hang from her
earlobe or a Mrs. Flewellyn "caught the last breath of her husband in a toy balloon, by his wish, and had it at home still—
most of it, until a Negro stole it" (p. 213). Rendering such oddities and harmless quirks as observers of small-town life can uncover appears to be the area in which Miss Welty excels most
dramatically as a writer.

In her clearly humorous stories, indeed, Miss Welty's debts
to southern local color become even more obvious. The debts
are important because the stories are important. As Ruth Vande

Kieft correctly implies, there is a sharpening "bite" and a dark-
ening vision in the stories "Lily Daw and the Three Ladies,"
"Why I Live at the P. O." and "Petrified Man."[32] But the humor
of all three originated in local color. Basic to the effects of all
three stories is the attitude permitted the reader, who stands outside the action, observing the absurdity of the characters, and
laughing especially at their ignorance of their own motives, their
extremely provincial outlooks, and their unsophisticated turns
of phrase. The characters embody not only foibles, but also
marked human weaknesses, which the reader remains free to
enjoy because of the very limitations of setting which keep the
character remote from him.

The satire of "Lily Daw" is directed against the three ladies
of the title, self-appointed protectors of morality, who meddle
officiously with the feelings and destiny of another whose
human rights they do not acknowledge, in the interests of preserving respectability and a rigid code of conduct in their town.
The humor is generated by contrasts between the respectable
ladies and the forces they seek to control. They are so obsessed
with sexual matters that they have decided to remove feeble-
minded Lily Daw from the temptations she might either experience or engender among the males of the town. They want to
place her in a mental institution. To their horror they discover
that they are too late, for Lily has apparently been seduced the
preceding night by a member of a traveling show. Torn by having to choose which of several alternatives is most respectable,
the ladies first convince poor Lily that she wants to go to the
Ellisville institution and then that she wants to stay and marry.
The situation becomes more humorous in the series of conversations and incidents in which Lily, though mentally retarded, still
manages to maintain her equilibrium while the ladies are constantly being shaken by facts with which they cannot cope. The
rigid moral code of the ladies is funny because it doesn't control
their consuming interest in sexual possibilities. And such strait-
laced strictness has, of course, been satirized fondly in southern
letters since Richard Malcolm Johnston's first stories. The last
scene of the story is especially revelatory of the origins of such
humor: the whole town, sensing an Event in the departure of
Lily Daw, waits on the train platform. Though Lily is jerked off
the train at the last minute, "The band went on playing. Some of

the people thought Lily was on the train, and some swore she wasn't. Everybody cheered, though, and a straw hat was thrown into the telephone wires."[33]

The knowledge that in a small enough place every personal event takes on a social significance, that private crises and joys are unknown because every incident is seen in a social context, again underlies the humor of "Why I Live at the P.O." In this story the narrator's complaints about the malice of her family reveal her own deeper pettiness. She is funny, as many characters created by local colorists were before her, primarily because she is incapable of doing serious harm and therefore can represent the worst in ourselves, yet evoke laughter, if only because of our superior ability to recognize such unattractiveness. Her reference to her younger sister's add-a-pearl necklace reveals her continuing jealousy and her lack of taste. Her assumption that Shirley-T is Stella-Rondo's daughter—"Stella-Rondo had her just as sure as anything in this world, and just too stuck up to admit it"[34]—suggests the excesses of prudery encouraged in the little hamlet, as well as the gross insensitivity of the narrator to the pathos of such an attitude. The utter selfish childishness of the family becomes clear when Uncle Rondo revenges himself by tossing a string of firecrackers into the narrator's room early one morning. And such revenge indicates another reason for the humor: Sister's victims are as full of petty malice as she is; consequently one feels no obligation to sympathize with them when Sister takes all she owns to the post office, including several items necessary for the family's comfort. The inventive meanness of provincials with limited funds but large imaginations has been a standard subject for southern humor since Longstreet's first *Georgia Scenes.*

"Petrified Man"[35] is surely one of the most effective humorous pieces of recent literature, simultaneously suggesting the frivolity of women and the plight of the males they symbolically emasculate—or petrify into stone. It is, of course, a serious story, but its theme is propelled by wickedly satiric humor. The humor is generated almost entirely by a heightened sense of incongruity, the same basis for the humor of "Why I Live at the P.O." and "Lily Daw." The seemingly aimless chatter of the beauty parlor, for example, fails to correlate with the intensity of passion which such chatter provokes. Mrs. Fletcher's outrage at someone's guessing she is pregnant is amusing because she feels disgraced by a normally happy physical condition. The women's open vindictiveness and anger are funny because of their incongruity with the artificial but ultra-feminine setting. The story proves that the traditional mode of satire in southern literature can be employed in trenchant criticism of modern society. Such satire is not automatically either genial or harmless, and it can serve a deeply serious purpose, if the writer has enough talent to make it work.

An equally serious effort to utilize traditional southern comedy for social commentary is to be traced throughout Miss Welty's recent novel, *Losing Battles.* The title suggests the book's major theme, the source of its intended poignancy: that though the Beecham and Renfro families continue their reunions in the face of every obstacle, their unquestionable solidarity fails to provide a bulwark against the impersonal economic and social forces slowly robbing them of all vestiges of prosperity. The novel certainly captures the pride and the foolishness, the dignity and the ignorance, the narrowness and the depth of mutual concern, the meanness and the love in such provincials. But the overwrought prose in which Miss Welty indulges—the excess of metaphors and similes and descriptive details—seriously mars what was perhaps designed to be her most philosophical work. And finally in her reliance on pettiness and backbiting for humor, she makes the poor but proud southern family too unattractive to sustain interest for the full length of the novel. They are the stuff of which "Why I Live at the P.O." and "Petrified Man" were made. But their types work best in short-story or novella-length pieces.

The possibilities inherent in forms, techniques, and targets of the humor traditional in southern literature are actually tapped best in Miss Welty's *The Ponder Heart.* This short novel is the quintessential product of the plain folk tradition, expertly manipulated by a talented writer. In virtually no respect does it differ in method from those local color stories explored in this study. It is simply the best of the genially comic works produced by southern writers over the years.

Miss Welty's method of narration is the first sign that she is writing within a very well-defined tradition. As in other of her best comic stories such as "Shower of Gold" or "Why I Live at the P.O.," the narrator is a garrulous provincial who has pounced on an unwitting passerby, an outsider who can presumably record her observations for the reader. As in countless other stories this narrator proceeds to spill all the local or family secrets as rapidly and indiscreetly as possible. Initially it is her idiom that is humorous. She uses local expressions which are vividly concrete or which indicate the provinciality of local life—for example, "I could tell by her little coon eyes, she was shallow as they come," or "There's been talk, I hear, of something civic—an arch to straddle the highway with the words in lights, 'Clay. If You Lived Here You'd Be Home Now.'"[37]

A second source of humor is the way in which the narrator unwittingly characterizes herself, becoming even more amusing because of her pretensions to wisdom or sophistication: "People get married beneath them every day, and I don't see any sign of the world coming to an end. Don't be so small-town" (p. 37). As Edna Earle Ponder points out repeatedly, she can't help it if she's so smart. Ineffective malice is always amusing, and Edna Earle has more than her share, which she displays incessantly. Such humor increases when the malice expressed is presented as the average condition of life in the town: "It was a perfectly normal household. Threats flew all the time" (p. 110).

Another familiar source of humor in local color is a discrepancy between the expected and the actual outcome of a train of events. For example, upon taking his son Daniel to the insane asylum to teach him a lesson, Mr. Ponder is incarcerated instead of Daniel, being in the judgment of the new attendant the more insane of the two. But it is Daniel's trial, the dramatic climax of the novel, that proves the culmination of a southern genre of humor—the courtroom scene—begun by southwestern humorists. Virtually every detail in Miss Welty's hilarious account can be traced to a precedent in nineteenth-century southern fiction. The affair begins with references to the heat and the unruly audience who have come to see the show. Mrs. Peacock, though maternal head of the family bringing murder charges against Uncle Daniel Ponder, is much more interested in making casual conversation with those sitting around her than she is in the finer points of the law. On order Miss Welty produces a casual judge, familiar enough with the defense attorney to address him by his first name, who soon gives up trying to maintain order in the

court. Next comes the series of more or less ignorant witnesses
who enjoy being the center of public attention, who perform
with zest and garrulity, who surrender the witness chair with
reluctance, but who if angered by the lawyer questioning them
speak their minds emphatically, regardless of protocol. Edna
Earle herself is proud of her performance and receives congratulations on it afterward: "I never lied in my life before that I
know of, by either saying or holding back, but I flatter myself
that when the time came, I was equal to either one" (p. 143).
The trial is marked by legal irregularities—the judge himself interrupts the proceedings to take dinner orders by a show of
hands, and eats his meal with Edna Earle, the chief witness for
the defense, at the witness's hotel. The defendant fires his own
lawyer and hires the prosecuting attorney to represent him, but
then brings his own case to a successful conclusion by bribing
not only the jury but also the entire courtroom, including the
spectators. Other standardized features include the "uppity"
outside lawyer who is defeated by the local, homespun boy and
the jury which is stacked with relatives of the defense attorney.
Throughout, of course, the happy outcome of the trial is assured.
But one could trace in *The Ponder Heart* nearly every humorous
device native to nineteenth-century southern fiction, for Miss
Welty's novel is designed, as was earlier local color, to amuse
and entertain. Although satiric barbs are directed at the culture
of which Edna Earle serves as spokesman (the coroner is blind;
the inmate of an asylum is allowed visits home to vote; the hotel
—center of the town's active life—boasts twelve rooms), the satire
remains genial.

No twentieth-century author has shown a more thorough
knowledge of traditional southern literature, or a more conscious
willingness to use whatever is helpful or amusing from that literature, than Eudora Welty. Miss Welty's undeniable originality
and talent often lie, in fact, in her skillful adaptation of older
motifs to more contemporary structures and narrative techniques. Particularly in her humorous work her debt to the older
writers who first defined "southern" is obviously great. She has
consciously created works which remain in the mainstream of
native southern fiction.

While Eudora Welty uses the details, situations, character
types, and motifs from the literature of the nineteenth century

to give a semblance of authenticity to her southern stories, and uses such traditions in a wide variety of ways, Flannery O'Connor narrows her focus almost exclusively to that group which can be identified as plain folk. Then she eviscerates their pretensions and dissects all she finds false about their values. To accomplish this devastation, of course, she must have a firm idea of what such folk are like. Thus she, as much as, or more than, any other writer, depends upon the definitions which she obsessively reveals to be false or inadequate. Recognizing her use of the plain folk tradition, with its assumptions about the typical southerner, his values and attitudes, his pleasures and antipathies, is a prerequisite for understanding Miss O'Connor's work; for by showing in virtually every story that some aspect of the tradition is false, she creates the ironic tone which dominates her style.

One also finds not only a remarkably consistent tone in Miss O'Connor's work, but also a uniformity of character types and settings. The majority of the characters in her stories are independent farm owners and their children, whose lives are struggles, to be sure, but who manage to maintain standards of living which they themselves consider decent. The settings of her best stories are these moderately-prosperous southern farms, and a remarkably large number of her characters are middle-aged women who run such farms with the aid of tenants. The women almost invariably voice the convictions of the society in which they live. And such convictions are the "standardized" ones associated with southern farmers since the local color period.

The major mark of a plain folk character as the local colorists drew him was his pride in himself. While Miss O'Connor takes a pointedly ironic view of such pride, it often dominates her protagonists. The speech patterns and opinions of the grandmother in "A Good Man Is Hard to Find" clearly reveal her to be less than aristocratic, for they are all pointedly vulgar. Yet she dresses and behaves as she feels the best group of southerners would surely do: "Her collars and cuffs were white organdy trimmed with lace and at her neckline she had pinned a purple spray of cloth violets containing a sachet. In case of an accident, anyone seeing her dead on the highway would know at once that she was a lady."[38] The same unquestioning sense of personal dignity enrages Julian, in "Everything That Rises Must

Converge," when his mother states, "Of course . . . if you know who you are, you can go anywhere. . . . I can be gracious to anybody. I know who I am."[39]

The southerner's pride in his family and his vanity about his relations gives Miss O'Connor the opportunity for some of her most sardonic humor. The tenant farmer's wife in "A Circle in the Fire," for example, explains as the story opens that a neighborhood woman who contrived to conceive and deliver a baby while in an iron lung "was a Pritchard that married a Brookins and so's kin to me—about my seventh or eighth cousin by marriage."[40] The same ironies are obvious in "A Late Encounter with the Enemy," when a profane, pretentious, and vain old man, who does nothing unless he can be the center of attention, becomes the focus of his sixty-two-year-old granddaughter's fantasies about his glory, which she will stand reflected in at her college graduation: "She meant to stand on that platform in August with the General sitting in his wheel chair on the stage behind her and she meant to hold her head very high as if she were saying, 'See him! See him! My kin, all you upstarts!'"[41]

Next to his pride in his own personal dignity and his family, the plain man was most proud of the accomplishments he had achieved through hard work. Miss O'Connor develops this theme too, in order to give pride in work the ironic twist her vision demands. The sentimental and unprincipled handyman in "The Life You Save May Be Your Own," for example, "said he had fought and bled in the Arm Service of his country and visited every foreign land and that everywhere he had seen people that didn't care if they did a thing one way or another. He said he hadn't been raised thataway."[42] But this hypocritical stranger withers no more before Miss O'Connor's irony than does the self-respecting Mrs. May, in "Greenleaf," who knows "Before any kind of judgment seat, she would be able to say: I've worked, I have not wallowed."[43]

While Flannery O'Connor leaves her readers in no doubt that her characters' analyses of their lives are short-sighted, the characters themselves see work in much the same terms as their literary forebears. It is the panacea for imaginary illness in "The Enduring Chill": "She knew that if he would get in there now, or get out and fix fences, or do any kind of work—real work, not writing—that he might avoid this nervous breakdown."[44] Work is also the avenue to upward social mobility. In "Greenleaf" Mrs. May frets constantly over the progress of her handyman's two sons: "They were energetic and hard-working and she would admit to anyone that they had come a long way—and that the Second World War was responsible for it." As Mrs. May tells her own two far less industrious sons, "and in twenty years . . . do you know what those people will be? *Society. . . .*"[45]

Belief in the personal progress which work, coupled with common sense, makes possible is as integral a part of the attitudes of Miss O'Connor's characters as of those of nineteenth-century southern fiction, though Miss O'Connor's stories make equally clear her convictions that such beliefs are amusing or absurd. The worried mother in "The Enduring Chill" thinks:

> When people think they are smart—even when they are smart— there is nothing anybody else can say to make them see things straight, and with Asbury, the trouble was that in addition to being smart, he had an artistic temperament. She did not know where he had got it from because his father, who was a lawyer and business- man and farmer and politician all rolled into one, had certainly had his feet on the ground: and she had certainly always had hers on it. She had managed after he died to get the two of them through college and beyond; but she had observed that the more education they got, the less they could do. Their father had gone to a one-room schoolhouse through the eighth grade and he could do anything.[46]

The kind of progress one can expect a southerner to recognize who considers hard work the path leading straight to a golden future is defined in "A View of the Woods" as synonymous with the crassest materialism. The sign of a "progressive" man's initiative, in the view of the property owner in this story, is the clutter of billboards announcing to highway motorists the steadily lessening distance to his business establishment. "He was an up-and-coming man—the kind, Mr. Fortune thought, who was never just in line with progress but always a little ahead of it so that he could be there to meet it when it arrived."[47] As a sign of faith in this kind of Progress, Mr. Fortune sells the lot in front of his house to the neighbor, to use for a filling station. His country common sense leads Mr. Fortune to realize that cutting off his porch view is unimportant: "A pine trunk is a pine trunk,

. . . and anybody that wants to see one don't have to go far in this neighborhood" (p. 70).

The same outlook which makes him value the progressive moves of his neighbor also make Mr. Fortune take a democratic view of others: "If his daughter thought she was better than Tilman, it would be well to take her down a little. All men were created free and equal" (p. 71). Such democratic spirit in "The Displaced Person" leads Mr. Shortley to argue for the firing of the foreign worker on the grounds that he creates a situation prejudicial to the rights of Mr. Shortley: "All men was created free and equal . . . and I risked my life and limb to prove it."[48] Finally the democratic attitudes Mrs. Hopewell cultivates in "Good Country People" are the basis for her pathetically short-sighted assessment of an itinerant Bible salesman. Mrs. Hopewell mistakenly assumes that the salesman, who characterizes himself as a "country boy," will have the same virtues she chooses to recognize in her tenants, the Freemans: "Mrs. Hopewell liked to tell people that Glynese and Carramae were two of the finest girls she knew and that Mrs. Freeman was a *lady* and that she was never ashamed to take her anywhere or introduce her to anybody they might meet. Then she would tell how she happened to hire the Freemans in the first place and how they were a godsend to her and how she had had them four years. The reason for her keeping them so long was that they were not trash. They were good country people."[49] Thus Miss O'Connor seems to imply that a blindly optimistic, democratic refusal to evaluate others can have as unfortunate results as a blindly pessimistic, undemocratic assessment of others.

As we have seen, one of the paradoxes of southern literature is that it insists on a democratic society while preserving the conventions associated with a socially rigid society in which whites must be classified as aristocrats or trash. Paradoxically those of a middle category are often the most class-conscious. Such contradictions provide Flannery O'Connor with the occasion and subject for extensive ironic commentary on southern society. Mrs. McIntyre of "The Displaced Person," for example, describes her employees by using the traditional categories: "The people she hired always left her—because they were that kind of people. Of all the families she had had, the Shortleys were the best if she didn't count the Displaced Person. They had been not quite trash. . . ."[50] The narrator explains that "Mrs. Shortley could listen to . . . [conversation about trash] with composure because she knew that if Mrs. McIntyre had considered her trash, they couldn't have talked about trashy people together. Neither of them approved of trash" (p. 208).

This assurance of social superiority shared by Mrs. McIntyre and Mrs. Shortley tortures Mrs. May of "Greenleaf" when she must admit that her handyman's boys are superior to her own. At one point she falls back weakly on the defense, "Well, no matter how far they go, they *came* from that."[51] Mrs. May signals her final defeat when in a weak moment she concedes to her own sons, "O. T. and E. T. are fine boys. . . . They ought to have been my sons" (p. 36). The class consciousness Julian's mother reveals in "Everything That Rises," when she proudly reviews their family history, protects her from facing the unpleasant implications of their living in a decaying neighborhood, just as Mrs. Shortley's class pride keeps her at first from considering the Guizacs a serious threat to herself in "The Displaced Person." As in other cases such pride in class appears ironically inappropriate, whatever character exhibits it.

Other attitudes associated with the southern plain folk also surface in Miss O'Connor's work, again with a uniformly ironic result. One finds, for example, the prejudice against Catholics which makes Asbury's requesting a priest to converse with so delicious a way of persecuting his mother in "The Enduring Chill." Or southern ladies exhibit their friendliness by striking up conversations with strangers, thereby infuriating their more anti-social offspring, in "Everything That Rises" or "Revelation." The conflict between farm and town and the assumption that rural life is purer while city life is more exciting (and probably more wicked) are basic to "The Artificial Nigger," "A Stroke of Good Fortune," *Wise Blood,* and *The Violent Bear It Away.* The belife that a respect for women constitutes a true gentleman explains the worth of the Greenleaf boys, who won't allow their mother to perform unpleasant chores at night, and conversely reveals that Thomas is not the gentleman he considers himself in "The Comforts of Home." In each of these works Flannery O'Connor reveals the ironies inherent in southern attitudes and culture. But in order to develop such irony, she accepts the definitions of *southern* current since the nineteenth century.

The themes and background Miss O'Connor explores most frequently reveal the same inversion for ironic effect that one notices in her characterizations. Perhaps the most sentimental element of southern local color is its portrayal of the happy families—the members doting fondly on one another—which populated the South during the Old Regime. Conversely the relationship most frequently examined in Miss O'Connor's work is the conflict between two generations of the same family. Indeed it appears that in her stories no child of any age can get along with his guardian or parent.

Another theme sacrosanct to nineteenth-century southern literature, of course, was the racial harmony and understanding possible in the South, primarily because its whites and blacks loved each other. In Miss O'Connor's reversal of this theme those whites who assume the conventional stance of gracious condescension to Negroes (such as Julian's mother in "Everything That Rises") are struck down by resentful blacks, either actually or psychologically. One of the funniest of such scenes occurs in "The Enduring Chill," when Asbury, seeking to annoy his mother by assuming a false intimacy with her black employees, calls the farm hands to his bedside in order to tell them goodbye before dying. He thus enacts a grotesque parody of the most sentimental southern local color, a parody which comes off so badly that Asbury is finally forced to call on his mother for help in ending it. In "Judgment Day," when the old man of the story behaves in New York as he would have in Georgia, he offends the Negro living next door so deeply that the black kills him. So much, Miss O'Connor seems to say, for the possibilities of racial understanding—and so much for the southern myth that such harmony is part of a southern pattern.

Even more fundamental or inclusive southern myths receive the same ironic treatment. Perhaps the most sacred of these myths centers about the beauty of the Old Way of Life before the War between the States—a myth Miss O'Connor thoroughly ridicules in several stories—perhaps most thoroughly in "A Late Encounter with the Enemy." Here an old man who participated in the Civil War as a boy—though he does not remember the war at all, much less his own part in it—is given a military uniform, dubbed a general, and introduced for the commercial benefit of a movie premiering in Atlanta. Although the vain old man loves such attention, and loves posing as an embodiment of southern nobility, the story suggests his total inadequacy for the role. If the "general" represents the southerner's systematic falsification of the past, his small grandson—who apparently cares only about Coca-Colas—represents the hope of the future. Thus the combination of the two underscores the irony of a commencement speaker's clichés: "If we forget our past, . . . we won't remember our future and it will be as well for we won't have one."[52]

In several stories well-meaning people are destroyed because of their adherence to Old Southern Values. The grandmother in "A Good Man Is Hard to Find" gets her whole family killed, for example, when she persuades them to turn off the main highway to look for a decaying old plantation mansion which she remembers belatedly was located in Tennessee, if indeed it ever existed anywhere. In "The Comforts of Home" a mother's insistence on acting in a manner consistent with her position of gentility finally destroys both her and her son.

All the assumptions about the genteel manners of southerners are contradicted by the violence that Flannery O'Connor presents as a central fact of southern life, as did southern writers of the previous century. In truth Miss O'Connor's work seems to consist of proportionately more violent episodes than any other southerner's. She especially associates such violence with southern fundamentalist Protestantism, perhaps because violence committed in the name of the Prince of Peace is the most ironic variety. At any rate both her novels and several of her best stories explore the violence which appears to be a natural outgrowth of the fierce, self-denying, hell-fearing fundamentalism which has dominated the South.[53]

The view of life such fundamentalism fosters is described in "Parker's Back." Sarah Ruth, the wife of the story, is daughter of "a Straight Gospel preacher . . . [who] was away, spreading it in Florida":[54] "One of the things she did not approve of was automobiles. In addition to her other bad qualities, she was forever sniffing up sin. She did not smoke or dip, drink whiskey, use bad language or paint her face, and God knew paint would have improved it, Parker thought" (p. 220). Miss O'Connor's view of rural religion seems directly related to the similarly critical or satiric attitude in southwestern humor sketches such as William Penn Brannan's "The Harp of a Thousand Strings," or in local color sketches such as Sherwood Bonner's "Sister Weeden's Prayer" or Will Harben's "The Heresy of Abner Calihan."

Even for those characters who do not concern themselves unduly with religious matters, however, religion remains important either because it institutionalizes middle-class virtues, as in "Greenleaf," or because it provides a reason for gathering socially, as in "The Displaced Person." In "Greenleaf" Mrs. May thinks of herself as "a good Christian woman with a large respect for religion, though she did not, of course, believe any of it was true."[55] But she feels confident that she can truthfully tell a prayer-healer, who moans and sways over buried newspaper clippings of disasters, "Jesus . . . would be *ashamed* of you. He would tell you to get up from there this instant and go wash your children's clothes" (p. 31). In "The Displaced Person" Mrs. Shortley "had never given much thought to the devil for she felt that religion was essentially for those people who didn't have the brains to avoid evil without it. For people like herself, for people of gumption, it was a social occasion providing the opportunity to sing. . . ."[56] However little Mrs. Shortley has analyzed her beliefs, she still condescends to Mr. Guizac's Catholicism, being sure "that these people did not have an advanced religion" (p. 202). As a matter of fact the violence occurring at the end of "The Displaced Person" is given pointedly religious implications when Mrs. McIntyre makes such comments as "As far as I'm concerned . . . Christ was just another D. P." (p. 243), or "I'm a logical practical woman and there are no ovens here and no camps and no Christ Our Lord . . ." (p. 245). In Miss O'Connor's stories, then, the social functions of southern churches appear as important a part of the institutions as they do in southern local color.

The plain folk tradition furnishes Flannery O'Connor with a systematic depiction of southern life which she can systematically examine for falseness or ironic contradictions. Because her themes are so somber, her view of life so sardonic, readers may easily overlook the elements of humor leavening virtually all of Miss O'Connor's fiction. It is such a tendency to take her work too earnestly that Miss O'Connor warned against in her note to the second edition of *Wise Blood:* "This book was written with zest and if possible, it should be read that way. It is a comic novel about a Christian *malgré lui. . . ."*

Though blacker than that of many southerners, Miss O'Connor's humor, like Faulkner's and Miss Welty's, is similar to that of nineteenth-century southern works. Basically it springs from a sense of the vulgar and grotesque. In such humor the author and reader share an aloof, condescendingly amused attitude toward the characters. In *Wise Blood,* for example, Enoch Emery's reading the legend above a building in the park as "Muvseevum" is, after all, the kind of mistake one associates with Bill Williams of Dukesborough. Readers who accept Miss O'Connor's characters in their vulgarity, without being appalled by their destructiveness, can still find them amusing in the traditional way.

One of Miss O'Connor's best stories exemplifies virtually every aspect of her uses of the plain folk tradition. "Revelation" illustrates her views of southern society as well as her literary methods, in a sense summarizing her debt to the past. The major character of the story perfectly exemplifies the southern plain woman. Mrs. Turpin occupies a stable, if commonplace, niche in the community; and she has achieved economic and social security through the prosperous little farm that she operates with her husband Claud. In the spectrum of southern society collected within the doctor's office setting of the first half of the story, she occupies a middle point: admittedly she lives with less prestige than the well-dressed woman with whom she talks, but she remains also confidently superior to the family she labels "trash." Social categories are an obsession with Mrs. Turpin, for she confuses economic and spiritual worth:

> Sometimes Mrs. Turpin occupied herself at night naming the classes of people. On the bottom of the heap were most colored people, not the kind she would have been if she had been one, but most of them; then next to them—not above, just away from—were the white-trash; then above them were the home-owners, and above them the home-and-land owners, to which she and Claud belonged. Above she and Claud were people with a lot of money and much bigger houses and much more land. But here the complexity of it would begin to bear in on her, for some of the people with a lot of money were common and ought to be below she and Claud and some of the people who had good blood had lost their

money and had to rent and then there were colored people who
owned their homes and land as well. There was a colored dentist in
town who had two red Lincolns and a swimming pool and a farm
with registered white-faced cattle on it.[57]

When such categorizing becomes complicated, Mrs. Turpin significantly escapes into sleep, but then has nightmares in which
all classes seem to burn in gas ovens, the earthly equivalent of
hell. In other words a confusion of social classes frightens Mrs.
Turpin because it threatens her sense of personal worth, which
is related in turn to her sense of her spiritual value and her
goodness.

In an attitude which is "typically" paradoxical Mrs. Turpin
insists that her own worth is determined by her personal character and accomplishments, while she believes with equal assurance in the existence of certain "classes" into which she can
automatically divide others. At the bottom of the white social
ladder she positions the trash, whom she labels because of their
appearance and manners. In the doctor's office Mrs. Turpin clas-
sifies and dismisses one set of characters because they appear to
belong in this group: "She could tell by the way they sat—kind
of vacant and white-trashy, as if they would sit there until
Doomsday if nobody called and told them to get up." One of
the group is "a lank-faced woman. . . . She had on a yellow
sweat shirt and wine-colored slacks, both gritty-looking, and the
rims of her lips were stained with snuff. Worse than niggers any
day, Mrs. Turpin thought" (p. 194).

Mrs. Turpin's smug self-satisfaction, particularly her loudly
announced gratitude that she was created as and who she is,
makes her intolerable to the ugly college girl who attacks her.
Thus Mrs. Turpin's joyful self-love leads directly to the revelation which crushes her: that she is like a wart-hog from hell.
Mrs. Turpin especially resents the vicious epithet's application
to her when "there was trash in the room to whom it might
justly have been applied. The full force of this fact struck her.
. . . There was a woman there who was neglecting her own
child but she had been overlooked. The message had been given
to Ruby Turpin, a respectable, hard-working, church-going
woman" (p. 210).

It is precisely Ruby Turpin's pride in her virtues, of course, which has made her obnoxious. As she thinks of herself, "To help anybody out that needed it was her philosophy of life. She never spared herself when she found somebody in need, whether they were white or black, trash or decent" (p. 202). Mrs. Turpin's virtues are in effect the standard virtues of the southern plain folk. But her story suggests that their pride in personal worth and beauty must be "burned away" before she and her kind—all the proud plain folk of southern fiction—can trail the rest of the saints into the kingdom of Heaven. Her final apocalyptic vision suggests Miss O'Connor's assessment of the plain people Ruby Turpin represents: "They were marching behind the others with great dignity, accountable as they had always been for good order and common sense and respectable behavior. They alone were on key. Yet she could see by their shocked and altered faces that even their virtues were being burned away. . . . In the woods around her the invisible cricket choruses had struck up, but what she heard were the voices of the souls climbing upward into the starry field and shouting hallelujah" (p. 218).

# *Conclusion*

*JOEL CHANDLER HARRIS* once wrote in the Chicago *Current*, "I think . . . that no novel or story can be genuinely American, unless it deals with the *common people*, that is, the *country people*."[1] Harris himself was one of the many southern local colorists who put this opinion into practice, who made it their business to record not only the world of the southern plantation but also the world of the plain folk—the common, ordinary country people who farmed their land and lived their lives unremarkably in the South during the nineteenth century. The respect which Harris, the professional conciliator of North and South, felt for this group of people is evident in his considering them the most genuinely American subjects available to the writer of fiction.

Even when local colorists were more interested in exalting distinctly southern over more national topics, however, they still turned for their material to the sizable body of plain folk which the South had always supported. Predictably they took sympathetic views of these commoners, for their writing often seemed to follow directly from the premise that all things southern were necessarily good. Out of their stories emerged a distinct, clear and detailed stereotype of the South's plain folk, as well as a record of the economic and social facts which described the typical southerner. The stories made clear that the plain folk lived on economic levels that varied extensively. Yet their worth was not directly related to their income, for social status was accorded on the basis of good character. And good character was determined by the possession of four major traits—pride, courage, common sense, and a willingness to work.

The record of the typical southerner which local colorists drew up was so detailed that it included not only the salient features of his character but also the important events of his life. Basically he considered any activity important which could serve as an excuse to gather a group together. He valued such gatherings because he normally lived isolated from others by the distances between farms and between small towns. Next to getting together with others the plain man loved sharing his roof with passersby and hearing the gossip which circulated around each neighborhood and which generally involved some romantic complication or development. But that average southerner had a less genial and easygoing side to his character, too, and could easily take offense at opinions expressed which differed from his own, or could even, under duress, lapse into violence.

The writers who portrayed plain folk almost invariably relied on stereotypes in populating their stories. The local color period, in fact, was historically important because so many stereotypes—and refinements of stereotypes—were added to southern literature. Though they wrote of aristocrats, local colorists soon turned their attention to the plain folk who were capable of a greater variety of action than aristocrats could indulge in. Soon the larger, more general plain folk stereotype broke down into subtypes, based on geographical locations. Thus the plain folk of the eastern seaboard—the Carolina tarheel and Georgia cracker—form one variety of plain folk, while the mountaineer formed another, and the Arkansas provincial a third. While most southerners were of Anglo-Saxon origin, the Acadians of French peasant stock, living on the Louisiana prairies, became still another variety of plain folk, distinguished by their national origin and their Catholic religion as well as the geographical location of their homes. But perhaps the most interesting plain folk type of all is the Creole, whom Cable first delineated as an aristocrat and then reduced to plain folk status.

Usually local colorists refused to question or criticize any aspect of southern society. But George Washington Cable, who so often was an exception to any rule fitting local colorists, wrote one good novel of pointed social criticism, *John March, Southerner.* Unsparingly dissecting southern life, institutions, morals, and manners, the novel implicated all southerners, including plain folk, in its indictments. For the most part, however, southern local colorists preferred that their works reflect the more pleasant aspects of the southern scene. To put as happy a face on matters as possible, writers often resorted to highly colored, verbose prose to describe idyllic scenes. Taking no chances that a character might appear odd, they also deemphasized characterization and utilized a narrative technique which functioned to keep the reader as far as possible from a knowledge of darker or more complex southern psyches. This technique included using double narrators to give to southern stories the semblance of an "oral" tradition and incorporating humorous incongruities. Many episodes were amusing because they made plain folk seem unintentionally funny. In so far as experimentation occurred at all in stories involving plain folk, it dealt with narrative technique and with symbolism based on natural scenes or settings.

Writers of the nineteenth century as well as historians of the twentieth recognized that the great majority of southerners, from the first years of the South's settlement onward, were neither rich aristocrats nor worthless white trash. Instead most southerners fell into a middle category, the outlines of which were constantly changing because the society was a very mobile and fluid one. Southern local colorists described this middle group of citizens often enough that before the nineteenth century was over, such descriptions had been standardized and a detailed literary tradition had emerged. Such a tradition inevitably affected the work of more recent southern writers. Three such writers—Faulkner, Eudora Welty, and Flannery O'Connor—all gained from the older literature a sense of what southern characters are apt to think or do as well as a sense of the most effective methods by which to present certain types of comic action. Recognizing this fact, perhaps students of contemporary literature can better comprehend the ideas that such selfconsciously southern writers bring to their work—ideas about their region and themselves.

# *Notes*

*THROUGHOUT THIS BOOK,* works which have been fully identified once will be cited thereafter only by title in the notes. When the context of my discussion makes a reference clear, page numbers to it will be given parenthetically. For full bibliographical details concerning primary sources, see the selected bibliography which follows.

## *Chapter I*

1. *Crumbling Idols: Twelve Essays on Art and Literature* (Gainesville, 1952), p. 64. Most of Garland's best work, of course, such as the stories in *Main-Travelled Roads,* must be classified as something other than local *color* because the stated purpose is to capture the *colorlessness* and ugliness of the locale—not its charm, beauty, or amusing qualities.

2. Bret Harte, Constance Fenimore Woolson, Alice French, Albion Tourgée, George W. Cable, and Joel Chandler Harris all wrote of areas in which they were not natives.

3. For a good summary of the relationship between the magazines and the writing of southern local color fiction, see Paul H. Buck, *The Road to*

*Reunion* (Boston: Little, Brown, 1938), pp. 220–228.

4. Most of the generalizations in the preceding discussion were formulated by Clarence Gohdes in *The Literature of the American People,* ed. Arthur Hobson Quinn (New York: Appleton-Century-Crofts, 1959), pp. 639–660.

5. *Crumbling Idols,* p. 58.

6. Claude M. Simpson, ed., *The Local Colorists: American Short Stories, 1857–1900* (New York: Harper, 1960), pp. 12–15.

7. Ibid., p. 10.

8. "The South as a Field for Fiction," *Forum,* 6 (December 1888), 405.

9. *The Literature of the American People,* p. 652.

10. This victory was no doubt made easier by the attitude of northern novelists toward the South in the years directly following the end of the

Civil War. Joyce Appleby read 400 novels written from 1865 to 1880 to discover what feelings toward the defeated South dominated writers from the victorious region. She concluded: "The puzzling fact remains that this body of fiction, with its marked spirit of charity toward the South, is a direct challenge to our idea of Northern hostility in the postwar period" ("Reconciliation and the Northern Novelist, 1865–1880," *Civil War History*, 10, 1964, 128).

11. *The Road to Reunion*, p. 219.

12. *Bricks Without Straw* (New York, 1880), p. 307.

13. The basis for such opinion is catalogued by Buck in *The Road to Reunion*.

14. *Origins of the New South: 1877–1913* (Baton Rouge: Louisiana State University Press, 1951), p. 154.

15. *The Southern Plantation: A Study in the Development and the Accuracy of a Tradition* (1924; rpt. Gloucester, Mass.: Peter Smith, 1962), p. 18.

16. *Cavalier and Yankee: The Old South and American National Character* (New York: Braziller, 1961), pp. 15–65.

17. *Origins of the New South*, p. 154.

18. *Pretty Mrs. Gaston and Other Stories* (New York, 1874), p. 26.

19. *In Ole Virginia, or Marse Chan and Other Stories* (New York, 1887), p. 6.

20. *A Golden Wedding and Other Tales* (New York, 1900), p. 81.

21. *The Southern Poor-White from Lubberland to Tobacco Road* (Norman: University of Oklahoma Press, 1939), p. xx.

22. *Origins of the New South*, pp. 109–110.

23. *Life and Labor in the Old South* (New York: Grosset & Dunlap, 1929), p. 340.

24. *Plain Folk of the Old South* (Baton Rouge: Louisiana State University Press, 1949), pp. 7–8.

25. *William Faulkner: The Yoknapatawpha Country* (New Haven: Yale University Press, 1963), p. 13.

26. Ibid., p. 11.

27. *The Southern Poor-White*, p. 106.

## Chapter II

1. *With the Bark On: Popular Humor of the Old South* (Nashville, 1967), p. 11.

2. Ibid., p. 48.

3. "The Fate of Pleasure," *Beyond Culture: Essays on Literature and Learning* (New York: Viking, 1965), pp. 57–87.

4. New York, 1957, p. 1.

5. *Streaks of Squatter Life, and Far-West Scenes* (Gainesville, 1962), p. 38.

6. Hennig Cohen and William B. Dillingham, eds., *Humor of the Old Southwest* (Boston, 1964), p. 303.

7. Ibid., p. 304.

8. *The Flush Times of Alabama and Mississippi* (New York, 1853), p. 93.

9. *Humor of the Old Southwest*, p. 220.

10. Ibid., p. xiii.

## Chapter III

1. Compare the elaborate class structure Mrs. Stowe attributes to her small community of Oldtown in *Oldtown Folks*, ed. Henry F. May (Cambridge, Mass., 1966), pp. 93–95.

2. Ruth McEnery Stuart, *Holly and Pizen and Other Stories* (New York, 1899), p. 195.

3. *Northern Georgia Sketches* (Chicago, 1900), p. 52.

4. *A Golden Wedding*, p. 311.

5. *The Primes and Their Neighbors: Ten Tales of Middle Georgia* (New York, 1891), p. 14.

6. Ibid., p. 52.

7. "Simon Becomes Captain," *Humor of the Old Southwest*, p. 228.

8. *The Primes and Their Neighbors*, p. 10.

9. Richard Malcolm Johnston, *Little Ike Templin and Other Stories* (Boston, 1894), p. 146.

10. Dukesborough Tales, *Harper's Franklin Square Library*, no. 290 (January 12, 1883), p. 53. Johnston published his first book, *Georgia Sketches*, in 1864 and reissued it in 1871 as *Dukesborough Tales*. It was enlarged and reissued by Turnbull Brothers of Baltimore in 1874. The edition used here contains sixteen stories, six more than in other available editions. A later edition comprised of the six best of these stories was published in 1892 and reprinted in the Americans in Fiction Series, ed. Clarence Gohdes (Ridgewood, N.J., 1968), No. 28.

11. *Otto the Knight and Other Trans-Mississippi Stories* (Boston and New York, 1891), p. 319.

12. *Bonaventure: A Prose Pastoral of Acadian Louisiana* (New York, 1901), p. 9.

13. Ibid., pp. 5–6.

14. *Northern Georgia Sketches*, p. 18.

15. *Mingo and Other Sketches in Black and White* (Boston, 1884), pp. 49–50.

16. *In the Tennessee Mountains* (Boston and New York, 1884), pp. 196–197.

17. *Bayou Folk* (Boston and New York, 1894), p. 194.

18. *A Night in Acadie* (Chicago, 1897), p. 190.

19. Acadians of French peasant stock were described by means of a positive stereotype discussed in Chapter VII.

20. *Bayou Folk*, p. 84.

21. Ibid., p. 223.

22. *Mingo*, p. 238.

23. Ibid., p. 239.

24. *The Wife of His Youth and Other Stories of the Color Line* (Boston and New York, 1899), p. 60.

25. *A Fool's Errand*, ed. John Hope Franklin (Cambridge, Mass., 1961), p. 99.

26. *Free Joe and Other Georgian Sketches* (New York, 1888), p. 73.

27. *The Phantoms of the Foot-bridge and Other Stories* (New York, 1895), pp. 6, 8.

28. *Northern Georgia Sketches*.

29. *A Night in Acadie*.

30. *Pretty Mrs. Gaston*.

31. "Mr. Bill Williams Takes the Responsibility," *Dukesborough Tales*.

32. *Elsket and Other Stories* (New York, 1896).

33. *Tales of the Home Folks in Peace and War* (Boston and New York, 1898), p. 385.

34. *Rodman the Keeper: Southern Sketches* (New York, 1880).

35. *Otto the Knight*, p. 1.

36. *Mingo*.

37. Owsley, *Plain Folk of the Old South*, p. 36. One finds even in the local color of Vermont an occasional character with respectable status (such as Roland Robinson's Sam Lovel) who is still primarily a hunter long after hunting has been rejected as an occupation by the community at large: " 'It does beat all natur' what cussed, foolish idees folks hes com tu hev abaout huntin' bein' low daown an' goo' fer nothin'. Don't they know 't huntin' was half folkses livin' in ol' times an' larnt 'em tu fight Injins as well as other varmints?' " (*Danvis Folks*, Boston and New York, 1894, p. 81).

38. "Up in the Blue Ridge" by Constance Fenimore Woolson, collected in *Rodman the Keeper* (1880), and five sketches by Sherwood Bonner, collected in *Dialect Tales* (1883).

39. Published in *Century Magazine* (May–June 1883) and collected in *Mingo* (1884).

40. This theme also appears in one of the first of Simon Suggs's adventures, "Simon Gets a 'Soft Snap' out of His Daddy." "The Reverend Mr. Suggs had once in his life gone to Augusta; an extent of travel which in those days was a little unusual. His consideration among his neighbors was considerably increased by the circumstance, as he had all the benefit of the popular inference, that no man could visit the city of Augusta without acquiring a vast superiority over all his untravelled neighbors, in every department of human knowledge" (*Humor of the Old Southwest*, p. 212).

41. *Old Times in Middle Georgia* (New York, 1898), p. 143.

42. *Mingo*, p. 238.

## Chapter IV

1. *Tales of the Home Folks*, p. 186.

2. *Oldtown Folks*, pp. 440, 93.

3. F. Hopkinson Smith, *Colonel Carter of Cartersville* (Boston and New York, 1893), p. 10.

4. Though such an attitude is certainly more to be expected in the West, Mark Twain mentions the same militantly democratic outlook among the communities described in *Roughing It*: "Those people hated aristocrats" (*The Complete Travel Books of Mark Twain*, ed. Charles Neider, Garden City, Hanover House, 1966, p. 691).

5. *Little Ike Templin*, p. 238.

6. *Bayou Folk*, p. 294.

7. "The Mortgage on Jeffy," *Otto the Knight*, p. 327.

8. *His Defense and Other Stories* (New York, 1969), p. 2.

9. *Balaam and His Master, and Other Sketches and Stories* (Boston and New York, 1891), p. 15.

10. *Mingo*, pp. 239–240.

11. *The Primes and Their Neighbors*, p. 11.

12. *Old Times in Middle Georgia*, p. 174.

13. *Little Ike Templin*, p. 43.

14. *Old Times in Middle Georgia*, pp. 14–15.

15. *Tales of the Home Folks*, p. 377.

16. Ibid.

17. "Among the peculiarly English ideas which the colonists brought to Massachusetts, which all the wear and tear of democracy have not been able to obliterate, was that of *family*. Family feeling, family pride, family hope and fear and desire, were, in my early days, strongly-marked traits" (*Oldtown Folks*, p. 258).

18. *A Fool's Errand*, p. 141.

19. Ibid., p. 157.

20. *Rodman the Keeper*, p. 319.

21. *Northern Georgia Sketches*, p. 13.

22. Harry Stillwell Edwards, *Two Runaways and Other Stories* (New York, 1922), p. 135.

23. *Mingo*, pp. 11–13.

24. *In the Tennessee Mountains*, p. 186.

25. Ibid., p. 132.

26. Ibid., p. 134.

27. *The Wife of His Youth*, p. 88.

28. *In Beaver Cove and Elsewhere* (New York, 1892), p. 18.

29. *Dialect Tales* (New York, 1883), pp. 149–150.

30. Ibid., p. 165.

31. Nor are they the exclusive property of southern writers. Mary E. Wilkins Freeman's "Catherine Carr" portrays a heroine almost identical to her courageous southern counterparts. The war, of course, is the American Revolution, but the plot seems Confederate: a clever aristocratic maid saves her home, her love, and her town by common sense, strategy, and courage, and outwits the English in successive encounters. See *The Love of Parson Lord and Other Stories* (Freeport, N.Y., 1969). Bret Harte also develops a western version of this stereotype in "M'liss: An Idyl of Red Mountain," *The Writings of Bret Harte* (Boston and New York, 1906).

32. *The Burial of the Guns* (New York, 1894), p. 27.

33. *Dukesborough Tales*, p. 91.

34. Ibid., p. 66.

35. In their portrayal of communities which assume the value of work, southern writers appear most similar to their New England counterparts. According to Harriet Beecher Stowe, "Work, thrift and industry are such an incessant steam-power in Yankee life, that society would burn itself out with intense friction were there not interposed here and there the lubricating power of a decided do-nothing...." Another character believes that "the purpose and aim of human existence were comprised in one word—work" (*Oldtown Folks*, pp. 74, 138).

36. For a neatly summarized explanation of the phrase and its implications, see Rod W. Horton and Herbert W. Edwards, "Progress: The American Dream," *Backgrounds of American Lit-*

*erary Thought* (New York: Appleton-Century-Crofts, 1952), pp. 72–73.

37. *The Library of Southern Literature* (Atlanta: Martin & Hoyt, 1907), v, 2112.

38. Ibid., p. 2113.

39. *Tales of the Home Folks*, p. 186.

40. *Otto the Knight*, p. 319.

41. Ibid., p. 176.

42. *Free Joe*, p. 170.

43. *Plain Folk of the Old South*, p. 36.

44. *In the Tennessee Mountains*, p. 183.

45. *Otto the Knight*, p. 23.

46. *The Primes and Their Neighbors*, p. 186. Johnston's autobiography recounts his college years, interrupted because of his poor health: "I was ready for the sophomore class half advanced, but my father saw fit to detain me at home for a year, and required me to work with the negroes four days in the week—from Monday morning to Thursday night. On Fridays and Saturdays I was allowed to hunt with my guns and dogs." He adds, "I hated it" (*Autobiography*, Washington, 1901, p. 27).

47. *Northern Georgia Sketches*, p. 287.

48. Ibid., p. 204.

49. *Flute and Violin: and Other Kentucky Tales and Romances* (New York, 1898), p. 100.

50. *Elsket*, pp. 66–67.

51. *Northern Georgia Sketches*, p. 53.

52. Ibid., p. 52.

53. Warping bars are instruments used to prepare yarn for weaving. The story is from *The Young Mountaineers* (Boston and New York, 1898).

54. *In Beaver Cove.*

55. *Mingo*, p. 242.

56. *The Burial of the Guns*, p. 10.

57. *In the Tennessee Mountains*, pp. 167–168.

58. *Old Times in Middle Georgia*, pp. 71–72.

59. *Two Runaways*, p. 76.

60. "A Born Inventor," *Two Runaways.*

61. "The Woman's Exchange of Simpkinsville," *A Golden Wedding*, p. 324.

62. *Dialect Tales*, p. 57.

63. When one remembers the increasing dependence on a one-crop system—usually cotton or tobacco—in the rural areas of the South, he can understand why the social structure would have to be fluid. W. J. Cash refers to "ravenous cotton" as a "voracious plant" (*The Mind of the South*, New York: Knopf, 1941, pp. 35, 382). Cotton could exhaust rich land in a matter of twenty years or so, and this fact militated against the establishment of wealthy old families who lived on one plantation for several generations. Ulrich Phillips explains in great detail that the cotton planter's only recourse, in the eastern seaboard states, was to fertilize extensively. "Reclamation, in fact, was done in Virginia and Maryland in the middle decades of the nineteenth century, with soiling crops and fertilizers, to such an extent as to bring a genuine rejuvenation of those old commonwealths" (*Life and Labor in the Old South*, p. 137). The primary settings for stories of the plain folk, however, are not Virginia and Maryland but Georgia, North Carolina, Arkansas, Louisiana, and the Tennessee mountains. According to Phillips, "The process of restoring soils lagged somewhat in the lower South, whether because the pinch of need was not as yet so sharply felt or because the call of the cotton West was more alluring to the cotton East" (p. 137). He adds that Georgia (the setting for more local color stories than any other state) was already suffering the consequences of improvident planting by 1830, when the South was just beginning to grow self-conscious. By 1830 lands directly bordering the Gulf of Mexico already furnished more cotton than the Atlantic seaboard sections; by 1860 the coastal areas along the Gulf furnished three of the four million bales produced by the United States (p. 104). With these facts in mind we can see why the Georgia social structure was anything but aristocrat-dominated, and why Georgia writers remembered it as "the most democratic region, socially, in the world" (*Tales of the Home Folks*, p. 186). The influence of the Georgia writers, not only of the southwestern humorist Longstreet but also of the popular Joel Chandler Harris, communicated that democratic vision of southern society to other local colorists who found it useful for their own work.

64. Stories portraying the friendly terms on which aristocrats and plain folk live side by side include Richard Malcolm Johnston's "Old Friends and New" (*Dukesborough Tales*), "The Two Woollys" (*Little Ike Templin*), Harris's "Little Compton" (*Free Joe*), Alice French's "Otto the Knight" (*Otto the Knight*), and Constance Woolson's "Up in the Blue Ridge" (*Rodman the Keeper*).

65. Plain folk and white trash visit sociably in Johnston's "Oby Griffin" (*Little Ike Templin*), address each other with familiarity in Harben's "The Whipping of Uncle Henry" (*Northern Georgia Sketches*), and treat each other with both tolerance and tact in Harris's "Azalia" (*Free Joe*).

66. *A Night in Acadie*, p. 130.

67. *Bayou Folk.*

68. *Mingo*, p. 21.

69. The blame for racial violence in the South has always been put on white trash. For example, a southerner writing for a popular publication said in discussing Neshoba County, Mississippi, after the murder there of three civil rights workers, "Many of [Sheriff Lawrence] Rainey's active supporters are the people called 'white trash' by the more independent farmers and middle-class townspeople, but the present crisis has made him 'the big man' not just for the poor whites but for the whole county" (Reese Cleghorn, "The Two Faces of Sheriff Rainey," *The New York Times Magazine*, February 21, 1965, p. 11). Yet the popular stereotype of white-trash emphasized either their "Indian-like content" (McIlwaine, *The Southern Poor-White*, p. xx) or their "burnt-out faces" which reveal "no hope for the future" (*Free Joe*, p. 177). In either case their total passivity is stressed. When a figure like Harris's Mrs. Bivins reveals passionate feeling, whether it is directed against the "Big-bugs" or the Negroes, she is no longer pas-

sive enough to be a convincing representative of the poor-white stereotype. What we have in Mrs. Bivins' case, as we will see, is resentment which not only erupts verbally, but also leads to positive (and according to Mingo, successful) efforts to improve her own situation. If Mrs. Bivins is able to save a little money each year, she is in effect no longer a poor white, but a rising member of the plain folk. Her antipathy towards Negroes is convincing because she has so fierce a concept of her own dignity. One who considers the matter will realize that the racial antagonism which leads to violence stems not from totally defeated poor whites, but from plain folk. According to a team of sociologists making a detailed study of the South: "Examples of the effect of class behavior in modifying caste controls were frequently seen in the case of lower-class whites and Negroes. In many instances it was noticed that lower-class whites living in Negro neighborhoods treated their Negro neighbors in much the same way as they did their white neighbors.... Evidences of neighborly relations were also apparent in comments by whites of rural areas.... Middle-class whites, on the other hand, even though living near Negroes, never developed neighborly relations and were generally antagonistic" (Allison Davis, Burleigh B. Gardner, Mary R. Gardner, *Deep South*, Chicago, 1941, pp. 30–52). Such facts perhaps explain why there are so few stories by local colorists which explore the relationship between plain folk and Negroes.

70. McIlwaine, p. xx.

71. The poor whites in "Free Joe," for example, conform completely to the stereotype, as do the Stuckeys in "Azalia."

## Chapter V

1. This category includes most local colorists except the Louisiana writers—Cable, Mrs. Chopin, Grace King, and Mrs. Stuart. Grace King lived part of her childhood in New Orleans, but was sent to an isolated plantation during the Civil War. Only Mrs. Chopin and Cable produced works with individualized characters.

2. *Mingo*, p. 238.

3. *The Primes and Their Neighbors*, p. 85. A remarkably similar Vermont militia day is described in Robinson's *Danvis Folks*, pp. 267–282.

4. Woodward, *Origins of the New South*, p. 61.

5. Constance Cary Harrison, *Crow's Nest and Belhaven Tales* (New York, 1892), p. 121.

6. *Bonaventure*, p. 58.

7. Woodward, p. 61.

8. Ibid., p. 400.

9. Page 37. Similar examinations are described in Bret Harte's "M'liss," *Writings*, pp. 268–269, and in Edward Eggleston's *The Hoosier School-Master* (New York, 1871), pp. 39–55.

10. *Oldtown Folks*, p. 88.

11. *Little Ike Templin*, p. 48. "The middle and lower classes, or nearly three-fourths of Southern

church-goers, in 1860 were Methodists and Baptists. The aristocratic churches were Episcopal and Presbyterian, although the former represented only about five percent of the church membership. Religion, especially among the masses, was a force of almost medieval intensity, and the churches were active in disciplining members and in enforcing creeds" (John Samuel Ezell, *The South Since 1865*, New York, 1963, p. 342).

12. *Mingo*, p. 238.

13. *Old Times in Middle Georgia*, p. 131.

14. *Northern Georgia Sketches*.

15. *Elsket*, p. 156.

16. *Northern Georgia Sketches*, p. 28.

17. *The Conjure Woman* (Boston and New York, 1899), p. 120.

18. "The Cause of the Difficulty," *Tales of the Home Folks*, p. 355.

19. *Old Times in Middle Georgia*, p. 205.

20. *Dialect Tales*, p. 86.

21. Ibid., p. 54.

22. *In the Tennessee Mountains*, p. 251.

23. Ibid., p. 182.

24. *The Phantoms of the Foot-bridge*.

25. *In the Tennessee Mountains*, p. 95.

26. The same kind of humor is also central to Harriet Beecher Stowe's "Laughin' in Meetin'," *Sam Lawson's Oldtown Fireside Stories* (Boston and New York, 1881).

27. *The Primes and Their Neighbors*.

28. *Holly and Pizen*.

29. *Two Runaways*.

30. Ibid., p. 60.

31. *The Burial of the Guns*, p. 20.

32. See *With the Bark On* for several excellent examples of early courtroom humor sketches. The humorous or irregular court scene may also be found in such western local color as Twain's *Roughing It*, pp. 584–587, or Bret Harte's "Tennessee's Partner," *Writings*, pp. 44–47.

33. *Old Times in Middle Georgia*, p. 186.

34. *The Primes and Their Neighbors*.

35. *Mingo*, p. 238.

36. *His Defense*.

37. *Elsket*.

38. *His Defense*, p. 6.

39. *The Phantoms of the Foot-bridge*.

40. *Northern Georgia Sketches*.

41. *In Beaver Cove*, p. 148.

42. *Otto the Knight*, p. 239. Arkansas prison scandals publicized in the spring of 1968 suggest that the statement may still be accurate.

43. *Balaam and His Master*, p. 115.

44. *Two Runaways*.

45. *The Wife of His Youth*, p. 87.

46. *In the Tennessee Mountains*, p. 51.

47. Ibid., p. 299.

48. The Thanksgiving feasting which Mrs. Stowe describes in loving detail in *Oldtown Folks* appears the equivalent ritual of the southern Christmas.

49. *Tales of the Home Folks*, p. 5.

50. *Little Ike Templin*, p. 157.

51. Ibid., p. 166.

52. *Solomon Crow's Christmas Pockets, and Other*

*Tales* (New York, 1898). Half the stories in this volume are resolved by the happy influence of Christmas.

53. *In Ole Virginia.*
54. *The Burial of the Guns.*
55. *Tales of a Time and Place* (New York, 1892).
56. *Otto the Knight.*
57. *Northern Georgia Sketches.*
58. *A Golden Wedding.*
59. *Holly and Pizen.*
60. *Solomon Crow's Christmas Pockets.*
61. *Old Times in Middle Georgia.*
62. *Little Ike Templin.*
63. *Bonaventure*, p. 68.
64. *Dukesborough Tales*, pp. 66–67.
65. *A Cumberland Vendetta and Other Stories* (New York, 1896).
66. *Dialect Tales*, p. 158.
67. The Southern Baptist Convention as a whole adopted no statement condemning dancing until 1921. At the convention in Chattanooga, Tennessee, the Social Service Commission reported on many things, among them "the Modern Dance": "Another gross and growing evil must be mentioned. It is the modern dance. One of the most serious and menacing byproducts of the World War is the great increase in the dance evil, and the extravagant extremes to which it has gone. Accompanied, as it is, by immodest dress, by close physical contact of the sexes, by its lack of restraint, it is undoubtedly doing much to undermine the morals of our young people. It is beyond question, that in many cases it leads to moral wreck and ruin. The time has come when, from every pulpit, strong and persistent protest must be made.... Your Commission would appeal, with all possible emphasis, to all our people, especially to the pastors and parents, that this growing menace shall be checked and abolished" ("13th Annual Report of the Commission on Social Service, Southern Baptist Convention, 1921," presented by A. J. Barton of Louisiana, p. 83). Church minute books, however, give accounts of individuals being turned out of the churches throughout the nineteenth century for dancing, card playing, gambling, sexual immorality, etc.
68. S. G. Hillyer, *Reminiscences of Georgia Baptists* (Atlanta: Foote & Davies, 1902), pp. 178–180.
69. *Dukesborough Tales.*
70. *The Primes and Their Neighbors.*
71. *Dukesborough Tales.*
72. *His Defense.*
73. *Flute and Violin.*
74. *In the Tennessee Mountains*, pp. 81–82.
75. *Dr. Sevier* (Boston, 1885), p. 345.
76. *Otto the Knight*, p. 265.
77. *A Fool's Errand*, p. 57.
78. *In the Tennessee Mountains*, p. 179.
79. Ibid., p. 158.
80. *New York Times*, February 22, 1965, p. 42.
81. *Free Joe*, p. 4.
82. *Flute and Violin*, p. 100.
83. *Free Joe*, p. 165.

84. New York, 1894, p. 1.
85. Discussed by Louis D. Rubin in "The Road to Yoknapatawpha: George W. Cable and John March, Southerner," *The Faraway Country: Writers of the Modern South* (Seattle: University of Washington Press, 1963).
86. Ibid., p. 42.

## Chapter VI

1. Foreword, *Main-Travelled Roads* (New York and London, 1899).
2. Willa Cather, ed., *The Best Stories of Sarah Orne Jewett* (Gloucester, Mass., 1965), pp. 257–258.
3. Ibid.
4. *Oldtown Folks*, p. 137.
5. Mary E. Wilkins Freeman, "Christmas Jenny," *A New England Nun, and Other Stories* (New York, 1891), p. 173.
6. "To attempt a portrayal of that era and that land, and leave out the blood and carnage would be like portraying Mormondom and leaving out polygamy" (*Roughing It*, p. 646).
7. *Deephaven* (Boston, 1877), p. 198.
8. *Dukesborough Tales.*
9. *Old Times in Middle Georgia*, p. 10.
10. *In the Tennessee Mountains*, p. 163.
11. *Dialect Tales*, p. 166.
12. Ibid., p. 174.
13. *The Phantoms of the Foot-bridge.*
14. Arlin Turner, ed., *Creoles and Cajuns: Stories of Old Louisiana* (Garden City, 1959), p. 189. This volume includes all the stories originally published in *Old Creole Days* (1879) as well as "Madame Delphine," the long story later added to the revised edition of Cable's stories. Since the stories are helpfully printed in the order in which they first appeared, it has seemed best to use this edition in the present study.
15. *The Grandissimes: A Story of Creole Life* (New York, 1957), p. 153. The first installment of this novel was published in 1879.
16. *Creoles and Cajuns*, p. 65.
17. *Little Ike Templin*, pp. 112–113.
18. *In the Tennessee Mountains*, p. 139.
19. *Free Joe*, p. 55.
20. *Crow's Nest and Belhaven Tales*, p. 147.
21. "The Woman's Exchange of Simpkinsville," *A Golden Wedding*, pp. 331–332.
22. *A Fool's Errand*, p. 119.
23. *Mingo*, p. 239.
24. *Old Times in Middle Georgia*, p. 42.
25. *Dukesborough Tales*, p. 39.
26. Ibid., p. 47.
27. *Two Runaways*, p. 131.
28. *Balaam and His Master*, p. 157.
29. *Free Joe*, p. 30.
30. Ibid.
31. *Tales of the Home Folks.*
32. *Balaam and His Master.*
33. *Rodman the Keeper.*
34. "The lover is always abject. Obedience to his lady's lightest wish, however whimsical, and

silent acquiescence in her rebukes, however unjust, are the only virtues he dares to claim. There
is a service of love closely modelled on the service
which a feudal vassal owes to his lord. The lover
is the lady's 'man'. . . . Only the courteous can love,
but it is love that makes them courteous (C. S.
Lewis, *The Allegory of Love*, New York: Oxford
University Press, 1958, p. 2).

35. A fact Constance Woolson noted with
annoyance: "In former days the South had a
literary taste of its own unlike anything at the
North. It was a careful and correct taste, founded
principally upon old English authors; and it
would have delighted the soul of Charles Lamb,
who, being constantly told that he should be more
modern, should write for posterity, gathered his
unappreciated manuscripts to his breast, and declared that henceforth he should write for
antiquity. Nothing more unmodern than the old-
time literary culture of the South could well be
imagined; it delighted in old editions of old
authors; it fondly turned their pages, and quoted
their choice passages; it built little libraries here
and there . . . and loaded their shelves with fine
old works . . . These Southern collections were
not for the multitude; there was no multitude.
Where plantations met, where there was a neighborhood, there grew up the little country library. . . . The books were generally imported, an
English rather than a New York imprint being
preferred; and without doubt, they selected the
classics of the world. But they stopped, generally,
at the end of the last century, often at a date still
earlier; they forgot that there may be new classics" (*Rodman the Keeper*, p. 284).

36. *Old Times in Middle Georgia*, p. 224.

37. The attitude Colonel Carter expresses still
has some currency: "Not long ago, Justice Tom P.
Brady of the Mississippi Supreme Court was
. . . the philosopher of Mississippi's racist White
Citizens' Councils and the polemical author of
*Black Monday*, a Negro-baiting tract attacking the
U.S. Supreme Court's 1954 school desegregation
decision. Brady, then a state Circuit Court judge,
insisted that . . . 'The loveliest and the purest of
God's creatures, the nearest thing to an angelic
being that treads this terrestrial ball is a well-
bred, cultured Southern white woman, or her
blue-eyed, golden-haired little girl' " (*Time*, October
22, 1965, pp. 94–95).

38. *Rodman the Keeper*.

39. *Old Times in Middle Georgia*.

40. *In the Tennessee Mountains*.

41. *The Primes and Their Neighbors*.

42. *Little Ike Templin*, p. 146.

43. *Dukesborough Tales*, p. 54.

44. *Rodman the Keeper*, p. 246.

45. *Old Times in Middle Georgia*, p. 174.

46. *Holly and Pizen*.

47. *The Burial of the Guns*, p. 12.

48. *Free Joe*, p. 31.

49. *A Fool's Errand*, p. 179.

50. *Mingo*, p. 237.

51. *The Wife of His Youth*, p. 269.

52. *Rodman the Keeper*, p. 309–310.

53. *Mingo*, p. 43.

54. *Hell fer Sartain and Other Stories* (New York,
1897), p. 56.

55. Woodward, *Origins of the New South*, pp.
158–159.

56. Ibid., pp. 159–160.

57. *Free Joe*, p. 31.

58. *Dialect Tales*, p. 11.

59. *Suwannee River Tales* (Boston, 1884), p. 201.

60. *Mingo*, p. 114.

61. *Colonel Carter*, p. 23.

62. *A Fool's Errand*, p. 255.

## Chapter VII

1. When they appear at all, it is usually in
the work of the New England women—Mary E.
Wilkins Freeman, Sarah Orne Jewett, and Harriet
Beecher Stowe.

2. *A Cumberland Vendetta*, p. 12.

3. *Hell fer Sartain*, p. 101.

4. Woodward, *Origins of the New South*, p. 299.

5. *Balcony Stories*.

6. *Dialect Tales*, p. 172.

7. *Tales of the Home Folks*.

8. *Free Joe*.

9. *Mingo*.

10. *Hell fer Sartain*, p. 57.

11. *A Cumberland Vendetta*.

12. *A Curtain of Green* (Garden City, 1941),
pp. 21–32.

## Chapter VIII

1. *Creoles and Cajuns*, p. 2. Since all of Cable's
Creole stories are collected in this volume, I will
not cite the volume again in this chapter.

2. Arlin Turner, *George W. Cable: A Biography*
(Durham: Duke University Press, 1956), p. 203.

3. *The Creoles of Louisiana* (New York, 1889),
p. 41.

4. Ibid., p. 42.

5. Ibid., p. 1.

6. *The Creoles of Louisiana*, p. 25.

7. Grace King, *Memories of a Southern Woman
of Letters* (New York, 1932), p. 60.

8. *The Creoles of Louisiana*, p. 167.

9. *The Grandissimes*, p. 181.

10. Ibid., p. 188.

11. Ibid., p. 19.

12. "Café des Exilés," p. 150.

13. *The Grandissimes*, p. 72.

14. *Dr. Sevier*, p. 284.

15. *The Grandissimes*, p. 192.

16. "'Sieur George," p. 53.

17. "Café des Exilés," p. 150.

18. *The Grandissimes*, p. 105.

19. Ibid., pp. 153–154.

20. Ibid., p. 36.

21. "'Tite Poulette," p. 81.

22. *Dr. Sevier*, p. 5.

23. "'Sieur George," pp. 49, 50, 52.

24. "'Tite Poulette," p. 80.

25. "Jean-ah Poquelin," p. 106.

26. "Posson Jone'," p. 181.

27. "'Tite Poulette," p. 83.

28. *The Creoles of Louisiana*, p. 42.

29. "'Sieur George," p. 48.

30. *George W. Cable* (New York: Twayne, 1962), p. 33.

31. Ibid., p. 31.

32. Ibid., p. 33.

33. Turner, p. 103.

34. Ibid., p. 104.

35. *The Writings of Lafcadio Hearn*, 16 vols. (Boston and New York: Houghton, Mifflin, 1923), I, 45–45.

36. That such a stereotype as the Creole does not automatically loosen its grip on the imagination because time passes, literary style changes, and a new philosophy gains currency is suggested by the work of Tennessee Williams. Williams more recently employed the type in forming Blanche DuBois in *A Streetcar Named Desire*. Though some details have changed drastically, Blanche remains a character whose literary origins go back at least as far as Cable's *Old Creole Days*. Although Blanche is from Mississippi, her French name, her aristocratic upbringing on the family plantation, and the setting of the play in the French Quarter of New Orleans link her with the Creoles. Once again the setting is a seedy, decaying neighborhood occupied by the poorest element of society, including among the residents a former aristocrat, Blanche's sister Stella. The difference between the two sisters is that Stella is happy here with her husband, Stanley Kowalski, while Blanche, like the many fictional Creole ladies before her, is determined to hold on to the outward graces and customs which typified the old way of life.

Belle Rêve, the "beautiful dream" which was the family plantation, has been lost "bit by bit," in "typically Creole" style, by the "epic fornications" of Blanche's ancestors. Yet Blanche, the lady, maintains her dignity even in her total defeat at the end of the play. She manages at last to evoke the respect of Kowalski and his cloddish companions: with the exception of the disillusioned Mitch, the card players in Stanley's apartment pay their respects, for the first time, by standing awkwardly as Blanche makes her last exit. Conventions have changed by Williams' time, and Blanche is now viewed as the victim of her compulsions. Even her nymphomania, however, has resulted from her valiant fight against crushing circumstances. When Blanche tells of her struggle to keep the plantation, and to nurse her dying relatives, she says, "Death ... death was as close as you are.... We didn't dare even admit we had ever heard of it!... The opposite is desire. So do

you wonder? How could you possibly wonder!" (Scene Nine).

*Streetcar* also contains traces of the old opposition between Creoles and Americans. Blanche's antagonist is Stanley Kowalski, whom she identifies with the apes and once calls a Polack. Stanley replies, "I am not a Polack. People from Poland are Poles, not Polacks. But what I am is a one hundred percent American, born and raised in the greatest country on earth and proud as hell of it, so don't ever call me a Polack" (Scene Eight).

It would be absurd to suggest that the heroine of Williams' famous play owes her dramatic power to the Creole stereotype. Yet we can see the shadow in the drama of Cable's romantic Creole stereotype, somewhat more "naturalistically" reformed to fit the requirements of the present. Thus the stereotypes which seem composed entirely of papier-mâché in the nineteenth century begin to seem the realities of the twentieth.

37. A third woman, Ruth McEnery Stuart, also included in her stories some Creole characters. Her Creoles are so vaguely aristocratic and otherwise so undistinguished, however, that it has seemed unnecessary to discuss them separately in this chapter.

38. *Memories of a Southern Woman of Letters*, p. 60.

39. Ibid., p. 61.

40. Ibid.

41. Quoted in Daniel S. Rankin, *Kate Chopin and Her Creole Stories* (Philadelphia: University of Pennsylvania Press, 1932), p. 4.

42. *Tales of a Time and Place*, p. 278.

43. "'Sieur George," p. 48.

44. *Balcony Stories*, p. 14.

45. Ibid., p. 205.

46. *The Grandissimes*, p. 31.

47. *Balcony Stories*, p. 198.

48. *Bricks Without Straw*, p. 164.

49. *Balcony Stories*.

50. Ibid.

51. *Bayou Folk*.

52. Ibid.

53. Ibid.

54. *A Night in Acadie*.

55. Chicago and New York, 1899, p. 145.

## Chapter IX

1. *Mark Twain and Southwestern Humor* (Boston: Little, Brown, 1959), p. 64.

2. Ibid., p. 68.

3. *Mingo*, p. 3.

4. *The Primes and Their Neighbors*, p. 187.

5. Examples are "Mutual School-Masters" (*Old Times in Middle Georgia*) and "Travis and Major Jonathan Wilby" (*The Primes and Their Neighbors*).

6. *Georgia Scenes*, p. 50.

7. *Dukesborough Tales*, p. 91.

8. Ibid., p. 8.

9. *Tales of a Time and Place*, p. 6.

10. *A Night in Acadie.*

11. While her first biographer heard nothing from her neighbors about Kate Chopin's personal life but "data beyond reproach," and her second biographer found nothing further (Per Seyersted, *Kate Chopin,* Baton Rouge: University of Louisiana Press, 1969, p. 71), one still cannot help suspecting an autobiographical element in these stories. Mrs. Chopin also wrote another story, "A Respectable Woman" *(A Night in Acadie),* in which a wife is tempted to love one to whom she is not married. In both "Athénaïse" and "A Respectable Woman" the man who almost becomes the matron's love is Gouvernail, a journalist who never holds it against his friends of either sex that they are married. It is interesting that Gouvernail appears momentarily for no apparent reason in *The Awakening.* While every other character has a definite function in the plot, Gouvernail is simply mentioned as a dinner guest of Edna's on the night she gives a banquet for her closest friends. The banquet celebrates Edna's final breaking away from her husband.

12. *A Night in Acadie.*

13. *Otto the Knight.*

14. *The Primes and Their Neighbors.*

15. *Dialect Tales,* p. 48.

16. Ibid., pp. 10–11.

17. Muriel Spark's "You Should Have Seen the Mess," Bernard Malamud's "Black is My Favorite Color," Ring Lardner's "You Know Me Al," and "The Golden Honeymoon" make clear, however, that southerners have no special corner on this technique.

18. Butcher, *George W. Cable,* p. 31.

19. *Mingo,* p. 132.

20. *Old Times in Middle Georgia,* p. 186.

21. *Dialect Tales,* p. 43.

22. *Two Runaways,* p. 86.

23. *Tales of the Home Folks,* p. 376.

24. *Dukesborough Tales,* p. 66.

25. *Free Joe,* p. 105.

26. *His Defense.*

27. *Solomon Crow's Christmas Pockets, A Golden Wedding.*

28. *Solomon Crow's Christmas Pockets.*

29. *Dialect Tales.*

30. *Little Ike Templin.*

31. *Two Runaways.*

## Chapter X

1. *Intruder in the Dust* (New York, 1948), p. 27.

2. *Sartoris* (New York, 1929), p. 20.

3. *Yoknapatawpha: Faulkner's "Little Postage Stamp of Native Soil"* (New York: Fordham University Press, 1969), pp. 249–250.

4. *As I Lay Dying* (New York, 1957), p. 363.

5. *The Hamlet* (New York, 1957), p. 5.

6. *The Town* (New York, 1957), p. 280.

7. Ibid., p. 307.

8. Ibid., p. 276.

9. Ibid., p. 41.

10. *The Hamlet,* pp. 4–5.

11. Ibid., p. 13.

12. Ibid., p. 372.

13. Ibid., p. 68.

14. *The Town,* p. 106.

15. *The Mansion* (New York, 1959), p. 87.

16. *The Town,* p. 33.

17. *The Hamlet,* p. 322.

18. Faulkner once told a friend that he ranked Anderson's "I'm a Fool" and Conrad's "Heart of Darkness" as "the two finest stories he had ever read" (Carvel Collins, ed., *William Faulkner: New Orleans Sketches,* New Brunswick: Rutgers University Press, 1958, p. 18).

19. *Absalom, Absalom!* (New York, 1936), p. 241.

20. *Selected Stories of Eudora Welty* (New York, 1943).

21. *The Bride of the Innisfallen, and Other Stories* (New York, 1955), p. 21.

22. "Place in Fiction," *Three Papers on Fiction* (Northampton, Mass., 1962), p. 5.

23. *Selected Stories.*

24. *The Bride of the Innisfallen.*

25. *Selected Stories.*

26. Ibid.

27. *The Bride of the Innisfallen,* p. 91.

28. Ibid., p. 115.

29. *A Season of Dreams: The Fiction of Eudora Welty* (Baton Rouge: Louisiana State University Press, 1965), pp. 240–241.

30. *Delta Wedding* (New York, 1945), p. 85.

31. *The Golden Apples* (New York, 1949), p. 215.

32. *Eudora Welty* (New York: Twayne, 1962), p. 72.

33. *Selected Stories,* p. 20.

34. Ibid., p. 98.

35. Ibid.

36. *Losing Battles* (New York, 1970).

37. *The Ponder Heart* (New York, 1954), pp. 35, 155.

38. *A Good Man Is Hard To Find and Other Stories* (New York, 1955), p. 11.

39. *Everything That Rises Must Converge* (New York, 1965), p. 6.

40. *A Good Man,* p. 130.

41. Ibid., p. 156.

42. Ibid., p. 57.

43. *Everything That Rises,* p. 51.

44. Ibid., p. 88.

45. Ibid., p 33.

46. Ibid., p. 87.

47. Ibid., p. 67.

48. *A Good Man,* p. 247.

49. Ibid., p. 170.

50. Ibid., p. 224.

51. *Everything That Rises,* p. 32.

52. *A Good Man,* p. 166.

53. The relationship of such fundamentalism to Miss O'Connor's fiction has been thoroughly explored by Louis D. Rubin, Jr., in "Flannery O'Connor and the Bible Belt," in *The Added Dimension: The Art and Mind of Flannery O'Connor,* ed. Melvin J. Friedman and Lewis A. Lawson (New York: Fordham University Press, 1966), pp. 49–72.

54. *Everything That Rises*, p. 229.
55. Ibid., p. 31.
56. *A Good Man*, p. 210.
57. *Everything That Rises*, pp. 195–196.

## Chapter XI

1. Julia Collier, ed., *Joel Chandler Harris, Editor and Essayist* (Chapel Hill: University of North Carolina Press, 1931), p. 182.

# Selected Bibliography
# of Primary Sources

Allen, James Lane. *Flute and Violin: and Other Kentucky Tales and Romances.* New York: Harper, 1898. (First published in 1891.)

Anderson, John Q., ed. *With the Bark On: Popular Humor of the Old South.* Nashville: Vanderbilt University Press, 1967.

Baldwin, Joseph G. *The Flush Times of Alabama and Mississippi: A Series of Sketches.* New York: D. Appleton, 1853.

Bonner, Sherwood [Katherine Sherwood Bonner McDowell]. "A Volcanic Interlude," *Lippincott's Magazine,* 25 (April 1880), 452–459.

———. *Dialect Tales.* New York: Harper, 1883.

———. *Suwanee River Tales.* Boston: Roberts, 1884.

Cable, George Washington. *Bonaventure.* New York: Scribners, 1901. (First published in 1888.)

———. *Creoles and Cajuns: Stories of Old Louisiana.* Edited by Arlin Turner. Garden City: Doubleday, 1959. (*Old Creole Days* was first published in 1879; "Madame Delphine," in 1881.)

———. *The Creoles of Louisiana.* New York: Scribners, 1889.

———. *Dr. Sevier.* Boston: Osgood, 1885.

———. *The Grandissimes: A Story of Creole Life.* New York: Sagamore, 1957. (First published in 1880.)

———. *John March, Southerner.* New York: Grosset & Dunlap, [1894].

Chesnutt, Charles W. *The Conjure Woman.* Boston and New York: Houghton, Mifflin, 1899.

———. *The Wife of His Youth and Other Stories of the Color Line.* Boston and New York: Houghton, Mifflin, 1899.

Chopin, Kate. *The Awakening.* Chicago and New York: Herbert S. Stone, 1899.

———. *A Night in Acadie.* Chicago: Way & Williams, 1897.

———. *Bayou Folk.* Boston and New York: Houghton, Mifflin, 1894.

Clemens, Samuel Langhorne. *The Complete Travel Books of Mark Twain.* Edited by Charles Neider. Garden City: Hanover House, 1966. (*Roughing It* was first published in 1872.)

Cohen, Hennig and William B. Dillingham, eds. *Humor of the Old Southwest.* Boston: Houghton, Mifflin, 1964.

Cooke, John Esten. *Pretty Mrs. Gaston and Other Stories.* New York: O. Judd, 1874.

Crim, Matt. *In Beaver Cove and Elsewhere.* New York: C. L. Webster, 1892.

Edwards, Harry Stillwell. *His Defense and Other Stories.* New York: Garrett, 1969. (First published in 1899.)

———. *Two Runaways and Other Stories.* New York: Century, 1922. (First published in 1889.)

Eggleston, Edward. *The Hoosier School-Master.* New York: O. Judd, 1871.

Faulkner, William. *Absalom, Absalom!* New York: Random House, 1936.

———. *As I Lay Dying.* New York: Random House, 1957. (First published in 1930.)

———. *The Hamlet.* New York: Random House, 1940.

———. *Intruder in the Dust.* New York: Random House, 1948.

———. *The Mansion.* New York: Random House, 1959.

———. *Sartoris.* New York: Harcourt, Brace, 1929.

———. *The Town.* New York: Random House, 1957.

Fox, John, Jr. *A Cumberland Vendetta and Other Stories.* New York: Harper, 1896.

———. *Hell fer Sartain and Other Stories.* New York: Harper, 1897.

Freeman, Mary E. Wilkins. *A New England Nun, and Other Stories.* New York: Harper, 1891.

———. *The Love of Parson Lord and Other Stories.* Freeport, N.Y.: Books for Libraries Press, 1969. (First published in 1900.)

French, Alice [Octave Thanet]. *Otto the Knight and Other Trans-Mississippi Stories.* Boston and New York: Houghton, Mifflin, 1891. (First published in 1882.)

Garland, Hamlin. *Crumbling Idols: Twelve Essays on Art and Literature.* Gainesville, Fla.; Scholars' Facsimiles & Reprints, 1952. (First published in 1894.)

———. *Main-Travelled Roads.* New York and London: Macmillan, 1899.

Harben, Will N. *Northern Georgia Sketches.* Chicago: A. C. McClurg, 1900.

Harris, Joel Chandler. *Balaam and His Master and Other Sketches and Stories.* Boston and New York: Houghton, Mifflin, 1891.

———. *Free Joe and Other Georgian Sketches.* New York: Scribners, 1888.

———. *Mingo and Other Sketches in Black and White.* Boston: J. R. Osgood, 1884.

———. *Tales of the Home Folks in Peace and War.* Boston and New York: Houghton, Mifflin, 1898.

Harte, Bret. *The Writings of Bret Harte.* Boston and New York: Houghton, Mifflin, 1906.

Harrison, Constance Cary. *Crow's Nest and Belhaven Tales.* New York: Century, 1892.

Hearn, Lafcadio. "Creole Papers: Quaint New Orleans and Its Inhabitants," *The Writings of Lafcadio Hearn.* 16 vols. Boston and New York: Houghton, Mifflin, 1923. Vol I.

Jewett, Sarah Orne. *The Best Stories of Sarah Orne Jewett.* Edited by Willa Cather. Gloucester, Mass.: Peter Smith, 1965. (First published in 1925.)

———. *Deephaven.* Boston: Houghton, Mifflin, 1877.

Johnston, Richard Malcolm. *Autobiography.* Washington: Neale, 1901. (First published in 1891.)

———. *Dukesborough Tales. Harper's Franklin Square Library.* Number 290 (January 12, 1883), pp. 1–92. (First published in 1864.)

———. *Little Ike Templin and Other Stories.* Boston: Lothrop, 1894.

———. *Old Times in Middle Georgia.* New York: Macmillan, 1898.

———. *The Primes and Their Neighbors: Ten Tales of Middle Georgia.* New York: D. Appleton, 1891.

King, Grace. *Balcony Stories.* New York: Century, 1892.

――――. *Memories of a Southern Woman of Letters.* New York: Macmillan, 1932.

――――. *Tales of a Time and Place.* New York: Harper, 1892. (First published in 1888.)

Longstreet, A. B. *Georgia Scenes: Characters, Incidents, etc., in the First Half Century of the Republic.* New York: Sagamore, 1957. (First published in 1835.)

Murfree, Mary Noailles [Charles Egbert Craddock]. *The Phantoms of the Footbridge and Other Stories.* New York: Harper, 1895.

――――. *In the Tennessee Mountains.* Boston and New York: Houghton, Mifflin, 1884.

――――. *The Young Mountaineers.* Boston and New York: Houghton, Mifflin, 1898.

O'Connor, Flannery. *A Good Man Is Hard to Find.* New York: Harcourt, Brace, 1955.

――――. *Everything That Rises Must Converge.* New York: Farrar, Straus and Giroux, 1965.

Page, Thomas Nelson. *The Burial of the Guns.* New York: Scribners, 1894.

――――. *Elsket and Other Stories.* New York: Scribners, 1896.

――――. *In Ole Virginia, or Marse Chan and Other Stories.* New York: Scribners, 1887.

Robb, John S. *Streaks of Squatter Life and Far-West Scenes.* Gainesville: Scholars' Facsimiles & Reprints, 1962. (First published in 1858.)

Robinson, Roland. *Danvis Folks.* Boston and New York: Houghton, Mifflin, 1894.

Smith, F. Hopkinson. *Colonel Carter of Cartersville.* Boston and New York: Houghton, Mifflin, 1893. (First published in 1891.)

Stowe, Harriet Beecher. *Oldtown Folks.* Edited by Henry F. May. Cambridge: Belknap Press of Harvard University Press, 1966. (First published in 1865.)

――――. *Sam Lawson's Oldtown Fireside Stories.* Boston and New York: Houghton, Mifflin, 1881.

Stuart, Ruth McEnery. *A Golden Wedding and Other Tales.* New York: Harper, 1900. (First published in 1893.)

――――. *Holly and Pizen and Other Stories.* New York: Century, 1899.

――――. *Solomon Crow's Christmas Pockets and Other Tales.* New York: Harper, 1898.

Tourgée, Albion. *A Fool's Errand.* Edited by John Hope Franklin. Cambridge: Belknap Press of Harvard University Press, 1961. (First published in 1879.)

――――. *Bricks Without Straw.* New York: Fords, Howard & Hulbert, 1880.

Welty, Eudora. *The Bride of the Innisfallen and Other Stories.* New York: Harcourt, Brace, 1955.

――――. *Delta Wedding.* New York: Harcourt, Brace, 1955.

――――. *The Golden Apples.* New York: Harcourt, Brace, 1946.

――――. *Losing Battles.* New York: Random House, 1970.

――――. *The Ponder Heart.* New York: Harcourt, Brace, 1954.

――――. *Selected Stories of Eudora Welty* (Containing all of *A Curtain Of Green, and Other Stories,* and *The Wide Net, and Other Stories*). Introduction by Katherine Anne Porter. New York: Random House, 1943.

———. "Place in Fiction," *Three Papers on Fiction.* Northampton, Mass.: Smith College, 1962.

Woolson, Constance Fenimore. *Rodman the Keeper: Southern Sketches.* New York: D. Appleton, 1880.

# *Index*

# McKinley's Bulldog:

## The Battleship OREGON

# McKinley's Bulldog:
# The Battleship OREGON

## Sanford Sternlicht

Nelson-Hall
Chicago

# Contents

# Preface

Port Merizo, Guam, languished under the mid-September sun. The heat waves rose like twisting, shimmering baroque columns from the quiescent sea, so that when viewed from seaward the scene—the huts on the beach, the jungle beyond, and the ancient volcanic hills that crowned the island and proclaimed its origin—took on the unreal quality of an old, faded postcard. It was 1944, and the Pacific war had twice flamed across the little island, destroying the town of Agana and many of the villages. The Japanese had sailed warships to Guam, a United States possession, and captured all the Americans by December 12, 1941. But, on July 20 of this year, the Americans had come back with many more ships, bombing and shelling with a vengeance as the terrified natives, the Chamorros—including the five hundred villagers of Merizo—hid in the hills. By August 9, the island was firmly in U.S. hands once more and the kindlier, less consistent, curious American rule again established. The villagers returned.

Guam no longer enjoyed the easy pace of life of happy, prewar days. The island throbbed with frantic energy, generated mostly by American seabees bulldozing long airstrips out of the jungle. Guam was needed as a base for the Superforts that would soon be hammering at the industrial cities of Japan herself. Already bombers were making daily runs from Guam to attack more westerly islands still in Japanese hands but destined to serve as stepping stones on the road to victory.

Guam was secure, or at least the official communiqués had said so, and a piece of American territory—taken from Spain by the United States cruiser *Charleston* during the Spanish-American War—had been returned to U.S. control. But some of the marines who had struggled to wrest the island from the Japanese during the bloody summer had been ordered to remain behind in the wake of the war to carry out the mean, dirty anticlimax called mopping up. They and the Chamorros of Merizo both knew that Japanese survivors, well armed and organized into foraging patrols, still constituted a military menace on the island. At any unguarded moment, a day-dreaming marine or a seabee dozing off for a moment in a shady clump of trees might find himself, for the remaining fraction of a second of his life, facing the business end of a Japanese bayonet held by a defeated but unconquered enemy soldier.

In the harbor one bright afternoon that September, a strange hull, ironbound in what seemed to be a belt of thick armor, was towed in under the escort of the LCI gunship 474 and moored by a bow anchor and by chains hauled out and bullnosed through a mooring buoy astern. The officer-in-charge of the port and the commander of Service Squadron 12 knew only that the vessel was the IX 22, a nondescript old hulk pressed into service as a dynamite barge, loaded stateside with 1,400 tons of 60 percent gelatin plus a lot of other high explosives, and towed out to Guam. The tow had been directed to Port Merizo instead of the main harbor at Apra to keep the "super firecracker" in quarantine —away from the other vessels supplying the airfield and the base construction. LCT's and LCVP's—the ubiquitous, workhorse "peter boats"—were lying off awaiting signals to come alongside and load dynamite for blasting at Apra and also for Tinian, Saipan, and Palau.

When the sun had sunk in the western sea and the evening breeze had cooled the harbor somewhat, the boatswain's mate of the LCI led a working party on board the barge to post an armed guard on the bow and on the stern, rig searchlights for night off-loading, and set windscoops to get some air through the seven hatches and into the holds. The LCI sailors manned a deck winch and hauled a few boxes of the dynamite topside so that the gunner's mate could inspect the condition of the cargo after the long, hot voyage.

Just as the lids were removed, a burst of Japanese machine gun fire from the beach only seventy-five yards away sprayed the deck of the huge barge, and bullets danced among the terrified sailors flying for cover in all directions, fumbling dynamite sticks like children with burning potatoes in their hands. The lights were doused, the sentries fired off a few rounds in the air, not knowing who or what was on the beach, and a port security detachment of marines shoved off to drive the Japanese back into the hills.

It had been a close call. One round might have set off an explosion that would have killed or injured dozens, ruined the port, leveled the village, wrecked the LCI and the lighters, and disintegrated one funny old dynamite barge. What almost none there knew was that the explosion of the barge's cargo would also have destroyed what little was left of the third modern battleship built for the United States Navy. It was the U.S.S. *Oregon* (BB-3), once the most modern, proudest, finest, and most successful warship in the American service.

Forty-six years before, a sleek, trim man-of-war had astounded the world and filled the hearts of Americans with great pride by making a record-shattering, glorious dash

around South America to join the American battle fleet in
time to meet the Spanish fleet at Santiago de Cuba. The *Oregon* had steamed 14,500 miles in sixty-six days, sometimes
coaling at sea, never stopping her engines for overhaul or
repair. In doing so, she had had to elude Spanish torpedo
boats searching for her and, in Caribbean waters, to avoid
the entire fleet of Adm. Pascual Cervera y Topete, who
would have delighted in the opportunity to chop up a single
American battleship.

For the first time, a steam vessel had bested the record
of the clipper ships in "rounding the Horn," and authorities
would not only remark on the newly realized seakeeping capacity of a ship like the *Oregon*, but also would and did
remark: "There should have been a canal across the Isthmus
of Panama. It should have been possible to bring the *Oregon* to the East Coast's defense even faster and without
sailing her around the whole of South America."

On Sunday morning, July 3, 1898, after a blockade of a
month, Admiral Cervera steamed the Spanish fleet out of
the harbor of Santiago de Cuba to its destruction and into
history. The American battleships were waiting, but only
the *Oregon* had boilers lighted off and all main machinery in
operation. It was the *Oregon* that overhauled and brought
to bay the last and fastest of the Spanish warships; it was
the *Oregon* whose thirteen-inch guns fired the last shots of
the battle, driving the *Cristobal Colon* into the beach. When
the mustachioed bluejackets of the other American ships
saw the great white bow wave of the *Oregon* looming up on
them as the swift battleship passed their slower vessels, her
thirteen-inch and eight-inch guns flinging shells furiously in
all directions at the fleeing Spanish battlewagons ahead and
the desperately maneuvering Spanish destroyers astern, the
men rose to the rails and shouted to each other, "There goes
the *Oregon* like a bulldog with a bone in her teeth!"

It might have been more fitting if the old battleship

had been blown to pieces under enemy fire at Guam instead of reaching the ignominious end she finally met. But that demise and the glory of a brave ship that served the United States Navy in three wars and for over fifty years form the story of *McKinley's Bulldog: The Battleship* Oregon.

McKinley's
Bulldog:
The
Battleship
OREGON

# 1

# The ABCD Navy

During the Civil War, the Union had built the finest, fastest, most powerful warships afloat. By 1880, the United States Navy had ceased to exist as a practical fighting force. Any one of several South American navies could have blown it to splinters—yes, splinters, for eighteen years after the *Monitor* stalemated the *Merrimac* (more properly the ram C.S.S. *Virginia*), only four American warships had iron hulls. The pattern of hurriedly and painfully achieved American military prowess, followed by public indifference and inevitable decay, had begun.

The Union navy once had seven hundred ships. It introduced armored combat vessels and proved their value under fire. It had perfected the rifled gun barrel, which fired projectiles farther and truer than the old smoothbore could toss a cannon ball, thus making possible modern gunnery ashore as well as afloat. The revolving gun turret, which could instantly make a protected gun a bow-chaser or a stern-chaser or a port or starboard broadsider at the whim of a commander and the turning of a steam-propelled table, was another Yankee innovation that should have made every wooden-hulled broadside ship-of-the-line obsolete. It really did, but conservative naval authorities were unable to realize that fact. During the war, the navy had introduced steam warships without sail rigging, yet steam warships constructed twenty-five years later would carry a full sail rig. After all, "machinery is unreliable (as well as dirty)," "coal is expensive," and "wooden ships make iron men."

Not only had the United States Navy been the first in the world to build a steamship, but it also had been the first to build one equipped with the screw propeller, which eliminated the cumbersome, vulnerable, speed-reducing side or stern paddles. And the U.S.S. *Wampanoag*, completed just after the Civil War, had been the fastest ship in the world. She had made nearly eighteen knots and, for the first time, a machinery-propelled vessel could outstrip the fastest clipper afloat.

And then the understandable antiwar feeling after the end of hostilities, the complacency of the inward-expanding continental power, and the indifference and shortsightedness of the Congress and the American people scuttled the navy. In 1881, the Royal Navy had more than 400 vessels on the active list, of which 56 were modern armored ships. The Japanese navy, which had purchased its first warship from the American government as late as 1866, had 5 new armored warships in a fleet of 19 fine vessels. The United States could "boast" a navy of all of 26 ships. Four of the smallest just happened to have iron hulls; the rest were wooden coffins. Up and down the East Coast, thanks to a foolish pork barrel policy, iron vessels had been "under construction" since 1865. In reality, they were obsolete rust piles. The entire American navy of 1880 could not have survived combat with one British predreadnought or the navy of Chile, let alone Spain.

The great energies of the United States were directed inward and westward for most of the last half of the nineteenth century. After the French fiasco in Mexico, Europe seemed quite willing to leave the Americas alone. There were enough spoils to be gathered in Africa and Asia. In addition, the growing continental rivalries among France, Germany, and Russia forced these nations to neglect, for the most part, the giant nation with a child's strength awakening across the Atlantic. And Britannia ruled the waves. Britain, although tempted to interfere in the Civil War on the side of the South and in the name of King Cotton, had nevertheless remained neutral, unable morally to support a nation of slave owners regardless of the economic advantages.

The Monroe Doctrine was in effect, but the United States was totally unable to enforce it without a significant fleet. It was the tacit support of the Royal Navy that prevented foreign incursions into the Western Hemisphere. The American payment for this support and cooperation was the existence of the Dominion of Canada. United States expansion remained south of the Canadian border, and European territorial ambitions were diverted by the British fleet.

In the 1870s and 1880s, it was inconceivable for most Americans that their nation might one day be a world power. Except for the possibility of expansion into the Caribbean, there was no thought of overseas colonial growth. After all, the United States was an importer of people, not an exporter. European immigrants were pouring into the Eastern cities at a rate unparalleled in the history of mankind. A great migration was taking place to fill up and develop a seemingly empty land whose native inhabitants were to have no say in determining the nature of the change and growth.

Furthermore, Americans looked back to the ideals of the founding fathers especially as the centennial of the nation approached and passed. The United States had long opposed the concept of standing armies and had made its military particularly weak and peculiarly subject to civilian control, at least in the view of most other nations. Military and naval forces were to be defensive forces. The militia, lightly trained but available, could be mobilized in time of war, and the professionals would quickly bring its training up to date. Since a navy need only defend the coasts, no deep draught, high fuel-capacity vessels were necessary. Slowly, in the final decades of the nineteenth century, American attitudes began to change. The frontier was closing. The nation had reached its continental limits. The oceans were the new frontier. Trade and communication with Europe and Asia became increasingly more significant. Imperceptibly but steadily, the notion grew that the United States might have to be prepared to protect its own lines of communication and trade routes. The concept of defense might thus include control, not only of the immediate coastal waters, but even of far-flung sea lanes.

In the decade prior to the war with Spain, the fighting ships of the world were categorized as battleships, armored cruisers, protected cruisers, unprotected cruisers, destroyers, torpedo boats, monitors, gunboats, and dispatch boats. The battleship was indeed the queen of battle, and the navies of the world were rated according to the number of such vessels they could muster. Battleships then were great floating gun platforms of up to 15,000 tons displacement, with wrought iron or steel armor up to twenty-four inches thick. They mounted a mixed bag of guns from main battery thirteen-inchers down to one pounder rapid-fires. Optics and range finding were still somewhat primitive, and smokeless powder was just finding acceptance (the United States fleet at Santiago would fire old-style brown powder; the Spanish would have new smokeless), and so the value of long-range batteries was considered limited. Better to have faster firing, smaller caliber guns for poor visibility and close-in fighting, as well as Long Toms for long-range battleship encounters, chases, and shore bombardments. Battlewagons were not fast, eighteen knots maximum, but they were not supposed to run. They were heavyweights built to stand and fight.

Before Alfred Thayer Mahan explained and popularized the basic tenets of sea power, the battleships seemed to many Americans a totally aggressive weapon. But we saw ourselves as a peace-loving people minding our own business behind the comfortable walls of two vast oceans. (All we nonaggressive Americans had done in the nineteenth century was to conquer most of the world's third-largest continent.) In reality, American business had become worldwide, and no port on the globe did not regularly see the American flag on the staffs and trucks of a vast merchant marine peddling the enormous surplus of goods pouring from the factories of New York and New England. An American battle fleet was inevitable. Whether it was to be adequate was another question.

After battleships, in naval ratings, came the fast, twenty-four-knot armored cruisers, which were much like the heavy cruisers of World War II vintage. The cruisers of the 1890s had some armor but much less than the battleships had. The main battery consisted of eight eight-inch or six-inch guns, and the usual host of smaller calibers and rapid-fire guns was also present. The armored cruiser could steam vast ranges, scout the enemy, hit the commerce, outrun the wagons, and take on anything its size or smaller. In actual warfare, this class of vessel was almost always misemployed. Again and again, squadrons of armored cruisers wound up being forced to slug it out with the heavily armored battleships until the inevitable destruction of the former occurred.

Whereas the armored cruisers displaced a wide range of tonnages and sometimes displaced as much as a battleship, the protected cruisers seldom displaced more than 5,000 tons. Along with the unprotected cruisers, they formed a class roughly equivalent in function to the light cruiser of World War II. Protected cruisers had an armored deck for protection against high trajectory fire but no side armor for broadside or torpedo fire. They made up to twenty knots and had a limited cruising range. When the American navy was rebuilding in the 1880s, these ships were the darlings of compromise. Their lack of cruising range made them defensive, while their single or twin eight-inch or six-inch rifles along with other smaller weapons appeared formidable and comforting.

Unprotected cruisers were not much smaller than protected cruisers, but they had no armored deck. For safety against shellfire, they depended on compartmentation and on coal bunkers placed around the vitals of the ship. (What was supposed to protect the ship that had to fight after heavy steaming and before recoaling?) The largest guns that unprotected cruisers carried were five-inchers. Unprotected cruisers as well as the heavier cruisers and even battleships carried torpedoes. This most dreaded naval weapon, of which more will be said later, made little sense on cruisers that would theoretically use it on battleships and other cruisers except that a cruiser made a suicidally large target at the 400-yard effective range of a Whitehead torpedo. The weapons made absolutely no sense on an eighteen-knot battleship.

Destroyers were a somewhat more natural home for torpedoes. This class of vessels was a rapidly evolving one. First had come the torpedo boat, which had been hailed as the great new naval weapon of the nineteenth century. Some naval authorities of the day thought this inexpensive craft, dubbed the "mosquito boat," had made battleships

obsolete, and at least one major European power had temporarily halted battleship construction. It is the law of war,
however, that every new weapon engenders its defense.
Soon navies developed a class called torpedo boat destroyers. These sturdy little tykes seemed quite lethal in
themselves, being armed with torpedo boat weapons and
possessing high speed, so designers developed a class called
destroyers of torpedo boat destroyers, which is not the easiest thing to say when maneuvering or changing station, so
the term was shortened to destroyers. These ships could
churn at thirty-five knots. Besides torpedoes, they carried
small rapid-fires. They displaced only 400 tons and had an
extremely limited range.

The torpedo boat from its inception in the nineteenth
century through its demise in World War II was the most
overrated weapon in modern military history. Not even the
zeppelin was so overestimated. The torpedo itself, of course,
was and is a most deadly and effective instrument of war,
especially when launched by a submarine. After all, German
submarines sank over 11 million tons of Allied shipping in
World War I and over 14 million tons in World War II. The
tin fish found its true home in the sub, not in its original car-
rier, the torpedo boat.

The torpedo itself developed from the mine, a most
effective passive weapon and the first to be called a torpedo.
In fact, the torpedoes that Farragut was "damning" at Mobile Bay were actually such mines. Then came spar torpedoes, which were basically mines on the end of forty-foot
spars projecting ten feet under water from vessels of the
Royal Navy. These weapons were charged with gun cotton
and electrically detonated from within the ship. The point
of it all was to hit an enemy vessel at or below the waterline,
and it was damned silly to have to throw one whole ship at
another to achieve the shot. The self-propelled torpedo
finally arrived on the naval scene in 1866 through the genius

of an English engineer, Robert Whitehead. His torpedo was cigar shaped, measuring eleven feet in length and fourteen inches in diameter. It weighed 300 pounds and ran on compressed air. Almost every naval power in the world took an interest in and bought Whitehead torpedoes—except the United States.

In 1891, off the coast of Chile, the torpedo achieved a spectacular success that shook the naval world. The British torpedo boat *Lynch,* which had gotten involved in a Chilean revolt, torpedoed and sank the armored ship *Bianco Encalada* with a fourteen-incher fired at a range of a hundred yards. The blast knocked the skipper of the *Bianco Encalada* into the sea. The reaction to the torpedo's dramatic success was similar to the reaction in world naval circles in 1967 when Russian-built Egyptian-manned, Komar-class patrol boats sank the Israeli destroyer *Elath* from over the horizon, at a distance of twenty to twenty-five miles, with Styx surface-to-surface missiles. Authorities began to take a second look at the defenses of expensive aircraft carriers and cruisers. In 1891, however, the point much ignored in the ensuing discussions was that a single hostile torpedo boat had no business being allowed within 1,000, let alone 100, yards of an ironclad. When in 1896 the Austrian naval officer Ludwig Obry invented the gyroscope and thus perfected the stabilization of the torpedo, the naval world shook again.

The torpedo boat itself would prove to be no match for the destroyer, rapid-fire guns, and the electric searchlight. Nevertheless, in 1890, when the American navy finally got its first torpedo boat into commission, there were nearly 1,000 such ships in service throughout the world.

Then there was that vessel that held a special place of honor in the hearts of Americans in general and tradition-bound Yankee naval officers in particular, most of whom were veterans of the great blockade of 1861–1865. It was the monitor, of course.

John Ericsson's brilliant invention had probably done more to save the Union than any other weapon of the Civil War. On the morning of Saturday, March 8, 1862, the *Merrimac*, rebuilt as the ironclad C.S.S. *Virginia*, steamed out into Hampton Roads and destroyed the wooden *Cumberland* and the grand old frigate *Congress*. It thus appeared that ironplated ships could destroy wooden vessels at will. The Union blockade was an almost totally wooden one, and in a few days it apparently would be reduced to a paper one. The next day "the cheese box on a raft," the *Monitor*—a low-freeboard, mastless, ironplated gun platform with two heavy cannon in a revolving steam turret—fought the *Virginia* to a standoff and caused the larger vessel to retreat. Northern despair turned to exultation and, under Ericsson's supervision, the shipyards of the North churned out cheap, quickly built monitors that were double turreted and more seaworthy than the original model.

The original *Monitor* foundered off Cape Hatteras in a fierce gale on December 31, 1862, causing the loss of sixteen lives. What was wrong with the first monitor was wrong with all subsequent versions. Their dangerously low reserve buoyancy, less than 20 percent, made them death traps. Other armored warships at that time were expected to have at least 80 percent reserve buoyancy. In other words, such a ship would remain floating even if it were 80 percent filled with water. But a monitor would sink if water filled only a fifth of it. A monitor's low freeboard, only 1½ to 2 feet (about what a respectable rowboat has), made the monitor an almost nonexistent target but also prevented the turret guns from firing in any kind of seaway. In other words, the monitor was a great coastal defense vessel and was used as such by other navies through World War II. To haul these slow, ungainly ships around the world or to try to incorporate them into a battle fleet—as Adm. William T. Sampson tried to do against the Spanish—was as foolish as using elephants against tanks. Yet the emotional attachment to the class of ships that had saved the Union blockade at Hampton Roads, at Charleston, and even at Mobile Bay was so strong that, as late as 1886, Congress approved the completion of the *Amphitrite, Monadnock, Puritan,* and *Terror,* double turret monitors planned at the close of the Civil War. These ships were all iron and filled with modern machinery, but they were still monitors. The navy, like the French in 1940, was still fighting the previous war.

Other vessels in the fleets of the last quarter of the nineteenth century were the lightly armed and very necessary dispatch boats; essentially swift yachts, which served as communicators between and among fleets and bases; and the ubiquitous gunboats, primarily riverine craft and blockaders displacing around 1,000 tons or less and heavily armed with four-inch or even six-inch rapid-fire guns.

The rapid evolution of naval weaponry in the late 1800s forced the United States to make a basic decision concerning goals. Should the nation protect its commerce, continue to enforce the Monroe Doctrine regardless of British support, defend two vast coastlines, and justify the growing self-image of Americans as a people whose "manifest destiny" would take them, rightly or wrongly, but seemingly inevitably, into the realm of imperialism and the world of international power politics? If so, then these new instruments of war, these swift and deadly iron boxes of power, were the costly temptations without which greatness and prestige could not come into being. The weapons would have to be built or bought with money that could have fed and housed and clothed and educated millions of immigrant children in the slums of New York and Chicago, millions of white and black children of the American rural poor, and the entire Indian nations of the West. The nation chose warships, and social services languished. But twentieth century America as we know her would not have existed or exerted her mighty influence on our days and our fathers' days if the nation had not, after great soul-searching, said "yea" to power.

It all began with the letters ABCD and a congressional act of March 3, 1883. Congress provided for four new steel-hulled vessels of American design. They were the cruisers *Atlanta, Boston,* and *Chicago* and the dispatch boat *Dolphin.* The four ships became known as the ABCD "fleet," or the "White Squadron." The vessels were provided with a full sail rig and had many shortcomings in design. Nevertheless, they were American made, and they became the proving ground for all subsequent modern naval construction. In 1885, Congress authorized two more cruisers, *Newark* and *Charleston,* and two gunboats, *Yorktown* and *Petrel.* We were on our way.

However, cruisers, like submarines in the later world wars, were primarily for raiding commerce. Monitors and other gunboats were for coast defense and riverine warfare. Only battleships could meet an enemy battle fleet on the high seas and defeat it before it reached the American coast. After all, in the War of 1812 the British had burned American seaboard cities at will. Neither the brilliant American single ship victories over British frigates nor the very effective privateering could prevent the burning of Washington or win the war.

The act of 1886 that provided for the completion of the four monitors also authorized the first two truly successful modern warships built in the United States. They were officially designated as second-class battleships. They took nine years to build and were not commissioned until 1895. American steel mills took three years to produce the required amount of nickel steel. The first of the battleships was the *Texas,* which was built from English plans. The second, of completely American design, had a brief career of only two and a half years after commissioning, but she was long remembered. She was named the *Maine*.

Captain Alfred Thayer Mahan's *The Influence of Sea Power upon History. 1660–1783* was published in May, 1890, after his lectures to the Naval War College—upon which the book was based—had already begun to have an effect on naval officers, expansionist politicians, and defense-minded government officials. The Secretary of the Navy in the Harrison administration (1889–93), Benjamin F. Tracy, became a disciple of Mahan. Like the military philosopher, he believed that a strong navy would exempt this country from war. If war did come, however, it would have to be fought with the fleet in being; there would be no time for new construction. Tracy was right, at least in regard to the forthcoming war with Spain, if not to subsequent conflicts. We are back to his viewpoint again today.

Tracy was helped by an event known as the Samoa Crisis. On March 15, 1889, a squadron of German warships, three antiquated American cruisers, and the H.M.S. *Calliope* lay at anchor in the middle of Apin Harbor of the island of Upolu in the Samoan group. The crews were at battle stations, with the superior German naval force about to invalidate the three way Samoan Agreement. The Germans had bombarded Apia and were preparing to make the islands a German possession—over the bodies of the crews of the inferior American and British forces. The skies darkened, the winds and seas rose in fury, and an unprecedented hurricane smashed the warships, tossing them against each other like matchsticks and heaving them up on reefs and rocks. The German ambitions were shipwrecked, but the American squadron also was ruined. Only the *Calliope*, with steam up in new engines, was able to beat her way out of the coral vise and into open sea. The incident showed Americans what sea power could do and what it had not done. A second-class, underpowered, undergunned navy was clearly no navy at all. The Samoan Crisis made the American public sea-conscious. The dispute was finally settled on June 14, 1889, when a tripartite protectorate over the islands was arranged. German ambitions had been thwarted, but by an act of God and not by the power of the United States Navy.

On June 30, 1890, the Republican administration pushed through a congressional act that provided for three battleships. They were called "seagoing coastal battleships" —a term for all seasons. "Seagoing" pleased the "Big Navy" expansionists, and "coastal" appealed to those who valued economy and defensive strategy. The battleships would displace about 10,000 tons each. The armor belt would be eighteen inches thick. Armament would consist of a main battery of four thirteen-inch guns and secondary batteries of eight-inch and six-inch guns. Unfortunately, the "coastal" compromise limited the speed to a little over sixteen knots and gave the ships coal capacity for a cruising range of less than 5,000 miles. Still, these ships could and would form the nucleus of the new battle fleet and indeed prove to be a lot more "seagoing" than "coastal."

Two of the new ships were built in Philadelphia and named *Indiana* and *Massachusetts*. The third contract was awarded to two energetic San Francisco shipbuilders, Irving M. Scott and Henry Scott of the Union Iron Works. Their ship would be named *Oregon*.

This *Oregon* would not be the first *Oregon* in the United States Navy. Number one was a brig of 187 tons, purchased in 1841 and used by Lt. Charles Wilkes, U.S.N., to survey the Columbia River. She was then sailed around the Cape of Good Hope to the east coast of the United States and sold in 1845. The second *Oregon* was a double-turret monitor, or would have been one had she ever been finished. Laid down in the Boston Navy Yard in 1864, she was to have two pairs of heavy guns mounted on fifteen-inch armored turrets. When the Civil War ended, work was halted, and she rotted and rusted for nineteen years as part of the "paper fleet." The Navy Department mercifully had the junk pile broken up in 1884.

No, the new *Oregon* would not be the first of her name, but she would prove to be the first of the new navy. At her birth, she would be the largest, toughest, most powerful American fighting ship built to that date.

# 2

# The Launching: "Like Crested Pallus Armed"

The shoring, cutting, hauling, heaving, hammering, riveting, and pounding had taken two years. Now the unchristened hull sat in her cradle and waited for her first caress from the element that would be her home for as long as she existed. Her keel had been laid on November 19, 1891, at San Francisco's Union Iron Works, then only six years old. Now, almost two years later, she was ready for launching. All of San Francisco was ready too.

The dawn of Thursday, October 26, 1893, was dull, with the not-unusual fog bank hovering over San Francisco Harbor. The sun beyond the layers of clouds made its presence known slowly but surely, as if it too did not wish to miss the gala event. By eleven-thirty, it would break through and splash a memorable scene with a brimming pot of golden light.

The *Oregon* sat on her slippery chute with her rudder lashed fore and aft like the blade of a cutting spade. Long before dawn, her decks swarmed with mechanics, dockyard workers, riggers, and nervous foremen putting on the finishing touches. The debutant *Oregon* looked like a plump girl of the fashionable Lillian Russell configuration wearing a bathing suit of bright red from her keel to the waterline and more somber lead gray above, except for the two turrets and the barbettes, which had also been given a coat of flaming red in honor of the occasion.

Alas, there had been a social dispute concerning the launching. Several young Oregon ladies, all daughters of prominent men, had vied for the honor of breaking the traditional bottle of wine over the bow of the new vessel and giving her her name. Fortunately, the fracas had been settled without bloodshed. Two young ladies would share the honor. Miss Daisy Ainsworth, representing the state of Oregon, would have the privilege of pressing a button commencing a Rube Goldberg series of causes and effects that supposedly would send a bottle of California (of course) champagne crashing against the bow of the vessel. At the same moment, Miss Eugenia Shelby, representing the city of Portland, would press her own electric button. It would cause a small guillotine to drop and sever a cord holding twenty-two five-pound weights in position. The weights would pound against the dog shores securing the ship in position and theoretically release the new princess of the seas and send her on her way. It was all to happen at precisely 11:45 A.M. Miss Ruth Dolph, daughter of Sen. Joseph Norton Dolph of Oregon, had been designated by Secretary of the Navy Hilary Abner Herbert to represent the service at the christening, but she chose not to attend, possibly because there was nothing left for her to do.

The customary christening platform had been built before the bow of the ship and draped with swirls and criss crosses of red, white, and blue bunting. A panoply of flags, banners, and pennants canopied the platform with a Gothic arch of color. On the platform and directly under the overhang of the bow stood a table holding some of the gimcracks of electric launching: the little guillotine with its sharp knife resting on a protecting block above the cord. Behind this machine stood a small gold-framed oil painting of Mount Hood, Oregon. A tiny card stuck into one corner of the frame was inscribed, "To the battle ship Oregon, compliments of Miss Eugenia Shelby." The picture was the first gift the *Oregon* would receive. There were many more to come, most more expensive, but none more touching. To the left of the painting was a small box surmounted with a photo of the *Oregon* and containing the electric signaling device that was to notify the platform guests when all was in readiness below. The signal buttons for the young ladies were there too. The bottle of champagne was hanging from the railing of the platform above the table, ready for the christening.

San Franciscans had been gathering from the early hours of the morning. Those fortunate enough to have tickets to enter the shipyard and perhaps sit in the stands could afford to arrive later, but the ordinary people of the city came early. A man named Benjamin Conger, shoved by the crowd, had his toes crushed by a cable car on his way to the launching. Kentucky Street, which led down to the shipyard, was aswarm with humanity on foot or in hacks. Men and women began to line the shore for half a mile below the *Oregon*'s berth, and the narrow street to the gate of the Union Iron Works was dangerously jammed and blocked by ten that morning. Fortunately, company officials threw open four gates to admit the general throng. This act caused a wild, trampling stampede for points of vantage near the ship's cradle. Boys and young men, like flies on meat, began to climb along the timbers of the stocks fifty feet above the superstructure of the ship. Shipyard guards had to force men back from beneath the very ways. The people perched and waited like patient gulls.

The roofs of the nearby Arctic Oil Works were filled with men and women, and some enterprising boys had obtained a long ladder to climb to the top of the tallest tank in the ironworks. Theirs was indeed a bird's-eye view.

In Mission Bay an immense fleet of vessels had congregated to honor the *Oregon*. In fact, never before had so many ships and craft gathered there. "Is there any room left for the launching?" many worried officials began to wonder. Giant ferry steamers, loaded to the guard rails with thousands of people, elbowed into the harbor. The excursion steamer *Ukiah* dangerously tested her passenger capacity; so did the stern-wheeler *Caroline*. Hundreds of men, women, and children clung to saucy-looking cutters, swift-sailing yachts, tugs, steam launches, punts, racing shells, and rowboats, all of which formed a crescent-shaped armada around the ironworks. The steamer *Walla Walla*, in the big dry dock at the ironworks, was full-rigged with people, some three thousand having scampered aboard and covered every inch of deck, superstructure, mast, and spar.

Foreign vessels tied up nearby displayed all the bunting and flags they could break out. The big Norwegian ship *Bredablik*, at Long Wharf, was a veritable Christmas tree of flags. In fact, every single harbor craft streamed with patriotic banners. Voices and whistles and cannon were ready to mark a great day for Uncle Sam and the United States Navy as well as California and San Francisco!

The United States Quartermaster's boat *General Mc-Dowell* hove into sight with the Presidio band aboard playing "Hail Columbia." Near the band stood the Presidio's commanding officer, Gen. Thomas Howard Ruger, and his staff, all decked out in their splendid full-dress blues with gold epaulets. The steam launch *Rockaway* shoved off from Mission Pier at 10:30 with a deckload of Union Iron Works officials, directors, and guests. The naval officers from Mare Island steamed down aboard the tug *Monarch,* while other government officials and their ladies rode on the revenue cutters *Corwin* and *MacArthur.* The tugs *Fearless, Vigilant, Active, Sea Queen,* and *Rescue,* which had been chartered by clubs and private parties, chugged as close to the official boats as they could get.

The big steamer *Bay City* carried hundreds of passengers to the scene of the launch for fifty cents a head. Several small steamers, including *Pride of the River,* had been chartered by enterprising speculators, who had sold passage to the launching for various fares and were reaping small fortunes.

Then the most important vessels of the celebration fleet hove into view. First came the fire tug carrying California governor, Henry Harrison Markham, San Francisco's mayor, Ellert, the city commissioners, and other officials. The tug was named the *Governor Markham,* of course. Gov. Markham had invited Gov. Sylvester Pennoyer of Oregon to attend the launching with him, but the latter official had declined. The snub caused the San Francisco *Chronicle* to complain that "had the battle ship been forwarded to East Portland and slid into the Williamette [*sic*] he might have consented to shed the lustre of his presence on the scene." Instead, Gov. Pennoyer had delegated Gen. G. Compton (Oregon Militia) of Portland as his proxy. The general would be one of the platform guests.

Following close astern of the *Governor Markham* was the red-stacked tug *Sea King.* Aboard were navy yard Comdnt. Captain Henry L. Howison, U.S.N.; his staff; and the Mare Island Marine Band. Within three years, Captain Howison would place the *Oregon* in commission on the Pacific station. From July, 1896, through March, 1897, he would serve as her first commanding officer.

By eleven-thirty, the crowd in the ironworks, along the beaches, in the overlooking buildings, and in the harbor was estimated at more than 100,000 people. It was indeed a great day for the navy, San Francisco, and the Eastman Kodak Company, whose new box cameras were everywhere in sight. When the sun broke to the masthead of the sky, the "Kodak fiends" shouted with joy and began snapping.

With the arrival of the platform guests, all but the last props and shores had been removed and the ways liberally slushed with tallow. The ship rested in her cradle. Each important guest was met and escorted to the platform by Irving M. Scott. The first to mount the ladder was General Ruger, whose full-dress blues and gold-tasseled sword had survived the voyage across the bay in fine style. He was followed by his staff officers, Colonel Moule, Colonel Miles, and Major Egan. Then up went General Compton in a cocked hat and sword, followed—at a respectable distance behind the dangling weapon—by Judge W. B. Gilbert of the circuit court.

Other distinguished visitors scampered aloft. Then came a navy band which quickly formed a circle, and played "The Star-Spangled Banner," followed by "A Home on the Rolling Deep" and other nautical and patriotic airs. In the middle of a number, the heroines of the day appeared, surrounded by a host of relatives, friends, and male admirers. Miss Ainsworth, a petite girl wearing a snug-fitting ankle-length red dress and clutching a bunch of lilies, was so eagerly aided in her ascent that she was practically hoisted aloft like a red ensign climbing to the main truck. Next came Miss Shelby, oppositely colored in a navy blue hat and a dress of the same color, with a large bunch of chrysanthemums on her ample, heaving bosom. She, too, with a little more effort on the part of the willing haulers, soon flew aloft.

The gallant General Compton, exerting the privilege of

rank, took the ladies in tow immediately and began to initiate them into the mysteries of ship launching. He explained the electric appliances at great length and assured the ladies of their safety from electrocution. They listened attentively as he told them how many pounds of pressure per square inch they should bring to bear on the buttons. The girls looked at the buttons and then at the great iron ship, not believing for one moment that they would actually be able to move that enormous hulk even a fraction of an inch. Miss Shelby was particularly concerned lest the bottle fail to break. Would they have to haul the vessel back into the cradle and up the ways to launch it again? Would she be held accountable?

More visitors arrived and soon the platform was filled, about half of those present being ladies. Irving M. Scott and Henry Scott piloted the guests around the platform, pointing out details of the ship and the ironworks. Irving M. Scott lectured to the assemblage on the cost, the construction, and the promise of the *Oregon:*

> When fitted out, the ship will have cost the United States Government well over $4,000,000. Her displacement loaded will be 10,288 tons. The *Oregon,* like her sisters, was designed with a view of meeting in battle vessels carrying the heaviest guns and armor. She was designed after a careful study of the vessels of other powers, and with a view to being operated upon the coasts of America. The *Oregon* is a vessel of great fighting power united with adequate protection in the shape of high-resisting armor. Her draught is sufficiently small to enable her to be operated in the shallow waters of the American coast.
>
> The following are the principal features of the *Oregon:* Length on the water line, 348 feet; beam, extreme, 69¼ feet; draught, forward and aft, 24 feet; eventual displacement, 10,200 tons; designed maximum speed, 16.2 knots; sustained sea speed, 15 knots.[1]

Now it was the turn of Henry Scott to play Cicero to the guests. He explained how the large vessel was held in check and how she would be set free. One lady asked, "Do you plan on anyone being killed in the launching?" to which Scott replied in the negative. Another timid lady wanted to know if the platform was attached to the ship and whether it would be carried along down the ways. She too was reassured. Meanwhile, the band sawed on lustily as the hammers clicked and thumped away on the ways below. It was time to start the ceremony.

First there was an original poem to be read. It had been written by one Samuel L. Simpson of Astoria, Oreg., in twelve stanzas and entitled, naturally enough, "The Launching of the Oregon." The poem had been telegraphed down to San Francisco by the board of trade of Astoria, along with the highest literary recommendations. The audience bared their heads in reverence as Mrs. M. J. Kinney of San Rafael hurled the lines at the defenseless vessel:

Oh, ship, like crested Pallas armed,

Oh, bride, the hoary god hath charmed. . . .[2]

The *Oregon* began to creak in her cradle and seemed to tug at the dog shores holding her.

The poem was loudly cheered upon its conclusion. Irving M. Scott then introduced the Reverend C. O. Brown of the First Congregationalist Church of San Francisco, who invoked the blessings of the Almighty in a short but moving prayer. The Reverend Mr. Brown had intended to speak at length, but a large bumblebee, attracted by the impressive floral arrangements on the platform, had somewhat nearsightedly attempted to light on the good pastor's upturned nose. Brown quickly shouted "Amen!" and retreated to the rear of the platform, waving his hat in front of him.

An electrician came forward to put the electric buttons in their proper places and set the guillotine. The ladies of the electric launching were ushered to their places before the table, and General Compton covered the rear to make sure they manned their guns and did not miss their cues.

More flowers were gallantly proffered: to Miss Daisy was given a large bunch of yellow chrysanthemums, while Miss Eugenia received an enormous bouquet of red roses.

The two Scotts held the positions between the table and the bow, where they could communicate with the man in charge of the men below. High up on the bow of the ponderous hull stood the riggers who were to take the ride down into the bay. Still higher up perched a vast audience of men and boys, clinging with tooth and nail to the timbers and waiting for the signal.

The exhausted band had stopped for lack of wind, and no sound was heard but the blows of hammers. Nearer and nearer came the thumps that were placing more responsibility on the dog shores. Shore after shore dropped with a crash, and then the perspiring workmen appeared under the bow. It was almost 11:45, the prescribed time for the launching, but there still remained a few blocks to clear away.

They were stubborn ones that refused to yield to hammer alone. Chisels were brought and, splinter by splinter, the forward keel blocks were chipped and hacked. As the last one gave way, the hull settled squarely on the ways, and the road to the sea was clear. Nothing remained but for the little guillotine to do its work.

"Are you ready below?" yelled Irving Scott.

The answer came with a click, and the word "Ready" showed in the electric box in front of Miss Ainsworth. With a steady hand, she pressed the button, and the keen-edged knife fell on the restraining rope. For a moment, the ship sat motionless, and the great throng watched for the first sign of life. Slowly the *Oregon* felt her weight and started. With never a quiver or jar, she moved off down the incline, but there was something amiss. The bottle of champagne still hung on its hook. Miss Shelby pressed away at her button, but the bottle refused to budge. The *Oregon* was about to escape this part of the ceremony and would have but for the prompt action of Henry Scott.

Just before the ship had traveled beyond reach, he leaped to the rail of the platform, grabbed the bottle from its hook, and dashed it against the bow of the ship.

"I name thee *Oregon*," murmured Miss Daisy Ainsworth as the huge hulk started down the toboggan ride, and a wild, glad cheer went up from more than 100,000 throats.

On the stroke of 12:00, the biggest iron battleship of them all glided gently into the waters of the bay. Flags and banners floated fore and aft, and her red bow was wet with the baptismal wine. A crash and a splash marked the instant that the ship rode down to the sea and jammed her stern into the mud flats—properly launched, named, and baptized.

The huge wave that ran ahead of the launch spoiled the view of those standing on the shore. The miniature tsunami rolled up the beach and rose to the waists of those in the front rank. There was a frantic rush to escape, but the jumbled mass of people, hacks, and peanut wagons in the background cut off the only way to safety.

Several people were carried off their feet and tumbled about in the mud by the playful tidal wave, and some were badly bruised. One William P. Vaughn was washed into the bay, and, before he was rescued, a raft struck one of his legs and broke it. He was carried to the Receiving Hospital.

The *Oregon* entered the water stern first. The rudder was in place and had to be clamped so that it might act as a cutwater when the vessel was launched. This it did nicely, and the wave that was raised by the big battleship was white capped.

No one can tell beforehand just what any vessel will do when launched, but the *Oregon* had been figured to a nicety, and, with credit to its builders and launchers, behaved wonderfully well. The Union Iron Works people had learned by experience what practical workings were. They had made mistakes in the past and were evidently trying to profit from former failures to score future successes in both building and launching all kinds of vessels.

For a month past, a dredger had been at work deepening the offing where the war vessel was to enter the water. It was supposed by many that, in the first plunge, the *Oregon* might take a dive and stick in the mud. However, the moment the big hull commenced to move in the water, it proved buoyant as a cork. The ship was sustained by the heavy-timbered cradle until well afloat. Then mooring chains braked the cradle while the *Oregon*, powered by its momentum, continued forward and floated by itself.

The cradle blocks and wedges floated in one mass while the *Oregon* was brought to an anchorage less than 150 yards from the stocks she was built on. She was a pretty sight, this mammoth warship, the bright red paint on the turrets, sponson, and topsides glistening in bold relief in the strong sunlight, while the dark lead color of waterline and bilge showed just how much deeper the ship must go when the engines and the boilers and the armament would be mounted and the vessel coaled.

The noise that greeted the big fighter as she plunged into the water was something terrific: "Its like was never heard on the borders of the vast Pacific before."[3] The hoarse siren of the big steamer blended its notes with the shrill treble of the tiny steam launch, and the volume of sound seemed to shake the very hills that surround the bay. The excitement among the spectators on board the big fleet was tremendous. Men shouted and waved their hats and the ladies hurrahed and waved their handkerchiefs as the *Oregon* came to rest after her maiden plunge. Small boys in small boats were out in force and vied with the sturdy boatmen for the post of honor on the occasion. This post, of course, was as close to the ship's stern as possible. The daring mariners remained there until the ship began to move, and then

there was a scurrying to get out of the way. Some succeeded, but a luckless few were caught by the big wave
thrown up by the battleship as she rushed into the water,
and several of the small craft were swamped. The occupants
of the inundated boats were quickly rescued by their
friends, and, except for a good ducking, no one was much
the worse for the accident.

Hardly had the big ship become stationary after her
plunge when she was surrounded by hundreds of the small
craft, the occupants of which eagerly inscribed their names
on her gray-painted sides. The immense fleet of vessels remained for a few minutes to gaze at the warship and then
headed back for the city again.

Those who were on the *Oregon* when she slid down the
ways were as follows: John Murray, foreman of the engineroom; James McKay, in charge of the fireroom and
boilers; Thomas Longworth, in charge of the deck, machinery, and ventilation; A. Martin, foreman of the construction
works; W. Donald, foreman of shipjoiners; Richard Sture,
foreman of riggers; W. Telfer, foreman of shipsmiths; A.
Donaldson, captain of the dry dock; and A. Smith, chief engineer, dry dock.

The knocking out of wedges and blocks—the task that
allowed the *Oregon* to rest in the cradle directly on the
shores—was performed by a gang of workmen under the supervision of James Dickie, superintendent of construction,
and E. T. Morris, chief engineer of the works. Other officials
actively engaged in the building of the vessel were George
Dickie, manager of the works; Robert Forsyth, assistant
manager; Hugo Frear, chief draughtsman; and R. Pengelly,
foreman of shipwrights.

It had been a good show. All parties were truly satisfied
—the navy, the builders, the officials, and, most of all, the
people of San Francisco. Slowly, the crowds melted off the
buildings, away from the beaches, and down from the ships

tied up at the ironworks. Some of the last spectators came down the ladders of the new cruiser launched only a year before at the Union Iron Works and still being fitted out. Her name was the *Olympia*, and one day she would lead Dewey's squadron to glory and victory at Manila Bay. Two months after that, the *Oregon* would prove to be the key ship at the Battle of Santiago.

These two ships, launched a year apart in the same shipyard and made by the same builders, influenced American history and changed American destiny more than any other warships ever built, with the possible exceptions of Perry's *Niagara* on Lake Erie in 1813, Farragut's *Hartford* at New Orleans and Mobile Bay, and Halsey's *Enterprise* during World War II.

The *Oregon* and the *Olympia*, waiting together that October day in 1893, would find their destiny less than five years later as instruments by which America won an empire and became an international power.

# 3

# At the Ready

The outfitting proceeded apace, but five years passed between keel and commission. The builders had to cast and turn and mount the guns, place and set the boilers and engines, and mount the armor plate. During both construction and outfitting, custom and regulation mandated continual government inspections.

The major problem was the shaping and installing of the plate, for only two American steel companies had begun to learn how to forge large quantities of armor to warship specifications. The Bethlehem Steel Corporation developed this capacity first, and the Carnegie Steel Corporation followed. In fact, the requirement for large amounts of armor plate for the United States Navy enormously increased the capacity and technical ability of the American steel industry.

Carnegie was awarded the armor plate contract for the *Oregon*. However, before the company could begin to manufacture the armor, the all-important question of the shape of the plate had to be answered. One school of naval construction argued for vertical armor—that is, armor without much curvature and set perpendicularly. It was relatively easy to make and install. Of course, the steel companies were in favor of this design. A second school, which included most naval constructors, insisted on inclined armor, which was set at an angle that theoretically would help deflect projectiles. The vertical won out and Carnegie produced Harveyized (carbon hardened) steel plate. This armor failed its first tests against close-range large projectiles. But Secretary of the Navy Herbert reduced the specification requirements and accepted the armor in December, 1894.

Finally, the Scott brothers notified the Navy Department that the *Oregon* was nearing completion. The department appointed a board of officers as a trial board to see that the contractors had met every detail of the agreement under which the ship had been built. The board had to certify that the vessel was seaworthy and able to carry specified weights without undue strain, and—of particular importance to both contractor and government—that she could develop contract speed or better. A bonus clause in the original *Oregon* contract offered $25,000 for each quarter knot of additional speed beyond the fifteen-knot specification.

The trial board's endlessly detailed inspection would determine the acceptability of the ship. The holds, passages, magazines, storerooms, watertight bulkheads and doors, and all movable parts had to be inspected and ascertained acceptable and functioning properly both at sea and in port. The ship had to be run at varying speeds to check the engines, the consumption of coal, the steam pressure produced, and the amount of vibration. Also, the ship had to be steered in circles to locate helm angles and tactical diameter and to test-exercise the three steering systems: hydraulic, steam, and hand. Most important of all was the measured course run for the full-speed trial.

In May, 1896, the Navy Department ordered Rear Adm. L. A. Beardslee, U.S.N., to head up the trial board "in addition to his other duties" and among his assistants, prophetically, were Capt. Charles Edgar Clark, U.S.N., and Chief Engineer Robert W. Milligan, U.S.N. Clark did not then dream that he would command the *Oregon* only two years later in one of the most fateful sea actions in American history, the brilliant run around the Cape to join Sampson's battle fleet and rout the Spanish at Santiago. Milligan would be in charge of the engineering spaces on that same epic voyage. More than to any other human beings, with the possible exception of the Scott brothers, the *Oregon* would owe her glory to these two naval officers. They would learn much about their future home in serving on the trial board for the U.S.S. *Oregon*.

Admiral Beardslee reluctantly commenced the additional duty. He was a busy man, and he shuddered at the potential paper work necessary in the "temporary additional duty" (TAD in modern naval terminology). Furthermore, the responsibilities were very great indeed.

The selection of a course for the full-speed trial was of great importance. The course had to be a thirty- or forty-mile straightaway in deep water not very far from the shore, fairly protected from the sea, and out of the track of tugs and sailing vessels. The board elected to use the Santa Barbara Channel, an almost ideal course that had been used in testing the *Olympia*, the *Monterey*, the *Charleston*, and other vessels. The channel extends between the southern coast of California and a group of four islands—Anacapa, Santa Cruz, Santa Rosa, and San Miguel—that lie parallel to the coast and some twenty to twenty-five miles distant from

it, thus affording partial protection from southeast to southwest. The water is deep nearly to the shore, so that between
Point Conception and Santa Barbara light—thirty-seven
miles along the coast—there is a straight east-and-west
course of thirty-one miles, at an average distance of four
miles from the beach, with a depth nowhere less than 100
fathoms. The coast, which consists of low foothills, included
many conspicuous and easily distinguishable marks, such as
lighthouses, windmills, and wharves. Furthermore, the positions of these landmarks were accurately charted. Thus, a
navigator was able by cross bearings to know his position at
any part of the course.

To doubly assure the navigator, the United States Coast
Survey had planted, at intervals of about ten miles, a number of pairs of tall stakes. The stakes of each pair were a few
hundred yards apart, and they were set on a line at right angles to the east-and-west course. The distance from one pair
of stakes to the next had been accurately measured, and all
measurements were verified before a trial was made. The
stakes had been freshly whitewashed for the occasion so
that they could easily be seen. As a result of all these preparations, a ship running on the course could readily determine its exact position. The officer of the deck would watch
the broad angle between the stakes of one pair until, when
the stakes were in line, the angle disappeared. Then the
officer prolonged this line until it intersected the course of
the ship.

On the morning of May 7, the inspection began. The
board, arrayed in overcoats (for it was a foggy and cold
California morning) mustered on a tug at the foot of Market
Street. The craft bore them over a very choppy sea to the
Union Iron Works, where the *Oregon* lay at anchor. As the
men drew alongside of her and gazed up with some little
awe at the high steel precipice they were about to scale,
their first sensation was one of littleness. As fixed as a rock

she lay, apparently in contempt of the nasty little sea, which kept the tug dancing to such an extent that the most expert boat jumper among them wished heartily that he were a better one. Their awe and dismay were not sensibly diminished when, on stepping over the side, they landed on an immense, wet, and considerably lumbered-up deck. The *Oregon* had just returned from a builder's trial to adjust compasses, and her deck was a confusion of enormous chains, hawsers, blocks, windlasses, guns, capstans, and pumps. For a couple of hours, the board wandered in small groups over and around the ship, lost in her immensity, and lost absolutely when they assayed the intricate passages of "down below." When the men assembled to plan and organize their work, a universal air of depression was plainly manifest, for the three officers had begun to realize the magnitude of the task before them. They listened with great interest to the suggestions of the official inspectors, who had gotten on familiar terms with the monster. However, as Beardslee, Clark, and Milligan buckled down to their work, the depression wore off.

After a day spent in inspection, they met to compare notes, finding themselves quite capable of disputing vigorously. Each proved to his own satisfaction that he understood what he was talking about.

Having divided themselves into subcommittees, the board members donned working suits and took up their task. Clark dived into holds, magazines, and shellrooms, crawled through double bottoms, and climbed into military tops and turrets. Milligan, in turn, toured engineering spaces. Beardslee remained in charge on the bridge. The ship's medical officer, who had nothing strictly professional to do until someone tumbled down a hatch or got stuck in a narrow passage, armed himself with a Kodak and crawled around for views. Each diver, crawler, and climber was provided by Union Iron Works officials with a brand-new memorandum book in which were pages headed "Defects Observed." When the inspectors reassembled to compare notes, those pages were in nearly all cases blank. At the most, they bore brief memoranda followed by question marks, which meant "to be referred for discussion." Every time someone proposed the question "Does this conform with the contract?" the vote was unanimously "aye." The board members were duty bound to take nothing for granted, but they were not to assume that all was wrong until proved right. Beardslee was authorized to accept the reports of preceding inspectors: otherwise his work would have been endless, for he could not judge the tensile strength and elastic limit of the millions of pounds of steel, nor the weights and dimensions of the thousands of parts that had entered into the composition of the ship and were now covered over. The board had confidence in the builders' ability and character, which had been demonstrated by good and honest work in building the *Olympia*, the *Monterey*, and the *Charleston*—three ships that later sailed with Dewey to Manila.

The *Oregon* left San Francisco early on May 9, not making a straight run to Santa Barbara, but devoting much time to experimental work—stopping at full speed and backing, running with one engine or both, and steering by different methods. When she did reach Santa Barbara, on the afternoon of the tenth, the board had a very fair idea of her performance under quite a range of varying situations—all, however, in fair-weather conditions. Beardslee and Clark longed (officially) for a gale.

The experiments continued until the thirteenth, when the final speed and endurance trial was to have taken place. A stiff breeze and a heavy swell from the southeast made a postponement necessary in order to secure a fair trial, so that day was spent at anchor. Some of the men wrote up notes, some enjoyed the hospitalities of the country club of Santa Barbara, some indulged in the delightful drives for which Santa Barbara was noted, and some worked at inspecting the deep holds.

Several United States vessels had been detailed to the service of the board, including the coast survey steamers *Gedney* and *McArthur*, the fishing commission's steamer *Albatross*, and the Mare Island tug *Unadilla*. A vessel was anchored at each end of the thirty-mile course, and the rest were stationed at intervals of ten miles along the channel. These ships served a twofold purpose. In the first place, their officers used special instruments to observe the direction and strength of the tidal and current flow during the trial and then corrected the speed record to allow for the flow. In the second place, the ships served as steering marks for the on-deck watch of the *Oregon*. With the mast of an anchored vessel for a front sight and the *Oregon's* jackstaff for a rear one, the helmsman could steer exactly.

At 7:00 A.M. on the 14th, Chief Engineer Robert Forsyth, a Union Iron Works man who superintended the engine department, reported all ready; and Irving M. Scott gave the word, "Go!" The *Oregon* was to run thirty sea miles to the westward, turn, and repeat to the eastward.

At 8:00 A.M., after a preliminary warming-up spin, the *Oregon* dashed across the first range line at a 17-knot gait. Passing Goleta Point, six miles beyond, she was going 17.5 knots (allowing for tidal correction, 17.34). The joyful ship leaped forward. She had her head. Everything was favorable. There was a light head swell that had no effect upon the ship; the accompanying moderate head wind gave her fires a good draft. It was a wonderful and exciting spectacle. Imagine the momentum and the pent-up energy of that ten-thousand-ton projectile with a velocity of thirty feet per second! The mere humans aboard were thrilled.

The run for the first thirty sea miles was at an average speed of over seventeen knots. As the *Oregon* neared Point Conception, the conditions grew less favorable. The head wind freshened, and the head swell increased considerably; the bow cut through instead of over, and the forward deck was afloat, which gave the board a chance to observe its freedom from leaks. A sea crashed hard! The jackstaff washed away, depriving the helmsman of his rear sight.

The sea was pouring over the bows in green masses and rushing aft in rivers, until, striking the foot of the forward turret, it deluged with spray everyone stationed there. Scott was comfortably seated under the lee of the pilothouse, apparently as unconcerned as though he were a passenger. As Beardslee, up to his eyes in business, was hurriedly passing Scott, the contractor detained the admiral a moment to chat about some matter of trifling importance. Beardslee, a man of nervous temperament, grew impatient. The unbroken train of successes on every trial of the ship had strongly biased him in favor of the *Oregon*. He dreaded that, at this crucial test, a journal might tear or something else go wrong. He was excited, and Scott noticed it.

"What's your hurry, Admiral? What are you excited about?" he asked.

"Great heavens, Mr. Scott," Beardslee answered, "why are *you not* excited? The breaking of a ten-cent bolt may cost you a hundred thousand dollars."

"Yes," retorted Scott, "I fully realize it; but *it isn't going to break. I know them all personally.*" Such sublime nerve could have been based only upon the utmost confidence in his own work.

However, after it was all over, Beardslee referred to this incident in correspondence with Scott, who replied, "Well, Admiral, I may have shown a smooth surface, but if you had only bored inside!"

The *Oregon* reached her western terminus some minutes ahead of schedule; so she ran a couple of miles farther before finally turning to port. The sea had by then increased, and the crew anticipated that when it got abeam

they should have a heavy roll. They therefore braced themselves and hung on for support; but the *Oregon* fooled them.
The roll was very slight, and there was not a moment when
every gun aboard could not have been used effectively. The
return to the eastward was but a repetition, except that the
draft was inferior because the ship was running with the
wind; the firemen were not so fresh; and the fires were
therefore less bright. As a result, the speed fell off a little.
The *Oregon* made her eastward run at an average of 16.49
knots, and the average for the entire sixty-two sea miles was
16.791 knots. This was the *Oregon*'s official record for four
hours, and it earned her builders a $175,000 bonus.

In observing the speed, Beardslee had noticed early in
the trial that the two patent logs did not agree. As the *Oregon* passed Goleta Point, they disagreed, not only with each
other, but with the distance by range. The logs were
promptly hauled in and put out of commission. Three groups
of officers were stationed to observe the ranges—one group on
the bow, one on the midship bridge, and one aft. When the
whitewashed stakes came into line at the bow station, the
officers there ordered, "Mark!" The midship station and the
aft station repeated the procedure, and with every shout of
"Mark!" the steam whistle gave a short, sharp blast. The
exact time of each blast was recorded. This sequence of
events was repeated at each station, and finally the figures
were averaged out. If the mean of the times of the first and
third blasts coincided with the time of the second, the cor-
rectness of the figures was confirmed. It always was, for
plenty of drill had made the boys accurate. For a few hours,
however, there was lively work. Sixteen and three-quarter
knots per hour means about twenty-eight feet per second.
The observing stations were only a little over a hundred feet
apart; so the *Oregon* passed a station every four seconds.
There was no time to make mistakes.

The board had no doubt as to the accuracy of the marking, but they were very glad of an additional and incontrovertible proof of speed: William R. Eckart, consulting engineer of the Union Iron Works, had contrived a very ingenious automatic device by which the steam of the second blast opened and immediately closed a shutter in a camera aimed shoreward. Each resulting photograph showed the whitewashed stakes in line.

After the speed test and the four-hour endurance trial, the *Oregon* was run another hour, slowing down by degrees, like a racehorse, to cool off. Then she steamed to her Santa Barbara anchorage, where Beardslee telegraphed the glad tidings to Washington and San Francisco. At 3:00 P.M., although the wind was strong from northwest and there was an ugly sea running, she weighed anchor for home.

Beardslee thought they had completed their tests, but he was mistaken. The gale he had officially longed for had arrived. By the time the *Oregon* reached Point Conception, he had all he wanted, and more, too; but the storm did not seem to make a great deal of difference to the *Oregon*. Beardslee took advantage of the new circumstances by conducting experiments at different speeds—stopping, backing, and so forth. In a couple of hours, he had found out all he needed to know about the *Oregon*'s performance in a gale. The results were admirable.

All were overcome by weariness and wetness, and the zeal of at least some board members abated. A hasty vote was taken, all agreed that they were satisfied, and they gladly ran into Santa Cruz Harbor for the night. Early the next morning, the gale having abated, the *Oregon* started for home.

During the passage from Santa Cruz, the weather was fair, and the crewmen devoted themselves to cleaning the ship and ornamenting her with flags. A broom was set at each masthead, a symbol that signified, as in Van Tromp's day, that the ship had swept the seas of all competitors. Unknown to Scott, the men also stretched along the boats a wide strip of canvas on which was inscribed, "Scotts Got the Cramps." The message referred to the comparative record of the sister ships *Oregon, Massachusetts,* and *Indiana,* the first built by the Scotts, the other two by the William Cramp and Sons Shipyard, Philadelphia. It was as follows: *Indiana,* 15.6 knots; *Massachusetts,* 16.15 knots; *Oregon,* 16.79 knots. The *Oregon* was in.

As the *Oregon* entered the Golden Gate, she was met by a tug crowded with enthusiastic Californians, friends of the Scotts. The ship stopped while a few passengers came on board, caught Scott, and removed him forcibly to the tug's deck, where for a few minutes he was the most thoroughly embraced, hugged, and even kissed man in the state. San Francisco went wild again that day.

July 15, 1896, was a warm bright day in San Francisco, and the *Oregon,* officially designated as the BB-3, was ready for commissioning. Capt. Henry L. Howison, U.S.N., who had witnessed the launching of the *Oregon* three years before, had been selected as the first commanding officer of the new ship.

The ceremony that commissioned the big, turreted sea monster into service was brief but impressive. The affair was scheduled for 11:00 A.M. and its importance attracted many civilians to the ship. The officers put on their full-dress uniforms and brought their families with them. The marines and bluejackets had polished up the guns, holystoned the decks, and burnished their own accouterments and shoes. All was shipshape and Bristol fashion. The ship looked smart.

At just 11:06, Lieutenant Commander Drake, the executive officer, ordered all visitors off the aft deck, and the ceremonies began. A bugle call brought the marines, who numbered sixty, from their quarters forward. They came aft two by two with the rhythmic tread of the sea soldier and

lined up in two rows along the starboard rail. A second blast
on the bugle, and the bluejackets came scurrying from
doors, hatches, turrets, scuttles, and even portholes—all
hands from the gunner's mate to the Chinese mess boy.
There were 250 sailors on board the vessel that day, and
they had been divided into two watches, which lined up on
either side of the big turret aft. Captain Howison and the
ship's officers took their places forward on the port side.

At a nod from Howison, two sturdy bluejackets quick-
hauled the ensign up the flagstaff. As the flag rose skyward,
its graceful folds fluttering on the morning breeze, the
officers and crew uncovered in the old navy salute. The male
spectators also removed their hats. Up on the main truck of
the ship's mast, Captain Howison's pennant was cast loose.
The long banner snapped in the wind. The captain stepped
to the center of the deck and read his orders from the Navy
Department, detaching him as special initiation officer of
the initiation ceremonies and appointing him to command
the proud new vessel. Following this, he made a speech. It
was short—very short—and to the point. "This ship," he
began, "has now been turned over to the navy yard and put
under our charge. She has been called the guns of the navy,
and is a credit to her builders. I only hope she will sustain
that reputation during her commission."

Everyone applauded, the bugle sounded, the ceremony
was over.

Irving M. Scott was the first to shake hands with Captain Howison after the commissioning was over.

"That was a good speech," said Scott. "Let me congrat-
ulate you." The builder and the ship's captain then walked
arm in arm to the wardroom while the spectators, who numbered about fifty, ranged all over the ship. As Scott and Howison left the weather deck they could be heard talking
about the most pressing military question then current: the
growing possibility of a war with Spain.

# 4

# The
# Captain
# and
# Castile

To American naval authorities in the last decade of the
nineteenth century, war with Spain seemed inevitable. Cuba
was the heart of the matter. Indeed, during both the nineteenth and the twentieth centuries, that island has been a
thorn in the American conscience and the source of a military threat.

During the first quarter of the nineteenth century,
Americans had sympathized with the various revolutionary
movements in Central and South America and seen the ex-
pulsion of Spain from her colonies in the Western Hemisphere as a natural and desired result of the impetus of their
own revolution against Great Britain. The Cubans, too, had
desired freedom from their European masters; yet, when in-
vasions of Cuba were planned, first by Simon Bolivar and
then, in 1825, by Mexico and Colombia, America used her

influence to block the expeditions. Cuban freedom would have meant the liberation of Cuban slaves, and the United States did not want millions of free Negroes living off her coast in proximity to the slave states. As late as 1843, Daniel Webster stated that the emancipation of Negroes in Cuba would strike a death-blow to American slavery. Then commenced a series of filibustering expeditions designed to annex Cuba as a slave state. They were supported by proslavery forces in the United States. President James Buchanan even attempted to purchase Cuba, but Spain refused.

After slavery lost its political power in the 1860s, America temporarily lost interest in Cuba. But the Cubans themselves would not let American concern for Cuban affairs die. Spain had put down a Cuban revolt as early as 1826, and, during the mid-1800s, a series of Cuban and foreign attempts to liberate the island all failed. The fiasco of the Bay of Pigs had several nineteenth century antecedents. During the Grant administration, Secretary of State Hamilton Fish again broached the possibility of American purchase, but Spain turned him down.

American sympathy for the Cuban revolutionaries began to grow once again, and the *Virginius* affair cemented American antagonism towards Spain's policies in Cuba and Puerto Rico and made the war of 1898 inevitable. In 1873, the gun-running, American-registered steamer *Virginius* was overhauled on the high seas by the Spanish gunboat *Tornado* and taken to Cuba, where some fifty of her officers and crew—American citizens for the most part—were summarily shot. The American people seethed with anger and demanded war. President Grant calmly and wisely chose arbitration, and the registry of the *Virginius* proved to be false. Compensation was paid to the United States, and the incident passed; but the affair left a deep distrust for Spain in the American mind. New York-based Cuban exiles soon began to attack Spain with a sensational propaganda campaign that rivals any of the twentieth century. They were greatly aided by the yellow journalism of two influential New York newspapers, Joseph Pulitzer's *World* and William Randolph Hearst's *Journal*. Spain was portrayed as the rapist, murdering monster of the Western Hemisphere. In actuality, her antiinsurrection methods were harsh indeed, but not as barbaric as they were made out to be. In fact, they were less severe than twentieth century counterinsurgency techniques.

The guerrilla war became more vigorous as the insurgents sensed that they might defeat the weakening imperial power if they could only be patient enough—and if they could draw on American aid. Furthermore, they were beginning to develop some adequate military leaders and field commanders, such as Antonio Maceo and Mario Garcia and the accomplished guerrilla leader Gen. Maximo Gomez. In 1895, the tide of battle turned towards the rebels, and they captured most of the countryside, but Spain held the cities. The situation formed a stalemate, for the Spanish could never take back the countryside and the rebels could never capture the fortified towns. The Cleveland administration, although sympathetic to the rebels, refused to take direct action. On July 13, 1895, the Cubans won a decisive victory in the Battle of Bayamo. The Spanish Captain-General of Cuba, Martinez Campos, was forced to resign and return to Spain. He had been a humane and reasonably intelligent viceroy. He was replaced by a harsher man.

Gen. Valeriano Weyler came to Cuba on February 10, 1896, with an odious reputation for repression, cruelty, and corruption in the governance of the Philippines and in the military suppression of disorders in Barcelona. In order to destroy peasant support for the insurrection, Weyler rounded up most of Cuba's rural population and herded the people into concentration camps created for them in the garrison towns. The suffering of the peasant internees, de-

prived of their already meager source of livelihood, was appalling, and it touched the conscience of the rest of the
civilized world. By the time the *Oregon* was launched, Spain
had one hundred fifty thousand troops in Cuba and more on
the way. In other words, a huge European army, far larger
than America's regular army (which consisted chiefly of Indian fighters), was camped on an island only ninety miles
from the coast of Florida, and this foreign army was engaged in brutally suppressing the political aspirations of the
indigenous population.

When Scott and Howison chatted after the commissioning ceremony in July, 1896, they surely discussed the
strength of the Spanish fleet and the possibility of the *Oregon*'s someday seeing action against Spanish units.

After the commissioning, Howison took the *Oregon* on
an eighteen hundred mile run to Acapulco, Mexico, to test
coal consumption at various speeds. In those days, such a
voyage was considered a long one, especially for a battleship
supposedly designed for coast defense. Upon her return to
the Golden Gate, on February 16, 1897, the *Oregon* was ordered to Puget Sound and again battled a severe storm
without damage.

On March 20, 1897, Capt. Albert S. Barker was given
command of the ship and, in June of that year, the *Oregon*
was ordered to proceed to Esquimalt, British Columbia, to
represent the government at the golden jubilee celebrating
the fiftieth year of the reign of Queen Victoria.

The *Oregon* returned to Seattle on July 6, 1897, and
was placed in dry dock for overhauling. Captain Barker and
his officers proceeded to Portland, Oreg., where a magnificent, $25,000, thirty piece silver punch set was pre-
sented to the officers for use on the state's namesake, the *Oregon.*

The schoolchildren of the state were given the honor of
helping to raise this sum by donating not more than ten

cents each. Adults were allowed to contribute twenty-five cents. Contributions rolled in from all parts of the state, and soon the order was placed in the hands of Feldenheimers Silversmiths of Portland.

Feldenheimers produced a service consisting of a large punch bowl and dipper, a slop bowl and dipper, a large tray, and twenty-four holders for the twenty-four crystal glasses. Each piece was beautifully engraved, the principal design being the beaver. On the side of the punch bowl was engraved the following:

FROM THE
CITIZENS OF THE STATE OF OREGON
TO THE
U.S. BATTLESHIP "OREGON"
1896

On July 6, 1897, the magnificent silver service was formally presented by Governor William Paine Lord on behalf of the people of Oregon to Captain Barker, who represented the officers and men of the *Oregon*.

Multnomah Field was chosen for the presentation, but, on account of inclement weather, the local armory was used. Because of the hurried change, a very small crowd witnessed the ceremony. The silver service was conspicuously placed on a large table, resting amid the folds of an American flag. Around the table were ranged representatives of the navy and of various state and city departments.

Mr. Dodd, chairman of the fund-raising project's committee, introduced Governor Lord, who made the presentation speech. Captain Barker accepted the service on behalf of the government and of the officers and men of the *Oregon*. After the silver service was carefully packed and ready to carry to Seattle, the floor was cleared, and an exhibition drill was performed by two hundred sailors from the monitors *Monterey* and *Monadnock*, which were anchored in Portland Harbor.

In the fall of 1897, the *Oregon* received money and authorization for the installation of rolling chocks and bilge keels, which would increase her stability in a seaway. The ship was ordered to the then-new navy yard at Bremerton, Wash., where the work was accomplished in the dry dock now designated as No. 1.

On January 17, 1898, Capt. Alexander H. McCormick, U.S.N., took command. A month later, on February 16, a shocking report, which had been rushed over the wires of the transcontinental telegraph, was hurried to the office of the Bremerton Navy Yard Commandant. He read it aloud in an incredulous tone to Captain McCormick. The United States battleship *Maine* had been destroyed in Havana Harbor by an explosion at 9:40 the night before!

In December of the previous year, the United States consul general in Havana, Gen. Fitzhugh Lee (a former Confederate officer and a nephew of Robert E. Lee), had become nervous about the potential threat to American lives and property in Havana. The Cuban situation had grown more and more ugly, and hotheaded young Spanish officers had begun to react to the propaganda barrages against Spain in the American press. Lee had requested Washington to have a warship made ready to come to Havana to support him and his office if it became necessary "to show the flag," and consequently the *Maine* had been put on alert in Key West. She was under the command of Capt. Charles D. Sigsbee, U.S.N., an intelligent, capable, bespectacled officer.

An incident by a few young Spanish officers in Havana was blown up all out of proportion by the rabid American press, and President McKinley ordered the *Maine* to sail to Havana on a "friendly" visit. At about the same time, the Spanish cruiser *Vizcaya*, so soon to be destroyed at Santiago, was dispatched to New York by her government "since courtesy visits had been resumed." The *Maine* had her orders on January 24, and she sailed even though Lee had misgivings and wished a postponement. On the morning of January 25, the *Maine* steamed by the Morro Castle of Havana, exchanging salutes with the fortification, and was courteously piloted by a Spanish pilot to an assigned mooring buoy. Sigsbee and some of his officers went ashore on official business, but there was no liberty for the crew, who were very unhappy indeed to be deprived of the well-known pleasures of a Havana shore leave.

Days and nights passed uneventfully, although Sigsbee kept the *Maine* on alert even to the extent of having a steam launch patrol the ship's perimeter. Then the unforeseen took place: on the evening of February 15, there was a muffled explosion below decks followed by a tremendous blast that sent the wrecked warship to the bottom with 266 men. Only her smashed and twisted superstructure remained above the dark waters of the old harbor. Sigsbee never lost his cool, and he began an immediate investigation. Unfortunately, neither his efforts nor the work of subsequent investigations could adequately determine whether the cause of the blast was a Spanish mine or an internal explosion. A navy board suspected a mine. When in 1911 the *Maine* was finally raised and towed to sea for an honorable burial, it was still impossible to determine the cause. Modern theory is that an internal blast probably set off a magazine.

Of course, the *World* and the *Journal* tried and condemned Spain immediately and shrieked for war. Left alone in the office of Secretary of the Navy John D. Long one afternoon, the brash, young jingoistic assistant secretary, Theodore Roosevelt, sent a cable alerting Comm. George Dewey and the Asiatic Squadron to be ready to destroy the Spanish Asiatic squadron as soon as war broke out.

The *Oregon* at Bremerton was in an embarrassing position as war clouds loomed. As was the custom, she had unloaded all her ammunition at Mare Island before heading to the northern yard, so she was ordered to proceed immediately to San Francisco to get that ammo back on board.

All coal at the Bremerton Navy Yard had been used to supply ships heading for Alaska in the Klondike gold rush; so Captain McCormick could not get the *Oregon* underway until more coal reached Bremerton on March 6. Three days later, he was in San Francisco, and the crew was turning to in furious fashion around the clock, taking on ammunition, stores, and coal.

Scuttlebutt had it that the *Oregon* would proceed to Callao, Peru, from which she could conveniently depart for the Philippines or the Atlantic, as the Navy Department might decide. For once rumor proved true, and the ship was ordered to proceed on March 18 to the Peruvian port to await further orders. Only two days prior to sailing, Captain McCormick, whose health had been deteriorating, became seriously ill and had to be relieved. On March 17, the *Oregon's* third and greatest commander hastily had his steaming gear hauled aboard his new command. It was Saint Patrick's Day and, as might have been expected, Chief Boatswain's Mate "Spud" Murphy piped the new commander aboard. The heavyset, fatherly looking officer with the walrus moustache was a fifty-five-year-old veteran of the Civil War. He knew the *Oregon*, and he knew the navy. Charles Edgar Clark was his name, and he was the right man at the right time.

Clark was born in Bradford, Vt., on August 10, 1843, into an old New England family with army traditions. As a youth, Clark had hopes of entering West Point. Unfortunately or fortunately, he was unable to secure an appointment to the military academy. As something of a consolation, his kindly congressman offered him one to the United States Naval Academy, which he first declined but later accepted. Thus, on September 29, 1860, the 17-year-old lad was appointed acting midshipman.

While Clark was at Annapolis, his family moved to Montpelier, Vt., the birthplace of Admiral Dewey. Some forty years later, a local Montpelier orator would, with traditional New England humor, refer to the conflict just concluded as "the war between the village of Montpelier and the kingdom of Spain."

When Clark reported in to the academy, the school and barracks ship for fourth classmen was the United States frigate *Constitution;* so the first navy deck the young midshipman trod was the main deck of "Old Ironsides." One of Clark's favorite instructors at the academy was Alfred Thayer Mahan.

With the onset of the Civil War, the naval academy was moved from Maryland far north to Newport, R. I., for safety, and all three classes above Clark's were ordered to active service. At the academy, one of Clark's best friends and classmates was Francis A. Cook, who would command the *Brooklyn* at the Battle of Santiago and receive the surrender of the Spanish cruiser *Colon.*

During the summer of 1862, as the Civil War raged, the young midshipmen made their first practice cruise in the sloop-of-war *John Adams*. They sailed to Hampton Roads, where they saw the wreckage of the wooden-hulled *Congress* and *Cumberland,* both smashed by the *Merrimac,* and heard the details of the *Monitor's* revolutionary success. Still, Clark was learning the trade of a windship sailor, and much of his career would be spent in wooden sailing ships— a clear example of technology being generations ahead of the imagination and practice of men.

Clark's second cruise and first trip across the Atlantic took place in the summer of 1863, as Gettysburg and Vicksburg boiled in death's cauldron. He shipped aboard the corvette *Macedonian,* commanded by the great Capt. Stephen

B. Luce, U.S.N. The *Macedonian* had been captured from
the British by the frigate *United States* in the War of 1812
and later rebuilt. She made for some interesting conversation in England.

In October, 1863, after only three years in the academy,
Clark and his class were graduated and received their pro-
motions to acting ensign. The young officer was assigned to
the sloop-of-war *Ossipee* on station with Farragut's West
Gulf Blockading Squadron. Clark joined the *Ossipee* lying off
Galveston, Tex., the day before Thanksgiving.

The *Ossipee*'s patrol was the Confederate coast west of
the Mississippi, and the chasing and overtaking of blockade
runners constituted Clark's first combat experience. His second combat experience was a first-class raking over by Adm.
David Glasgow Farragut himself, when the unfortunate ensign had to present a request for unauthorized supplies to
the Flag on behalf of his own out-of-favor commanding
officer. It was the only attention Farragut ever paid to
young Clark, who faithfully avoided the old warrior for
safety's sake from then on.

The high point of Clark's Civil War service came on the
morning of August 5, 1864, when the *Ossipee* fell into line to
pass the Confederate forts and attack the Southern fleet at
the entrance to Mobile Bay. Clark was in charge of a division of four guns, including the forecastle pivot gun, the first
of the *Ossipee*'s cannon to open fire. The ship passed the
gauntlet of fire from Fort Morgan with only a few casualties
and light damage, and she was equally fortunate in her passing encounter and exchange with the ram *Tennessee*. But
Adm. Franklin Buchanan, senior Confederate naval officer
at Mobile Bay, brought the *Tennessee* back for more. Farragut was determined to destroy the Confederacy's only
capital ship, and so he ordered his squadron, one by one, to
broadside, ram, and sink the damaged ironclad. The *Richmond* and the *Brooklyn* closed and poured shot and shell

into the enemy vessel. Then the *Hartford* struck with her bow and was herself seriously damaged. She fired her guns furiously and at a fantastic rate.

Tied to the rigging of the *Hartford,* Farragut waved the *Ossipee* on. The *Ossipee*'s throttle was wide open, and the wooden ship raced to a collision with the ironclad. On the forecastle, Clark suddenly saw a Confederate officer appear above the casement of the *Tennessee,* waving a white flag. Clark raced aft to the captain to report and then transmitted to the *Tennessee* the captain's order: "Put your helm to starboard! Ours is to port." But it was too late, and anyway the wheel ropes of the *Tennessee* had been shot away. The *Ossipee,* her engines backing full, nevertheless struck hard, but neither ship sank. The *Tennessee,* the last hope of the Confederate navy in the gulf, then surrendered to the *Ossipee.*

After the war, Clark began thirty-three years of peacetime duty as a naval officer serving a nation that had little interest in sea power or military affairs but preferred to expend its energies in the westward movement, in binding up the nation's wounds, and in prodigious economic expansion. His career was typical, his advancement unspectacular within the shackles of a most rigid seniority system.

Clark's first duty after the war was in the U.S.S. *Vanderbilt,* a side-wheeler donated by Commodore Vanderbilt to the United States government during the Civil War. Clark had two promotions on the *Vanderbilt,* to the grade of master on May 10, 1866, and to lieutenant on February 21, 1867. His next ship was the U.S.S. *Sewanee,* a double ender. Aboard the *Sewanee,* he passed the examination for promotion to lieutenant commander and reached that grade on March 12, 1868, at the age of twenty-four. It would be thirteen years until his next promotion.

At six o'clock on the morning of July 7, 1868, the *Sewanee* was cruising off the northern end of Vancouver Island with Clark the officer of the deck. Running at full speed with a following current of almost three knots, she struck an uncharted rock and was instantly ground into a total wreck. All the crew made it ashore, and Clark soon found himself in charge of a party of shipwrecked sailors on Hope Island waiting for rescue and holding off hostile Indians. Clark's group was eventually rescued by the Royal Navy.

Clark was detached from the Pacific Fleet and ordered home. On his way to Montpelier, he stopped off at Greenfield, Mass., to renew his acquaintance with the family of his classmate George T. Davis and particularly with Davis's youngest sister, Louisa. They were married on April 8, 1869: a naval officer generally has little time to waste. They would have two daughters, both of whom married officers in the United States Navy.

In July, 1870, Clark was assigned as navigator of the monitor *Dictator* with the Atlantic Fleet. Two months later, he left the *Dictator* and began his first shore duty, as an instructor and assistant to the commandant of midshipmen at the naval academy, where he stayed until 1873. After the academy tour, Clark was assigned as executive officer on another monitor, the U.S.S. *Mahopac*. Ordered to the Asiatic Squadron in February, 1874, Clark and his family rode the trains across country to San Francisco and then sailed on the S.S. *Colorado* to Yokohama. There Clark reported to Rear Adm. Alexander Mosley Pennock, who was flying his flag on Farragut's beloved *Hartford*. Pennock assigned Clark to the U.S.S. *Yantic* as executive officer. She was lying off Shanghai, and Clark had to leave his family at Nagasaki.

After seven months on the *Yantic*, Clark was ordered to the *Hartford* as executive officer and later wound up as executive officer of the U.S.S. *Monocaci*, a light draft paddlewheeler. The *Monocaci* was one of the first of the Yankee gunboats on the China Station, and Clark finished his Asiatic tour in the Yangtze upwater.

In August, 1881, after two years of shore duty at the Boston Navy Yard, Clark reported to the U.S.S. *New Hampshire*, an old ship-of-the-line that was fitting out for the training of naval apprentices. The old sailing ships were the boot camps of the day. On November 15, Clark was promoted to commander and given control of the *New Hampshire*, usually a captain's billet.

Clark's next duty afloat was the command of the U.S.S. *Ranger*, a bark-rigged, screw propeller steamer fitted out for survey work in the North Pacific. Among his subordinate officers involved in the hydrographic work was Ensign Albert A. Ackerman, U.S.N., who would command one of the *Oregon*'s turrets at the Battle of Santiago. The work on the *Ranger* was grueling, and, when his cruise was completed, Clark welcomed five years of shore duty, mostly as a lighthouse inspector on the Great Lakes.

In May, 1894, Clark was given command of the steam sloop-of-war *Mohican* and placed at the head of the Bering Sea Patrol, a squadron of ten vessels, with orders to enforce the sealing regulations recently agreed upon by arbitration in Paris. Clark's service in this capacity was outstanding. On June 21, 1896, he was promoted to captain. Other duty on the Pacific coast followed, including command of the receiving ship *Independence* and of the monitor *Monterey*, from which he was detached on March 15, 1898, with emergency orders to leave San Diego as soon as possible and proceed to San Francisco to take immediate command of the battleship *Oregon*.

# 5

# "Six Thousand Miles to the Indian Isles"

Clark had only forty-eight hours on board the *Oregon* before she had to shove off for the long and dangerous run to the east coast to join the American Battle Fleet. (The crew, for security reasons, did not know whether they were heading for Cuba or the Philippines.) Forty-eight hours to take on the last of 1,600 tons of coal, 500 tons of ammunition, and enough stores for six months. The ship stepped deep into the water. All hands toiled around the clock. Clark himself was exhausted when, early on the morning of March 19, 1898, the *Oregon*—displacing almost 12,000 tons and short twenty-seven men in the black gang and sixty-seven hands on deck—departed her birthplace and began a voyage that would live in history.

The officers of the *Oregon* on this voyage are listed in Appendix B. William D. Leahy, an engineer cadet on the cruise, became one of the nation's great military leaders of World War II.

Orders were to make for Callao, Peru, four thousand miles away, as fast as possible. The *Oregon* would average 250 nautical miles per day, an excellent cruising clip for a ship supposedly designed as a coast defense battleship. The one problem that arose as she moved towards the equator was that of ventilation in the firerooms and other engineering spaces, where temperatures rose to the range of 110 to 150 degrees.

As soon as the *Oregon* cleared San Francisco Bay and all divisions reported secure for sea, Clark commenced such battle drills as clearing ship for action, gunnery drill, and damage control. The drills would continue all through the voyage and, indeed, up to the very day of battle in July. As with Isaac Hull and Thomas Truxtun, drill was Clark's text and sermon of military service. The only day off in the sixteen-day run to Peru was when the *Oregon* crossed the line. King Neptune was piped aboard to receive his customary honors due.

However, Clark did allow the ship's band to present a concert each evening on the boat deck before tattoo. It played the popular dance tunes of the Gay Nineties. Also, Clark would gather his officers in the wardroom for a game of whist. From the beginning, Clark evidenced that superb but rare mixture of humaneness and strength that forms the core of the kind of leadership that evokes devotion.

A week out of San Francisco, Chief Engineer Milligan informed Clark that, with the boilers continuing to make a full head of steam, the supply of fresh water for the crew would have to be severely limited. The engineer rightly did not wish to impair the efficiency of his boilers by contaminating them with salt water. Clark was deeply concerned for the health and endurance of his crew, for not only would drinking water be limited, but it would be available only in the form of hot, distilled feed water. He called all hands, except those on watch, topside to explain.

In his autobiography, *My Fifty Years in the Navy,* Clark would write:

> When I explained to the men, however, that salt water in the boilers meant scale, and that scale would reduce our speed, delay us in getting to the seat of war, and might impair our efficiency in battle, the deprivation was borne without a murmur. The very small quantity of ice that was made on board went to the firemen and coal passers, and however much the rest of us may have longed for a little to cool the lukewarm drinking water, I know that it was not only willingly, but cheerfully given up.[1]

Milligan had another idea: Why not save for an emergency the best coal on board, the "dusky diamonds" from Cardiff, Wales, taken on board in San Francisco? The quality of coal was an extremely important factor in a warship's ability to operate to her maximum capability. Purer coal meant hotter fires, more steam, and thus more speed. It also meant less ash to be hauled topside and "deep sixed." Clark agreed, and, underway and at night, the willing crew redistributed the coal in the bunkers so that Cardiff coal was in a standby position. Coaling ship—that most filthy, backbreaking, and despised job—was miserable even in port with unlimited water available for washing; but handling vast amounts of the black fuel at sea, aboard a rolling ship and without fresh water to wash with, was even more miserable. After the job was finished, decks, equipment, and men were all flushed down with salt water dipped from the sea.

On arriving at Callao, Clark was disappointed to hear that the board of inquiry appointed to look into the circumstances that led to the sinking of the *Maine* had not yet announced its findings. He was informed by the Navy Department that the Spanish torpedo boat *Temerario* had been reported off the east coast of South America but that its destination was unknown. When this intelligence reached the crew, the word was passed that, if the *Oregon* were ordered to the Atlantic and the *Temerario* were met in the Strait of Magellan, Captain Clark intended to sink the Spanish ship, war or no war.

The Peruvians seemed to strongly favor the United States in her threatened war with Spain. But it was also reported that some of the Spanish residents of Callao and Lima were plotting to sink or blow up the *Oregon*. Rumor or fact, Clark took no chances and ordered the sentries doubled. During the hours of darkness, a steam launch patrolled around the ship to detect and investigate approaching boats, and its searchlights were kept at the ready.

On April 6, Clark received word that the board of inquiry had blamed Spain for the *Maine* disaster. With this news came word that the Navy Department had definitely decided to use the *Oregon* and the *Marietta* in the Atlantic. The bunkers of the battleship were immediately filled with 1,100 tons of coal that Commander Symonds, captain of the U.S. gunboat *Marietta,* had purchased for the *Oregon* before her arrival in Callao.

The *Oregon* set sail on the morning of April 7, 1898, after fifty hot, backbreaking, tense hours in Callao. Clark knew that Spanish intelligence had made inquiries as to the day and time of the ship's intended departure, and so she slipped out quietly, aided by a fog bank, with only Clark aware of her destination. She would try to slip past the Spanish Atlantic squadron, commanded by Adm. Pascual Cervera y Topete, and join the American fleet assembling off the Florida coast. This fleet would soon be under the command of William T. Sampson, who would be promoted from captain to rear admiral and ordered by President McKinley to blockade Cuba. While the *Oregon* was still en route to Florida, diplomatic relations between the United States and Spain would break down, efforts at international mediation

*Oregon*, 1898 (U.S. Bureau of Ships)

*Oregon* 13-inch gun breech (Oregon Historical Society)

*Oregon* Fireroom (Oregon Historical Society)

Moving the *Oregon* to Marine Park at the foot of S. W. Jefferson Street, Portland, September 11, 1938 (Oregon Historical Society)

Removing the mast for the Battleship *Oregon* Park, 1942 (Oregon Historical Society)

would fail, last-minute Spanish concessions to Cuba would prove unacceptable to an enraged American public, and Congress would declare on April 25 that a state of war existed between the United States and Spain as of April 21.

Heading south, the *Oregon* forced 12 to 13.5 knots and handled beautifully, even when shipping heavy seas from the steadily worsening weather along the coast of Patagonia. Despite the storms, the gun crews were exercised each day with subcaliber firing and small arms practice. On April 16, the *Oregon* was running before a moderate gale, visibility extremely limited, and trying to make the entrance to the Strait of Magellan. Finally, the weather broke for a moment, and Clark could see the Evangelistas and Cape Pillar. He ordered full speed to try to make the safe anchorage at Tamar Island while there was still some light left, but the storm increased to a full gale, and the ship could not make the anchorage before nightfall. Clark was worried. He knew the shores were littered with the wrecks of a hundred ships, sail and steamer. He ordered soundings from the chains, but to no avail. The seas prevented accurate readings. Clark decided to try to anchor and ordered one let go. With a wild rush and a shattering roar, the anchor cable flew out 125 fathoms before the smoking brakes could check it. At last, it bit into the ground, and the other anchor was paid out under foot. The anchors held, and the *Oregon* was safe, but not a sailor undressed or slept a wink that night.

At first light the next morning, the anchors were weighed, and the *Oregon* was soon racing through the narrowest reaches of the strait, chased by a heavy snow storm, with sheer black cliffs looming to port and starboard. Towards evening, the crew sighted Cape Froward, the extreme tip of the continent, and at night the ship came to anchor at Sandy Point. The passage of 165 miles had been made in eleven hours with the fireroom blowers increasing the natural draft of the funnels. A remarkable speed for a battleship of the day.

Now the crew expected to meet the Spanish torpedo boat *Temerario,* and all guns were loaded and manned, while constant lookout was maintained "below and aloft." Coaling proceeded at Sandy Point or Punta Arenas. The fuel was purchased from a Scottish agent and had to be taken from a hulk in which wool had been stored on top. The crew worked hard, and the agent made things more difficult by insisting that the hoisting buckets be frequently weighed. As one bucket reached the *Oregon's* weather deck, Chief Murphy, in Irish exasperation at Scottish tightness, yelled down to the agent: "Here! Lower again for another weigh! There's a fly on the edge of that bucket!"

The gunboat *Marietta,* mounting six guns, joined the *Oregon* at Sandy Point. She coaled too and participated in the security patrol by launches.

At first light on April 21, the two vessels sailed in consort under sealed orders. That afternoon, the *Oregon* spoke to an American steamer en route from Montevideo to the Klondike. The steamer signaled that there were "prospects of peace." It was the day on which hostilities would officially be considered to have begun.

The ships, however, sailed on a strictly war footing: no lights carried, guns loaded, searchlights ready, the crew sleeping at their battle stations. Clark was taking no chances. The *Marietta,* a slower ship than the *Oregon,* was nevertheless ordered to scout ahead. The *Marietta* tossed barrels in her wake, and Clark had his gun crews at target practice whenever possible, using small arms inserted in the barrels of the big guns so as to test aim and accuracy without wasting precious large-caliber ammunition.

The gunboat could only make ten knots in calm seas, and the South Atlantic slowed her to eight. Nearing Rio de Janeiro, their next port of call, Clark ordered the *Marietta* to proceed independently and sent the *Oregon* racing ahead. The *Oregon* made Rio on the afternoon of April 30, with the rail manned, "The Star-Spangled Banner" and "Hail Columbia" blaring from the ship's band, and cheers broadsiding the Brazilian fleet and waterfront. The battlecry was "Remember the Maine!"

There the *Oregon* learned that war had been declared. Another ship was waiting to join Clark's armada, and a supply of coal was ready. The additional consort was the dynamite cruiser *Nictheroy*, purchased from the Brazilians for $1 million (to buy friendship as well as a warship) and later renamed the *Buffalo*.

It was back to the coal barges for the crew. The dispatches from the Naval War Board in Washington, on which Alfred Thayer Mahan was sitting, again said, "Beware the *Temerario*." The enemy vessel supposedly had left Montevideo and was headed for Rio. The *Oregon* would never see the *Temerario*.

Clark moved the *Oregon* to an unusual anchorage in mid-harbor, where no vessel would have an excuse to approach. He informed the Brazilian admiral that Brazil was expected to prevent any hostile acts by Spanish vessels in neutral waters, and that the *Oregon* would sink any Spanish vessel that approached within half a mile of her anchorage.

The Brazilian government proved friendly and readily agreed to the demands. The American steam cutters patrolled all night, the searchlights were in use, and the rapid-fire guns were always manned. The *Marietta* anchored as picket vessel in a position to cover the entrance to the harbor. At night, the Brazilian admiral sent a cruiser to patrol outside the harbor entrance, and with her searchlights and those from the forts, it would have been impossible for a Spanish ship to enter the harbor unseen. Sentries were placed on the coal barges, for Spanish sympathizers with bombs in their possession had been apprehended near them, and all coal was carefully examined before it was put on board.

On May 2 came the news of Dewey's superb victory in Manila Bay. The great commodore, with a small squadron of cruisers led by the *Olympia,* had crushed the Spanish Asiatic squadron in a single morning and won an empire for his country. Only one American life had been lost. Clark himself heaved a deep sigh of relief: his son-in-law was serving with Dewey.

The scene that followed the publication of this news in Rio might be likened to an Indian war dance, for the coal-blackened men fairly went wild. They danced on the coal barges and decks. The entire American colony, including the American minister, came on board to celebrate.

Meanwhile, the officers were carefully and secretly considering the dispatch from the Navy Department: "Four Spanish armored cruisers, heavy and fast, three torpedo-boat destroyers sailed April 29 from Cape de Verde to the west. Destination unknown. Beware of and study carefully the situation. Must be left to your discretion entirely to avoid this fleet and to reach the United States by West Indies. You can go when and where you desire. *Nictheroy* and *Marietta* subject to the orders of yourself."[2]

Captain Clark's answer to the department was as follows: "The receipt of telegram of May 3 is acknowledged. Will proceed in obedience to orders I have received. Keeping near the Brazilian coast, as the Navy Department considers the Spanish fleet from Cape de Verde superior, will be unsuitable. I can coal from the *Nictheroy,* if necessity compels it, to reach the United States. If the *Nictheroy* delays too much I shall hasten passage leaving her with the *Marietta.* Every department of the *Oregon* in fine condition."[3]

A last exchange of dispatches with the Naval War Board in Washington led to some confusion as to orders, and

Clark's final dispatch read, "Don't hamper me with instructions. I am not afraid, with this ship, of the whole Spanish fleet."

Mahan and other members of the Naval War Board were deeply concerned about the lack of security in Washington and the refusal of American newspapers to keep the movements of naval vessels a secret. Therefore, the board decided that the best way to ensure the *Oregon*'s safety was to leave Clark at loose ends and allow him to make his way to Florida as best he could without requiring him to clear his itinerary with Washington. The *Oregon* was a vital and exposed portion of the American naval force.

Thus, at seven o'clock on the morning of May 4, the *Oregon* and the *Marietta* steamed majestically out of Rio's harbor. Many of the good people of Rio believed the ships were going to certain destruction, for the city's newspapers had printed startling rumors that Admiral Cervera's fleet awaited the Americans outside the harbor. The Brazilian admiral even sent a cruiser out ahead of the *Oregon* and the *Marietta* to prevent an engagement in his nation's territorial waters.

At the request of the government of Brazil, the *Oregon* and the *Marietta* had agreed to sail twelve hours before the *Buffalo* did. The vessels went about fifty miles and then returned to meet the *Buffalo*. Both ships lay off the harbor entrance all night and left before daylight to prevent detection; but the *Buffalo* did not come out, and so Clark sent the *Marietta* back towards Rio to wait another twelve hours. After Clark had waited thirty-six hours in all, he sighted the *Buffalo* coming out with the *Marietta;* but as the *Buffalo* could not make more than seven knots, the question arose whether the *Oregon* and the *Marietta* should remain with this slow vessel or continue northward at high speed. The *Oregon* would be an important addition to Admiral Sampson's fleet; the department had been urging Clark to make a quick passage; the enemy's fleet was supposed to be seeking the *Oregon*, and Clark felt that she could make a better fight single-handed than if accompanied by slow vessels that would have to be protected. The captain weighed all these considerations and decided to part company with the two other vessels and proceed north at full speed. So, in the middle of the night, Clark signaled the *Marietta*, "Proceed with the *Buffalo* to Bahia, and cable the department." The *Marietta* answered, "Good-by and good luck." Then the *Oregon* went ahead full speed.

The following day, upon the high seas, Clark summoned all hands aft to the quarterdeck and read the men part of a message from the Navy Department stating that the Spanish fleet was supposed to be in search of the *Oregon*. A scene of great enthusiasm followed: five hundred men joined in an outburst of cheers for the *Oregon*, her captain, and her officers. Every preparation was made to meet the enemy's fleet. The ship was cleared for action. All the woodwork was torn out. Even the expensive mahogany pilothouse was reduced to a skeleton to prevent its being set on fire by Spanish shell. The ship was painted the dull gray war color, and the graceful white vessel that had steamed out of Rio harbor was transformed into an ugly lead-colored fighter. To lessen the danger of conflagration, preparations were made to throw all boats overboard upon sighting the enemy's fleet. Everybody was eager for action at any odds.

Before leaving Rio, the *Oregon*'s men had purchased a large supply of red ribbon and used it to make cap bands. Letters cut from brass and attached to the bands spelled out the inspiring words, "Remember the Maine." The cap of every *Oregon* man bore this legend throughout the war.

The battleship steamed northward along the coast of Brazil, intending to touch at Bahia or Pernambuco to communicate with the Navy Department. One forenoon was spent at target practice. All the guns were fired and the shooting was excellent.

On May 8, after dark, the *Oregon* anchored in the harbor of Bahia, and early next morning Clark sent the following cable message to Washington: "Much delayed by the *Marietta* and the *Nictheroy*. Left them near Cape Frio, with orders to come home or beach, if necessity compels it, to avoid capture. The *Oregon* could steam fourteen knots for hours, and in a running fight might beat off and even cripple the Spanish fleet. With present amount of coal on board will be in good fighting trim, and could reach West Indies. If more should be taken here I could reach Key West; but, in that case, belt-armor, cellulose belt, and protective deck would be below water-line. Whereabouts of Spanish fleet requested."[4] Clark made arrangements for coal, but in the evening this answer to the captain's message was received: "Proceed at once to West Indies without further stop Brazil. No authentic news the Spanish fleet. Avoid if possible. We believe that you will defeat it if met."[5]

And so, in the middle of the night, the ship went to sea, standing well off the coast in order to make a wide sweep around Cape St. Roque, where Admiral Cervera's fleet was rumored to be lurking. Captain Clark's plan of battle was as follows: Upon sighting the Spanish fleet, the *Oregon* would sound general quarters, go ahead full speed under forced draft, and head away from the enemy. The purpose of this maneuver was to "string out" the enemy's vessels in their chase. When their leading vessel came within close range, the *Oregon* would turn on her and attack her with heavy broadsides. Clark hoped to destroy the first enemy vessel and then devote attention to the others in succession. He was confident that not more than two of these vessels could equal the *Oregon*'s speed; by making a running fight, he expected to eliminate the possibility of the enemy's surrounding and either ramming or torpedoing the American vessel.

About eight o'clock on the evening of May 12, off Cape St. Roque, the *Oregon* sighted a number of lights, which had the appearance of a fleet sailing in double column. Not a light was burning on the *Oregon*, and she passed right through the midst of the vessels undetected, for she could not have been seen a hundred yards away. What those lights were has never been ascertained, but, according to the log of the *Colon*, one of Cervera's fleet, the enemy's squadron was not off Cape St. Roque at that time.

Of course, the *Oregon* passed many sailing vessels. They included the tiny sloop *Spray*, in which one of history's greatest mariners, Capt. Joshua Slocum of New Bedford, Mass., was making the first solo voyage around the world. Slocum described the passing:

> On the 14th of May, just north of the equator, and near the longitude of the river Amazon, I saw first a mast, with the Stars and Stripes floating from it, rising astern as if poked up out of the sea, and then rapidly appearing on the horizon, like a citadel, the *Oregon!* As she came near I saw that the great ship was flying the signals "C B T," which read, "Are there any men-of-war about?" Right under these flags, and larger than the *Spray*'s mainsail, so it appeared, was the yellowest Spanish flag I ever saw. It gave me a nightmare some time after when I reflected on it in my dreams.
>
> I did not make out the *Oregon*'s signals till she passed ahead, where I could read them better, for she was two miles away, and I had no binoculars. When I had read her flags I hoisted the signal "No," for I had not seen any Spanish men-of-war; I had not been looking for any. My signal, "Let us keep together for mutual protection," Captain Clark did not seem to regard as necessary. Perhaps my small flags were not made out; anyhow, the *Oregon* steamed on with a rush, looking for Spanish men-of-war, as I learned afterward. The *Oregon*'s great flag was dipped beautifully three times to the *Spray*'s lowered flag as she passed on.[6]

Meanwhile, in the inferno of the battleship's firerooms, the carbon filament electric light bulbs glowed red in a haze of coal dust, with which the ventilators, wind funnels, and port hold scoops were unable to cope. Grimy stokers, stripped to the waist and streaming with sweat, threw shovelsful of coal on the fires, slammed the furnace doors, and winced with pain as the muscles in their backs protested their efforts to straighten up.

On May 15, the *Oregon* made 375 miles, her longest one-day run of the voyage. At daylight on May 18, she came to anchor in the harbor of Bridgetown, Barbados.

The first news that greeted Clark was that the American navy had bombarded San Juan, Puerto Rico, and had been repelled. Actually, the attack, under Admiral Sampson's command, had been of an exploratory nature. Bridgetown placed the *Oregon* in quarantine because she had been in two yellow fever ports—even though no one had been allowed on shore in those ports and all on board were in good health. The white inhabitants of Barbados were strongly pro-American, and boatloads of them pulled around the ship, cheering and wishing her success. The blacks shouted, "American bully boys! You knock Spanyard in a cock hat, and then we give you a good time."

Her Majesty's officials were most friendly and gave Clark a cordial welcome, but they rigidly enforced the neutrality laws. The *Oregon* was allowed sufficient coal to reach a home port, but she could remain in Bridgetown only twenty-four hours. Neither of the belligerents was supposed to receive cable messages until twenty-four hours after the ship's departure. Before the government censor reached the cable office, the American consul had managed to send a dispatch to the State Department announcing the *Oregon*'s arrival. Therefore, the Spanish consul was permitted to cable news of the *Oregon*'s arrival to his government. In Bridgetown, Clark heard a rumor that a Spanish fleet of sixteen vessels was at Martinique, only ninety miles away, and that Spanish vessels had been seen cruising off Barbados the previous day. He seemed to have the enemy's vessels all around him.

The *Oregon* began coaling as soon as possible, and, to the anxious inquiries of a few shore people—most likely Spanish informers—Clark stated that he should probably sail next morning. But about nine o'clock that night, the *Oregon* suddenly cast off the coal barges and steamed out of the harbor. She kept all lights burning brightly and set a course direct for Key West, so that the Spanish spies could see the lights and report to the Martinique fleet the direction in which the *Oregon* had sailed. But when she was five miles from the harbor, she suddenly extinguished every light, turned about, made a sweep around Barbados, and laid a course well to the east of all the islands. This strategic move was designed to frustrate any night attack by the enemy torpedo boats and armored vessels that were believed to be at Martinique. The *Oregon* passed north of the Bahamas and after dark on May 24, anchored off Jupiter Inlet, Fla. From there she sent the Navy Department the following dispatch: "*Oregon* arrived. Have coal enough to reach Dry Tortugas or Hampton Roads. Boat landed through surf awaits orders." The announcement of her safe arrival soon sent a thrill of joy and thanksgiving throughout the United States.

About two that morning came this answer: "If ship is in good condition and ready for service, go to Key West, otherwise to Hampton Roads. The department congratulates you upon your safe arrival, which has been announced to the President." The anchor was hove up in a hurry, and, with light and happy hearts, the crewmen were soon on their way to Key West, planning to eventually join Admiral Sampson's fleet in Cuban waters. The *Oregon* reached Key West on the morning of May 26 and anchored off Sand Key. She had made the run of 14,500 miles in just sixty-six days; passed through two oceans and circumnavigated a continent; endured most oppressive heat and incessant toil; dem-

onstrated to the skeptics of Europe that heavy battleships of
the *Oregon* class could cruise with safety under all conditions of wind and sea; and, at the end of this voyage, had
the pleasure to report the ship in excellent condition and
ready to meet the enemy.

Clark, who had so ably executed his trying task, received congratulatory messages from every part of the
United States, including this telegram from Secretary of the
Navy Long: "The department congratulates you, your
officers and crew, upon the completion of your long and
remarkably successful voyage."

All hands were called to muster on the evening of May
26, and Captain Clark read the congratulatory telegram
from the Secretary of the Navy. Almost immediately, the
U.S.S. *Wilmington* crossed the bows of the battleship and
gave her the first "Three cheers for the *Oregon*."

The distances made on this long voyage are taken from
the official log of the *Oregon:*

San Francisco to Callao, Peru ......4,112.0 nautical miles
Callao, Peru, to Port Tamor
   (western end of
   Strait of Magellan) .............2,549.0 nautical miles
Port Tamor to Punta Arenas
   (eastern end of
   Strait of Magellan) ...............131.4 nautical miles
Punta Arenas to
   Rio de Janeiro, Brazil ............2,247.7 nautical miles
Rio de Janeiro to Bahia, Brazil ...... 741.7 nautical miles
Bahia to Barbados,
   British West Indies .............2,228.0 nautical miles
Barbados to Jupiter Inlet, Fla. ......1,665.0 nautical miles

Forty-one hundred tons of coal were used during the
voyage, and the average speed was 11.6 knots per hour. The

*Oregon* traveled a total distance of 14,500 miles from Bremerton, Wash., to Jupiter Inlet, Fla.

The *Oregon's* nautical achievement had many repercussions in naval circles. It was now realized that battleships could swiftly steam to any part of the world. If a battleship was well built and properly kept up, it could be ready for immediate service upon arrival and need not be dry-docked for extensive repairs. Battleships could be coaled in port or from rendezvousing colliers upon the high seas. The ship's performance hinged on the quality of its machinery; its engineers' skill in preventing machinery breakdowns from poor maintenance or ill usage; and the structural integrity of the hull. The *Oregon* excelled in all these factors.

Naval theoreticians like Mahan, however, began to wonder if the voyage around the tip of South America should have taken place at all. If American ships of the Pacific Fleet were to be called to action in the North Atlantic, they should not have to sail fourteen thousand miles to do so. The race of the *Oregon* and its strategic implications were not lost on military thinkers. Nor would Theodore Roosevelt (who had recently resigned as Assistant Secretary of the Navy and, as a lieutenant colonel of volunteers, was raising a regiment of cavalry) forget the voyage of the *Oregon*. The lesson of her race—against the storms of the South Atlantic, the Spanish enemy, and time itself—would be one of the major arguments for the building of the Panama Canal. The navy would have to be able to proceed rapidly between the Atlantic and the Pacific.

# 6

# Into Battle

The nation had greeted Dewey's Manila Bay victory of May 1, 1898, with joyful abandon. For the first time since the Civil War, Americans had a great naval hero to celebrate. But along the east coast, the jubilation quickly turned into a fearful hysteria. The Spanish fleet (commanded by Adm. Pascual Cervera y Topete, a dignified, white-haired, experienced naval officer) was on the high seas headed west, destination unknown. At any moment it might appear off an American city and shell the community to rubble. "Where is the navy?" every coastal village from Maine to Florida inquired. Congressmen began to pressure the navy to distribute units of the fleet along the seaboard to protect the cities. But such a policy would have been disastrous.

Alfred Thayer Mahan had shown the American nation the importance of a united fleet, or a "fleet-in-being." Scattered units would be unable to stop an attack by a concerted enemy naval force, for fleets could only defeat other fleets in mass action. Fortunately, the navy had not forgotten the lessons of the War of 1812. United States vessels won many individual actions in that war, but the American navy was ultimately defeated because its units were foolishly assigned to the protection of ports. The Royal Navy bottled up American ships in the ports, and as a result won local superiority anywhere it wished to be. The coastal settlements and even the capital of the United States became playthings for British landing parties. In 1898, the Atlantic Fleet was divided into squadrons, but it would finally assemble when Cervera was located and would fight and win as a battle unit.

At the beginning of the Spanish-American War, neither the American navy nor the Spanish navy had overwhelming superiority on paper. The United States had four fast, armored cruisers; Spain had seven. Spain's torpedo boats were considered among the best in the world, and torpedo boats in general were thought of as most deadly and even decisive weapons. However, the Spanish were unable to get their one battleship out of dry dock in time for service in the war. In addition, their state of readiness, their logistical support, and their leadership would prove far below the standards of the United States Navy.

Since February 15, when the *Maine* was destroyed, the U.S. naval force in southern waters had been stationed on war footing at Key West and the Dry Tortugas. The men were already well trained in gun mechanisms and manuals, for such training was usual in time of peace. To this training was added constant daily target practice with subcaliber fire. The practice consisted of firing a small projectile from a large gun, employing the pointing and aiming mechanisms of the latter. A small gun was placed inside the breech of the large gun, precisely in its center, and was held there by a special fitting. The axes of the small and large pieces therefore coincided and, except for the shock and recoil, normal firing conditions with full charge were imitated. One-pounders were ordinarily placed inside the heavy turret guns, and rifle barrels were used with the secondary batteries.

During those waiting days at Tortugas and Key West, fluttering flags a few hundred yards from each ship showed the targets, and for hours each day the splash of bullets followed the rifle reports with monotonous regularity. After each shot, the gun was swung off the target, brought back, and aimed anew, thus making each shot an independent exercise. It was not inspiring or dramatic, this steady burning of powder in small quantities during the sultry afternoons; but it was the sort of work that makes war deadly, and it bore its fruit in the swift and terrible destruction of Cervera's fleet.

The Navy Department had directed that all vessels should be painted a uniform gray, the "war color," to diminish as much as possible their visibility under the varying conditions of the atmosphere. The complement of each vessel was increased to its war-time number, and the commander in chief, Rear Adm. William F. Sampson, U.S.N., awaited his instructions. A number of additions to the squadron had arrived, for the government had already begun to purchase and equip auxiliaries.

In addition to Sampson's force, which was known as the North Atlantic Squadron, a second force called the Flying Squadron had been organized at Hampton Roads and placed in command of Com. Winfield S. Schley, U.S.N. The Flying Squadron was intended as a compact force for expeditionary work. The cruiser *Brooklyn* was the flagship of this squadron, which also included the battleships *Massachusetts* and *Texas* and the fast cruisers *Columbia* and *Minneapolis*. Later, a third squadron, known as the Northern Patrol Squadron, was formed under the command of Com. J. A.

Howell, who was recalled from the Mediterranean. His principal vessels were the flagship *San Francisco*, the ram *Katahdin*, and a few steamers that had been purchased from the Morgan Line and converted to armed auxiliaries. The Northern Patrol Squadron was to protect the northern Atlantic coast from Spanish raids. But neither the Flying Squadron nor the Northern Patrol Squadron actually saw service until they were sent to Cuban waters after the appearance of Cervera in the West Indies. At that time, they ceased to exist as independent commands and were placed under the orders of Admiral Sampson.

The double-turreted monitors were fitted out as speedily as possible and sent to Key West. The old single-turreted monitors, which had long been lying in the back channel at Philadelphia's League Island and were useless except as floating batteries, were placed in the northern ports. There, manned by naval militia and aided by armed tugs and other improvised auxiliaries, they formed an inner line of naval defense and a psychological placebo for nervous coastal dwellers.

The war began for the Atlantic Fleet of the United States Navy on April 26, 1898, when Sampson's squadron of eleven ships and four torpedo boats weighed anchor and departed Key West to blockade Havana. By May 1, it was known that Cervera's squadron of four armored cruisers and two torpedo boats had sailed from Cape Verde, presumably for the West Indies. Cervera's first port of call was likely to be far to the east of Cuba at San Juan, Puerto Rico, a Spanish fortified port with a good harbor and ample supplies of coal. The San Juan expedition was organized in the hope of finding Cervera's fleet in San Juan or of meeting it in that vicinity. The expedition consisted of the flagship *New York*, the battleships *Iowa* and *Indiana*, the monitors *Amphitrite* and *Terror*, the cruisers *Detroit* and *Montgomery*, the torpedo boat *Porter*, the armed tug *Wompa-*

*tuck*, and the collier *Niagara*. The vessels rendezvoused north of Bahia de Cadiz light, near Cardenas, and sailed at midnight on May 4. But Cervera was not at San Juan. Lacking a naval foe, Sampson bombarded the city on May 12. It was an indecisive, perhaps even an unnecessary, action.

The squadron steamed slowly back to Key West, the slow and unwieldy monitors being taken in tow. Instructions were sent to the auxiliary cruisers employed as scouts, and the naval base at Key West was cabled to have coal ready for all the ships.

By this time, Admiral Cervera had reached the Caribbean. His four cruisers were heavily armed and armored ships, rated at a trial speed of twenty knots and presumably capable of making sixteen knots under service conditions. His torpedo boats were new, very fast, the best product of English yards. They were twice as large as their American counterparts, the *Dupont* and the *Porter*, and were also more seaworthy. For their class, they were heavily armed. The destination of this squadron was unknown to the Americans. Cervera was probably heading for Cienfuegos or Havana, but he might have been planning to reach Santiago de Cuba or San Juan.

Cervera's purpose, if he knew his business, would be to raid the blockade and break it at various points, but especially at Havana; to avoid action with U.S. battleships; to destroy cruisers and auxiliaries; and perhaps, if he could maintain his coal supply, to make a dash at points upon the northern coast. It was difficult to estimate the damage such a squadron might do, with good luck and bold and skillful handling. Therefore, it was vitally important to find Cervera's fleet and either destroy it or shut it up in a closely blockaded port. The search for Cervera became the paramount object of the war.

On May 17, Sampson's flagship *New York*, which was heading for Key West, put on a full head of steam and left the remainder of the squadron to follow. At six that evening, she met the torpedo boat *Dupont*, which carried important dispatches confirming the impression that Cervera would attempt to get into either Cienfuegos or Havana. Arriving at Key West at 4 P.M., May 18, Sampson found Schley's vessels coaling. The *Iowa* arrived at dark, and the other ships of the San Juan expedition early the next morning. All the vessels coaled as quickly as possible. The light vessels on the blockade had been warned against surprise, and the *Cincinnati* and the *Vesuvius* were scouting the Yucatan Channel.

Plans were at once made for new dispositions. Commodore Schley, with the cruiser *Brooklyn*, the *Massachusetts*, the *Texas*, and the *Scorpion*, sailed on the morning of May 19 for Cienfuegos by way of Cape San Antonio, the western end of Cuba. The next day, the *Iowa*, the gunboat *Castine*, the collier *Merrimac*, and the torpedo boat *Dupont* were dispatched to Cienfuegos to join him, and, on May 21, the cruiser *Marblehead*, the yacht *Eagle*, and the auxiliary gunboat *Vixen* were sent on the same business. The resulting U.S. force on the southern side of Cuba was strong enough to destroy Cervera or to blockade him in Cienfuegos. Cervera was known to have left Curaçao on May 15. If his destination were either Santiago or Cienfuegos, he had already arrived. He had in fact entered Santiago at about the hour of Schley's sailing from Key West.

When the *Oregon* reached Key West on May 26, Sampson's hand was strengthened. On May 27, the ship's crew was increased by the arrival of sixty young men of the Chicago naval reserves. They remained with the *Oregon* until she went to New York after the war, and they won the respect and esteem of the battleship's regular officers and men. Several years after the war, they formed an organization named the Clark Club, which royally entertained Captain Clark on two occasions when he visited Chicago.

At Key West or later off Santiago, the crew was augmented by Lt. C. M. Stone, Ens. L. A. Bostwick, and Naval Cadets P. B. Dungan, E. J. Sadler, C. C. Kalbfus, H. J. Brinser, C. G. Hatch, C. Schackford, and T. C. Dunlap. All served through the war. A. G. Magill, a naval cadet who sailed on the *Oregon* from San Francisco, had become seriously ill on the run from the Pacific and been sent home.

The *Oregon* was coaled and supplied, and she weighed anchor once more at 1:04 A.M. on May 29. She had had less than three days in port after a 14,500-mile cruise. Her engines were fully functioning, her boilers reasonably clean, and her crew healthy and in high spirits. She had not needed an overhaul. The *Oregon* was indeed a superb ship, probably the finest ship the United States had built to that time.

Clark was under orders to join the blockading squadron off Havana led by Com. John Crittenden Watson, U.S.N., who had been Farragut's flag lieutenant on the *Hartford* during the Civil War. The *Oregon* arrived off Havana on May 29, a bright Sunday morning. She was greeted with enthusiasm by the ships of Watson's squadron, and her crew was cheered wildly as she passed down the line of warships to the blare of the bands of the blockading ships. Still tired and dirty from coaling ship, Clark's men beamed with satisfaction at their reception: once the elusive Spanish fleet had been located and brought to bay, they'd show the other ships of the United States Navy what the *Oregon* could really do.

They did not have long to wait! Soon after daybreak the next morning, May 29, Commodore Schley's Flying Squadron, after much unnecessary delay, steamed in toward the Morro at the entrance to the harbor of Santiago on the southern coast of Cuba and discovered three ships lying at anchor near Smith Key. One of them had a military mast between her two smokestacks and was immediately identified as the *Cristobal Colon,* one of Admiral Cervera's biggest ships. The Spanish fleet was in the harbor of Santiago de Cuba!

The *St. Paul*, a former liner that had been acting as a scout for Schley's squadron, was immediately dispatched to St. Nicholas Mole, Haiti, where the nearest cable office was located, to telegraph the news to Washington and to Admiral Sampson in Key West. Sampson received the message at lunchtime and immediately ordered the flagship *New York* and the converted yacht *Mayflower* to prepare to get underway. The two ships sailed from Key West on May 30, contacted Commodore Watson's squadron off Havana that afternoon and, after ordering the *Oregon* to accompany them, steamed around the eastern tip of Cuba and joined Commodore Schley at Santiago at six on the morning of June 1.

Soon after the arrival of the three ships off the steaming tropical coast, Commodore Schley went aboard the *New York* to make his report to Admiral Sampson. While the two officers were conferring, Captain Clark signaled the *Brooklyn*, the flagship of Schley's squadron, requesting orders. He was told to "proceed six miles to the southward and report names of strange vessels." The order was actually an assignment to a station in the southern part of the blockading line, but Clark took the wording literally and set out in the direction indicated. The *Oregon* soon spotted smoke on the horizon ahead. In a moment, the battleship was off in full pursuit, with her boilers under forced draft. As she gained speed and closed in on her "prize," a lookout incorrectly reported that the stranger was a large steamer and that cargo was being jettisoned. A few minutes later, the "enemy ship" was close enough for the officer of the deck to identify her as a large tug. When a blank charge was fired across her bow, the tugboat came about and hoisted the Stars and Stripes. She was a newspaper boat with a number of correspondents aboard, bound for Jamaica with dispatches for their papers. A battleship chasing a tug! The crestfallen *Ore-*

*gon* turned back toward the blockading line and, at the half-way mark, met the cruiser *Marblehead,* which had been sent in pursuit as soon as the flagship had discovered the *Oregon's* mistake. Although steaming at fifteen knots, the fast cruiser had been unable to overtake the battleship, and, as the two ships passed, the *Marblehead's* men sent up a cheer for the battleship they couldn't catch.

The Navy Department was unwilling to expose Sampson's fleet to the fire of the Santiago shore batteries, which the ships would have to pass in order to engage the Spanish warships. For this reason, the admiral continued Commodore Schley's blockade. The American ships arranged themselves in a semicircle facing the mouth of the bay. If the Spaniards appeared, the Americans were to converge on the bay's outlet and engage the enemy's ships as they came out. Admiral Sampson decided to try to "put a cork in the bottle" at Santiago, even though he had witnessed the futility of a similar maneuver at Charleston, S.C., during the Civil War. At Charleston, the federal commander had tried to obstruct the entrance to the bay by scuttling in the channel a number of old New Bedford whalers loaded with stones. Sampson proposed to prevent the escape of the Spanish fleet by sinking the collier *Merrimac* in the fairway at Santiago.

From the hundreds who volunteered for the risky mission, a crew of seven was finally selected, and Lt. Richmond P. Hobson of the Naval Construction Corps was placed in command. The seven took the old collier into the narrow passage at 4:00 A.M. on June 3. The ship was detected by the Spanish batteries, which opened fire and damaged the *Merrimac's* steering gear so badly that she overshot her mark, failed to turn athwart the channel, and sank too far inside to block the entrance. The volunteers took to the boats and were rescued by Cervera himself, who gallantly reported their safety to Sampson next morning. Hobson would re-

ceive the Congressional Medal of Honor for his great courage.

The tedious, month-long blockade was underway, with
no end in sight. The ships were cauldrons of steam and
sweat. The men wore as few clothes as they could get away
with; the officers wore unpressed, pajama-like dress whites,
made limp and shapeless by the moisture. Engineroom or
boilerroom duty was hell. Most of the captains shut down
boilers to relieve the black gang and save coal, but Clark
wisely kept all fires lighted throughout the blockade. When
the Spanish finally made their break for freedom, only the
*Oregon* was able to get up full steam during the course of
the battle.

Clark suggested to Sampson that the semicircle of
American ships off the harbor entrance did not constitute a
tight enough ring and that picket boats should be employed
close in. Sampson agreed, and the *Oregon,* the *Massachusetts,* and the *New York* provided the boats and crews.
Sampson also wisely decided to use the ships' large searchlights to illuminate the harbor entrance at night. This time
the *Oregon,* the *Massachusetts,* and the *Iowa* got the duty.
The *Oregon* in her turn steamed well within enemy rifle
range and turned her light to the harbor. It was dangerous
duty, but Cervera would later say that the light prevented
him from trying a nighttime escape.

Meanwhile, the United States Army was gathering at
Tampa. The regular army had been called in from the West,
and volunteer units poured in. They included the Rough
Riders—the First United States Volunteer Cavalry under
Col. Leonard Wood and Lt. Col. Theodore Roosevelt.

There were not enough supplies to keep the men in
Tampa and not enough transports to take them anywhere
else. After the government finally decided that Sampson
should not brave the batteries and mines at Santiago's harbor, the army was ordered to attempt an amphibious opera-

tion near the city to take the forts and guns by land. Each army unit had to scramble for a place on the limited number of transports (chartered merchant vessels for the most part), and the Rough Riders found themselves embarked on June 8 sans horses and most of their equipment. The rest of the army fared no better.

To make things worse, the loaded convoy did not get underway until June 14 due to a false report of a Spanish raiding squadron in the vicinity. The poor soldiers had a week of hell, crammed aboard overloaded ships in the Florida sun.

On June 10, before the Army could shove off, the first American troops landed in Cuba. They were the United States Marines. The United States had only one more requirement to assure the successful maintenance of the blockade, and that was to possess a safe harbor near Santiago for shelter, coaling, and repairs. Admiral Sampson secured this indispensable adjunct by sending the *Marblehead* and the *Yankee* to Guantanamo. On board the former was the *Oregon*'s marine guard under the command of Capt. Randolph Dickens, U.S.M.C., and Lt. A. R. Davis, U.S.M.C. Sampson's ships drove the Spanish gunboats to the inner harbor and secured the outer harbor, which was excellently suited to the needs of the fleet. To make possession both useful and complete, it became necessary to gain a position on shore and drive back the enemy so that the Spanish could not annoy the ships and boats in the bay. This work was assigned to the *Marblehead* and *Oregon* marine guards and to the First Marine Battalion, which left Key West on June 7 and arrived in Guantanamo Bay on June 10 aboard the transport *Panther*.

The marine guards spearheaded the amphibious assault under cover provided by the *Marblehead*'s guns. They splashed ashore closely followed by the First Marine Battalion in boats from the *Panther*, supported by shore bombardment from the *Yankee*. The marines established themselves on a low hill where a Spanish blockhouse had been destroyed by the guns of the *Yankee*. The next evening, they were attacked by Spaniards concealed in the chaparral, and two men on outposts were killed. The attack was renewed in the night by the unseen enemy, and Surgeon Gibbs was killed and two privates wounded. The next day, the camp was shifted to a better position, and some sixty Cubans joined the Americans. The Spanish bombarded the camp all that night, and Sergeant Good was killed, but on the thirteenth, with the aid of the Cubans, who knew the country, the Spanish were easily repelled. On the fourteenth the Americans took the offensive. Two companies of marines, supported by the Cubans, left the camp at nine o'clock that morning to destroy the well at Cuzco, which was the Spaniards' only water supply within twelve miles. They failed to cut off the enemy as they had hoped, but they drove the Spaniards steadily before them, reaching the intervening hill first and carrying the crest under a sharp fire. As the marines descended into the valley, the Spaniards broke cover and retreated rapidly, and at three that afternoon the fight was over, the well filled with earth, and the heliograph signal station captured and destroyed. One Spanish lieutenant and seventeen men were captured, and the prisoners reported a Spanish loss of two officers and fifty-eight men killed and a large number wounded. On the American side, one marine was wounded and about a dozen were overcome by heat. This engagement marked the end of the Spanish attacks at Guantanamo. The Spaniards had had enough and withdrew, leaving the American post undisturbed to the end of the campaign. The marines had done their work admirably. For three days and nights, they had met and repelled the attacks of a concealed enemy. Then they had taken the offensive, and they had marched and fought for hours under the tropi-

*Oregon*, 1898 (U.S. Bureau of Ships)

Captain Charles E.
Clark in his cabin,
April, 1898 (Oregon
Historical Society)

President and Mrs. Wilson boarding to review the Pacific Fleet, August 21, 1919 (Navy Department)

Captain Charles E. Clark with Naval Cadet Over-
street and the captain's orderlies: Marine Corps
privates Haight (rear left) and Ellis, on the
bridge of the *Oregon* during battle with the
Spanish Fleet, July 3, 1898 (Oregon Historical
Society)

*Oregon* at the Union Iron Works, San Francisco, preparing for
sea trials, March 8, 1896 (San Francisco Maritime Museum)

Dress Ship, 1918 (Navy Department)

Hull of *Oregon*, Guam, 1948 (Oregon Historical Society)

cal sun and through dense brush with the steadiness and marksmanship of experienced bushfighters.

The guard from the *Oregon* seemed destined to see stormy service, for, after the Spanish-American War, at least half the guard was assigned to the legation guard at Peking. In the siege of the Chinese capital during the Boxer Rebellion, many of these men were killed and hardly one escaped unwounded. Lieutenant Davis was killed at Tientsin.

The army finally arrived off Santiago at daybreak of June 20, and Sampson immediately met with the army commander, Gen. William R. Shafter, U.S.A., as well as with the Cuban generals Garcia and Castillo. The point of the operation was to take the forts around Santiago and thus capture the Spanish ships by land or flush them out into the range of the waiting American guns offshore. Shafter, however, refused to land his men just beyond the Morro as Sampson demanded. Instead, the force landed some ten miles down the coast at Daiquiri and had to drive through the jungle against a courageous Spanish rearguard action. The Americans were struck down by bullets, heat, and fever, and they gained less than a mile a day.

But first the troops had to be landed. The army had neither lighters nor launches. They had been omitted, forgotten, or lost, and no one knew exactly how or where; so the work of disembarking the troops fell to the navy. The ships provided a cover of a heavy fire, and the landing was effected without any resistance from the enemy. On an open coast, without any harbor or shelter, with nothing but an iron pier so high as to be useless, smoothly, rapidly, efficiently, through a heavy surf, on the beach and at an unfloored wooden wharf, the boats and launches of the navy landed fifteen thousand soldiers with a loss of only two men. It was a neat piece of work, thoroughly and punctually performed, and it excited admiration among foreign observers,

who had recently beheld with disbelief the comic perform-
ances connected with the embarkation at Tampa.

The next morning Gen. Joseph Wheeler, commanding a
division of dismounted cavalry under direct orders from
General Shafter, rode forward, followed by two squadrons
of the First Volunteer Cavalry and one each of the First and
Tenth Regular Cavalry. The campaign had begun.

To lighten the monotony of blockade duty and to soften
up the defenses of the bay, Sampson decided to stage a full-
dress bombardment of the forts at the harbor entrance. On
June 26, he formed his fleet into parallel lines some eight
hundred yards apart and steamed the ships toward the island until a scant two miles of water separated them from
their objective. Breakfast was served, and, at 8:00 A.M., the
flagship *New York*, leading the eastern line which was
directed at the Morro fort, sent an eight-inch shell curving
toward the ancient stronghold. Commodore Schley's flagship
*Brooklyn*, which was leading the western line, followed suit
in less than a minute with a shot aimed at Socapa Point. As
the firing became general, the two lines of ships began maneuvering with faultless precision, Sampson's squadron turning toward the east and Schley's toward the west.

The lighter ships stayed out of range of the shore batteries, but the battleships steamed slowly in toward the
land, firing as they advanced, until the range had been reduced to eighteen hundred yards. The replies from the forts,
weak at first, became hotter as the gunners evidently gained
confidence. But the Spaniards' marksmanship was poor, and
none of the American ships received material damage while
scoring again and again on the coquina and masonry walls
of the fortifications.

An eyewitness described the scene:

It was hard for the untrained eye looking under the
smoke from the cannon's discharge, to follow the course

of the shell; but there was no mistake as to where it landed. When the shells hit soft spots on the cliffs and exploded, they sent reddish earth and stones hurtling skyward. Others struck point-blank and burst into radiating fragments, which left thin lines of bluish smoke trailing after them. Sometimes a shell plunged into a huge crevice and exploded out of sight, but in a moment huge boulders that had been loosened would tumble downward into the sea. At one point the cliff was like flint, and shells rebounded and hurled off without producing any effect. Occasionally these deflections were in straight lines, and again a vicious, corkscrew whirling gave a vivid idea of the fearful force of the projectile. The terrific impact made the shells glow with heat as they spun upwards into the clouds, or bounded straight back as if seeking to return to the ships from which they had been fired.

The cannonading was continued for 2½ hours before Admiral Sampson signaled the fleet to retire. During the engagement, the military mast of the *Oregon* was struck by a piece of shell, and the mast of the *Massachusetts* received a direct hit without suffering serious damage. One seaman injured by a bursting shell was the only casualty in the fleet. The Morro fort was badly hit by the bombardment. Some of the shells landed uncomfortably close to the cells in which the men of the *Merrimac* were confined, but none was hurt.

A mood of quiet satisfaction reigned aboard the *Oregon* that evening as her crew went about the task of cleaning up after the morning's work. After the final engagement at 6:30 P.M., Seaman R. Cross found a secluded spot in the shelter of the after thirteen-inch turret, drew a stub of pencil from the pocket of his jumper, and settled himself to make an entry in his diary:

June 26. Started in this morning to see if we coulden knock down that Spanish old Morro or else knock something cruckit around it. Well we pelted away for an hour or more and the flag ship signalled over to the Iowa to close in and pump at the Smith Key Battry. The Iowa signalled back that her forward Turret was out of order, so it fel to us, we went in to 700 yards of the shore Battry and did knock down the Spanish flag with an 8-inch shell and knocked over one of the three Big Guns. I believe if the flag ship had not called us off Capt. Clark would have went in along side of old Morro and give him a tutching up.

Two days later Seaman Cross made another entry:

June 28. I am getting tired to trying to keep cases on this thing. There is nothing doing but laying around here like a lot of sharks watching for a fish.[1]

For the Army the taking of the blockhouse on San Juan Hill (actually Kettle Hill) on July 1, 1898, by the Rough Riders under Roosevelt (now a full colonel and commanding officer of the regiment) was the most distinguished action of the brief and confused but successful campaign. During the battle on July 1, the *Oregon* joined the other ships of the combined squadrons in supporting the army by bombarding the city of Santiago. At 5:00 A.M. on July 2, she took part in a second bombardment of the batteries on both sides of the entrance to the harbor. This bombardment succeeded in silencing the batteries along the shore line. The shelling completely destroyed the Punta Gorda battery behind the Morro and further damaged the fort.

Sunday morning, July 3, 1898, dawned clear and bright off the harbor of Santiago. The red ball of the sun rose swiftly in the eastern sky, and the day promised to be fiercely hot and breathless. The glossy surface of the blue sea reflected the gray hulls of the warships swinging lazily at anchor. At 8:45 A.M., Admiral Sampson's flagship, *New York*, made signal, "Disregard movements of commander in chief," and headed eastward with the *Hist* and the *Ericsson*. Sampson was on his way to a conference with General Shafter at Siboney, a few miles down the coast. The *Massachusetts* was coaling at Guantanamo.

The United States fleet was formed in a semicircle three miles off the harbor. With the departure of the *New York,* the semicircle tightened and drew in. Lined up from east to west were the auxiliary gunboat *Gloucester;* the battleships *Indiana, Oregon, Iowa,* and *Texas;* the cruiser *Brooklyn;* and the auxiliary gunboat *Vixen.* Commodore Schley on the *Brooklyn* was senior officer present afloat and nominally in charge, although for the most part the ensuing battle was a captain's fight.

The men on the American vessels were carrying out the Sunday morning routine that had been followed since the squadrons had arrived on station. Breakfast had been eaten, and the final morning tasks of cleaning ship before mustering at quarters were nearing completion. A press boat passed the *Oregon,* and a reporter shouted the news that the army had suffered heavy losses in the previous day's attack on the city.

Three bells in the forenoon watch were about to be struck as the clock in the pilot house of each ship stood at 9:28. The bugle sound of "quarters" had just been carried away on the breeze. Clad in spotless white uniforms, the men of the fleet mustered in divisions on their ships to listen to the monthly ritual of the reading of the Articles of War, which would normally be followed by church call and divine services. On the *Oregon,* Clark was in his cabin buckling on his dress sword and putting on his cap to go on deck when suddenly the brass gongs of the ship's alarm rang furiously and Clark's orderly burst into the compartment shouting: "The Spanish Fleet, sir! It's coming out!"

The *Oregon's* sharp-eyed chief quartermaster had spotted the masthead of a ship slipping out from behind Smith Cay. "Battle Stations!" The signal "enemy is escaping" was rushed aloft, and a six-pounder gun fired as a warning to the other vessels. After thirty-four days of waiting and watching, the moment of battle had arrived. The *Oregon* bluejackets rushed to their guns and stations with almost child-like eagerness and anticipation as well as a sense of relief that the long watch was at last over. They threw themselves down scuttles and ladders, desperate to get to battle stations at the boilers, engines, hoists, and guns.

Clark rushed on deck. Men shouted to him as they pointed shoreward: "There they come! There they come! You'll see them in a minute, Captain. She's behind the Morro now!" The armored cruiser *Infanta Maria Teresa* appeared, Cervera's blue flag and her great red and yellow battle ensigns standing out sharply against the green jungle behind her. It was forced draft and full speed for the *Oregon,* the only American ship ready for emergency speed.

The orders poured from the conning tower now:

"Turn on the current for the electric hoists!"

"Steam and pressure on the turrets!"

"Hoist the battle flags!"

"Lay aloft range finders in the top!"

"Range to the lead ship!"

"Set sights for 4,000 yards!"

Commodore Schley signaled: "Clear ship for action" and "Close up."

Down the shore, Sampson heard the first cannon firing and ordered the *New York* to turn about and steam for the sound of the guns. As Cervera's flagship cleared the Morro, she turned westward, and the *Oregon* opened up with her eight-inch guns. The armored cruiser *Vizcaya,* the second-class battleship *Cristobal Colon,* and the armored cruiser *Oquendo* followed the *Maria Teresa* in a column, each opening fire as her guns would bear. The American vessels nearly collided with each other in their eagerness to close with the enemy. The *Brooklyn,* at the western end of the line, suddenly found the entire Spanish squadron pointing for her midships, and she was forced to turn away to star-board, narrowly missing the American battleships as she turned 360 degrees to reengage the enemy outboard of the equally speedy *Oregon,* the leading American battlewagon.

As the *Oregon* passed Santiago Harbor, the Spanish torpedo boat destroyers *Pluton* and *Furor* made a most ill-timed appearance and received a full volley from the *Oregon's* six-inch guns and rapid-fires. The other battleships hit too. The small ships were crushed by a hail of projectiles. The *Furor* disappeared as a lump of twisted iron beneath the waves, taking Adm. Fernando Villaamil down with her. The *Gloucester*—under Comdr. Richard Wainwright, U.S.N., former executive officer of the *Maine* at Havana—closed with the *Pluton* and drove her ashore. The Spanish torpedo boat destroyers had lasted twelve minutes in battle. The *Oregon* was all speed. An officer of the *Iowa* would later describe her thus:

> The *Oregon* came racing across the *Iowa's* bow and charged right down on the Spanish fleet, letting go first at one vessel, then at the other, and all the time carrying a great white bone in her teeth, that told of her engine-power and wonderful speed.

Clark ordered the *Oregon's* head a point more westward. "Head them off, and let the land trap them," thought Clark, almost like an old Indian fighter. To his surprise, the *Oregon* was not only passing through the pack of the American battleships that had started the engagement west of his ship, but she was also overtaking the supposedly speedier Spanish cruisers! He could not know how much damage the Spanish vessels had suffered in breaking out of the harbor. In fact, the American shells had not hulled them but had smashed their wooden decks and superstructure. Horrible fires were beginning to make torches of the fleeing vessels, their speed fanning the infernos. Also, the Spaniards' main propulsion machinery was in poor repair, and the hulls were foul.

Seeing all but the *Brooklyn* falling back, Clark grinned and said to his navigator, "Well, Nicholson, it seems we shall have them on our hands after all." The men of the *Brooklyn*, the most lightly armed vessel of the American squadron, saw the *Oregon* coming on strong and fast and shouted, "Here comes the *Oregon!* It's the *Oregon*, God bless her!"

Schley's flagship was skippered by Clark's old Annapolis roommate, Capt. F. A. Cook, U.S.N. At Schley's order, he signaled, "Follow the flag." It wasn't necessary.

Suddenly the *Teresa* seemed to slow, and the other Spanish ships steamed past her. Was she mortally wounded or was the gallant Cervera sacrificing himself and the flagship to make a stand and perhaps save the other three ships of his squadron? At 10:00 A.M., the Spanish flagship was the prime target of the *Oregon* and the pursuing battlewagons. At two thousand yards, the forward guns of the *Oregon*, with the *Teresa* sharp on her starboard bow, poured everything into the wounded vessel. By 10:10, the *Teresa* was a roaring hellfire, her guns silenced, smoke and flame leaping from her upper works. The stricken ship turned and limped to the beach and grounded at Juan Gonzales, only six miles from the harbor of Santiago. She had seen only forty minutes of actual combat. The *Brooklyn* and the *Oregon* leaped on for further prey. The *Iowa* and the *Texas* followed, and the *Indiana* trailed far behind. Last of all was the *New York*, puffing up coast as fast as she could to get a piece of the action Sampson had so long awaited and planned for. Passing the *Indiana*, Sampson ordered that ship to turn back to the harbor to watch for the *Reina Mercedes*, which had remained in port.

With the *Teresa* a burning wreck, the *Oregon* turned her attention to the *Almirante Oquendo* and began firing on the cruiser with her forward guns and all those in her starboard broadside that could be brought to bear. Closing to a range of nine hundred yards, the American battleship subjected her victim to "the hottest and most destructive fire of the eventful day." Within twelve minutes, the *Oquendo* was ablaze and headed inshore. The *Oregon* drew up abeam of the Spanish ship and raked her unmercifully. The *Oquendo* continued to fire until her torn and battered hull came to rest on the beach only a half mile west of the *Teresa*. Captain Clark shouted over the noise of the guns, "We have settled another; look out for the rest." The *Oregon's* gunners answered him with a cheer that was repeated down through the ammunition passages and the magazines to the steaming boilerroom and engineroom below.

Lt. R. F. Nicholson suggested that they turn about and completely destroy the *Oquendo*. Clark answered, "No, that's a dead cock in the pit. The others can attend to her. We'll push on for the two ahead." And so the bones of the *Oquendo* were left for the slower ships astern to pick over.

It was all bulldog determination now on the *Oregon*. The Americans had the Spanish on the hip and could end the war in a day.

The *Vizcaya* was next in line and two miles away when the *Oregon* turned her forward thirteen-inch guns on the fleeing cruiser. The *Brooklyn*, which had been on the battleship's port bow since the chase began, had been firing on the *Vizcaya* for some time and was taking hot fire from the Spanish ship. When the signal "close up" broke on the flagship's signal halyards, the *Oregon* repeated the message to the ships astern and increased her speed to sixteen knots. The range had dropped to 3,000 yards when the *Vizcaya* swung offshore and headed across the *Oregon's* bow while continuing to fire her forward guns at the *Brooklyn* and those on her port side at the *Oregon*. This maneuver brought the *Vizcaya* broadside to the battleship, but after a thirteen-inch shell from the *Oregon* struck the port bow of the Spanish ship, she turned back on her original course. A few minutes later, another thirteen-inch shell struck the *Vizcaya* amidships, causing her to heel to starboard while a column of steam and smoke erupted from her superstructure. To the accompaniment of cheer after cheer from the men of the *Oregon*, the *Vizcaya* headed for shore with flames bursting from her hull.

While the *Vizcaya* was under fire from the *Oregon* and the *Brooklyn*, Captain Clark had been moving about the deck of his ship commending his gunners for their accuracy and warning the men not to expose themselves unnecessarily. At the moment the Spanish ship turned toward the beach, Clark was talking to the after turret's gunnery officer, who was deploring the fact that he could not bring his guns to bear while the quarry was so far ahead. When Clark saw the Spanish cruiser change course, he cried, "There's your chance! There's your chance!" and the six-inch guns of the *Oregon*'s starboard broadside and the thirteen-inch guns of the after turret blasted the *Vizcaya*'s upper works. By the time the *Oregon* had the cruiser to starboard, the *Vizcaya* had had enough. Her colors came down on the double, and she ran ashore at Aserraderos, eighteen miles from the Morro—the third burning wreck in ninety minutes. Commodore Schley promptly acknowledged the battleship's support with the signal "*Oregon*, well done."

Clark stood on the top of the forward thirteen-inch turret, his favorite conning position during the chase. He felt no great sense of jubilation or victory. He was a sensitive, compassionate, and fatherly man. Later, he would reminisce about the *Vizcaya:*

> As this last battle-torn wreck of what had once been a proud and splendid ship fled to the shore like some sick and wounded thing, seeking a place to die, I could feel none of that exultation that is supposed to come with victory. If I had seen my own decks covered with blood, and my officers and men dying around me, perhaps resent-

ment would have supplied the necessary ingredient, but as it was, the faces of the women and children in far-away Spain, the widows and orphans of this July third, rose before me so vividly that I had to draw comfort from the thought that a decisive victory is after all more merciful than a prolonged struggle, and that every life lost to-day in breaking down the bridge to Spain might mean a hundred saved hereafter.[2]

The unfortunate *Vizcaya* had caused the only American casualty of the action. A shell from one of her guns struck Chief Yeoman George Ellis, U.S.N., of the *Brooklyn* and killed him instantly. He had been taking ranges with the stadimeter for the forward turret and had stepped out to try to see beyond the smoke of battle. The shell passed over the *Brooklyn* herself.

Suddenly, for the *Oregon* and the *Brooklyn*, the great chase began. The *Cristobal Colon* was escaping. She was Spain's newest and fastest vessel. The *Oregon* poured on the coal and was soon making over sixteen knots. The *Brooklyn*, sheering off somewhat to port in order to intercept the enemy at a distant headland, signaled, "She seems built in Italy." Clark retorted, "She may have been built in Italy but she will end on the coast of Cuba." He was not wrong.

The *Cristobal Colon* was six miles ahead of the *Oregon*, but the American vessel was overtaking. The Spanish ship was running out of her good coal, and her second-rate fuel was inadequate to keep up the necessary steam pressure. Also, the Spanish crewmen were exhausted because they had been serving as infantry against the American army until the day before. The Spaniards had been stiffened up by large rations of alcohol, which now was taking its toll.

Clark sent his men to dinner by watches; but, after getting a bite, they returned on deck to follow the exciting chase and take a pull at their pipes. As the *Oregon* dashed onward, slowly gaining and soon to be within range, the enthusiasm reached high pitch. Old Boatswain's Mate

Murphy, stationed in the fighting-top, gave way to his excited feelings and yelled through a megaphone, "Oh, captain, I say, can't you give her a thirteen-inch shell, fer Gawd's sake!" The men in the engineer force, ever unmindful of the frightful heat, were straining every muscle to its utmost, and the engineering officers were helping the exhausted firemen feed the roaring furnaces.

Several times, the *Colon* turned in as if looking for a good place to run ashore; but, each time she changed her mind and continued to run for her life. It was 12:50 when Captain Clark gave Lt. (jg) E. W. Eberle orders to "try a thirteen-inch shell on her," and soon a 1,100-pound projectile was flying after the *Colon*. The chief engineer was just coming on deck to ask the captain to fire a gun in order to encourage the exhausted engineer force; when the men below heard the old thirteen-incher roar, they knew they were within range and made the effort of their lives.

The scene on the *Oregon*'s decks was one of unbridled enthusiasm. The chase was nearly over. Officers and men were crowded on top of the forward turrets, and some were aloft—all eager to see the final work of that historic day. The *Brooklyn* fired a few eight-inch shells, and the *Oregon* fired two of the missiles; but all fell short, and the eight-inch guns ceased firing. The *Colon* returned a few shots, but they fell far short of their mark. *Oregon*'s forward thirteen-inch guns continued to fire slowly and deliberately, with increasing trajectory. The sixth shot, at a range of ninety-five hundred yards (nearly five miles), dropped just ahead of the *Colon*, which then suddenly turned and headed for the shore. The men were cheering wildly. A few minutes later, at 1:12, a thirteen-inch shell struck under the *Colon*'s stern. It was a near miss, close aboard. Immediately, the *Colon*'s colors dropped in a heap at the foot of her flagstaff. Her bugle sounded, "Cease firing!" The Spanish ship had surrendered, and the last shot of July 3 had been fired.

Suddenly, the thunder of heavy guns was replaced by the strains of "The Star-Spangled Banner" from the *Oregon*'s band. On the forward deck, 550 men—mostly bare to the waist, and begrimed with powder, smoke, and coal dust —were embracing one another and cheering with the fervor and joy that mark the outpouring of the hearts of men who have looked into the face of death and known unequivocal victory. There were rousing cheers for Captain Clark; cheers from the *Brooklyn*, which signaled, "Congratulations upon the glorious victory"; and a wildly enthusiastic return in kind from the *Oregon*.

After lowering her colors, the *Colon* ran ashore at Rio Tarquino, one of the most beautiful spots on the south coast of Cuba, about fifty miles west of Santiago and thirty-two miles beyond the *Vizcaya*'s resting place. The *Colon*'s demoralized crew fell to destroying her armament and equipment.

At the time of the *Colon*'s surrender, the *Brooklyn* was off the *Oregon*'s port bow. Between six and seven miles astern and hull down were the *New York* and the *Texas*. These two vessels and the *Vixen* joined the *Oregon* at about 2:20, just as the *Brooklyn*'s boat was returning from the *Colon*. All commanding officers were ordered to report on board the *New York*. As Captain Clark's gig approached the flagship, he received an ovation from the crew of the *New York*. Clark rose in his boat, tipped his hat, and ordered his boat crew to rise and receive the cheers of their fellow sailors.

Clark soon returned from the flagship with orders to head east with the *Brooklyn* and blast the Spanish battleship that was reported off Siboney. But just as they were ready to start, the *New York* learned that the reported Spanish battleship was an Austrian vessel. The flagship signaled, "*Oregon*, take charge of prize and haul her off the beach."

It was after 4:00 P.M. When the prize crew reached the

*Colon*, they found fifteen feet of water in her enginerooms
and all valves open. The prisoners were immediately sent aft
on the quarterdeck and were soon transferred with their
effects to the *Resolute*.

Five cows were found tied up on the *Colon's* forecastle,
and some of them succeeded in swimming ashore after the
*Oregon's* men had cut them adrift. Souvenirs taken included
several battle flags, pictures of the ship and officers, a captain's gig, two cutters, a dog, two cats, some chickens, and a
black pig. The *Colon's* pig became the *Oregon's* mascot and
was promptly named Dennis Blanco: *Dennis* because all his
predecessors in the navy had borne that name, and *Blanco—*
well, probably because he was of the opposite color, so very
black.

Officers and men worked furiously to keep the *Colon*
afloat; but their efforts were in vain, for, at 11:00 P.M., she
listed to starboard and turned over on her side. The *Oregon's* officers left just as she went over. The American flag
had been hoisted and went down with her. The *Texas* and
the *Oregon* remained by the wreck all night, and the next
morning they started for their station at Santiago. The *Oregon* slowly steamed up the bend past a scene of horror that
silenced all hands. The burning and battered wrecks strewn
along the beach made too pitiful a picture for rejoicing.
Floating about were uniforms, boxes, trunks, planks, and the
bloated bodies of the Spanish dead.

When the *Oregon* reached Santiago, Commodore
Schley greeted her with the signal "welcome back, brave
*Oregon*." It was July 4, and although the officers and men of
the squadron didn't know it then, they had won the war on
a summer morning.

Engineer in Chief George W. Melville, U.S.N., Chief of
the Bureau of Steam Engineering, discussed the *Oregon's*
achievement in his annual report of 1898:

It has not been customary to call special attention to the performance of vessels except on trials under maximum conditions, but that of the *Oregon* is so exceptional that it deserves a record in the Bureau's report. She was ordered from the Pacific to the Gulf before war was declared, and leaving Puget Sound 6 March, arrived at Jupiter Inlet 24 May, having steamed over 14,500 miles, stopping only for coal, and not being delayed an hour anywhere through any derangements of the machinery. Stopping at Key West only long enough to coal, she took her place in the blockading fleet at Santiago, and was always ready for service.

This alone would have given her an unparalleled record among battleships but the culmination came in the great battle of 3 July, when she surpassed herself. Always ready for action, she speedily attained a power greater than that developed on the trial, giving a speed (on account of greater displacement and foul bottom) only slightly less than then attained, and distancing all the other ships except the *Brooklyn,* which is 5 knots faster. Every official report comments on her wonderful speed, and it is generally believed that but for it, one at least, and possibly two, of the Spanish ships might have escaped.

The whole record is thus one which has never been equaled in the history of navies, and it will remain the standard for a long time to come. The credit is due, in the first place, to the builders—the Union Iron Works—for the excellence of the material and workmanship, but still more, and chiefly, to the engineering department of the vessel. The Bureau, therefore, takes great pleasure in commending to the Department's most favorable consideration Chief Engineer Robert W. Milligan, the executive head of the department, for his professional ability, untiring care, and excellent discipline, and also the junior engineer officers and the enlisted men, whose faithfulness and zeal, and under most trying circumstances, have enabled our Navy to add this to the other brilliant records of our vessels.[3]

# 7

# Mopping Up

On July 4, 1898, the victorious American ships were back on station off Santiago. The blockade had to be maintained because the army was closing in on the city and Spanish transports might attempt an evacuation. Most important of all for the navy, one Spanish cruiser, the *Reina Mercedes*, remained in the harbor. That night, the Spanish decided to block the harbor they had so assiduously attempted to keep open when Hobson had brought in the *Merrimac*. The *Reina Mercedes* steamed to the channel entrance and was scuttled. In the process, the *Massachusetts* and the *Texas* opened up on her, and the *Mercedes* too failed to block the channel. This brief action completed the destruction of Cervera's ill-fated squadron.

With the Spanish fleet a mass of twisted and smouldering metal, General Shafter generously entered into an armistice with the Spanish commander in order to avoid further bloodshed. The armistice remained in effect until July 17, when the Spanish surrendered to Admiral Sampson in Santiago. The Cuban action was over.

The American fleet was ordered to prepare to cross the Atlantic to deal with the remaining Spanish warships, including Spain's sole battleship. The Americans were to engage the Spanish fleet on the Iberian coast or follow it through the Mediterranean and the Suez Canal if the Spaniards should attempt to relieve Manila by this route. The American ships were divided into two squadrons, the Eastern Squadron, which would go all the way to Manila if necessary, and the Covering Squadron, which was prepared to escort the first squadron across the Atlantic and through the Mediterranean and then stay in those waters to protect the Eastern Squadron's flank and rear. Commodore Watson shifted his broad pennant from the *Newark* to the *Oregon* and took command of the Eastern Squadron.

The preparations proved to be unnecessary. Peace negotiations had begun with the fall of Santiago, and, on August 7, the Spanish accepted the American surrender terms. The war was over on August 12, and the United States of America had become a world power with an empire in the Caribbean and the Pacific.

But Captain Clark had fallen seriously ill with a tropical fever. The continuous stress of the long and tension-ridden voyage around South America, the intense heat of tropical blockade duty, and the final strain of battle had broken Clark's health. The shocked and saddened men of the *Oregon* learned that, although both had seemed indestructible, their good ship was stronger than their plucky fifty-four-year-old skipper.

On August 6, 1898, Captain Albert S. Barker, U.S.N., again took command of the *Oregon*, and Clark was ordered home on the *St. Louis* for medical treatment. In his modest autobiography, written twenty years later, Clark recalled his departure from the *Oregon:*

> There are a few occasions in a man's life which will remain with him always. . . . One . . . I can never forget was the day when, broken in health, I left the *Oregon.* It was a pleasure to find that the boat in which I was to be rowed to the northbound steamer was manned by my officers. That is an honor deeply appreciated by any captain. But I was surprised and hurt, as we left the ship's side, that none of the men were visible. Suddenly, as if moved by one spring, they rose from the decks where they had been lying concealed, and led by old Murphy, the chief boatswain's mate, joined in a ringing shout of "God bless our captain." So the last impression I had of the *Oregon,* as we rowed away, was a forest of waving arms and tossing caps, seen through a mist, although the day was clear and bright.[1]

When the people of the state of Oregon learned of the victory at Santiago and of Clark's illness, a subscription was taken up to buy him a gold sword. The precious weapon was manufactured in Portland and sent to Clark with the admiration and gratitude of the people of the state.

Clark recovered but never saw sea duty again. In March, 1899, he was assigned command of the navy yard at League Island. It was not until 1901 that the Navy recognized his distinguished service on the *Oregon* by advancing him six numbers on the captains list "for eminent and conspicuous conduct in battle." His next billet was as governor of the naval home in Washington, D.C. Finally, on June 16, 1902, four years after Santiago, he was promoted to rear admiral. His last assignment was as the president of the Naval Examination and Retirement Boards in Washington, from which he retired himself on August 4, 1905.

The *Oregon*'s great commander lived with his granddaughter in California until his death in 1922 at the age of seventy-nine. Toward the end, the aged hero was little remembered by any save his old shipmates. In 1915, as the Panama Canal neared completion, there had been talk of having Clark take command of the *Oregon* once more, with as many of the old *Oregon* hands as could be mustered, and traverse the canal to officially open the waterway inspired by the ship's great race. But the trip never took place. The Great War in Europe had darkened all festivities, and the Spanish-American War seemed almost as distant and forgotten as the Second Punic War. Clark, however, died as he lived, a man without bitterness, glad to have had the opportunity to serve his beloved country.

On August 14, 1898, the *New York,* the *Brooklyn,* the *Iowa,* the *Massachusetts,* the *Indiana,* and the *Oregon* weighed anchor and departed Cuban waters at long last. The victorious battle squadron headed for New York City and arrived there on August 20 to a tumultuous victory celebration. Arranged in line of column order, the vessels steamed into New York Harbor, all flags flying, whistles shrieking, and surrounded by harbor craft, pleasure boats, and sail. The sailors were given their long awaited and much deserved liberty, and there was hardly a jack among them who had to buy his own drinks that week in Old New York.

It was time for the *Oregon*'s long-neglected overhaul. Over a year had passed since the ship was last in dry dock, and her hull was foul with tons of barnacles, seaweed, and other debris that had accumulated in the tropical waters off Cuba. Therefore, Captain Barker ordered the ship into the Brooklyn Navy Yard, where the overhaul began on August 20. There, hundreds of people visited the vessel daily.

Meanwhile, affairs were not going so smoothly in the new American empire. To the surprise of the American people, the Filipinos had no desire to see their hated Spanish masters merely replaced by American masters. The United States Army commander in the Philippines, Maj. Gen. Wes-

ley Merritt, U.S.A., and the naval leader Admiral Dewey
had their hands full with the guerrillas under Emilio Agui-
naldo. The unfortunate war against the people of the Philippines would go on for three years.

Dewey asked the Navy Department to reinforce his
squadron at Manila, and the department agreed. The admiral was less concerned with Filipino military activities than
with the possibility of foreign—particularly German—inter-
vention in the islands. He wanted the fabulous *Oregon,* and
he got her.

The ship was painted peacetime white once more. The
naval militiamen were detached and sent home with the
thanks and good wishes of the navy and their regular navy
shipmates. Some men whose enlistments had expired took
their discharges and returned to civilian life. Still others left
the *Oregon* through routine transfers of personnel. Always
with ships and men, the faces change one by one until all
are different, but the ship and the spirit live on.

On October 12, 1898, the *Oregon* was underway once
more. She headed for the Pacific via the Strait of Magellan
in company with the *Iowa,* the supply ship *Celtic,* the collier
*Scindia,* and the distilling ship *Iris.* Captain Barker was senior officer present afloat for the expedition.

The cruise to the Pacific was more leisurely than the
*Oregon's* previous race to the Atlantic. The *Oregon* and the
*Iowa* arrived in Rio de Janeiro in time to participate in fes-
tivities celebrating the anniversary of the founding of the
Republic of Brazil. Then the vessels rounded the tip of
South America and headed for Callao, Peru, where they re-
ceived a resounding welcome on December 12. The *Iowa*
then headed north to San Francisco for repairs. The collier
and the supply ship had been detached previously, and so
only the *Oregon* and the *Iris* were left for the journey to
Manila. They arrived there at sunset on March 18, 1899. A
Navy band from Dewey's squadron hailed the vessels with

"The Star-Spangled Banner" as they glided to anchor firing their salutes to the revered admiral.

The *Oregon* had once more performed superbly under-way, making the journey without any engineering difficulty and arriving in perfect condition. Dewey cabled the Navy Department, "The *Oregon* and the *Iris* arrived today. The *Oregon* is in fit condition for any duty."

The beleaguered naval officer—who was administering a large city and an enormous colony and fending off foreign sharks—was delighted to have the *Oregon* at his side. She was the first battleship assigned to his Asiatic Squadron. All his other major ships, including the *Olympia,* were of course only cruisers. The *Oregon* relieved the *Olympia* as flagship. Captain Barker wrote Secretary of the Navy John D. Long that Dewey was at last confident that no foreign power would dare to attack the Philippines. One battleship had shifted the balance of power in the Far Pacific.

On November 7, the *Oregon* joined a squadron that landed General Wheaton in Lingayen Gulf and on the fifteenth, she supported a column of troops sent north along the shore. Then she attacked Vigan, some hundred miles to the north, at the request of General Young; on the twenty-sixth, she landed a party of sailors and marines under Commander McCracken to seize the port.

The annexation of the Philippines after payments to Spain placed the United States in the midst of the Far East trade muddle. Anti-Western and antiimperialist resentment was growing in weak, corrupt, and faction-torn China. Russia and Japan were already beginning the light sparring that would lead in 1905 to Japan's knockout victory in the Russo-Japanese War, and the two nations were bent on carving out large pieces of Chinese territory for themselves.

The Chinese people under Boxer leadership rebelled against their own corrupt government and the foreign con-cessionaires. Peking, including the embassies of the imperialist nations, was quickly placed under siege by the Boxers. In the summer of 1905, the trading nations gathered an invasion army to relieve the city. The *Oregon* was reluctantly detached from Philippine duty to serve as both transport and support ship for the growing American presence in China. She would first sail to Taku and then patrol the China coast.

# 8

# Disaster
# and
# Rescue

The *Oregon*, now under the command of Capt. George F. F. Wilde, U.S.N., made for Hong Kong to pick up extra sailors and marines who had been shipped there previously from Manila and who were needed at Peking. The *Oregon* departed Hong Kong on June 23, 1900, and steamed north towards Taku, the nearest port to Peking. Captain Wilde was under orders to make haste. Unfortunately he took the shortest and least safe route. The *Oregon* rounded the Shantung Peninsula and, on June 28, was about to enter the Gulf of Pechili when Wilde decided to anchor in a dense fog three miles south of Now-Ki Island Light in the Chang-Shan Channel, approximately 38 degrees north latitude and 121 degrees east longitude. The next morning, the weather cleared, and Wilde put two boats over to take soundings. They reported 5½ fathoms in the channel eastward. But the ship was hardly underway when it struck Pinnacle Rock, an obstruction twenty-five feet high and encircled by a shoal. The forward compartment was flooded, the skin of the ship was cut through to frame nineteen along the side, and there were small holes through the bottom. Any rough weather and the *Oregon* was lost.

Despite the fact that it was the stormy season, the weather and the *Oregon's* luck held good for three key days. Rescue ships rushed to her aid, the vessel was lightened, and temporary repairs were made. The *Oregon* was not to die on that distant Chinese rock. The ship desperately needed dry-docking and major hull repairs, but the nearest American dry dock was of course on the west coast of the United States. The Russian naval facility at Port Arthur was only sixty miles away from where the *Oregon* had been refloated. The Russians, however, declined to help the *Oregon*, stating that their dock was too narrow and that, furthermore, they were too busy to assist. It was the Japanese who came to the rescue. Their cruiser *Akitisushima* was the first foreign vessel to arrive at the scene. Another early arrival was the Chinese cruiser *Mai Chi*, which had been detailed to protect foreigners in the nearby coastal town of Tengchow. The Chinese assistance was outstanding, and, in return for the aid, Wilde permitted the *Mai Chi* to hoist the American flag when threatened with capture by Russian vessels spearheading Russia's expansion of her sphere of influence in North China. Three years later, Peking would formally thank Washington for this protection.

The Japanese were most anxious to help the Americans, especially since the Russians had turned them down. The *Oregon* eased her way slowly out of Chinese waters and limped under escort to the Japanese naval base at Kure. There, the Japanese provided every assistance possible, even though they needed their large dry docks for their own busy vessels. Meanwhile, the *Oregon*'s marine detachment joined the expedition for the relief of Peking.

Capt. Wilde was relieved by Capt. Francis W. Dickins, U.S.N., on February 22, 1901, and on April 7, Capt. Charles M. Thomas, U.S.N., took over command of the *Oregon*. The *Oregon*'s material condition was not perfect even after the dry-docking, and Thomas's orders were to bring his ship home. Preparations were made to sail the Pacific again.

The *Oregon*'s first port of call upon her return home was to be San Francisco. When the people of that city learned that their home-built, world famous battleship was returning for the first time since her great race around South America and her glorious day at Santiago, a massive celebration was planned for the estimated day of arrival, June 13, 1901. Unfortunately for the city fathers as well as the ship, the *Oregon* steamed into the Golden Gate a full twenty-four hours ahead of schedule. She still was the fastest American battleship afloat, perhaps the fastest battleship in the world at that time. In spite of the *Oregon*'s early arrival, the San Franciscans celebrated her return. They especially honored her great builders, the men of the Union Iron Works, eventually to be the Bethlehem Steel Company's Shipbuilding Division. From San Francisco, the *Oregon* steamed north to the Bremerton Navy Yard once more. There she was laid up in ordinary and refitted.

By 1902, tensions were mounting in the Far East. China's government was disintegrating because of internal problems as well as external pressures from the voracious trading powers, particularly Russia and Japan. The *Oregon* was put back into commission and sailed for the China Sea under the command of Capt. Joseph Giles Easton U.S.N., to commence four years of showing the flag and supporting American "interests" in China.

On February 8, 1904, the Imperial Japanese Navy attacked the Imperial Russian Fleet at Chemulpo without warning, and the Russo-Japanese War was on. The *Oregon* was involved in one incident during the conflict. Anchored off Shanghai one evening under the command of Capt. John P. Merrell, U.S.N., she watched Japanese destroyers chase the Russian warship *Askold* into the bay. The bay formed a part of neutral Chinese waters, and the Russian ship was theoretically safe, but the Japanese had little respect for such niceties and deployed for a torpedo attack. Captain Merrell ordered the *Oregon's* searchlights turned on the Japanese destroyers, and the lights blinded and confused the Japanese long enough to allow the Russian ship to escape up the river. The Japanese protested this violation of international law in illuminating their vessels. Merrell growled back that he would turn more than lights on them if they did not respect the neutrality of the port. The thirteen-inch guns of the Bulldog of the Navy could still bite.

Anti-American sentiment in China was on the rise, partly due to the general hatred of the exploiting "foreign devils," but mostly due to the exclusion of Chinese immigrants from the United States, a policy that clearly implied prejudice. On July 20, 1905, Chinese Nationalists instituted a boycott of American goods in Shanghai. The boycott was successful and quickly spread through all of South China, then to the Philippines, Hawaii, and even to the Japanese ports. American businessmen roared for protection. President Theodore Roosevelt on November 15 ordered the Secretary of the Navy to concentrate "as strong a naval force as possible" off China. Preparations were also made for an Army expedition of fifteen thousand troops. The Chinese would buy our goods or else.

Therefore, in February, 1906, the *Oregon* was belligerently patroling off Hong Kong while the American gunboat *El Cano* was steaming on the Yangtze River. On February 26, Roosevelt submitted a set of humiliating demands to the Imperial Chinese Government. The Emperor gave in and issued an edict forbidding expressions of antiforeign sentiments by his subjects everywhere. Unfortunately, the United States had learned how to use gunboat diplomacy.

Now Merrell could bring the *Oregon* home again, and the ship was placed out of commission at the Bremerton Navy Yard once more. She stayed there for five years, from April 26, 1906, to April 26, 1911. The navy had less need for the *Oregon* than formerly. Newer battleships, more heavily armed, more heavily gunned, were coming into commission as the United States began to build a world fleet. Significantly, the *Oregon* was out of commission during the voyage of the Great White Fleet.

After the *Oregon* was put back in commission, under the command of Capt. Charles F. Pond, U.S.N., she rejoined the now formidable Pacific Fleet. But the *Oregon* was now too old-fashioned to be part of the battle fleet. Her role was merely supportive. She was a famous ship, and others were proud to stand in company with her, but her fighting days seemed over.

The years washed by. Theodore Roosevelt's great strategic dream, the Panama Canal, was soon to open. Many Americans felt it would be a grand, sentimental gesture to have the *Oregon,* manned by her Spanish-American War crew under old Admiral Clark, sail first through the canal. In June, 1913, sixty thousand state of Oregon schoolchildren petitioned President Wilson to allow "their ship," the *Oregon,* to lead the parade through the new waterway. But when the canal opened in 1914, the terrible war in Europe prevented large-scale celebrations. No one was in much of a mood to celebrate any international event when Europe was tearing herself to bits and millions of humans were slaughtering one another.

The opening of the Panama-Pacific Exposition at San Francisco in 1915 found the *Oregon* on duty in the Golden Gate under the command of Comdr. Joseph M. Reeves,

U.S.N., who later became an admiral. Reeves had served as assistant engineer in the port engineroom in 1898. Thousands of fair goers visited the old war relic. The *Oregon* was still the most famous ship in the navy. In 1916, the entire United States Pacific Fleet passed in review for the second year of the exposition, and the *Oregon*, under Comdr. G. W. Williams, U.S.N., served as reviewing ship.

After the United States entered World War I, the *Oregon*, under command of Comdr. C. P. Snyder, U.S.N., was ordered once more to the Bremerton Navy Yard. The vessel was overhauled and modernized at a cost of $1 million and then had a short wartime career as a west coast training vessel, providing training and experience in navigation, seamanship, and gunnery for officers and men soon to be assigned to combat ships in the war zones. For part of this time, the *Oregon* served as designated flagship of the Pacific Fleet.

A unique assignment came to the *Oregon* with the Bolshevik Revolution and Russia's withdrawal from the world war. The *Oregon* was selected as an escort vessel for an expedition of American troops to Siberia. The men, under Gen. William Sidney Graves, U.S.A., joined with other allied forces, ostensibly to try to prevent Allied war supplies in Russia from falling into German hands, but actually to help White Russian counterrevolutionaries. America's "Siberian adventure" has been long forgotten by Americans and long remembered by the Russians. The expedition failed, and the Allied troops withdrew, the Japanese most reluctantly. They had sent the largest number of troops and had the most to gain by maintaining a military presence in Siberia.

After returning to the United States, the *Oregon*, under Lt. Comdr. W. E. Madden, U.S.N., was temporarily placed out of commission on June 16, 1919, after two thirds of her crew were attacked by influenza during the terrible epidemic of April, 1919.

On August 21, 1919, the *Oregon* was once more taken out of the reserve fleet and put back into commission to serve as the reviewing ship when President Woodrow Wilson and the Secretary of the Navy Josephus Daniels gave a postwar welcome to the Pacific Fleet under Adm. Hugh Rodman, U.S.N., at Seattle. A bronze tablet was placed on the deck where the president had stood during the review. The use of the *Oregon* as reviewing vessel was a sentimental gesture, for the Navy had long realized that the fighting days of the old ship were over and her military value in the age of the fifteen-inch-gun dreadnaught was nil. The *Oregon* was decommissioned for the last time on October 4, 1919. Her final commanding officer was Capt. I. C. Wettengill, U.S.N.

It was planned that the old Spanish-American War battleships *Oregon, Indiana, Iowa,* and *Massachusetts* be used for target practice and sunk at sea. However, the United Spanish War Veterans and other civic organizations mounted a campaign to save the *Oregon.* In 1920, they won temporary success when that great naval buff, Assistant Secretary of the Navy Franklin D. Roosevelt, intervened and the *Oregon* alone of the old battleships survived the gunfire and scrap heap.

Under the terms of the Washington Conference on Limitation of Armaments, 1921–22, the *Oregon* was again scheduled for the scrap yard. If the United States were to limit its number of battleships, then "BB-3" could not be an old Spanish-American War relic. Again the public uproar commenced, this time louder and clearer. The people of the state of Oregon particularly wanted the old ship saved, and they wanted her nearby so that their children could see the proud old conqueror and walk her decks.

In 1925, the state of Oregon officially petitioned the United States Government to have the vessel preserved as a memorial and berthed in Portland. Oregon governor Ben

Wilson Olcott personally wrote to the Navy Department
requesting that the plea of the state legislature be granted.
He pledged that the state would live up to any agreement
the Navy might require, including a guarantee that adequate sums would be appropriated annually for the maintenance and preservation of the *Oregon* Memorial.

The Navy Department agreed at last, with the proviso
that the state create an acceptance fund to maintain the vessel in a condition that would safely allow visitors to board
her. The legislature of the state of Oregon enacted a law
creating a permanent *Oregon* fund. The veteran would be
brought to Portland.

At Bremerton, the propeller shaft of the *Oregon* was
cut in two, and the engines were dismantled. Then, with a
regular navy crew aboard and commanded by Capt. Robert
T. Menner, U.S.N., the old ship was pushed and pulled by
navy tugs down Puget Sound and out into the Pacific. At the
mouth of the Columbia River, she was met by the veteran
pilots Capt. O. P. Rankin and Capt. N. Hampson, who took
command of the *Oregon* and the navy tugs on their trip up
the Columbia and Willamette rivers. The *Oregon* was flying
the old "homeward bound" pennant for the last time. Just
below Portland, she was boarded by the queen of the 1925
Rose Festival and her court. The reception given the old
ship on her arrival at a berth at the east end of Portland's
Broadway Bridge was glorious and long remembered. Her
arrival officially opened the 1925 Rose Festival.

State officials signed for the ship when she arrived in
Portland on July 14, 1925. She had been officially accepted
from the Navy Department, represented by Captain Menner, on July 3, 1925, the anniversary of the Battle of
Santiago, by Gov. Walter M. Pierce on behalf of the people
of the state of Oregon.

Some years before, on May 8, 1919, the ship's newspaper, *The Bull Dog,* had summed up the bluejackets' feeling about the ship:

> She's been sailing the seas for Uncle Sam since 1896, and in that time she has won a name as one of the historic ships of the Navy. At present it seems as though her days are numbered. There is a newspaper report that she is to continue in service with the Pacific Fleet, but our orders to return to Bremerton and put "The Bull Dog" in a comfortable kennel for a long rest have not been revoked at this writing. But whether she keeps on sailing or ties up in the Navy Yard, we'll say that we are proud to have had duty aboard her. It is a privilege to serve on a ship with such a record and it will be a distinction to boast of in the future years when one reads in history of the good old *OREGON* who romped around the Horn and fought the good fight to victory at Santiago, that we once swung our hammocks between her decks. In this war she was too old to be in the first line but she guarded the nation on this coast, has trained many gun crews who peppered the suds with accurate fire from the decks of ships which carried our men and the necessary food and gear to France, and has sent out many sons with commissions to serve on other ships and to command sub-chasers, and she is winding up her duty in this war with this important mission to boost the Victory Loan on the West Coast that Uncle Sam may pay his debts and go forward to new achievements to peace as important as his glorious accomplishments in war.
>
> So, once again, "Here's to the grand old *OREGON.*"

# 9

# Fiasco
# and
# Final Glory

In 1925, the governor of the state of Oregon appointed
a commission of five members to manage the affairs of the
battleship *Oregon*. The original members of the commission
were Col. Carle Abrams, Col. U. G. Worrell (retired), and
Howard Waddell, all veterans of the Spanish-American War
and World War I; Lafe Manning, a Spanish-American War
veteran who had seen service on the battleship; and Mrs.
Cora A. Thompson, wife of a Spanish-American War veteran. In 1928, Mrs. Thompson resigned from the commission
to assume the duties of secretary and business manager of
the battleship commission.

The possibility of establishing a National War Museum
aboard the ship was taken up by the Battleship *Oregon*
Commission in August, 1925, and Mrs. Thompson was
placed in charge of this work. Progress was slow until 1928,

when the United Spanish War Veterans, at their national encampment in Havana, Cuba, passed a resolution instructing each state department of the organization to send all its members a request for gifts and loans to the museum. The following year, the National Auxiliary, United Spanish War Veterans, passed a similar resolution. Then material began to arrive, not only from the United States but also from England and Canada.

The old warship became very much a part of the civic structure of the city of Portland. Various organizations, such as the Boy Scouts, held meetings aboard, and schoolchildren scurried through the ship on fall and spring outings. It was a good fate and a good life for a retired old veteran, but bleak days were approaching.

In 1938, the Battleship *Oregon* Commission sponsored a project that would have saved the vessel from its later, ignominious fate, had the plans been carried to completion. The idea was to dig a short channel shoreward, warp the old ship in, and permanently encase it in concrete at a place to be called the Battleship *Oregon* Marine Park. The *Oregon* would be the historic jewel in a recreational setting. Unfortunately, Portland and the state of Oregon were too enmeshed in the struggle with the Great Depression to provide funds for the entire worthwhile project, but the ship was at least moved to safer quarters. That year, the United Spanish War Veterans held their national convention in Portland, and one of the ceremonies was the towing of the old battleship from the northeast end of the Broadway Bridge to the southwest end of the Hawthorne Bridge. There the *Oregon* was floated in a basin roughly carved from the bank and bed of the Willamette River, completely out of danger from the regular channel traffic. Later in the day, the basin and the site of the future Battleship *Oregon* Marine Park were dedicated.

A few months later, the public-spirited citizens of Port-

land and the state raised enough money to complete the
basin and a seawall, lay out the park, and build a long,
solidly railed gangplank from street level to the deck of the
battleship.

But the *Oregon,* unfortunately, was still afloat, still
movable, and worst of all, still in the possession of the federal government. She was still officially only on loan to the
people of the state of Oregon.

Now begins the mystery and embarrassment of a great
ship's demise through misplaced patriotic zeal, stupidity, av-
arice, and indifference. Almost immediately after the Japanese attack on Pearl Harbor, the governor of Oregon,
Charles A. Sprague, who obviously knew little about modern naval warfare, offered to return the *Oregon* to the navy
so that she might serve for "coastal or other defense use."
The offer, although generous and high minded, was absurd.
The *Oregon* had no military value whatsoever. The navy at
first declined the offer, indicating rightly that the historical
importance of the *Oregon* outweighed any possible opera-
tional value the ship might have. Still, rumors of her immi-
nent scrapping began to circulate widely, and patriotic organizations deluged the navy with letters and petitions of
protest over such a fate for the vessel.

On September 15, 1942, the beleaguered Navy Department released to the nation a statement headlined, "Navy
Knows of No Plans to Scrap USS *Oregon.*" The statement
read in part, ". . . the maintenance of this historic shrine
remindful of the resourcefulness, perseverance and loyalty
of the old Navy remains an inspiration to our fighting
forces." Fine words, but a bundle of lies, for plans had indeed been laid to scrap the *Oregon.* The United States War
Production Board, zealously and sometimes fanatically
searching for scrap steel to feed the voracious and insatiable
furnaces of war production, had eyed the ship. Knowing
that the navy would soon be forced to reverse its decision

concerning the ship, Under Secretary of the Navy James Forrestal informed Governor Sprague that, due to the "great necessity for scrap metal and the pressure exerted upon us to make every possible contribution toward the building up of an adequate stockpile, this decision will probably have to be reconsidered."[1]

The matter was referred to President Franklin D. Roosevelt. The president surely felt bad about the situation. He was a naval buff and an amateur historian. Furthermore, he had helped to save the *Oregon* after World War I. Finally, Roosevelt wrote to Secretary of the Navy Frank Knox:

The White House

October 26, 1942

Dear Colonel Knox:

It is with great reluctance that I authorize the Navy Department to turn the USS *Oregon* over to the War Production Board for reduction to scrap metal.

It is my understanding that the Department will take immediate action toward the preservation of the USS *Olympia* as a naval relic of the Spanish-American war period.

Sincerely yours,

Franklin D. Roosevelt

Even the *Olympia*, as it turned out, was not preserved by the navy. Dewey's flagship was finally saved by the continuing efforts of private charity. Knox was clearly not surprised at Roosevelt's decision. In fact, he had anticipated it, for, on October 24, he had written a letter to a group of concerned *Oregon* supporters—the Battleship *Oregon* Naval Post No. 1478, Veterans of Foreign Wars—stating somewhat fatuously that: "despite the fact that I, like yourselves, would like to preserve the *Oregon*, the necessity for utilizing all available strategic material makes it imperative that the metals of the *Oregon* be utilized. Far from being scrapped, the strategic materials of the *Oregon* will be reclaimed and converted into war material, and thereby again join in battle, a choice I am sure the good ship would make, were it within her power to do so."

With almost immodest haste, Knox had the vessel stricken from the navy list and put up for sale on November 2, just a few days after he received the president's letter. The business of her sale proceeded circumspectly. Special invitations were sent out to those selected to bid for her scrapping contract. These invitations stated somewhat mysteriously that "due to the fact that this ship is of inestimable sentimental value, bidding and award of this ship for scrapping will not be handled under the usual circumstances. . . . Award will be predicated not only upon the highest bid, but also upon other factors which will be discussed with the bidders at the opening of bids on board the vessel."

These "factors" were never defined. Only the single military mast of the *Oregon* was allowed to be saved, and it is all that remains of the ship today. It occupies a place of honor on the Portland seawall. On December 7, 1942, (O Irony!) the old ship was knocked down for only $35,000 to two Portland businessmen, Edwin M. Ricker and William O. McKay. The *Oregon* was towed to Kalama, Wash. Work on the ship began almost immediately, and it seemed at first that her steel might indeed make its tiny contribution to the war effort. However, steel scrap became less and less critical, and the dismantling slowed down. The navy yard at Mare Island, Calif., became interested in some of the *Oregon*'s machinery, and, for a while, there were some negotiations between the yard and the wreckers.

As September, 1943, began, only the superstructure and internal machinery had been removed from the vessel. Concerned citizens and navy historians were totally disgusted with what by then appeared to be either vandalism or crude wartime speculation and profiteering. The navy was extremely embarrassed and stopped the little work being done on the dismantling project. The ship was requisitioned back from her owners. The *Oregon* was not officially returned to the navy list, for such action would have been absurd, but she was again referred to by her previous designation, IX-22. The IX stood for *miscellaneous vessel*, a designation given to such historic ships as the *Constitution* and the *Constellation*.

The navy decided that there was still some military use in the *Oregon* after all, although not of course as a combat vessel. The American island-hopping campaign in the Pacific was proceeding apace, and a vessel was needed to carry blasting material and ammunition out to Guam and store the explosives. The *Oregon* was going to war again. Her armored hull was perfect for dynamite stowage and so she was ballasted with gravel and loaded with 1,400 tons of explosives. The seabees were waiting for her on Guam.

In July, 1944, the *Oregon* was on the high seas, under tow this time, back in those familiar Pacific waters. She was taken to Port Merizo, where Japanese stragglers took her under fire one evening. The seabees continued the work of blasting and harbor clearing. Each day, the commander of Service Squadron 12, to which the *Oregon* was assigned, would send LCT's and LCVP's alongside for loads of dynamite, which were then transported to Apra Harbor, Tinian, Saipan, or Palau. The LCI(G)474 served as the *Oregon's* permanent tender.

The *Oregon* was moored at Port Merizo for safety's sake, to keep the floating bomb away from more populated areas. But the crew who worked aboard the *Oregon* did not feel much danger, for they assumed that, with prescribed precautions, no serious accidents would result. Hourly temperature readings were taken in the holds, windscopes were rigged for circulation of air through all hatches, and of course no smoking was allowed on the ship. Armed guards were maintained on the bow and stern of the old battleship and heavy use was made of searchlights at night. The work was done at night because the extremely hot weather made work on the steel decks unbearable during the day. Each night, about fifteen tons of dynamite were unloaded from the ship. The boxes were brought up from the holds to the main deck by a deck winch and then sent down a chute to the landing craft.

During the stay at Port Merizo, part of the ship's work consisted of establishing good will among the native inhabitants. The village of Merizo had about five hundred Chamorro people. When the *Oregon* first arrived, many of the villagers began coming out to the ship, anxious to talk to the men and tell of their experiences during the Japanese occupation of the island. It was against the rules to provide civilians large quantities of food, but they were given small rations of flour and other baking materials, and some of the men also provided the Chamorros with clothing. The village had a grade school with a principal and four teachers. All the boys of the school belonged to Boy Scout troops, and the boatswain's mate and the signalman were assigned to spend spare moments instructing the scouts in handling lines, tying various knots, and signaling with flags and blinkers. One of the officers began instructing the teachers on the U.S. government and the Constitution. The Chamorros were welcome guests, and it was not unusual to have about ten to fifteen at the mess. A small native orchestra, which had two violins, a banjo, and a ukelele, often came out to the ship on Sundays after divine services on the island. The Chamorros were invited to the services. At first, only the women attempted to join in the religious songs, but, on succeeding Sundays, more and more Chamorros learned the words and melodies. It was not long before every man, woman, and child sang without hesitation and with full confidence. For better or for worse, the *Oregon* had brought American civilization back to Port Merizo.

As the fighting passed to the east, the islands that had been dearly won in American blood grew less and less important until even Guam became a backwater to the war. All the *Oregon*'s dynamite and ammunition had been requisitioned, and she languished and rusted in the now almost silent harbor of Port Merizo.

After the war ended, the *Oregon* was placed under the jurisdiction of the commanding officer of the Naval Operations Base, Apra, who had no idea what to do with the ship. There was some talk of sinking her to form part of a breakwater, but nothing ever came of the plan.

Then, on November 14, 1948, Hurricane Agnes ravaged the Marianas. Fifty-knot winds and high seas pounded and tore at the old ship until, in torment, she broke free from her moorings, and unmanned, moved swiftly out to sea. The dawn of November 16 found the hurricane blown out and the *Oregon* out of sight and presumably resting peacefully on the bottom of the Pacific Ocean. However, search planes were dispatched just to make sure the old relic was not still afloat and menacing the sea lanes.

On December 8, 1948, a very surprised naval aviator spotted a great steel hull seemingly underway, five hundred miles southeast of Guam and heading for the Philippines. The *Oregon* had simply taken a month's unauthorized leave to pay a last visit to some of her old haunts.

Hastily, the commanding officer at Guam dispatched a fleet tug to lasso the AWOL and tow her home to Apra Harbor. He then reported that the ship had suffered "no apparent damage during unscheduled voyage."

In the United States, the *Oregon*'s escapade once more drew attention to her existence. Many people who had once been interested in the vessel had forgotten her, but the solo voyage reminded them that she was still alive. Oregon legislators, particularly United States Senator Wayne Morse, remembered all the hot air expended over the *Oregon's* "noble sacrifice" in 1942 and demanded that the vessel be brought back stateside and restored to her former condition. While this effort was being made, other groups of Americans interested in the historical heritage of their nation were mounting campaigns to save other vessels, including the frigate *Constellation,* which would indeed be saved, and the steam sloop *Hartford,* which would be destroyed.

Alas, the *Oregon* was now almost beyond restoration. In 1953, some people suggested the ship be rehabilitated at Guam, but even this plan proved impractical. All that was left of the old warrior was the hull, with its original steel plates riveted together in San Francisco in the last decade of the nineteenth century. The millions of dollars needed to bring the ship back to her pre-World War II condition would have had to come out of naval appropriations, and the funds could not be spared from a peacetime budget. Still, the cost would not have been more than that of a new jet fighter plane. Finally, Congress decided in the name of the American people. The Eighty-third Congress, in Public Law 523, ordered the Secretary of the Navy to dispose of the *Oregon.* All that her many friends had accomplished in eight years of effort to save her was an ignominious death. They could not even force the government to tow her out to sea and let her sink beneath the waves.

On March 15, 1956, the *Oregon* was sold to the Massey Supply Corporation for $208,000—a considerable hike from the $35,000 the vessel had brought in 1943, when she was in good shape. Massey quickly turned around and resold the hulk to the Iwai Sanggo Company, a Japanese scrap and salvage firm. The Japanese sent a tug to Guam, made fast their towing cables, and dragged the hull to Kawasaki, Japan, where the ship was quickly broken up and her pieces were fed into the giant steel mills of Japan.

In some ways, the former enemy was kinder to the ship than her own people had been, for just inside the main gate of the Yokosuka Naval Base of the Japanese Maritime Defense Force may be found some anchor links from an old, old ship and a plaque with this inscription in Japanese and English:

IN MEMORY OF A GALLANT SHIP
U.S.S. OREGON
1896–1919

This section of anchor chain from the historic U.S.S. Oregon was presented to the U.S. Naval Base at Yokosuka, Japan, through the generosity of Ryozo Hiranuma, the Mayor of Yokohama, in cooperation with Lionel M. Summers U.S. Consulate General, Yokohama. Presented 26 February, 1957.

And thus lived and died McKinley's Bulldog, the battleship *Oregon*. She was born in an exuberant America that was just beginning to turn its eyes from the closed frontier and the problems of internal expansion to the heady, dangerous dreams of colonialism and world power. The ship was superbly built and gave tribute to American technological progress and the growth of heavy industry in California. In war, no American vessel ever served her country better. In peace, she showed the flag, trained thousands of naval officers and enlisted men (several of whom went on to distinguished and formative military careers), and then was a floating historical museum. Except for the *Constitution*, no ship has been more revered and loved by the American people.

The *Oregon* died in a period of post-Korean War disenchantment with things military, although in truth she had been needlessly ruined by misguided patriotism during World War II. The old lady should have been allowed to live. Her inspiration is sorely needed now and will be needed even more in the future. But, surely, she has a secure place in history and in the heart of any American who has ever read of the great race around Cape Horn and the chase of the *Cristobal Colon.*

# Appendix A

**U.S.S.** *Oregon's* **Characteristics**
**at Commissioning**

The hull of the *Oregon* was protected at the waterline by belts of the strongest available armor, 18 inches thick. The belts rose 3 feet above the water and extended to a depth of 4½ feet below the water. They turned in forward and aft to sweep around the oases of the armored redoubts. The armored area accounted for about 75 percent of the water plane. The belts were backed by 6 inches of wood, two ¾-inch steel plates, and a 10-foot belt of coal. Forward and abaft of the side armor belts were heavy underwater protective decks that sloped at the sides to 4½ feet below the water. Over the armor belt was an armored deck that had belts of water-excluding material worked on its slopes. Above the belt armor and from redoubt to redoubt, the sides were protected by 5 inches of steel.

The vessel was cut sharp up forward, making a powerful ram bow and doing away with excessive bow waves on account of the easier lines so obtained. This feature aided greatly the maneuverability of the ship.

Below the waterline, the *Oregon's* bow swept forward to form a pointed ram. Above the ram, the bow was pierced for a surface torpedo tube. At the level of the deck, the bow bore a striped red, white, and blue shield. On billboards on each side of the forecastle rested a bower and a sheet anchor, whose chains were led through hawse pipes to a steam winch just forward of the huge forward thirteen-inch gun turret. The anchor davits and two ventilators, all of which could be unshipped when clearing for action, and a scuttle were also located in the bow.

Rising from the waterline belt at each end of the ship were armored redoubts made of steel 17 inches thick. These redoubts extended above the main deck 3½ feet and gave an armored freeboard of 15 feet 2 inches. They protected the turning gear of the turrets and all the operations of loading. The turrets were designed to be inclined. They were 17 inches thick and were powerfully strengthened. The horizontal thickness of the inclined turrets was 20 inches. The conning tower had armor 10 inches thick; a tube of 7-inch thickness protected the voice pipes, electric wires, and steering connections.

The battery of the *Oregon* was made up of four thirteen-inch breechloading rifles, eight eight-inch breechloading rifles, four six-inch breechloading rifles, twenty six-pounder rapid-fire guns, two Gatlings, and six torpedo tubes. The Navy Department believed that this battery represented a weight of armament superior to that of any battleship laid down by a foreign power.

The thirteen-inch guns were nearly eighteen feet above the water and had large arcs of train. The six-inch guns were almost fifteen feet above the water and fired across the center line of the ship. The eight-inch guns were mounted across the middle line of the ship. All these guns could pierce at two miles the armor of many of the best armored cruisers and could also be used with great effect against the lightly armored and unarmored parts of a heavier battleship. The guns could be brought into action early in an engagement, on account of their great height. The guns of the powerful secondary battery were so disposed that a stream of projectiles might radiate from the vessel. Such a stream would lead to the almost certain destruction of any light boat venturing within range.

Fixed torpedo tubes were carried at the bow and stern and two training tubes, firing through five inches of protection, were carried on each broadside.

The 8-inch guns had barbettes made of steel 10 inches thick, inclined turrets of 8½-inch thickness, and cone bases and loading tubes of 3-inch thickness. The 6-inch guns were protected by 5 inches of armor. Ammunition was sent up inside 2-inch splinter bulkheads worked around the deck of these guns. Some of the six-pounder guns were mounted between decks and had 2-inch armor worked around them. Other six-pounders were exposed and had the usual service shields. The one-pounder guns were protected by 2 inches of steel.

The navy had paid special attention to the ammunition and had secured a rapid, efficient, and thoroughly protected supply that was believed to represent an advance upon all systems then in vogue.

Great care had been taken to dispose the *Oregon's* great battery so that one gun might not interfere with the line of fire of another. In addition the small boats had been stowed amidships, where the blasts could not reach them. The sides and decks had been especially strengthened so as to withstand the great strains brought upon them by the fire of the larger guns. The thirteen-inch guns were kept six feet above the deck at the middle line so as to reduce strain on the deck.

The *Oregon* carried a seventy-foot, conical military mast, which rose above the conning tower. This mast carried two tops for rapid-fire and machine guns. The ammunition was sent up to the tops inside the mast. The military mast was surmounted by a tall signal mast, and the enclosed pilot house and signal bridge stood at the foot of the military mast. Aft of the mast were two funnels some forty feet high, with two boat cranes and an array of ventilators between them.

The engines of the ship were of a twin screw, vertical, triple expansion, direct acting, inverted cylinder type. The engines were placed in water-tight compartments and separated by bulkheads. The diameters of the cylinders were: high pressure, 34½ inches; intermediate, 48 inches; low pressure, 75 inches; stroke, 42 inches.

The condensers were of composition and sheet brass, each main condenser having a cooling surface of 6,353 square feet. The circulating pumps were centrifugal and independent. There were four double-ended and two single-ended auxiliary steel boilers of the horizontal return fire-tube type. The main boilers were about 15 feet in outside diameter and 18 feet long. The auxiliary single-ended boilers were about 10 feet 2 inches in diameter and 8½ feet long.

The *Oregon*'s bunkers carried 1,800 tons of coal which, it was calculated, would permit her to cruise 16,000 nautical miles at a speed of ten knots. Her crew would consist of 30 officers and 438 men.

# Appendix B

**The Officers of the Oregon during the Race around the Horn.**

Captain . . . . . . . . . . . . . . . . . . C. E. Clark
Lieutenant Commander . . . . . J. K. Cogswell
Lieutenants . . . . . . . . . . . . . . R. F. Nicholson, W. H. Allen,
                                     A. A. Ackerman
Lieutenant junior grade . . . . . E. W. Eberle
Ensigns . . . . . . . . . . . . . . . . . . C. L. Hussey, R. Z. Johnston
Captain of Marines . . . . . . . . . R. Dickins
Second Lieutenant
    of Marines . . . . . . . . . . . . . A. R. Davis
Naval Cadets . . . . . . . . . . . . . H. E. Yarnell, L. M.
                                     Overstreet, A. G. Magill,
                                     C. S. Kempff
Chief Engineer . . . . . . . . . . . R. W. Milligan
P. A. Engineer . . . . . . . . . . . . C. N. Offley
Asst. Engineers . . . . . . . . . . . J. M. Reeves, F. Lyon
Engineer Cadets . . . . . . . . . . H. N. Jenson, W. D. Leahy
Surgeon . . . . . . . . . . . . . . . . . P. A. Lovering

| | |
|---|---|
| Assistant Surgeon | W. B. Grove |
| Paymaster | S. R. Colhoun |
| Chaplain | P. J. McIntyre |
| Paymaster's Clerk | J. A. Murphy |
| Boatswain | John Costello |
| Gunner | A. S. Williams |
| Carpenter | M. F. Roberts |

# Notes

### Chapter 2: The Launching

1. *San Francisco Chronicle,* 27 October 1893.
2. Ibid.
3. *San Francisco Examiner,* 27 October 1893.

### Chapter 5: "Six Thousand Miles . . ."

1. Charles Edgar Clark, *My Fifty Years in the Navy,* p. 262.
2. Ibid., p. 270.
3. Ibid., p. 274.
4. Ibid.
5. Ibid.
6. Captain Joshua Slocum, "Sailing Alone Around the World," p. 593.

### Chapter 6: Into Battle

1. Charles Edgar Clark, *My Fifty Years in the Navy,* pp. 332–333.
2. Ibid., p. 296.
3. Records of the Bureau of Ships, United States Department of the Navy, Washington, D.C.

### Chapter 7: Mopping Up

1. Charles Edgar Clark, *My Fifty Years in the Navy,* pp. 300–301.

### Chapter 9: Fiasco and Final Glory

1. John D. Alden, "Whatever Happened to the Battleship *Oregon?*," p. 147.

# Bibliography

Alden, John D. "Whatever Happened to the Battleship *Oregon?" United States Naval Institute Proceedings* 94 (September 1968): 146–149.

Beardsley, C. A., Rear Admiral, U.S.N. "The Trial of the *Oregon." Harper's New Monthly Magazine* 98 (1899): 699–707.

Braisted, William Reynolds. *The United States Navy in the Pacific: 1897–1909*. Austin: University of Texas Press, 1958.

Bryant, Samuel W. *The Sea and the States*. New York: Thomas Y. Crowell Co., 1947.

Cannon, Joseph C. *The U.S.S.* Oregon *and the Battle of Santiago*. New York: Comet Press, 1958.

Cassard, William G. *Battleship* Indiana *and Her Part in the Spanish-American War*. New York, 1898. Compiled and published for the *Indiana* ship's company by Everett B. Mero, chief yeoman, U.S.N.

Clark, Charles E. *My Fifty Years in the Navy*. Boston: Little, Brown & Co., 1917.

Eberle, Lieutenant Edward W., U.S.N. "The *Oregon's* Great Voyage." *Century Magazine* 58 (May–October 1899): 912–924.

Graves, Major General William S., U.S.A. *America's Si-*

*berian Adventure: 1918–1920.* New York: Peter Smith Co., 1941.

Harbaugh, William Henry. *Power and Responsibility: The Life and Times of Theodore Roosevelt.* New York: Farrar, Straus & Cudahy, 1961.

*Harper's Pictorial History of the War with Spain.* New York and London: Harper Brothers, 1899.

Harris, Brayton. *The Age of the Battleship: 1890–1922.* New York: Franklin Watts, 1965.

Hayes, John D. "Admiral Joseph Mason Reeves, U.S.N.: Part I." *Naval War College Review* 23 (November 1970): 48–57.

Lewis, Charles Lee. *Famous American Naval Officers.* Rev. ed. Boston: L. C. Page, 1945.

Lodge, Henry Cabot. "The Spanish American War." *Harper's New Monthly Magazine* 98 (1899): 449–464, 505–523, 715–733, 833–858.

Mahan, Alfred Thayer. *Lessons of the War with Spain.* 1899. Reprint. Freeport, New York: Books for Libraries Press 1899 ed. 1970.

*New York Times.* 1893–1956.

Puleston, W. D. *Mahan.* New Haven: Yale University Press, 1939.

Sampson, William T. Rear Admiral, U.S.N. "The Atlantic Fleet in the Spanish War." *Century Magazine* 57 (November, 1898–April, 1899), 886–913.

*San Francisco Chronicle.* 1893–1896.

*San Francisco Examiner.* 1893.

Slocum, Captain Joshua. "Sailing Alone Around the World: Being a Personal Narrative of the Experiences of the Sloop 'Spray' on Her Single-Handed Voyage of 46,000 Miles: Part VI, The Homeward Trip from the Cape of Good Hope." *Century Magazine* 59 (February 1900): 589–600.

Staunton, J. A. "The Naval Campaign of 1898 in the West

Indies." *Harper's New Monthly Magazine* 98 (1899): 175–193.

Wilson, H. W. "The Naval Lessons of the War." *Harper's New Monthly Magazine* 98 (1899): 288–297.

# Index